ENGLISH PLACE-NAME SOCIETY. VOLUME IV.

THE PLACE-NAMES OF
WORCESTERSHIRE

ENGLISH PLACE-NAME SOCIETY

The English Place-Name Society was founded in 1924 to carry out the survey of English place-names and to issue annual volumes to members who subscribe to the work of the Society. The Society has issued the following volumes:

I. (Part 1) *Introduction to the Survey of English Place-Names.*
(Part 2) *The Chief Elements used in English Place-Names.*

II. *The Place-Names of Buckinghamshire.*

III. *The Place-Names of Bedfordshire and Huntingdonshire.*

IV. *The Place-Names of Worcestershire.*

V. *The Place-Names of the North Riding of Yorkshire.*

VI, VII. *The Place-Names of Sussex,* Parts 1 and 2.

VIII, IX. *The Place-Names of Devonshire,* Parts 1 and 2.

X. *The Place-Names of Northamptonshire.*

XI. *The Place-Names of Surrey.*

XII. *The Place-Names of Essex.*

XIII. *The Place-Names of Warwickshire.*

XIV. *The Place-Names of the East Riding of Yorkshire and York.*

XV. *The Place-Names of Hertfordshire.*

XVI. *The Place-Names of Wiltshire.*

XVII. *The Place-Names of Nottinghamshire.*

XVIII. *The Place-Names of Middlesex (apart from the City of London).*

XIX. *The Place-Names of Cambridgeshire and the Isle of Ely.*

XX, XXI, XXII. *The Place-Names of Cumberland,* Parts 1, 2 and 3.

XXIII, XXIV. *The Place-Names of Oxfordshire,* Parts 1 and 2.

XXV, XXVI. *English Place-Name Elements,* Parts 1 and 2.

XXVII, XXVIII, XXIX. *The Place-Names of Derbyshire,* Parts 1, 2 and 3.

XXX, XXXI, XXXII, XXXIII, XXXIV, XXXV, XXXVI, XXXVII. *The Place-Names of the West Riding of Yorkshire,* Parts 1–8.

XXXVIII, XXXIX, XL, XLI. *The Place-Names of Gloucestershire,* Parts 1–4.

XLII, XLIII. *The Place-Names of Westmorland,* Parts 1 and 2.

The volumes for the following counties are in an advanced state of preparation: *Berkshire, Cheshire, the City of London.*

All communications with regard to the Society and membership should be addressed to:

THE HON. SECRETARY, English Place-Name Society, University College, Gower Street, London, W.C.1.

ENGLISH PLACE-NAME SOCIETY. VOLUME IV.

DA
645
.A4
1969
v. 4

THE PLACE-NAMES OF
WORCESTERSHIRE

By

A. MAWER *and* F. M. STENTON

IN COLLABORATION WITH

F. T. S. HOUGHTON

CAMBRIDGE
AT THE UNIVERSITY PRESS
1969

Published by the Syndics of the Cambridge University Press
Bentley House, 200 Euston Road, London, N.W.1
American Branch: 32 East 57th Street, New York, N.Y. 10022

Standard Book Number: 521 07501 7

First published 1927
Reissued 1969

First printed in Great Britain
at the University Press, Cambridge
Reprinted in Great Britain
by William Lewis (Printers) Ltd, Cardiff

PREFACE

WHEN we presented the Bedfordshire-Huntingdonshire volume to our subscribers just twelve months ago, it was our pleasant duty to show how the choice of those counties had been largely determined by generous help offered by other scholars. This year again the very difficult task of selecting a county for treatment while the Survey is still young and the time-factor is all-important has been settled for us by even more generous help on the part of Mr F. T. S. Houghton. For many years past he has been collecting material for a study of the place-names of the county of Worcestershire. He placed all that material unreservedly at our disposal, but also rendered us an even more indispensable service when he undertook the initial work of identifying the various place-names recorded in the large masses of new MS material which we were able to submit to him. Here, and again when it came to a question of interpreting the material gathered from various sources, his knowledge of the topography of the county, of its political, ecclesiastical, and manorial history proved of the utmost value. So intimate has been his share in the production of the work that it would be idle to attempt to define the exact limits of his help, even if such definition were desirable in a co-operative scheme of this kind. As an example however of what the volume owes to him we should like to draw special attention to the article upon the Saltways, for that article except for a few insignificant details is entirely his. No scholar could have been more generous in his help or more untiring in the working out of the details of any problem which suggested itself or was presented by us to him. No more happy vindication of the possibilities of co-operative study could have presented itself to the authors of this volume and we sincerely trust that our readers may find themselves equally sensible of it.

Next to the help received from Mr Houghton we must record our indebtedness to the British Academy for the grant which has enabled us to have a large amount of work done on unpublished documents and to secure early forms for a great number of names which would otherwise have been entirely undocumented and also for many names for which the material to be gathered from printed sources was late or unsatisfactory. This volume finally confirms the conclusion we had arrived at long since, viz. that no satisfactory book can be published upon the place-names of any county unless it includes a large amount of material drawn from unpublished documents. For the most part that work must be done by paid workers. The scholars who have the equipment to do it almost invariably have other work of a kindred nature to which they must devote their time and skill. In this county we were however fortunate enough to receive a large measure of help from one of these scholars. Mr R. R. Darlington, who is working on the early Life of St Wulfstan, very generously placed at our disposal his transcripts of the documents spoken of as Evesham A and Evesham B in our text (v. xxvi) and also transcribed and dated with the utmost care all the place-name material from the MS Register of Worcester Priory which had been deposited at the British Museum by the Cathedral authorities for his use.

In the preparation of the volume certain printed works have been of great service. The county is fortunate, to a degree equalled by few other English counties, in having a large number of its early documents in print, thanks to the excellent work of the Worcestershire Historical Society. Our indebtedness to their volumes is apparent in almost every article. Next to these volumes must be mentioned the Victoria History of the County of Worcester. This has been of constant service, not only for its wealth of information, but for its careful indication of the sources of all its material. In many cases this has led to the discovery of rich stores of place-name material. The usefulness of the volumes has been very greatly enhanced by the index-volume recently issued by Mr Page. Finally we must pay our meed of sincere tribute to the work of the late Mr W. H. Duignan, the pioneer of these studies in the counties of Worcestershire, Warwickshire and Staffordshire. The Worcestershire volume is undoubtedly the best of the three and it has been our pleasure to record in more than one instance the happy intuitions which suggested to him the right solution of certain of the most difficult names in the county. He was an amateur in these studies but an amateur in the oldest and best sense of the word. The time at which he worked and the conditions under which all place-name students then had to work made it impossible for him to have at his disposal even the raw material which would have enabled him to write a book of the kind here attempted. Forms have now been found for many names which were undocumented in his book or not included at all and for a large number of those which were documented new forms have been found which compel us to reconsider their whole history.

The county presented, in proportion to the number of its place-names, more cruces than any county hitherto attempted. Certain of them still remain entirely unsolved and for others only tentative solutions can be offered. For the solution of some of the cruces we are again deeply indebted to scholars both at home and abroad. Direct witness to that is to be found in the numerous references in the ensuing pages to Professor Ekwall, Professor Zachrisson, Dr Ritter and Mr Bruce Dickins. Equally helpful, though less capable of explicit acknowledgement in separate articles, has been consultation with Professors Collinson and Glyn Davies of the University of Liverpool especially upon points of Celtic and Comparative Philology.

Others we can but refer to in the alphabetical order of their names:

Mr F. B. Andrews, F.S.A., for help with reference to the Pershore district in particular, and in various questions affecting the rest of the county.

Mr St Clair Baddeley for help with many problems presented to him in connexion with his own county of Gloucestershire and also with reference to Herefordshire.

Mr W. B. Bickley for helping in the solution of certain problems which arose with regard to names on the Warwickshire-Worcestershire border, especially of Balsall Heath.

Mr E. W. Bowcock for information with regard to the forms of the names of places in Shropshire and their topography.

Mr John Dowty for valuable information with reference to the local pronunciation of place-names in the county.

Mr H. C. Gabb for valuable information with reference to the local pronunciation of place-names in the county.

Major-General Davies for similar services.

Mr J. E. B. Gover for use of his extensive collections, largely drawn from MS sources, for Cornwall, Devon, Middlesex, Surrey.

The Rev. R. G. Griffiths, F.S.A., of Clifton-on-Teme, for forms derived from unpublished documents and for help with numerous problems arising from the study of place-names in his district.

Mr C. F. Hardy for identification of places recorded in Ogilby's *Itinerarium Angliae*.

The Rev. J. B. Hewitt, of Stanford-on-Teme, for information with regard to the place-names of his parish and the surrounding districts.

The Rev. Canon Holden for valuable information with reference to the local pronunciation of place-names in the county.

Mr John Humphreys, F.S.A., for information on certain points in which botanical problems presented themselves.

Major J. de Courcy Laffan for the forms of names in the four counties of Berkshire, Oxfordshire, Northamptonshire and Warwickshire.

The Rev. E. E. Lea, rector of Eastham, for forms derived from unpublished parish-documents and for other information with regard to his district.

Mr Percy Park for valuable information with reference to the local pronunciation of place-names in the county.

Mr P. H. Reaney for help with the forms of various place-names in the county of Essex.

Dr O. K. Schram for the forms of Norfolk place-names and for help of various kinds.

Dr Serjeantson, of Lady Margaret Hall, for the transcription of Worcestershire place-name forms from unpublished charters in the Bodleian.

Mr C. A. Seyler some time since placed at our disposal his notebooks dealing with the topography of a large number of the Anglo-Saxon charters and, more especially and in full detail, with certain charters belonging to the borders of Gloucestershire and Worcestershire. Several references are made to his notable discoveries, especially in the survival in present-day field-names of names found in the ancient charters. He has shown how much there is to be gleaned by those who will study the charters on the land itself.

Dr A. H. Smith for the forms of place-names in the North Riding and for help of various kinds.

Professor A. Hamilton Thompson for certain forms for Worcestershire place-names from unpublished Episcopal Registers.

The Rev. Dr Whitley for help with forms derived from the Borough Records of Droitwich and for information with regard to details of the topography of the Droitwich district.

Mr Lort Williams, K.C., for valuable information with reference to the local pronunciation of place-names in the county.

Miss K. M. Wilson for valuable information with reference to the local pronunciation of place-names in the county.

The Rev. R. A. Wilson for valuable information with reference to the local pronunciation of place-names in the county.

Once again, the Director's Secretary, Miss E. G. Withycombe, has rendered very valuable help in the preparation of the volume for the press and to her is due in large measure any degree of accuracy in its details which it may possess. It was a matter of great loss and regret that her departure from Liverpool before the completion of the printing of the volume made it impossible for her to see it all through the final stages. To Miss Scroggs, who did the work on unpublished documents made possible by the Academy grant, our best thanks are due for skilled and careful service.

The proofs of this volume have been read by Professors Ekwall and Tait and by Mr Bruce Dickins. They have made valuable additions and saved us from many faults, but are in no sense responsible for the volume as it now stands. To Dr Grundy we are also much indebted for his care in going through the volume especially from the topographical point of view, on the basis of his unpublished studies of the Worcestershire charters, carried through on lines familiar to place-name students from his published work on the charters of Wiltshire, Hampshire and Berkshire.

In addition to the specific acknowledgements already made, we wish to record our general sense of indebtedness to Professor Ekwall. He continues to be an invaluable help and stand-by to the editors in all their difficulties and is continually bringing to their notice undiscovered treasures from the collections that he has amassed.

To the care and skill of the Ordnance Survey Office and especially of Captain Withycombe and Mr O. G. S. Crawford we owe many services, including the map which accompanies this volume.

To the Cambridge Press and its printers we stand, as always, deeply indebted for their skill and care.

A. M.
F. M. S.

Whitsuntide, 1927

The collection from unpublished documents of material for this volume has been made possible by a grant received from the British Academy.

CONTENTS

Introduction . . . . *page* xiii

Notes on the dialect of Worcestershire . . . xxvii

Changes in the county-area xxx

Abbreviations xxxi

Phonetic Symbols xxxvi

Notes xxxvii

Addenda et Corrigenda:

    Vol. I, Part I xxxix

           Part II xxxix

    Vol. II xxxix

    Vol. III xl

Addenda: Vol. IV xliii

District, Road and River-names 1

The Worcestershire Hundreds 17

The Place-names of Worcestershire . . . 19

The elements found in Worcestershire place-names 367

Notes on the distribution of these elements . . 377

Personal-names compounded in Worcestershire
    place-names 380

Feudal names 387

Manorial names 388

Field and other minor names 388

Personal-names in field and other minor names . 394

Indexes 401

MAP

Map of Worcestershire   *In pocket at end*

INTRODUCTION

IN passing from the region of the middle Ouse to that of the middle Severn, the Survey is entering a very different field and is confronted by new and in some ways more difficult problems. In Bedfordshire and Huntingdonshire the English settlement at least began early, and the pre-English element in the surviving local nomenclature is of insignificant extent. In Worcestershire, everything points to a later settlement, and the number of names which cannot be explained as English is considerable. The county contains none of those place-names, characteristic of the earliest settlement, in which a personal name is followed by a final element *ingas*. The rarity of English burial grounds of the heathen time suggests that the settlement of the county was followed at no great interval by conversion to Christianity[1]. The number of place-names derived from feminine personal names suggests a late settlement. Moreover, on geographical grounds, the occupation of Worcestershire is not likely to have taken place before the invaders were securely established in Gloucestershire, and if ancient West Saxon traditions may be trusted, Gloucester and Cirencester were still British towns in 577. It seems safe to assume that the settlement of Worcestershire did not begin before the last decades of the sixth century, when the first energy of the invasion was past, and it was possible for a surviving British population to transmit some material fragments of its ancient local nomenclature to its conquerors.

It should at once be said that the interpretation of these fragments presents great difficulty. No conclusive explanation can at present be offered of Worcester itself, or of Mamble,

[1] Two Worcestershire place-names, Arrowfield and Weoley, denote sites where heathen worship was practised. The latter, in the extreme north of the county, is more likely to be due to Mercian immigrants from the Trent or Teme valleys than to Saxon settlers from the south. The occurrence of this name in north Worcestershire, like that of Wednesbury (OE *Wodnesbeorh*) in south Staffordshire, shows that specifically heathen place-names might arise in districts which cannot have been reached in the first phase of the English occupation. They cannot be regarded as proof of early settlement, though they all doubtless arose some time before the middle of the seventh century.

Tardebigge or Pendock. The history of the familiar name Bredon is not in all respects simple. This difficulty, though unfortunate, is not indeed remarkable. These names were presumably of high antiquity. They were transmitted, under conditions of which nothing is known, to an invading race by whom they were not understood. It is not strange that their development should be obscure. It can only be hoped that the comparative material to be obtained from other counties, especially those along the Welsh border, may in time throw light upon Worcestershire problems which at present seem insoluble.

It may be assumed that the English invaders of Worcestershire entered the county from the south. It is only towards the south that Worcestershire lies widely open to the adjacent country, and it is only in the south, at Upton Snodsbury, Bricklehampton, Bredon's Norton and Little Hampton, that archaeological evidence of heathen English settlement has been found within the county. No serious argument has yet been brought against the accepted opinion that the English occupation of Worcestershire was a result of the battle of Dyrham in 577, by which Ceawlin, king of the West Saxons, conquered the towns of Gloucester, Cirencester, and Bath, and brought his people to the Severn. It is, no doubt, possible, it is even probable, that further fighting was necessary before the West Saxons could advance northwards. It may have been the battle of 'Fethanleag'[1] in 584 rather than the battle of Dyrham which brought the invaders into Worcestershire. In any case, a people established at Gloucester must soon have attempted expansion up the Severn valley. For more than thirty miles

[1] No form has yet been discovered in field or place-names which affords any clue to the identification of this place. It may however be observed that a Worcestershire or Warwickshire site would agree better than any other suggestion with the history of West Saxon movements in so far as they are recorded in the *Chronicle*. All that we know of the battle is that it gave to Ceawlin many towns and great booty, but that within a year the king returned 'in anger' to his own country. Whatever reverse or treachery may have lain behind Ceawlin's return, the capture of many towns in the battle points to something more than a merely local success. It indicates the conquest of a considerable territory, and an advance up the Severn valley had been made almost inevitable by the conquest of Gloucester. Apart from the evidence of place-names, of which something will be said later, a sixth-century Saxon occupation of south Worcestershire is virtually proved by the character of the objects found in burial grounds in this district.

there was no obstacle to their settlement until the open country
on either side of the river was ended by Wyre forest to the west,
the forests of Morfe and Kinver to the north, and the Clent
and Lickey hills to the east. In historic times, this broken and
wooded country formed the natural boundary between the
Hwicce, the men of Gloucestershire, Worcestershire, and west
Warwickshire, and the Anglian peoples to the north, just as
Wychwood forest, which preserves their name, divided them
from their Saxon neighbours to the south.

Little that is definite can be said about either the origin or
the meaning of the folk-name *Hwicce*. It is even uncertain
whether the name was borne by the first settlers of this region
or arose locally at a later time. Its antiquity is nevertheless
suggested very strongly by the fact that personal names were
formed from it far back in the Old English period. None of
them is recorded in independent use, but at least three examples
are found in local compounds. Wichnor in Staffordshire, near
Burton on Trent, OE *Hwiccenofre*, certainly contains a weak
personal name *Hwicca*[1]. Witchley Green near Ketton in
Rutland, the meeting-place of a Hundred in the eleventh century, appears as *Hwicceslea* in a document of approximately
the year 1072[2]. That similar names were being formed at a
time much earlier than the eleventh century is shown by the
remarkable form *Hwiccintunae* for Whiston in Northamptonshire, which must go back to an OE *Hwiccingtun*[3]. There are
good parallels to this creation of a personal name from a folk-
name. The element *Swǣf*, common in compound names, is
certainly derived from the national name *Swǣfe*, and there is
reason to believe that the element *Gēat* represents the name of
the *Gēatas*. But personal names are only likely to have arisen
from the names of ancient and important folks. A folk-name
of purely local significance could not have produced a personal
name recorded in somewhat distant parts of England. That
the Hwicce were important is clear from the fact that in the
eighth century they were reckoned to contain 7000 tribute-

---

[1] O.S. Facs. iii. Anglesey MSS, ii.

[2] The 'Northamptonshire Geld Roll' printed by Ellis, *Introduction to
Domesday* 1, 184–7, from a late twelfth-century manuscript.

[3] This form is derived by Thorpe (382) from an 'Inspeximus' of a confirmatory charter of Edward the Confessor to Ramsey Abbey.

paying families[1]. And the more ancient their name the easier it is to understand its adoption as a personal name by men who founded settlements far from their territory.

It would appear that the original English settlers of Worcestershire were West Saxons. It is therefore remarkable that in the seventh century, when the definite history of this region begins, its inhabitants already form part of the great complex of peoples who owned the supremacy of the Anglian kings of the Mercians. The first definite evidence of Mercian authority in Worcestershire occurs in a document of approximately the year 680, which expresses the ancient traditions of Gloucester abbey[2]. In this document, which is very corrupt but should not be rejected, Aethelred, king of the Mercians, appears as granting land to two *ministri* of noble race. To one of them, named Osric, the king grants three hundred hides 'at Gloucester,' while the other, Oswald, Osric's brother, receives an equal amount of land 'at Pershore'[3]. Nothing more is known of Oswald, but Osric is certainly identical with the man of that name whom Bede describes as king of the Hwicce in a passage which refers to the years between 680 and 690[4]. For the next hundred years there is good evidence of a succession of local rulers acknowledging the overlordship of the Mercian kings.

A brief entry in the *Chronicle* under the year 628 seems to mark the date at which the region of which Worcestershire forms part ceased to be West Saxon. It records that Cynegils and Cwichelm, kings of the West Saxons, 'fought with Penda at Cirencester,' and there came to an agreement. Of its terms

---

[1] It is probable that the limits of the territory of the Hwicce are represented with substantial accuracy by the boundary of the medieval diocese of Worcester. A map of this diocese such as is given in the Record Commission ed. of the *Valor Ecclesiasticus* vol. III, shows the important part of this territory which is now included in Warwickshire. The distribution of heathen burial grounds suggests that the English who entered Worcestershire from the south spread eastwards up the Avon before they proceeded to occupy the country north of Worcester. It should be interesting to see if the place-names of Warwickshire bring out the division of the county between Saxons and Angles which is suggested by the ecclesiastical map.

[2] BCS 60.

[3] The fact that the charter describes Osric and Oswald merely as *ministri nobilis generis* is a strong argument in favour of its authenticity. A later forger would almost certainly have followed Bede, and described Osric as *rex*. There are other indications of an ancient origin in the document.

[4] *Historia Ecclesiastica* IV, 21.

nothing is known, but all the subsequent history suggests that the West Saxon kings resigned to Penda their lordship over the people then or later called the Hwicce. There is no trace of any claim by later kings of Wessex to authority over this people, and the West Saxon expansion of the next generations was directed not towards the north, but the south-west. Five years after the battle of Cirencester, Penda became king of the Mercians, and the opportunity had passed for the recovery by the West Saxon dynasty of any territories lost towards the north[1].

There can be no question that these events were followed by an Anglian movement into the Severn valley, whatever its extent may have been. As to this, there is, of course, no direct evidence. But Osric, the *minister* or *gesith* of king Aethelred, must have been accompanied by companions of his own race into the province over which his lord had set him. The tradition that the monastery of Bredon was founded by Eanwulf, grandfather of Offa king of the Mercians, is very early[2]. Eanwulf must have been living in the first part of the eighth century. In view of recent work on early Germanic genealogy, it is permissible to suggest that some family connexion may have existed between Eanwulf and the brothers Eanfrith and Eanhere, who, according to Bede, were ruling the Hwicce in the third quarter of the seventh century. It is difficult to suppose that within the somewhat narrow territory of the Hwicce there existed two separate families of the highest rank, each of which employed the stem *Ēan-* to form the names of its members[3].

---

[1] Despite the entry in the *Chronicle* under 626 which is usually taken to record Penda's accession, it is clear from Bede's language that he did not become king of the Mercians before the overthrow of Edwin of Northumbria in 633 (*Hist. Eccl.* II, 20).

[2] In BCS 234 Offa states that Eanwulf his grandfather had founded the church *æt Breodune* in honour of St Peter. There is no material reason for doubting this charter, which is preserved not only by Heming but in the fragmentary Wollaton cartulary of *circa* 1000. In BCS 272, which is certainly genuine, Offa asserts that Æthelbald king of the Mercians had given other lands to Eanwulf. The latter must therefore have been living after 716, when Æthelbald became king.

[3] The same stem reappears at the middle of the eighth century, when a certain *Ean*berht appears as the first of three brothers who as *reguli* make a gift *æt Onnanforda*, apparently near Andoversford in Gloucestershire, to an abbot named Headda (BCS 187, an original text). There is, unfortunately, no evidence to connect these brothers with earlier rulers of the Hwicce. The

It is, no doubt, true that the Anglian element represented by Osric and Eanwulf was aristocratic, and does not by itself prove a movement of peasantry from Anglian territory to the Severn plain. But the aristocratic element is of particular significance for the history of local nomenclature in regions like Worcestershire, whose occupation belongs, in the main, to the later phases of English settlement.

Moreover, this element does not stand alone. Two at least among the place-names of Worcestershire prove a definite migration of Anglian peoples into the county. There can be no doubt of the connexion which exists between the unique name Phepson (*infra* 137) and the folk-name *Feppingas* preserved by Bede[1]. That the Feppingas were an Anglian people is fortunately made clear by Bede's explicit language. He definitely states that Diuma, bishop of the Middle Angles and Mercians, died *apud Mediterraneos Anglos in regione quae uocatur Infeppingum*. As it is in every way unlikely that another folk existed bearing this very abnormal name, the *Fepsætan* whose name forms the first element of Phepson can safely be regarded as a community of Anglian migrants into what is now Worcestershire. The importance of this name lies in the proof which it affords that the Anglian movement into Worcestershire was something more than the settlement of individual nobles. The word *sætan* should not be pressed too far, but it certainly

persistence of *reges* or *reguli* of the Hwicce under the supremacy of such powerful Mercian kings as Wulfhere, Æthelred, Æthelbald and Offa is easier to understand if the local dynasty really formed a branch of the great Mercian royal house.

[1] *Hist. Eccl.* iii, 21. The Feppingas are presumably identical with the folk whose name appears in the Tribal Hidage in the form *Færpinga*, though it is curious that the *r* appears in all the forms of this name in the different manuscripts of this record. It apparently results from confusion of the OE forms of *r* and *þ*, a confusion which, common at a later time, must in this place have occurred in the Old English period itself, for the oldest manuscript of the Tribal Hidage cannot well be later than the early eleventh century. The only clue to the position of the 'Færpingas,' and therefore to the original home of the Worcestershire *Fepsætan*, lies in the arrangement of the Tribal Hidage, which places them before a folk named 'Bilmiga' who are followed by another named 'Widerigga.' If the names of the last two folks are now represented by Billing and Wittering in Northamptonshire, the Færpingas will naturally fall into the western part of the latter county. If they were really seated in this quarter, in the extreme west of Middle Anglian territory, a migration of only forty miles would have brought a party of them to Phepson.

denoted a group of settlers, a community which did not merely
consist of a lord and his household but included peasants of
free condition. A name like *Fepsetnatun* belongs to a different
order of ideas from names like *Doddan-ham* or *Aelfsiges-tun*[1].

Another ancient Anglian folk-name, from which a similar
conclusion may be drawn, is preserved in one of the obscurer
local names of Worcestershire. The preservation of a pre-
Conquest form shows that the stream-name now known as
Whitsun Brook (*infra* 16) represents an Old English *Wixena
broc*, and contains the folk-name *Wixan* recorded in the archaic
document called the Tribal Hidage. Like the *Fepsætan* of
Phepson the *Wixan* of Whitsun Brook must have been a
detached portion of a distinct folk. The region from which
they had migrated to what is now Worcestershire is indicated,
roughly, by the position assigned to them in the Tribal Hidage.
In that record they come immediately after the Gyrwe, the
inhabitants of the country around Peterborough. There is no
evidence to fix their position more closely, but the sequence of
other names suggests that they lived in the parts of Kesteven
in the modern Lincolnshire or in the country immediately to
the west. The migration of even a small section of this people
to so remote a region as Worcestershire is a very remarkable
fact. It illustrates the complexity of the races which composed
the Early English kingdoms. And for the student of Worcestershire history it helps to make more plausible the suggestion
that a community of Kentishmen settled at Conderton (*infra*
115), in the angle between Avon and Severn.

The task of identifying specifically Saxon elements in Worcestershire place-names is far from easy. The folk-names of
Wessex and the other Saxon kingdoms are so imperfectly
known that there is little chance of tracing them in other parts
of England. The most hopeful line of inquiry would be an
investigation of the personal names compounded in Worcester-

---

[1] It is possible that the appearance of the element *bold*, 'building,' in three
Worcestershire place-names is due to Anglian influence. It occurs frequently
in the north and northern midlands but seems to be unknown in southern
England. On the other hand, the word was certainly familiar in Wessex.
It occurs in Alfred's laws, c. 37, in the compound *boldgetæl*, of which the
most natural rendering is 'collection of dwellings,' 'village.' It is remarkable that it should not have been used to form local names in Wessex.

shire place-names in order to establish the local use of personal-
names of Saxon as against Anglian origin. At present, the study
of the personal names which occur in local nomenclature is
not sufficiently advanced for any far-reaching conclusions to
be drawn. It may, indeed, prove to be the case that no general
conclusions can ever be obtained. The Saxon and Anglian
peoples, closely associated from the time of the Migration, had
from the earliest period a closely similar nomenclature. The
remarks which have been offered on the names Phepson and
Whitsun Brook will have shown how easily personal names
might be introduced from one part of England into another.
The *Cantware* of Conderton might have introduced Kentish
personal names into Worcestershire at a date early enough to
have permitted the formation of place-names from them. All
that can be attempted here is an indication of certain place-
names containing personal names recorded in Wessex, but
apparently not at present found within Anglian territory.

   The preservation of an unusually early form shows that the
first part of the name Chaceley (*infra* 192) is a personal name,
Ceatwe, of an archaic and indeed extremely rare type. It has
not been recorded from the Midlands, East Anglia or the
North, but a corresponding weak form Ceatwa occurs in the
compound *Ceatwanberge* in the boundaries of Chesilborne in
Dorset[1]. Another connexion between Worcestershire and this
part of England is made by the personal name *Streng* or *Strenge*
which forms the base of Strensham (*infra* 229). It appears
again in the Somerset place-name Stringston, and in a remarkable local name of early type, *Strengesburieles*, on the boundary
of Dauntsey in Wiltshire. Elsewhere in England it is only
found in the lost *Strengesburna* near Pensax. The references
given in the note on the difficult name Ombersley (*infra* 268)

---

[1] No other examples of the suffix -*w(e)a*, or -*we*, is known to occur in local
nomenclature. It is important in the present connexion to note that the
list of archaic names which includes *Sceldwea* and *Tætwa* among the ancestors
of Woden, the one definite piece of evidence for the existence of Old English
names in -*wa*, comes from the genealogy of the West Saxon royal house.
This list, whatever its ultimate origin, is certainly very ancient. Regarded
in connexion with the Dorset *Cetwanberge* it makes the West Saxon origin
of the Worcestershire *Ceatewes leah* virtually certain. Conversely, the existence of these compounds of personal names in -*wa* is a serious argument
against the view that the names above Woden in the West Saxon genealogy
are fictitious.

show that the name-element *Ambre*, found in Wiltshire, Sussex, and Oxfordshire, has not yet been observed in regions of Anglian settlement. The Oxfordshire example, Ambrosden near Bicester, is particularly noteworthy, for it occurs in a district which, according to the *Chronicle*, was conquered by the West Saxons in 571, six years before the battle of Dyrham which brought them to the Severn. More difficult problems are presented by the name of Eastbury in Hallow (*infra* 129), but it certainly seems to contain a personal name *Ēar* of highly archaic, and indeed semi-mythological character. From the present point of view, its interest lies in the fact that the only other place-name in which it is known to occur, *Earomundesleah*, the original name of Appleton in north Berkshire, belongs to the district from which the West Saxons must have set out on the movement of 577. The personal name *Cifa*, from which Chevington in Pershore (*infra* 219) is derived, forms another link between Worcestershire and the ancient Wessex, for it occurs again in the Berkshire place-name Chieveley. It is also found in Surrey and Devon, but not in Mercia, Middle or East Anglia, or beyond the Humber. On the left bank of the middle Thames, Bensington near Wallingford derives its name from a personal name *Bænisa*, a mutated derivative of a name *Bana*, formed from the word *bana*, 'slayer.' A mutated patronymic based on the latter name, which from its form must be very ancient, forms the first part of the name of Banbury Stone in south Worcestershire (*infra* 196). Of all these names, *Ceatwe* is perhaps the only one which from its antiquity amounts to proof of a Saxon element in the present county. But the cumulative effect of the series which has been quoted is certainly considerable, and confirms in a remarkable manner the historical tradition of an early West Saxon movement into the Severn valley.

The evidence for Anglian settlement in Worcestershire is less definite, but is still suggestive. There is an exact duplicate of the name Fladbury (*infra* 126) in Fledborough on the left bank of the lower Trent in Nottinghamshire. The personal name *Flǣde*, which must be feminine, is only known from these two local examples. If, as is possible, an examination of Warwickshire material shows that Birmingham contains the personal name *Breme* from which Bromsgrove (*infra* 336) is derived, another, and an important link will be established between Worcestershire and Mercia. Pickersom and Pixham (*infra* 225, 266) contain a name *Pīcer*, which otherwise seems only to occur in Pickering in Yorkshire. The name *Pybba* found in Pedmore, Pepper Wood, and Pepwell (*infra* 245, 277, 305), probably also occurring in a diminutive form in Peopleton (*infra* 216), appears in the genealogy of the Mercian royal house. It was borne by the father of Penda, and was therefore current in the generation immediately preceding the Anglian movement towards the Severn valley. It is hard to avoid the suspicion that the occurrence of three if not four examples of this difficult and anomalous name within a limited area is due to the deliberate adoption of this name by the Anglian settlers who had entered the county under Penda, Pybba's son[1]. With somewhat more assurance, a similar explanation may be suggested for the occurrence of the name of Penda himself at Pinvin and the lost *Pendiford* (*infra* 223, 397) in Worcestershire and at Pinbury in Gloucestershire. In any case, these names clearly point to an Anglian as distinct from a Saxon element in the former county. Even if historical evidence were lacking, an analysis of the place-names of Worcestershire would suggest that Angles as well as Saxons had combined to form the Old English population of the county.

The personal names compounded in Worcestershire place-names are of exceptional interest for a different reason. The importance in place-name study of the type of personal-name in which a name-element is followed by a derivative suffix such as *il*(*a*) or *el*(*a*), *uc* or *ic*, has always been recognised. The *Aemela* of Amblecote, the *Ippel* of the lost Ipplesborough, and the *Wēaloc* of *Walloxhall* (*infra* 299, 309, 319) are Worcestershire names of this type. But recent work has brought out the wide distribution over England of other suffixes, of which, -*t*, -*n*, and -*r* are the most important. The place-names of Worcestershire make a notable contribution to the list of English personal-names formed in this way. There are only two instances, and

---

[1] If the *Pubbewurth* of the Book of Fees II, 853 relates to Pibworth Farm in Aldworth, Berkshire, it affords a West Saxon example of this name. This isolated instance does not, however, affect the argument from the triple occurrence of the name in Worcestershire.

one a somewhat doubtful one, of the -*t* suffix, the *Inta* of Inkberrow and the *Basta* or *Bæsta* of Bastenhall (*infra* 82, 324), but the -*r* and -*n* suffixes are well represented. Examples of the former are the *Dudra* of Dodderhill, *Ceadder* of Chaddesley, and the *Pīcer* of Pixham and Pickersom (*infra* 225, 234, 266, 281). If Kidderminster contains a personal name *Cydera* (*infra* 247), as the modern form and several early spellings suggest, it affords another instance of the same type. The -*n* suffix occurs in the *Peden* of Pensham and the *Cūlna* of Cookley (*infra* 221, 258). Names of this type are, as a class, early. By the end of the seventh century, the -*l* suffix was normally employed in diminutive formations, and therefore the other suffixes under consideration are rarely found in personal names derived from written sources. It is therefore interesting to note that the latest example of the -*r* suffix found in English materials comes from a document relating to the region of the Hwicce. In 759, a charter made jointly by three *reguli* of the Hwicce is witnessed by a certain *Dilra*[1]. The ultimate source of this name is at present obscure, but it certainly belongs to the same type as *Pīcer* or *Dudra*, and its survival illustrates the conservatism of the men of this region in regard to personal nomenclature.

It is in regard to the problems of an early time that place-names make their chief contribution to the history of Worcestershire. The later Scandinavian element in the county, strong enough for an eleventh-century bishop of Worcester to refer to all the thegns of Worcestershire, both English and Danish[2], has left few traces on the local nomenclature which have survived

---

[1] BCS 187. As this is an original eighth-century text, the form should not be explained away as due to a scribal mistake. A similar formation, *Hymora*, occurs in another original eighth-century text (BCS 148). The late survival of the -*r* suffix, proved by the example which has been quoted, removes the difficulty caused by the appearance of names of this type in regions which cannot have been settled before, at earliest, the middle of the seventh century. The name Huddersfield, for example, must contain a personal name of this form. West Yorkshire cannot have been occupied before the conquest of Elmet by Edwin of Northumbria, but if the -*r* suffix was used among the Hwicce in the eighth century it may well have been used among the men of Deira a hundred years earlier. The -*n* suffix was discussed by Ritter, *Vermischte Beiträge*, p. 193 (cf. IPN 171), but the -*r* suffix, equally important, has received less attention than it deserves.

[2] Earle 242.

to the present day. A few Scandinavian personal names, such as *Swein* and *Thorkell*, will be gathered from the list of field-names which ends this book. Others could no doubt be obtained from further study of this kind of material. The rarity of Scandinavian names is in itself a noteworthy fact, suggesting as it does that the local nomenclature of the county was already established when Cnut and his earls introduced a Danish aristocracy into Worcestershire. At the least, it disproves the suggestion which has sometimes been made that Clent, one of the most important place-names in the county, is a name of Scandinavian origin.

It is, on the other hand, probable that *Clent* (*infra* 279), and *Lench* (*infra* 148), like the *bult* of Bouts (*infra* 325) in Inkberrow and the *beall* of Cakebole (*infra* 236), are survivals of ancient words which had passed out of common use before written records became frequent. Such a survival is analogous to the local persistence of those early forms of personal nomenclature to which reference has already been made. It is intelligible enough in a county like Worcestershire, lying far towards the western limits of early English settlement and bounded towards the east by hills and woods which, though far from impassable, were still a hindrance to intercourse in early times. The local nomenclature of Worcestershire is that of a region in comparative isolation. The well-marked group of *hamtuns* (*infra* 378), the *ingtun*-names compounded with north, south, east (*infra* 379), the triple occurrence of *weardsetl* in place-names (*infra* 253, 292, 335), the use of *maþþum*, 'treasure,' to form the place-name which is now Mathon (*infra* 65), the very curious application of what in form are personal names to a brine pit in the *Helperic* of Helpridge Farm, and to a river in *Tilnoth* just over the Gloucestershire border (*infra* 282) are good illustrations of this local individuality. Similar names can, no doubt, be found in other counties. If Kimble (PN Bk 163) really means 'royal bell,' and no better interpretation has yet been suggested, it illustrates the same tendency to apply artificial descriptive names to natural objects which is present in *Helperic* and *Tilnoth*. It is possible that too little allowance has been made in the past for the deliberate creation of artificial names of this type. At present, they certainly seem to be commoner in Worcestershire than elsewhere, and they help to give the nomenclature of the county the distinctive character which it undoubtedly possesses.

The materials on which the following pages are based differ in one fundamental respect from those which were used in earlier volumes. The number of Old English documents which relate to Worcestershire is very large. Quite apart from a considerable body of original texts, the late eleventh-century cartulary of Worcester Cathedral, written by the monk Heming at the command of Bishop Wulfstan, has preserved much material in a form almost unaffected by the French influences which entered England at the Conquest. Even if some of the documents copied by Heming prove on examination to have been composed at a later date than that which they themselves bear, their value for place-name study remains high. The greater part of any fabrication or interpolation of charters which may have been carried on at Worcester was done before the Conquest. No English cartulary except the *Textus Roffensis* is of higher authority than Heming's register. At the beginning of the eighteenth century a learned antiquary could write of Worcester Cathedral: ' As this Church was one of the most flourishing in the whole Island under the Government of our *Saxon* Kings; so it had the fortune to preserve its Charters and other Instruments (relating to those Times) much better than its Neighbours[1].' The muniments of Worcester Cathedral have suffered heavy loss since these words were written. Thanks in the main to Heming, the loss is not irremediable.

In sharp contrast to the Worcester texts are the gross forgeries which come from the abbey of Evesham. But it is the subtle forger who does the most harm to history, and the methods employed at Evesham were crude[2]. It is for the Norman rather than the Old English period that Evesham materials are valuable. Among the miscellaneous records which were collected into the two twelfth-century cartularies of Evesham which survive are included two lists of villages, giving the details of their

[1] Nicholson, *The English Historical Library*, ed. 1714, p. 134.
[2] Two of the Evesham charters which purport to come from the seventh and eighth centuries seem on diplomatic grounds to be substantially genuine, BCS 116, which relates to Ombersley and proves that this important name is early, and BCS 146, which relates to Acton Beauchamp.

assessment to the Danegeld, of which the older seems to be an independent version or abstract of the Domesday returns, the younger coming from the earlier part of the twelfth century. These are the records which are quoted in the present book under the abbreviations Evesham A and B. Until they have been printed and discussed in relation to other documents of their class it would be premature to discuss their real nature more closely. It will however be evident that they supply a great store of place-name forms of unusually early date. As a body of evidence they are outweighed by the mass of earlier material which comes from Worcester, but they form a most valuable supplement to the Domesday forms of place-names for which no Old English spellings survive and they occasionally include the names of places which the Domesday Survey ignores.

The work of many students, and especially the publications of the Worcestershire Historical Society, supply an unusual number of forms illustrating the development of Worcestershire names in the twelfth and thirteenth centuries. Few counties possess such a record as the Worcestershire Subsidy Rolls 1275 and 1327. Most of the sources of later forms belong to familiar types. One very notable record relating primarily to the county still remains unprinted. The early thirteenth-century cartulary of Worcester Cathedral, the sequel to Heming, still awaits an editor. Through the kindness of the Dean and Chapter it has been possible to use the forms which it contains in the present volume, which thus derives from the archives of Worcester Cathedral materials ranging from the reign of Aethelred of Mercia to the reign of Henry III.

NOTES ON THE DIALECT OF WORCESTERSHIRE
AS ILLUSTRATED BY ITS PLACE-NAMES

OE *æ* appears as [æ] in modern names, without exception, and the ME forms as a rule also show *a*, very rarely *e*.

OE *a* (Anglian) before *ld* is lengthened and then rounded to ME [ɔ·] as in *Cotswolds* and *Upton Wold*.

Anglian *æ* for WS *ie* before *l* followed by a consonant. Eleven of the names which end in *wielle*, *wælle* scattered all over the county, show no signs of ME *wall*-forms. Littals in Clifton-on-Teme and Dorhall in Chaddesley Corbett are the only ones which have only *wall* and those which vary between *well* and *wall* (with a large preponderance of *well*-forms) are confined to the parishes of Kidderminster, Droitwich, Hartlebury, Little Kyre and Lower Sapey, except that we have one OE charter form in -*wælle* for Blackwell in Tredington. Walmspout in Mathon has *welm* in the only ME form that has been noted. The evidence for the whole county confirms Ekwall's doubts, at least so far as its southern half is concerned, whether Worcestershire was ever really a wall-county: v. *Contribution to the History of OE Dialects* 62.

OE *ǣ* has given ModEng [i] in *Snead* and *Sneachill*. When the vowel is shortened it gives ModEng [æ] as in *Fladbury*, *Hatfield*, *Madresfield*, or [e] as in *Headley* (2), *Spetchley*, *Meneatt*, *Menith*. *Stratford* in Ripple has only *stret*-forms to 1649.

OE *a* before *m*, *n* often shows the characteristic West Midland development to *o*. This has persisted in the modern form in *Conderton*, *Monyhull*, *Ombersley*, *Romsley*, *Longdon* (3), *Cromer*, and practically so in *Caunsall*. In *Mamble* and *Ham Green* in Feckenham we get *om* as late as 1591 and 1656. *Frankley* always has *an*. *Langmore* and *Langley* show *lang*- after some hesitation and *Ankerdine* similarly decides in favour of *ank*-. In an unstressed suffix, -*hamm* by no means always appears as -*hom* so that that cannot be used as a criterion for distinguishing names in ham and hamm.

OE *ĕa* in *Chad*-names and also in *Hadzor* hesitates between ME forms in *a* and *e*; v. *Chadwick, Chadbury, Chadwich*.

OE *ēa* when shortened appears regularly as *a* as in the numerous *Ast*-names and in *Abberley, Walloxhill, Hanbury, Hampton, Radford* (2), *Nafford*. Occasionally in *read*-names, as in *Redstone, Redditch, red*-forms have prevailed, probably under the influence of the independent word.

OE *ĕo* appear in ME as *e, o, u, eo*. Generally we have *e* in ModEng, but we have *u* in *Hurtle* Hill in Rock, *Sturt* Coppice in Leigh, *o* in *Dorhall* in Chaddesley Corbett and (at least in pronunciation) in *Cherkenhill* [tʃɔknəl] and *eo* in *Beoley, Weoley*. The only ones for which we have only *e*-forms are *Netherton* in Dudley and Kidderminster, *Netherend* in Cradley, *Lightwoods* in Warley Salop and *Hartle* in Belbroughton, all in the north part of the county.

OE *ĭe* (Anglian *ĕo*) give *Hursley* and *Hurcott* with the regular development of the Anglian vowel. *Sherridge* and *Heightington* show occasional ME forms in *u* and *Hardwick* in Eldersfield one *o*-form. In Bredon's *Hardwick* and in *Harborough* we have only *e* and *a* forms in ME, apparently from the more usual form *herde*.

The development of OE *ī(o)w* in the *New*-names in the county is worthy of note. For *Newnham* we have forms *Neowcham, Noweham* (c. 1240), *Nowenham* (1542), for *Naunton* in Ripple, *Nounton* in 1182. For *Naunton* Beauchamp and *Naunton* in Severn Stoke the *Naunton*-forms only appear in the 16th cent., but for *Nobury* we have *Nubery* in 1280 and there is an unidentified *Nowedich* in Charlton (c. 1220). *Neubold* is pronounced locally as [noubəld]. These suggest that in this county there was a tendency to shift the stress in the diphthong from *ío* to *ió*, leading to a characteristic sound-development, which certainly goes over into Gl in certain *Naunton*-names. It should be noted that these are found only in the north of the county, in the Cotswold area.

OE *o* has been unrounded to *a* in *Atterburn, Clattsmore, Dadsley, Cladswell, Gladder Brook*, in each case in the neighbourhood of a point-consonant.

OE *ŭ* are unrounded and fronted to *i* in *Cinders, Diglis, Sinton* (3), *Sindon's* Mill, *Ismere* and in several forms of *Sodington*. The change is in every case associated with point-consonants.

OE *y̆* should regularly appear as ME *u, o* in this county and commonly does so. It is only however in *Hull Fm, Rodge Fm, Bushley, Hurst Fm* (2), *Rugg's Place, Horns Hall* that we have any sign of the rounded vowel in the present-day form of the name. *Peopleton* shows it in spelling but not in pronunciation. Only in *Kinnersley* and *Kidderminster* have we no sign in ME or ModE of a *u*-form.

OE **ceald** always appears as ME *cald, cold,* but **cealf** as *chalve, chelve.*

OE *f* becomes *v* in *Edvin, Pinvin,* in *Vardroe* for *Foredraught,* and in field-names such as *le Vallyng, Vroggemore, Vasterne.*

Prefixing an *n* as the result of a misdivision of words in such names as *Atten asshe* is very common in this county and we have as a result *Napleton, Noke, Noken, Nash* (3), *Neight* (2), *Norchard* (2), *Noverton, Nurton.* Less common is the prefixing of *r* as in *Rock, Rashwood, Rea* (2), *Ryknild Street.*

Initial *w* has developed before ME *o* as in occasional *Wold* for *Old* Swinford, *Warstock, Whorenap,* and the field-name *Whorwode* for *Horwode.* It has been lost in Upton *Old* for *Wold* and [ustər] for Worcester; cf. EDG 236.

Initial [*j*] has been lost in *Hagtree, Edvin.* It has been added in *Yarnold, Yessel,* and the one-time pronunciation of *Eardiston.*

The inflexional *n* of the suffix of the weak form of the adj. is preserved as in *Newnham, Naunton* (3), *Hanley* (2), *Hampton, Whitnells End.*

WMidl genitival *-us* for *-es* is illustrated under Gumborn Fm and Trotshill and is common in field-names, e.g. *Bollucus croft* (1373), *Eylwardushale* (13th).

CHANGES IN THE COUNTY-AREA

Certain areas once in Worcestershire have now been transferred to other counties, viz. Acton Beauchamp, Edvin Loach and Mathon to Herefordshire (1893-7), Alstone, Church Iccomb and Little Washbourne to Gloucestershire (1832–44), Oldberrow to Warwickshire (1894). Northfield and part of King's Norton were incorporated in Birmingham in 1911.

Other areas once in other counties have now been transferred to Worcestershire: Upper Arley from Staffordshire (1895), Stoke Bliss from Herefordshire (1897).

Broom and Clent were in Staffordshire from the 13th cent. to 1844.

Halesowen, at first in Worcestershire, was in Shropshire from the 13th cent. to 1832–44.

Tardebigge was in Staffordshire from c. 1100 to 1266 and then in Warwickshire till 1844.

The changing bounds of the county offered some difficulties. In face of them we have been inclusive rather than exclusive. For the historical student we felt it necessary to include all that had once been in Worcestershire. For the present-day general public we felt it necessary to include all that has been added to Worcestershire from other counties.

ABBREVIATIONS

Abbr	*Placitorum Abbreviatio*, 1811.
AC	*Ancient Charters* (Pipe Roll Soc.), 1888.
AcctsWo	*Accounts of the Priory of Worcester* (WoHS), 1907.
AD	*Catalogue of Ancient Deeds.* (In progress.)
AlmBk	*Almoner's Book of the Priory of Worcester* (WoHS), 1911.
AN	Anglo-Norman.
AnnMon	*Annales Monastici* (Rolls Series), 5 vols., 1864–9.
AOMB	*Augmentation Office Miscellaneous Books* 61 (PRO).
ASC	*Anglo-Saxon Chronicle.*
Ass	Assize Rolls (unpublished) for Worcestershire for 1221, 1255, 1275 (PRO).
Bardsley	*Dictionary of English and Welsh Surnames*, 1901.
BCS	Birch, *Cartularium Saxonicum*, 3 vols., 1885–93.
Berks	Berkshire.
BiblWo	*Bibliography of Worcestershire* (WoHS), 3 pts., 1898–1907.
Bk	Buckinghamshire.
BM	*Index to the Charters and Rolls in the British Museum*, 2 vols., 1900–12.
Bodl	Worcestershire Charters (unpublished) in the Bodleian.
Bowen	Emmanuel Bowen, *The Large English Atlas*, c. 1760 and 1763.
Bracton	*Bracton's Note-book*, 1887.
BT	Bosworth-Toller, *Anglo-Saxon Dictionary*, 1882–98.
C	Cambridgeshire.
Cary	Cary, *English Atlas*, 1787.
Ch	*Calendar of Charter Rolls.* (In progress.)
Ch	Cheshire.
ChancP	*Chancery Proceedings in the reign of Elizabeth*, 3 vols., 1827–32.
ChancR	Variant Readings from Chancellor's copy of Pipe Rolls, as noted in Pipe Roll Society's editions.
ChronEve	*Chronicon Abbatiæ de Evesham* (Rolls Series), 1863.
Cl	*Calendar of Close Rolls.* (In progress.)
ClR	*Rotuli Litterarum Clausarum*, 2 vols., 1833–44.
Co	Cornwall.
Comp	*Calendar of Committee for Compounding*, 5 vols., 1889–93.
CompR	*Early Compotus Rolls of the Priory of Worcester* (WoHS), 1908.
	Compotus Rolls of the Priory of Worcester (WoHS), 1910.
Ct	*Court Rolls of the Manor of Hales* (WoHS), 2 pts., 1910–12.
Cu	Cumberland.
Cur	*Curia Regis Rolls.* (In progress.)
D	Devon.
D	*Letters and State Papers Domestic*, 12 vols., 1856–72.
Dan	Danish.
DB	*Domesday Book.*
Db	Derbyshire.

Do	Dorset.
Du	Durham.
Dugd	Dugdale, *Monasticon*, 6 vols. in 8, 1817–30.
Earle	Earle, *Handbook to the Land-charters*, 1888.
EcclVar	Ecclesiastical Commission Various (PRO), chiefly an Extent of 9 Hy 4.
EDD	*English Dialect Dictionary.*
EDG	Wright, *English Dialect Grammar*, 1905.
EHR	*English Historical Review.*
EPN	*Chief Elements in English Place-names*, 1923.
Ess	Essex.
EveA and *B*	Early Worcestershire Surveys in Cotton Vesp. B xxiv (Date of copy, c. 1190.)
FA	*Feudal Aids*, 6 vols., 1899–1920.
Fees	*Book of Fees*, 2 vols., 1922–3.
FF	Feet of Fines, 7 Ric. 1 to 50 Edward 3 (PRO). Calendar of Fines, Edward 3 (Lansdowne MS).
FF	*Index Pedum Finium pro Com. Wigorn*, 1865.
FF	*Worcestershire Fines*, 1649–1714 (WoHS), 1896.
Fine	*Calendar of Fine Rolls.* (In progress.)
FineR	*Excerpta e Rotulis Finium*, 2 vols., 1835–6.
For	*Forest Proceedings*, Excheq. K.R. (PRO).
Forssner	Forssner, *Continental Germanic Personal Names in England*, 1914.
Förstemann	Förstemann, *Altdeutsches Namenbuch, Personennamen* (PN), *Ortsnamen* (ON), 2 vols. in 3, 1901–16.
Fr	French.
France	*Calendar of Documents preserved in France*, 1899.
FW	Florence of Worcester, *Chronicon ex chronicis*, 2 vols., 1848–9.
G	Greenwood, *Map of Worcestershire*, 1820.
Ger	German.
Gerv	*Gervasius Cantuariensis* (Rolls Series), 2 vols., 1867–9.
Gl	Gloucestershire.
Gough	Camden's *Britannia*, tr. Gough, 3 vols., 1789. (Used for the maps by Cary.)
Ha	Hampshire.
Hab	Habington, *A Survey of Worcestershire*, (WoHS), 2 vols., 1895–9.
Hanley Charters	Hanley William Charters (MS).
Harl 3763	Evesham Cartulary.
He	Herefordshire.
Heming	*Hemingi chartularium Eccl. Wigorniensis*, 2 vols., 1723.
Heref	*Hereford Episcopal Registers* (Canterbury and York Soc.), 1906–14.
Herts	Hertfordshire.
Hickes	*Linguarum vett. septentrion. Thesaurus*, 2 vols., 1703–5.
Higden	*Polychronicon* (Rolls Series), 9 vols., 1865–86.
HMC	*Historical MSS Commission Reports.* (In progress.)
Inq aqd	*Inquisitiones ad quod damnum*, 1803.
Ipm	*Calendar of Inquisitions post mortem.* (In progress.) *Inquisitions post mortem for the county of Worcester* (WoHS), 1894.
IpmR	*Inquisitiones post mortem* (Record Commission), 4 vols., 1806–28.

IPN	*Introduction to the Survey of English Place-names*, 1923.
John of Worc	*The Chronicle of John of Worcester*, ed. Weaver, 1908.
K	Kent.
KCD	Kemble, *Codex Diplomaticus Aevi Saxonici*, 6 vols., 1839–48.
Kelly	*Directory for Warwickshire, Worcestershire*, etc., eds. of 1855, 1892.
Knowle	*The Register of the Guild of Knowle*, 1894.
Kyre	*Kyre Park Charters* (WoHS), 1905.
L	Lincolnshire.
La	Lancashire.
Lat	Latin.
Layamon	Layamon's *Brut*, 3 vols., 1847.
Lei	Leicestershire.
Lewis	*Topographical Dictionary of England*, 4 vols., 1841.
LGer	Low German.
LibAlb	*Liber Albus of Worcester Priory* (WoHS), 1919.
LibPens	*Liber Pensionum of the Priory of Worcester* (WoHS), 1925.
LOE	Late Old English.
LP	*Letters and Papers Foreign and Domestic.* (In progress.)
LVD	*Liber Vitae Dunelmensis* (Surtees Soc.), 1841.
LWS	Late West Saxon.
LyttCh	*Charters of the Lyttelton Family*, ed. Jeayes, 1893.
Marr	*Worcestershire Parish Registers* (Marriages to 1837), ed. Phillimore, 2 vols., 1901–10.
ME	Middle English.
Middleton	*Report on the Middleton MSS* (HMC), 1911.
MinAcct	*Ministers Accounts* (PRO).
Misc	*Calendar of Inquisitions Miscellaneous*, 2 vols., 1916.
MLG	Middle Low German.
Mon	Monmouthshire.
More	*Journal of Prior More* (WoHS), 1913–14.
Mx	Middlesex.
Nash	*Collections for the History of Worcestershire*, 2 vols., 1781–2.
Nb	Northumberland.
NED	*New English Dictionary.*
Nf	Norfolk.
NI	*Nonarum Inquisitiones*, 1807. Also in WoHS, 1893–1902.
NoB	*Namn och Bygd.* (In progress.)
Norw	Norwegian.
NQB	*Notes and Queries for Bromsgrove.*
Nt	Nottinghamshire.
Nth	Northamptonshire.
O	Oxfordshire.
O	Early ed. (c. 1830) of 1-in. O.S. map.
ODan	Old Danish.
OE	Old English.
OFr	Old French.
Ogilby	Ogilby, *Itinerarium Angliae*, 1699.
OHG	Old High German.
ON	Old Norse.
OrdBk	*The Old Order Book of Hartlebury School* 1556–1752 (WoHS), 1904.

c

Orig	*Originalia Rolls*, 2 vols., 1805–10.
O.S.	Ordnance Survey.
OSw	Old Swedish.
(p)	Place-name form derived from personal name compounded with *de*, *atte*, etc.
P	*Pipe Rolls* (Record Commission, 3 vols., 1833–44, Pipe Roll Soc. (in progress), Great Roll of the Pipe for 26 Hy 3, ed. Cannon, 1918.
Pap	*Calendar of entries in Papal Registers*. (In progress.)
Pat	*Calendar of Patent Rolls*. (In progress.)
Pat	Perambulation of the Forest of Feckenham, Pat. Rolls (Supplementary) (PRO).
p.n.	place-name.
PRO	Public Record Office.
QSR	*Calendar of Quarter Sessions Papers* (WoHS), 1900.
QW	*Placita de Quo Warranto*, 1818.
R	Rutland.
RBB	The Red Book of the Bishoprick of Worcester (PRO), transcribed from a lost volume by Dr Wm. Thomas in the 18th century. It included the Worcester Domesday of Bishop Baldwin (1182) and an extent taken in 1299.
RBE	*Red Book of the Exchequer*, 3 vols., 1896.
Redin	*Uncompounded Personal Names in Old English*, 1915.
RG	*Metrical Chronicle of Robert of Gloucester* (Rolls Series), 2 vols., 1887.
RH	*Rotuli Hundredorum*, 2 vols., 1812–18.
Ritter	*Vermischte Beiträge zur Englischen Sprachgeschichte*, 1922.
s.a.	sub anno.
Sa	Shropshire.
Saints	*Die Heiligen Englands*, ed. Liebermann, 1889.
SaltSoc	*Salt Society's Publications*. (In progress.)
Saxton	*Map of the County of Worcester*, 1577.
Scand	Scandinavian.
Schönfeld	*Wörterbuch der Altgermanischen Personen und Völkernamen*, 1911.
Searle	*Onomasticon Anglo-Saxonicum*, 1897.
Sf	Suffolk.
So	Somerset.
Speed	*Map of the County of Worcester*, 1611.
SR	*Lay Subsidy Rolls* for 1275, 1327, 1332, 1603 (WoHS), 1893–1902.
Sr	Surrey.
St	Staffordshire.
StEng	Standard English.
Stevenson MSS	Collections bequeathed to St John's College, Oxford by W. H. Stevenson.
StratGild	*Register of the Gild of the Holy Cross etc. of Stratford-upon-Avon*, 1907.
StSwith	*Charters from St Swithin's, Worcester* (WoHS), 1912.
Surv	*Parliamentary Survey* (1649) *of the lands of the Dean and Chapter of Worcester* (WoHS), 1924.
Surv	An early Worcestershire Survey (c. 1150), in VCH i.
Surv	Parliamentary Survey (1650) of certain lands in Worcestershire (PRO).

Sw	Swedish.
Sx	Sussex.
T	Isaac Taylor, *Map of the County of Worcester*, 1772.
Tax	*Taxatio Ecclesiastica*, 1802.
Thomas	*Survey of the Cathedral-church of Worcester*, 1736.
Townsend	*Diary of Hy Townsend* (WoHS), 3 pts., 1915–20.
VCH	*Victoria History of the County of Worcester*, 4 vols. and Index, 1901–26.
VE	*Valor Ecclesiasticus*, 6 vols., 1810–34.
VisitWo	*The visitation of the co. of Worcester*, 1569 (Harleian Society), 1888.
	The visitation of the co. of Worcester, 1682–3, ed. Metcalfe, 1883.
W	Wiltshire.
Wa	Warwickshire.
WCy	West Country.
We	Westmoreland.
Wigorn	*Worcester Episcopal Registers* (WoHS), 4 vols., 1897–1907.
Wills	*Calendar of Worcester Diocese Wills* (WoHS), 2 vols., 1904–10.
WillsP	*Wills proved in the Prerogative Court of Canterbury* (British Record Soc.), 6 vols., 1888–1912.
WoC	Register of Worcester Priory *pen.* Dean and Chapter of Worcester Cathedral.
WoCh	*Original Charters relating to City of Worcester* (WoHS), 1909.
WoHS	Worcestershire Historical Society. (In progress.)
WoP	*Registrum Prioratus B. Mariae Wigorniensis* (Camden Soc.), 1865.
Wt	Isle of Wight.
Wulst	*Annals of the Hospital of St Wulstan, with Cartulary*, ed. F. T. Marsh, 1890.
Y	Yorkshire.
ZONF	*Zeitschrift für Ortsnamenforschung*. (In progress.)

Reference is made to the various county place-name books (*v.* summary bibliography in EPN) by using the abbreviation PN followed by the recognised abbreviation for the county, e.g. PN Gl for Baddeley's *Place-names of Gloucestershire*.

PHONETIC SYMBOLS USED IN TRANSCRIPTION
OF PRONUNCIATIONS OF PLACE-NAMES

p	*p*ay	z	*z*one	r	*r*un	e	r*e*d
b	*b*ay	ʃ	*sh*one	l	*l*and	ei	fl*ay*
t	*t*ea	ʒ	a*z*ure	tʃ	*ch*urch	ɛː	th*ere*
d	*d*ay	θ	*th*in	dʒ	*j*udge	i	p*i*t
k	*k*ey	ð	*th*en	ɑː	f*a*ther	iː	f*ee*l
g	*g*o	j	*y*ou	ɑu	c*ow*	ou	l*ow*
ʍ	*wh*en	χ	lo*ch*	ai	fl*y*	u	g*oo*d
w	*w*in	h	*h*is	æ	c*a*b	uː	r*u*le
f	*f*oe	m	*m*an	ɔ	p*o*t	ʌ	m*u*ch
v	*v*ote	n	*n*o	ɔː	s*aw*	ə	*o*ver
s	*s*ay	ŋ	si*ng*	oi	*oi*l	əː	b*ir*d

Examples:
Harwich (hæridʒ), Shrewsbury (ʃrouzbəri, ʃruːzbəri),
Beaulieu (bjuːli).

NOTES

(1) The names are arranged topographically according to the Hundreds. Within each Hundred the parishes are dealt with in alphabetical order and within each parish the place-names are arranged similarly. The only exceptions to this rule are that the river-, road- and district-names are taken at the beginning as also the place-names in Worcester City itself.

(2) After the name of every parish will be found the reference to the sheet and square of the 1-in. O.S. map (Popular Edition) on which it may be found. Thus, Alfrick 81 E 8.

(3) Where a place-name is only found on the 6-in. O.S. map this is indicated by putting 6″ after it in brackets, e.g. Field Farm (6″).

(4) Place-names now no longer current are marked as 'Lost.' This does not necessarily mean that the site to which the name was once applied is unknown. We are dealing primarily with names and the names are lost.

(5) The local pronunciation of the place-name is given, wherever it is of interest, in phonetic script within squared brackets, e.g. [ɑ·frik]. Where the old spellings indicate a local pronunciation which cannot now be traced but which must have prevailed at an earlier stage in the history of the name, that pronunciation is given in phonetic script as in the case of the other names, but it is preceded by the word *olim*, e.g. Salwarpe, *olim* [sæləp].

(6) In explaining the various place-names summary reference is made to the detailed account of such elements as are found in the *Chief Elements in English Place-names* by printing those elements in Clarendon type, e.g. Hawkbatch, *v.* **heafoc, bæc.**

(7) In the case of all forms for which reference has been made to unprinted authorities, that fact is indicated by printing the reference to the authority in italic instead of ordinary type, e.g. *Ass* 1275 denotes a form derived from a MS authority in contrast to SR 1275 which denotes one taken from a printed text.

(8) Where two dates are given, e.g. 1040 (12th), the first is the date at which the document purports to have been composed, the second is that of the copy which has come down to us.

(9) Where a letter in an early place-name form is placed within brackets, forms with and without that letter are found, e.g. *Ar(e)leye* means that forms *Areleye* and *Arleye* are alike found.

(10) All OE words are quoted in their West-Saxon form unless otherwise stated.

ADDENDA ET CORRIGENDA

VOL. I, PART I

p. 122, l. 17. Mr P. H. Reaney (*Englische Studien* lxi. 80) points out that Warley Semeles is now Little Warley and appears as *Warle Setmoles* (1252-8 AD). *Septem molarum* is a Latinisation of the surname (cf. William *de Septem molis* or Setmoles 1242-59 AD) of a family owning land in Warley in 1212.

p. 125, l. 9. Mr P. H. Reaney (*u.s.* lxi. 80) writes '*Beauchamp Albrich* is not identical with Belchamp (*not* Beauchamp) Walter but survives as Allbrights formerly (*in*) *Bello Campo Sancto Ethelberti* (1294 FF), a small chapelry in Belchamp Otten.'

VOL. I, PART II

p. 13, s.v. calf. For 'Cawston' read 'Causton.'

p. 15, s.v. ceorl. For 'Chalgrave' read 'Chalgrove'

p. 17, s.v. clæg. Clayhanger (Ess) does not actually survive. It is perhaps identical with the present Claybury or Clayhall (P. H. Reaney).

p. 19, s.v. crouche. Delete 'Crutch (Wo)'

p. 20, l. 6 from bottom. Dr Grundy points out that *deopan delle* survives as the field-name *Dibdell* and that there is a quarry in it.

p. 22, l. 1. After Dordon read 'Wa' for 'Wo'

p. 23, l. 21. 'Eton (Bk)' belongs under eg and not under ea.

p. 25, l. 7. For '*airidh*' read '*airigh*'

p. 34, s.n. healh. Mr F. T. S. Houghton draws attention to the fact that the word *appellatur* in the quotation in l. 4 of the article is not in the text of the charter as printed in BCS 225 but is found in Sweet's *Oldest English Texts* 427, with no use of brackets to suggest that any letters not in the MS have been supplied (*v.* Preface vi). Birch gives *appro...supremum* after *healh* and this is nearer the truth. Mr J. P. Gilson, who very kindly collated the MS for us, reports "I do not feel sure of the second *p* in *app*. It might be *apr* but is not I think *app* in spite of our official facsimile editors. The surface beyond this is hopelessly gone. There is room for four letters (e.g. *appetit*) before *supremum*, but not for more, so both *appropinquat* and *appellatur* seem to me to be excluded." It is clear from this that all reference to this passage should be omitted in any attempt to determine the meaning of healh.

p. 41, l. 9 from bottom. For 'Barling' read 'Barlings'

p. 46, s.v. mapel. Maplestead (Ess) belongs rather under mapuldor (P. H. Reaney).

p. 59, l. 17 from bottom. For *competum* read *compitum*

VOL. II

p. 43, FOSCOTT. Mr A. H. Cox suggests that places called *Foxcote* or *Foxcott* and the like may originally have taken their name from an actual fox-earth.

p. 155, HOLMER GREEN. Mr A. H. Cox tells us that *Homers* is in Hambleden and must not be identified with this place.

p. 179, LUXTERS. The Rev. A. H. Stanton calls our attention to the faulty transcription made for us in the extract from the Fingest Terrier quoted here. The '5' is simply the number of the item in a series and the entry is simply 'Lucksters which is about ten acres.' *Luxters* is simply the name of the farm, deriving probably from a pers. name.

p. 212, WOODROW. Mr A. H. Cox suggests that the meaning of this name is simply 'row of trees.'

p. 265 (Index), s.n. Eton. For '235, 236' read '236, 237'

VOL. III

p. xl, AKEMAN STREET. The form *Accemannestrate* Hy 2 (c. 1200), Lee, *History of Thame*, 372, is conclusive in favour of a shortening of the vowel.

p. 2, l. 15. For 'Aketon' read 'Acton'

p. 7, l. 11 from bottom. Dr A. H. Smith calls our attention to a passage in the Chartulary of St Johns of Pontefract (*Yorks. Arch. Soc. (Rec. Series)* xxv, 281) in which the name *Watlinge Strete* is applied to the Great North Road, in the neighbourhood of Allerton Bywater, in the beginning of the 13th cent.

p. 9, l. 18. For 'Herefordshire' read 'Shropshire'

p. 43, n. 2, l. 2. For 'Clifton' read 'Stanford'

p. 46, s.n. *Stevington*. The same pers. name is found in Steventon (Ha, Berks).

p. 68, l. 16. Dr Ritter calls our attention to the fact that the right reading in BCS 1229, as shown by the BM Facsimile, is *crangfeldinga*. This means that *cranoc* alone must have been the form in early days, and that *cran-* is due to early loss of *c(g)* in the cons. group.

p. 73, s.n. DENEL END. Dr Ritter points out to us that the OE adj. *dunn*, 'dun-coloured,' was used as a topographical term, cf. *dunnan hole* (BCS 687, 699) and *on þone dunnan stan* (ib. 734).

p. 75, s.n. KEMPSTON. The forms of Kempstone (Nf), DB *Kemestun*, c. 1100 *Camestone*, c. 1140 *Kamestuna*, c. 1145 *Chemestuna* and a study of the history of Kempsey (Wo) make it probable that in all three we have an OE pers. name *Cemmi*. For its history and for the vowel *v*. PN Wo. The *b* in the forms of the Beds p.n. must then be taken as due to early epenthesis.

p. 92, s.n. MOGGERHANGER. Dr Ritter suggests with much likelihood that the first element here is the LOE name *Morkere*. The triple *r* of the compound in which it was found may have led to a first development of *Morker-* to *Moker- Moger-*, becoming later *Moke-, Mog(g)e-*.

p. 110, s.n. SWADING HILL. Dr Schram suggests to us that the family may have come from Swathing (Nf).

p. 114, s.n. WENSDON HILL. Delete the reference to Wendling (Nf).

p. 124, l. 12. Delete the reference to Harleston.

pp. 175–6, PEGSDON. A further example of OE *peac* is to be noted in Peake Fm (Ha). Mr C. A. Seyler has identified this with the *lytlan weac* of BCS 758, with the common confusion of the OE symbols for *p* and *w*. Just to the east of it is a hill with two peaks, one of 673 ft., the other of 615 ft.

p. 200, s.n. WASHINGLEY. Delete 'and also a lost *Wasincham* in the Norfolk Domesday'

p. 212, s.n. RAMSEY. Dr Ritter calls attention to the omission of early and important forms *Hramesege* (BCS 1306) of c. 975, *Ramesige* (Saints) of c. 1000 and *Hramesige* (*Anglia*, viii. 300) of c. 1000. These make it certain that we cannot have to do with OE *Hræfn*, for we should not thus early have had forms with single *m*. He takes the first element to be OE *hramse, hramsa*, 'garlic, rams, ransom.' This is found in OE in the forms *ramese, hramese* (B.T. Supplt.) and in the p.n. compounds *rameslea* (BCS 801) and *hramæs hangra* (KCD 658). Since he wrote, Mr J. J. Kneen, quite independently, in his *Place-Names of the Isle of Man*, 306, has suggested a similar etymology for Ramsey (IOM). This is *Ramsa* in the *Chronicle of Man* (c. 1250), i.e. 'garlic stream,' containing the cognate Scand. *rams*, and the Manx name for the stream, viz. *Strooan ny craue*, 'stream of the wild-garlic' (Irish, *creamh*), aptly confirms this suggestion.

p. 217, RAVELEY. Dr Ritter suggests with much probability that the earliest *Ræflea* is for *Hræfnlea* with the same loss of *n* that we get in OE *elboga, Bretwalda, Dorsetæn, æfsweorc* for earlier *elnboga, Bretnwalda, Dornsætan, æfesnweorc* and that the whole name means 'raven-clearing.'

p. 252, s.n. ABBOTSLEY. Mr Bruce Dickins points out to us that the advowson of Abbotsley was forfeited by the Abbot of Jedburgh in 1321 (HMC App. iv. 448) and the change of form of the name may have been in part due to his connexion with the place.

p. 266, s.n. BOUGHTON. Dr Ritter rightly prefers to start from an OE pers. name *Būca* as more readily explaining the subsequent forms, with later voicing of *c* to *g* and development of spirant *g* from earlier stop *g*.

p. 290, l. 18 from bottom. Delete reference to Ramsey.

p. 315, first column, l. 5. For 'He' read 'Sa' and delete the reference to Oxmead in l. 13.

ADDENDA

TO VOLUME IV

p. 3, FOSSE WAY. The ditch-origin of this road-name would be readily explained on the view, set out by Mr R. G. Collingwood (*Antiquity*, March 1927, p. 16), that the Fosse was originally a frontier line studded with forts.

p. 54, s.n. CORNWOOD. It should be noted in connexion with this difficult name that the charter from which the OE form comes contains a number of peculiarly unsatisfactory forms. *Suðintuna gemæru* is ungrammatical. *Stilladun* is almost certainly an error for *Stillandun* (cf. s.n. Stildon *infra* 74), in *Eardgulfestun*, OE þ has been misread by Heming as ʒ. These curious forms suggest that in interpreting Mamble (*infra* 60) we should not assume that the *momela gemæra* in the same charter is necessarily correct.

p. 63, l. 9 from bottom. Delete the article on HOLME. The form here given is almost certainly an error for *Holine* and refers to Holling Fm.

p. 67, PENSAX. As the volume was being passed for press we received an interesting suggestion from Dr Ritter with regard to this name. He would take (*to*) *Pensaxan* as LOE for (*to*) *Pensaxan* and would interpret the name as denoting a settlement of Saxons at a place or in a district called *Penn* (cf. Penn Hall in this parish *infra* 68). For such a compound he adduces the parallels of the OGer *Moinwinidi* (9th) explained by Förstemann (ON ii. 1570) as 'Main-Wends,' i.e. settlement of Wends on the Main, and Strasswalchen, OGer *Strazwalaha* (8th), *Strazwalachon* (9th), presumably a settlement of 'Welsh' men on some important road. Such a name, 'Saxons at Penn,' suits not only the topography but also the historical conditions. From the bounds of Pensax as given in Heming (246) it is clear that that name was applied to a considerable area and not merely to the present parish. This area lay in the extreme north-west of the county, it extended as far as the Teme, which here forms the natural boundary to the west against what was always Anglian territory, so that the area to the east might naturally be described by a name containing reference to its Saxon population.

p. 71, Add FALKLANDS (6″) in Rock. This is *Farkland* in 1545 (LP) and is probably another example of the rare folcland dealt with in EPN.

p. 91, CUTMILL. Dr Schram calls our attention to another example of this name in a Fine of 1197 (Arch. Cantiana i. 235) concerned with Boxley (K). The form there is *Cucciddemille* but the *cc* is clearly an error for *tt*. The name is now lost. There is an undocumented Cutmill in Chidham (Sx).

p. 92, s.n. GOLDENWICK. Professor Ekwall (PN La 81) had already noted the mention in WoP of both *acra Goldgive* and *Goldgivewik*, suggesting an OE pers. name *Goldgiefu*.

p. 94, RUSHWICK. Professor Ekwall calls attention to the possible identification of this place with the stream called *Rixuc* in the bounds of Cotheridge (BCS 1106). The bounds here seem to run due south following a now unnamed stream roughly parallel to the combination of footpath-road-footpath which runs straight down to Bransford Bridge, forming the *stræt* which in the charter runs down to Bransford. (The present bounds of Cotheridge are very little different from these.) This puts Rushwick a mile east of the *Rixuc*, but there is a feeder of the *Rixuc* rising very near Rushwick and it is possible, as was so often the case, that both arms of the stream bore the same name. If that was the case, Rushwick is probably to be explained as a later folk-etymologising of earlier *rixuc*. That word itself is a derivative of **rysc** and must, as Professor Ekwall suggests, mean 'rushy place' or 'rushy brook.'

With this word in mind, Professor Ekwall suggests with much likelihood that we should give a different explanation of Rushock (*infra* 255). The Elmley Brook at this point in its course may have also been called *Rixuc* and the full name of the place have been *rixuc-hoc*, which would explain the curious DB form *Russococ*.

p. 101, BREDON. Mitton in Bredon was granted to Bishop *Heaberht* (BCS 433). William of Malmesbury (*Gest. Pont.* § 136, Rolls Series) calls him *Herebeorht* while Habington (i. 525) has *Herebert*. Possibly Bredon *Herberd* is Mitton.

p. 104, FOXBATCH. Dr Grundy points out that this survives in two or three field-names on the western boundary of Broadwas, just east of the village of Doddenham, where there is a little valley.

p. 124. Further examples of the association of members of a guild with place-names are to be found in the 13th cent. *Gildenegore* in Castle Acre, and the 13th cent. *Gildene Halfakyr* in Felthorpe and *Gildeneaker* in Ashby in Flegg, all Nf examples provided by Dr O. K. Schram. It is of course just conceivable that some of these last names and even one or two of the earlier names may contain the OE adj. *gylden* and the reference be to the colour of the crops or to that of gorse or broom growing on the land, but we have no definite evidence for such a usage and it would not explain such forms as *Ildeberg*, *Ildenebrugge* or *Ealing* Bridge. Equally doubtful is Guildenhurst in Pulborough (Sx), *Guldenhurst* in 1332 (SR). This may be 'golden wood' or 'guildsmen's wood.'

p. 155, QUEENHILL. Counthorpe (L), with forms *Cunnigetorp* (1208 FF), *Cointhorp* (1234 ib.), *Coynthorp*, *Quenithorp* (1265 Ipm) furnishes an interesting parallel for the confusion of initial *c* and *q*. We may note also (*ex inf.* Dr Schram) *Quenhill* in Lexham (1197 FF), *Quinhill* in Burgh by Aylsham (1234 Broomholme Cartulary) in Norfolk.

p. 188, RAMSDEN should be dealt with under Pershore Holy Cross (217) and not under Besford. It is in the former parish.

p. 232, under YARDLEY add
BROOMHALL *Bromhalas* 972 (c. 1050) BCS 1282, *Bromhale* 1275, 1327 SR, 1314 *FF*, all (p), *Bromhales* 1420 IpmR, *Bromwall* 1552 Ct, *Bromhall* 1662 FF. 'Broom-covered nook(s),' *v.* brom, healh.

p. 294. Under CRADLEY add
OLDENHALL. *Holdenhale, Holdenhall* 1275 SR (p), *Oldenhale* 1277 Ct, 1327 SR, both (p). 'Ealda's nook,' *v.* healh.

p. 357, s.n. TESSALL. Dr Ritter suggests that the first element is an OE pers. name *Tǣse* from the adj. *tǣse*, 'pleasant.' Cf. *tǣsan mǣd* BCS 390. Hence 'Tæse's nook of land' (*v.* healh).

WORCESTERSHIRE

Worcestershire

Wireceastrescire c. 1040 (12th) KCD 757
Wigercestresire 1066 (c. 1250) KCD 829
Wircestrescire n.d. (c. 1250) KCD 830
Wihracestrescir 11th (1038 C) ASC
Wirecestrescire 1086 DB
Wiðreceastrescir 12th (1087 E) ASC
Wigreceastrescir 12th (1119 E) ASC
Wirecestresira Hy 2 (1312) Ch
Wicestressire c. 1300 RG

For the origin of the name of the county, *v.* Worcester *infra* 19.

DISTRICT NAMES

THE COTSWOLDS

The earliest form for this name[1] is to be found in Giraldus Cambrensis' *Speculum Ecclesiae* (Opera, iv. 106, Rolls Series) where he passes through *montana de Codesuualt* in travelling from Blockley to Evesham. Mr Baddeley (PN Gl 50–1) gives forms *Coteswolde* (1318) and *Cotteswolde* (1360). We may add *Coteswaud* and *Coddeswold* (Pat 1250, 1269). It is clear that this name, like Cutsdean *infra* 120, contains a personal name *Codd*, *v.* PN Bk 74. Whether it was actually the same man who gave his name to Cotswold, Cutsdean and the *Codeswelle* in Cutsdean it is impossible to say with certainty, but as Cutsdean is in the heart of the Cotswolds it is quite possible. The second element is weald, probably used here simply of high open ground. The name was almost certainly used in the original instance of a much smaller area than that to which it is now applied. The earlier name for the larger area was 'hill of the Hwicce' (*v.* Introduction xv), as *in mons Huuicciorum* (BCS 236), *in monte Wiccisca* (BCS 1135).

WYRE FOREST

foresta de Wira 1177 P
v. Worcester *infra* 19 for this name.

[1] Stevenson MSS.

ROAD-NAMES

BUCKLE STREET

> *Buggildestret* 709 (c. 1200) BCS 125
> *Buggan stret* c. 860 (c. 1200) KCD 289 (iii. 396)
> *Bucgan stræt* 967 (11th) BCS 1201

In the charter-references here given the name is applied to a road running from Bidford Bridge (Wa) to Aston-sub-Edge (Gl) and now called Buckle Street. This is part of the road called Icknield or Ryknild Street *infra* which runs from Wall, near Lichfield, southward to join the Fosse Way near Bourton-on-the-Water (Gl). The first element in the name is OE *Burghild*, a woman's name. This, by assimilation, became *Buggild*, and *Bucge* is a pet-form for it, cf. *Bucge* for *Ēadburg*. We must suppose that she was a prominent landholder somewhere on the line of the street. It may be that we should identify her with *Burgenhilda* (i.e. *Burghild*), whom Florence of Worcester names as a daughter of Cœnwulf, king of Mercia (796–821). There was also a *Bucge*, with a daughter *Heburg*, i.e. *Hēahburg*, who had an interest in land at Evenlode (BCS 209) and another who was a nun at Withington (ib. 156).

It should be added that the charter of 709, our earliest authority for this name, is a gross forgery. For the modern form we may compare Bucklebury (Berks), earlier *Burghildebiri*.

ICKNIELD STREET, RYKNILD STREET

> *Ykenilde Strete, Ikenildestret* 1275 *Ass* (p), 1289 Wigorn,
>   1299 (18th) *RBB*, 1319 Pat
> *Ikeneldestrete* 1314 *FF*, 1327 Pat, both (p), 1546 AD iii
> *Ikelyngestrete* 1340 NI (p)
> *Rikenildstret* c. 1400 Higden, *Polychronicon* ii. 46
> *Ekelingstrete* 1535 VE
> *Ikelyngstreyte* 1547 Pat

In the above entries (except that from Higden) we have reference to the course of this road (*v.* Buckle Street *supra*) in the neighbourhood of Alvechurch and perhaps that is the stretch of the road to which it was originally applied. The name is really borrowed from the more famous Icknield Way, under conditions which are fully explained in PN BedsHu 4–5 and it is certainly of post-conquest origin. The form *Rikenild* is first found in Higden and is used of a road running from St Davids by Worcester, Birmingham and Lichfield to York. The *r* is due to corruption of ME *at there Ikenilde strete* to *at the Rikenilde strete*.

FOSSE WAY

The bounds of Tredington (KCD 620) run *in fos...ondlong fos*. Other references to this road in OE charters are *Fosse streat* (BCS 1257) near a lost Clifton by Bath[1], *on þan olden fosse and lang fosse* (BCS 112) near Shepton Mallet and *in foss...æfter foss* near Donnington (Gl). There can be little doubt that this is the Lat. *fossa*, which must have been inherited by the English from the Romanised Britons, the road having presumably come to be so called because it had a prominent 'ditch' on one side or both. In Blockley (*v.* Ditchford *infra* 98) the road seems to have been known as *dic*, 'ditch, dyke.'

PORTWAY

In the bounds of Wolverton (KCD 612) we have reference to the *portweg*. This must be the Worcester-Pershore road as it forms the boundary of the present Stoulton parish. The name is preserved a little further east on the Worcester-Alcester road, which branches off at Spetchley, in *Portway* Fm (6") in Kington. There is a *norðmæstan port weig* (BCS 356) in the bounds of (a part of) Hallow. The *sealt stræt* of that charter is almost certainly the north and south main road from Grimley. Possibly the portway in question was the road running north-west in the direction of Wichenford from just west of Greenhill. The southern portway (not mentioned) may be the road through Shoulton in the direction of Wichenford. This southern portway is probably identical with the *portstræt* of BCS 1108 which runs to Greenstreet Fm (*infra* 131), the *grenan wege* which follows it in the bounds. In BCS 1240 there is another *portstræt* in the bounds of the lost 'Perry' (cf. Perry Wood in St Martins). This must be the east road out of Worcester, leading to Bredicote. There is also a *portstræt* near the bounds of Ombersley (KCD 627) and a Port Street in Bengeworth (*infra* 96). In these

---

[1] *ex inf.* Dr G. B. Grundy.

compounds with *port* as the first element the road must have been so called as leading to some prominent *port* or town (*v.* port). In all the cases except the last it is clear that the *port* must be Worcester itself. In the last case it is probably Evesham, though the road does ultimately come from Worcester[1].

RIDGE WAY

The Ridge Way runs from Headless Cross, south of Redditch, forming the boundary between Warwickshire on the one side and Feckenham and Inkberrow on the other. This road is referred to in the Metes of Feckenham Forest (*Pat* 1300), where the bounds run along *Foxhunteweye* (i.e. foxhunters' road) *que a quibusdam vocatur le Rugwey*, i.e. called by some the Ridge Way. It is referred to in 1464 (Pat) as *Le Riggeway*. For these 'ridge ways,' *v.* Grundy in *Arch. Journ.* lxxiv. 87 ff. There was another *Ruggewey* in the neighbourhood of Pershore (*AOMB* 61) which Dr Grundy identifies with the Stoulton-Defford road.

In addition to these we may note two roads mentioned in the bounds of Yardley (BCS 1282). These are *Leommanincg weg* which seems to be the present Birmingham-Stratford-on-Avon road and *Dagarding weg* the Birmingham-Coventry road. These must take their name from unknown persons named *Leofmann* and *Dægheard* respectively.

SALTWAYS

Droitwich and its neighbourhood were the only places in Central England where salt was produced in the Middle Ages. The salt there produced was carried on packhorses to the places where it was in demand along roads or tracks, some of which acquired the designation of *Saltways*. The roads commonly so called are (i) the ancient road running north from Droitwich and joining the Ryknild Street a little south of Birmingham and south to Worcester, Tewkesbury and Gloucester, (ii) the road from Droitwich through Feckenham and Alcester to Stratford-on-Avon. These came to be known respectively as the *Upper* and the *Lower Saltways*, though the authority for these names is comparatively modern.

---

[1] In KCD 627 we have a *portstræt* in Waresley in Hartlebury which would seem to be the road running west to Redstone Ferry.

In the Saxon charters and in other ancient records there is however evidence for several other salt-roads. In DB there were 36 vills[1] in the county which had salt-rights in Droitwich. In addition to these there were ten vills each in Gloucestershire and Herefordshire, six in Warwickshire, two in Oxfordshire and one in Buckinghamshire which had similar rights. It seems probable that for the supply of salt to these places there were some dozen or more salt-ways. Their routes were as follows:

A. A track from Droitwich by Martin Hussingtree[2] passed near Spetchley (KCD 683 *to þære saltstræte swa west...to Swæchæme* (sic) *gemære*), then over Low Hill (KCD 612 *of Oswaldes hlawe ondlong þære sealtstræt*) and so (KCD 645 *on þone salt herpað and swa ondlong þæs herpaðes on salteredene...on saltere wellan...on salt broc*)[3] by Saw Brook to Pinvin and Wyre Piddle (S). Here it turned south-east and crossed the Avon at *Perryford* (*infra* 120) and ran between Elmley Castle and Netherton, where it is named *Saltway* on the 1″ map, and on it is *Saltway* Barn (1″). The direction is then near the western boundary of Hinton-on-the-Green (Gl), as in KCD 764 (*æfter hinhæma gemæru...in salt-wyllan*), thence past Ashton-under-Hill, west of Dumbleton, past Salters Close, over Alderton Hill, through Toddington (S) and past Stanway (S) to Hailes (named *Saltway* in Taylor's Map), past *Salters* Hill (1 mile east of Winchcombe), Hawling and Salperton[4] to Hazleton. Then, diverging from the Cheltenham-Oxford road 1 mile west of Northleach, it crosses the Fosse Way 1 mile south-west of that town and drops upon *Saltway* Barn (6″). South-west of that it passes on by Crickley Barrows to *Saltway* Fm, 2½ miles south-west of Northleach. Near here it is marked *Salt Way* on the 1″ map. Thence it

---

[1] Marked with an (S) in the ensuing pages.

[2] As this road left Droitwich and passed Witton it seems to have been called *le Ermyngwey*, for in AD i we have mention of land called *le Wychfeld* by the road called *le Ermyngwey* (1346). This would seem to be an adaptation of the old name *Erming* or *Ermine* Street, dealt with in PN BedsHu 3 ff.

[3] The compound *saltbroc*, like *saltwyllan*, *saltuuelle*, might of course refer to waters which were in themselves salt, but as the *saltbroc* immediately follows a *salterewellan* and is called *saltaresbrok* in the 12th cent., and as the *saltuuelle* comes topographically very close to a *sealterawyllan* and both are undoubtedly on a salt-way, we may take *saltbroc* and *saltwielle* as loosely constructed terms for brooks and springs on the line of saltways.

[4] It is just possible that the first element in this difficult name may have something to do with *sealt* (PN Gl 132–3).

D

reaches another *Saltway* Barn (Old 1″) below Pitcher Well Copse on the high ground between the Leach and the Coln, where the old 1″ map marks *Saltway* Road. From here it continues midway between Coln St Aldwyn and Hatherop direct to Lechlade.

A′. From Hailes a branch ran through the Guitings (S), Aston Blank and Sherborne by *Saltway* Plantation (2½ miles south of Sherborne) and east of the Eastleaches, where the track is a county boundary for 4 miles, to Lechlade.

B. Through Worcester[1] by the 'King's Highway called *Saltway*' (1426 Pat) to Tewkesbury (S), Cheltenham (1½ miles south is *Salters* Hill) and Leckhampton (1½ miles south is *Salter*ley), by the edge of Birdlip Hill past the *Salt*-Box (PN Gl 133) and *Salt*ridge Hill (2 miles north-east of Painswick)[2], and thence by Stroud to Wotton-under-Edge, where it would fork south-west to Thornbury (S) and Rockhampton (S) and south to Chipping Sodbury (S), all in Gloucestershire[3].

B′. A deviation at Tewkesbury (S) to Gloucester (S), where the monks of St Peter had salt rights, and thence to Awre (S) on the Severn.

C. Through Wychbold (S) and Upton Warren (S) to Bromsgrove (S) and Birmingham. There would be a branch to serve Tardebigge (S), Alvechurch (S) and the lost *Osmerley* (S), with another to serve Halesowen (S).

D (presumed). To Hampton Lovett (S), Horton (S), Elmley Lovett (S), Rushock (S), over Bradford in Chaddesley to Kidderminster (S), with branches to Chaddesley Corbett (S) and Belbroughton (S).

D′ (presumed). To Doverdale (S), Redstone Ferry, Astley (S) and Holt (S) by a deviation.

E. To Hadzor (S), Hanbury (S) (*Saltway* on 1″ map), Holloway (S), Feckenham (S) and Studley (S) in Wa, possibly

---

[1] The present Castle St was known as *La Sauteweye, Saltway* 1343, 1480 (WoCh) and by it salt could be diverted from the main road, thus avoiding tolls and traffic, and taken down the Severn to Gloucester etc.

[2] The Cheltenham-Stroud road up till 1795 ran along the top of the ridge from Birdlip. The new road forks from it at Water Edge (1″) and takes lower ground. The old road, marked *Saltway* on the old 1″ map, went by The Camp, Stancombe Fm and Lypiatt Park to Stroud.

[3] For help with the course of the Saltways in Gloucestershire we are much indebted to the kindness of Mr St Clair Baddeley.

with a branch to Haselor (S), also in Wa. This is the *Saltweia* of a Wo fine of 1227[1].

F. To Phepson (S), Shell (S), Stock Wood and on to the north of Inkberrow (S), called *Salterestret* in 1275 (*Ass*) and *Saltar Street* in an 18th cent. map of Inkberrow parish. From this section a branch would go to Abbots Morton (S). Continuing, the track went by Cook Hill, Arrow, and Oversley to the existing main Alcester-Stratford road, from which there would have been branches to Haselor (S), Hillborough (S) and Binton (S), all in Warwickshire, and so to Shottery (KCD 725 *in þa sealtstret, of þære stræte innon Scotbroc*, i.e. Shottery Brook) and Stratford-on-Avon. From thence Wasperton (S) and Brailes (S), both in Warwickshire, would have been reached. Traces of this may be found in the *saltstret* (c. 1200) of *AOMB* 61 in Sibford (O), a mile or two east of Brailes.

G. Droitwich to Oddingley, Tibberton and Crowle, all places with salt-rights. We have no documentary evidence in support of this saltway but its existence may be presumed.

H. A saltway which parted from A between Wyre Piddle and Perryford, crossed over *Luddesbroc* (KCD iii. 396) and then went *of Ludes broce on ða sealtstræt* and so due east across the Avon at Twyford[2]. Thence it went by Bretforton and along Buckle Street to Broadway, Buckle Street being known indifferently as *sealt stræt* or *Buggilde stret*, as is clear from a comparison of BCS 1282, 125 and KCD 1368. Thence it went to near Stow-on-the-Wold (BCS 229 *innon þere salt stret*), on by Maugersbury (KCD 1365 *sealtera wyllan*) to Iccomb (BCS 240 *Saltuuelle*). An alternative route from Broadway passed near the Four Shire Stones (BCS 1238 *andlang sealt stræte to þam stane*), thence near Broadwell (KCD 1359 *anlong þere sæltstræte*) to Maugersbury. From Evesham, Mickleton (S) could also be reached.

I. From the Four Shire Stones (see route H) there would be a route to Chipping Norton. This passed the village of Salford, *Salteford* in BCS 222. Thence there are the remains of a direct

---

[1] There is a lane leading from the direction of Droitwich into Redditch, marked *Salters* Lane on the 6″ map. This may have been the real route from Droitwich to Studley, or an alternative to that through Alcester.

[2] As Evesham Abbey had salt-rights, there must have been a branch into Evesham itself, just before Twyford.

track to Bampton (S), 15 miles due south of it, with *Salters Corner* (6″) in Widford two-thirds of the way along this stretch. Three miles north of Chipping Norton there is a branch road to the Rollrights (S). All these places are in Oxfordshire.

Princes Risborough (S) in Bucks may have been reached by an extension from Chipping Norton. There is an old track leading south-east to Stonesfield (O), where it joins Akeman Street. The Roman road was probably used for some 14 miles, to a point 5 miles east-south-east of Bicester, whence there is an almost uninterrupted course along minor roads, leading in another 14 miles to Risborough. Alternatively, there may have been a road from Stratford-on-Avon, via Eatington, Oxhill, Upper Tysoe (Wa), by the Red Horse on Edgehill to Wroxton and North Newington (O), where we have a *Salt Way* (1″), thence by Adderbury (O) and Aynho (Nth) to Akeman Street and so by the same route to Risborough.

K. In BCS 1282, in the bounds of Acton Beauchamp, the bounds go from the Leadon *in linleahe, of linleahe in saltera weg*. This saltway must have come via Worcester through the south part of Suckley. From Acton there is a fairly direct road west to Moreton Jeffreys (S), Ullingswick (S), Marden[1] (S) and Wellington (S), all in Herefordshire. A deviation from this road leads to Tupsley (S), just east of Hereford.

L. Eastnor, Ledbury and Much Marcle and Cleeve in Ross, all places in Herefordshire with salt-rights, would be reached by the Wyche[2] cutting through the Malvern Hills.

M. In the Subsidy Roll (1275) for Bockleton there appears a pers. name Joh. de *Saltereswelle*. As Bockleton is on the straight line from Droitwich to Leominster (S) this probably points to a saltway from Droitwich through Great Witley, across the Teme at Stanford and thence by Kyre, Bockleton, Pudleston to Leominster.

N. The metes of Redmarley d'Abitot (BCS 1109) run *of sealterforda* and those of Pendock (BCS 541) on *sealt leage*.

---

[1] From Ullingswick to Marden some two or three miles of the way are little more than a lane or track, which has now fallen out of use, and we are indebted to Mr St Clair Baddeley for the information that local tradition has it that this was once used by the 'salt-people.'

[2] Has this name anything to do with *Wich* or *Droitwich* itself, being so called because it carried a road from that place? Equally curious is the *Saltwhiche* in Cirencester (Baddeley, *History of Cirencester*, 225).

These, or at any rate the first of them, may indicate an alternative saltway from Tewkesbury to Ledbury.

O. The metes relating to Hallow (BCS 356) refer twice to a *s(e)alt stræt*. The bounds are difficult to follow but the street referred to seems to be the north and south road through Grimley and St Johns to Powick and onwards. This was possibly an alternative route to B, used to avoid passing through the city of Worcester and paying toll there[1].

RIVER-NAMES

The forms of the river-names, so far as they are found in early documents, are as follows. Their interpretation is reserved for the present, as they can only satisfactorily be dealt with as a whole.

ARROW, R.

Arue 710 (14th) BCS 127
arwan stream 11th Heming 362
Arwe 1244 FF

This is the same river-name as the *Ar(e)we* of the ASC (1016 D, E), now known as the Orwell R. (Sf). The Arrow in Herefordshire (*erge* in BCS 1040) must be of different origin.

AVON, R.

Afen(e) 705 (12th) BCS 123, 780 (11th) BCS 235, 873 (11th) BCS 537
Avena, Auene 709 (12th) BCS 125, c. 860 (12th) KCD iii. 396
Eafene 845 (11th) BCS 845

This is a common river-name in Old English and we have early forms for the present Avon-rivers which flow out by Avonmouth, Christchurch, and the Severn estuary at Berkeley.

BELL, R. (lost)

v. Belbroughton *infra* 275.

BODY BROOK (6″) in Dodderhill

Bottebroc, Bottebroke 1275 SR, *Ass* (p)
Bottybroke, Boddybroke 1456 VCH iii. 79, n. 95, 17th Nash

---

[1] There is also a Salter Street (parish and hamlet) in Tanworth (Wa). It must be the north and south road passing through the hamlet, for this road is marked as Salter Street on the original 1″ map. It is difficult to see what place having salt-rights it could serve and for the present its relation to the other saltways must remain uncertain.

Probably OE *Bottan-brōc*, 'Botta's brook.' The modern form shows curious retention of the inflexional syllable, such as is uncommon except in Devonshire. Cf. Caddecroft *infra* 218.

Bow Brook olim Himble Brook

> *hymel broc* c. 840 (11th) BCS 428, 884 (18th) ib. 552, 956 (11th) BCS 937, 972 (c. 1050) BCS 1282
> *Humelbroc, pontem de Humelbroke* 1237 Ch, 1275 *Ass*
> *Hymmylbrooke, Hymbell Brook* 1501 VCH iv. 28, 1579 FF

The present name of the stream is derived from the bridge mentioned above. That bridge was called Stone*bow*, *v. infra* 167 and the fuller name of the stream was at first *Stone Bow* Brook (Ogilby 1675). For the first element in the name *v.* Himbleton *infra* 135.

Carrant Brook[1] in Bredon

> *Carent* 778 (18th) BCS 232
> *Cærent* 780 (11th) BCS 236, 987 Earle 208
> *Kærent* 875 (11th) BCS 541
> *Garren, R.* 1763 Bowen

This stream has a continental parallel in the *Carantonus* or *Carentonus*, now the Charente in France; cf. Holder, *Alt-keltischer Sprachschatz*, 770.

Chind, R. (lost)

> *v.* Chyndhouse *infra* 352.

Cole, R. in Yardley

> *Colle* 849 (11th) BCS 455, 972 (c. 1050) BCS 1282

This is the stream from which Coleshill (Wa) takes its name.

Corn Brook in Knighton-on-Teme

> *Cornabroc* c. 957 (11th) BCS 1007
> *v.* Cornwood *infra* 54.

Dowles Brook

> *v.* Dowles *infra* 47 for this stream-name.

---

[1] There may have been a second Carrant Brook in Worcestershire for there are 13th cent. field-names *Carenforlong, Carentemede* in Hartlebury (VCH iii. 381) which look as if they contained this stream-name.

ENNICK, R. (lost)
  v. Ennick Ford *infra* 222.

ERSE, R. (lost)
  Yrse 972 (c. 1050) BCS 1282, 987 (11th) KCD 612
  Eourse, Ursa 13th (15th) *AOMB* 61
  For this stream *v.* Ersfield *infra* 179.

EVENLODE, R.
  Bladaen 718 (11th) BCS 139
  Bladen, riparia de Bladene 1005 (13th) KCD 714, 1238 Cl
  The present name of this stream is a back-formation from the village of that name. The old name is still preserved in the names Bledington (Gl), DB *Bladintune* and Bladon (O), on its banks.

GLADDER BROOK in Ribbesford
  Gloddre 1332 SR, 1340 NI, both (p)
  water of Gloddere, Glodderebrugge 1366 Cl
  Glodder brook 1595 AD v

GLEDEN BROOK in Warndon
  to þære glædenun 978 (11th) KCD 618
  This perhaps contains the OE *glædene*, the name of the yellow flag.

GLYNCH BROOK in Redmarley
  Glenc, Glencing, Glencincg 963 (11th) BCS 1109, 970 (c. 1050) BCS 1282
  Glench 1276 RH
  le Glynge 15th VCH iv. 214

GRIMLEY BROOK
  in bæle, ondlang bæles, on bæle, onlong bæle 851 (11th) BCS 462, 962 (11th) BCS 1087
  Bale Broke 1534 More
  Here we have the old name of the brook, repeated in *la burne de Bale* in Alvechurch (1244 *FF*) and preserved in *Ball* Mill *infra* 141.

HONEYBROOK (6″) in Wolverley

Hunigbroc 866 (11th) BCS 514

Of similar character to this stream-name are Honeybourne *infra* 264, a lost *Honeyborne* in Droitwich, a *hunigbroc* in Rimpton in Somersetshire (KCD 1174), *hunigwiellæs weg* (BCS 624) in the bounds of Ashmansworth (Ha), Honeywell in Ilsington (D), Honeychild (K), cf. *celde* in EPN, and *hunighomm* (Heming 347). In all these cases we must have reference to the sweetness or general pleasantness of the water or pasture.

HORSEBROOK (local) in Wolverley

Horsabroc 866 (18th) BCS 513, 964 (11th) BCS 1134
Horsebroke 1354 LibPens

The name is self-explanatory. It lies just by a *Horseley* in the same parish *infra* 258.

INKFORD BROOK in King's Norton and Beoley (Old 1″)

Merebrok 1275, 1327 SR (p)   *Inkford Brook* 1649 Surv

The brook lies on the Warwickshire boundary so it is clear that the first name is 'boundary brook,' *v.* (ge)mære, broc. The forms of Ennick Ford *infra* 222 suggest that the old brook-name here also may have been *Hennuc*. For further forms *v.* Inkford in King's Norton *infra* 354. It forms part of the river Cole and the whole extent of the river now bears that name.

ISBOURNE, R. in Hampton

Esegburna 777 (16th) BCS 223
(Bi)esingburnan 872 (11th) BCS 535
Esing(e)burna 930 (c. 1200) BCS 667
Eseburne 988 (c. 1200) KCD 662

This stream must have taken its name from the people who settled on its banks, viz. the *Ēsingas* or 'people of Esa.' For this pers. name *v.* PN Bk 121.

KYRE BROOK

For this stream-name, *v.* Kyre *infra* 55.

LAUGHERN BROOK

Laure 816 (11th) BCS 356
Lawern 816 (11th) BCS 357, c. 970 (11th) BCS 1139
Lawrne 1636 VCH iii. 565

LEADON, R.

Ledene 972 (c. 1050) BCS 1282, 978 (11th) RCD 619, 1392
BM

LITTLE BROOK (6″) in Huddington

lytlan broc (acc.) 884 (18th) BCS 552
Littlebrook 1649 Surv

Self-explanatory. It separates Huddington from Himbleton.

MARL BROOK

Mæra broc c. 957 (11th) BCS 1007
Merebroch c. 1200 (c. 1240) *WoC*
Marbrook 1787 Cary

v. (ge)mære, broc. This is one of the varied corruptions under
which the old name for a 'boundary' brook now appears. This
one separates Lindridge and Mamble. *v.* Merry Brook *infra*.
We may also note Marbrook (6″) on the bounds of Blockley,
Mary Brook (6″) on the bounds of Pershore St Andrew and
Mere Brook on the bounds of Hanley. For none of these have
we early forms, but they certainly all have the same origin.

MERRY BROOK in Charlton

Merebroc 709 (c. 1200) BCS 125
Mærbroc 998 (c. 1200) KCD 662

'Boundary-stream,' *v.* (ge)mære, broc.

PARRET, R. (lost)

Pedredan (dat.) 988 (12th) KCD 662
Pederedan (acc.) 1003 (12th) KCD 1299
Peodredan (dat.) n.d. (12th) KCD 1358

This stream, which seems to have formed the north part of
the boundary between Hampton and Bengeworth, flows into
the Avon half a mile south-west of Bengeworth Church. The
name must be identical with that of the Parret R. in Somersetshire, *Pedride* ASC, s.a. 658, *Pedrede* ib. s.a. 894, *Pedredistrem* in
BCS 143 and *Peddredan* (dat.), KCD 839.

PIDDLE BROOK

> *Pidele* 708 (c. 1200) BCS 120, (water called) 1229 Ch
> *Pidwuella, Pidwellan* (dat.) 930 (c. 1200) BCS 667
> *Pidelan* (dat.) 963 (11th) BCS 1110, 972 (c. 1050) BCS 1282
> *Piduuella, Pidwyllan, Pidwellan* 1002 (11th) KCD 1295
> *Pydelebroc* 1182 (18th) *RBB*

There is also a lost *pydewellan* (BCS 1201) near Bickmarsh (Wa) and a Piddle R. in Dorset, *Pidelen stream* (BCS 1186), *Pydele* in KCD 656.

REA, R. in Bayton

> *in ðære ea nen* c. 957 (11th) BCS 1007, *le Ree* 1523–1619 Kyre
> *the Ree* 1310 LibPens

This was originally a river Nen(e) which has given its name to the villages of Neen Sollars and Neen Savage (Sa). The formation of the modern name is explained in EPN s.v. æt.

The old name of the Rea river in Birmingham is unknown. From 1480 onwards it is variously known as 'the old Ree,' 'the Ree,' 'the Raye,' and we have mention of *Rebridge, Reybridge* in the 16th cent.

SALWARPE, R.

> *v.* Salwarpe *infra* 306.

SAW BROOK (6″) in Stoulton

> *Saltbroc, Saltbrok* 11th Heming 360, 1408 *EcclVar*
> *Saltaresbrok* 1182 (18th) *RBB*

For this name *v.* Saltways *supra* 5.

SEELEY BROOK in Hanbury

> *Syleye mead* 1253 AD iii　　　*Syley* 1545 LP

The forms are hardly adequate for any certain explanation, but the first element may be from OE *Siganlēage*, 'Siga's clearing,' *v.* leah.

SEVERN, R.

> *Sabrina*[1] Tacitus c. 115 (11th), 814 (11th) BCS 350
> *Sæfyrne* 706 (12th) BCS 116

[1] The form in Ptolemy in all MSS except one is Σαβριανα. One has Σαβρινα. This is of the 14th cent. but none is earlier than c. 1200.

Sæferne c. 770 (11th) BCS 219, 816 (11th) BCS 356, 884
(11th) BCS 551, c. 900 (894 A) ASC, 908 (11th) BCS 608,
929 (11th) BCS 665, 956 (12th) BCS 927, 969 (11th) BCS
1242, 972 (c. 1050) BCS 1282, 1042 (18th) KCD 765,
1017 KCD 1313
Sæbrine (Lat.) 816 (12th) BCS 357, 855 (11th) BCS 487
Sefærn c. 1100 (910 E) ASC
Seferne 751 (11th) BCS 462
Sæuerne 956 (12th) BCS 928, 962 (11th) BCS 1087, 1088,
c. 965 (11th) BCS 1139
Seuerne 986 (14th) KCD 654
Seuarne c. 1200 Layamon
Syuerne 1307 FF

SMITE, R. (lost)
  v. Smite Hill in Hindlip *infra* 140.

STOUR, R.
  There are two river Stours with which we are concerned in
Worcestershire. The first is that in the east of the county,
partly a Warwickshire river, which flows into the Avon and the
second in the north-west of the county, which joins the Severn
at Stourport, the ancient Lower Mitton (*v. infra* 254). For the
latter we have a form *Stur* in an original 8th-cent. charter
(BCS 154). For the former we have a similar form in BCS 123,
a 12th-cent. copy of an 8th-cent. charter. Further forms seem
unnecessary as there is no variation in them. We have Anglo-
Saxon charters proving the genuineness of this river-name as
found in Dorset, Kent and Essex and in all cases the old form
is the same.

TEME, R.
  Tamede c. 770 (11th) BCS 219
  Temede c. 770 (11th) BCS 219, 816 (13th) BCS 357, c. 950
  (11th) BCS 1007, c. 965 (11th) BCS 1139

TIRLE BROOK in Teddington
  Tyrl 780 (11th) BCS 236
  Further examples of Tirle as a river-name are probably to be
found in (i) Tirle Mill in Ombersley, on a brook flowing into
the Severn, (ii) the Tirle Way, near Bordesley Abbey (1520 LP)

which probably took its name from a brook which flows into the Arrow close to the Abbey. The stream-name appears in metathesised form in the *tril* stream (Do), BCS 1214. Possibly Trill Fm in Clifton Mabank (Do), on an unnamed stream, has the same origin.

TRAPNELL BROOK in Knighton-on-Teme

In a Knighton charter in *WoC* (c. 1210) we have mention of a *domum Tropinel*. The house and brook must take their name from the same person. Professor Zachrisson suggests that it is an *el*-diminutive of OFr *Tropin*, a variant of OFr *Turpin*. For OFr *Torpin*, *Trepin*, v. Kalbow, *Die Germ. PN des Altfr. Heldenepos* 104 and Bardsley, s.n.

WENFERTH, R. (lost) in Kidderminster

Wenferð 866 (11th) BCS 514

This is the old name for a brook which, rising near Yielding-tree, flows past Wannerton, which contains the name (*v. infra* 253), Hurcott, and Podmore Pool to join the Stour. It is probably identical in name with the *Winfrith* in Dorsetshire from which the village of that name (DB *Wenfrode*) takes its name; cf. Bradley in *Essays and Studies* i. 32 for this latter name.

WHITSUN BROOK in Flyford Flavell

Wixenabroc 972 (c. 1050) BCS 1282   *Wyxebroke* 1280 *For*
In considering this name we must take count of *Eastwixna*, *Westwixna* (gen. pl.) in the Tribal Hidage (BCS 297). In this record they stand between the *Gyrwe* and the *Spalde* and were therefore apparently settled in the country near the Lincolnshire Fens. Elsewhere in the county we have examples of people from other districts forming settlements in this county (cf. Phepson *infra* 137 and probably also Conderton *infra* 115) and such are not unknown outside the county as in Exton (Ha), *Eastseaxnatun* in BCS 758, a settlement of East Saxons (Mawer, *PN and History* 10). Here, in similar fashion, we probably have a settlement of people from a tribe whose name is only found elsewhere in an entirely different district. The modern forms show the common confusion of *k* and *t* with consequent development of *x* to *ts*.

Windrush, R.

Uuenrisc 779 BCS 230, c. 1000 Saints
Wenris, Wænric 949 BCS 882
Wenric, Wænric 958 (12th) BCS 1036, 1044 (12th) KCD 775

Wyndbrook in Pendock

Wenbroc 963 (11th) BCS 1109, 967 (11th) BCS 1208

The same stream is referred to in BCS 542. Hearne in Heming prints *wenbroc* and Birch *penbroc*. There is no doubt that the former is the correct form.

THE WORCESTERSHIRE HUNDREDS

Following the precedent established in our previous volumes we have grouped the parishes and vills of the county under the Domesday Hundreds, as the nearest approach that it is possible for us to make towards the original grouping of villages in the county. It must be borne in mind however that this county, more perhaps than any other, has undergone extensive hundredal re-arrangement, most of which took place soon after the Norman Conquest. The present Doddingtree, Pershore, and Oswaldslow Hundreds are by no means co-terminous with the districts so named in Domesday Book. Four of the Domesday Hundreds are now lost and two of the present Hundreds—Blackenhurst and Halfshire—are post-Conquest creations. The details of the changes are set forth below at the head of each of the DB Hundreds. It will be convenient here to note the history of the two non-Domesday Hundreds.

Halfshire

This is spoken of already as a unit (*Hundredum de Dimidio Comitatu*) in the Pipe Roll of 1176. In 1191 (P) a curious mixture of Latin and French gives *Hundredum Dimidii Conte*. It is called the 'half county of Wych,' i.e. Droitwich, in 1298 (Ipm), the *dimidium comitatus de Wych* in 1275 (SR) and the *Demy Counte* in 1315 (Ipm).

Blackenhurst

Blacahurste c. 1105 VCH i. 330 n. 6
Blakehurste Hy 1 (1241) Ch, 1255 *Ass*, 1276 RH
Blakenhurste 1315 Ipm, 1327 SR

The name means 'black wood,' *v.* blæc, hyrst. Nothing is known as to the meeting-place of the Hundred. For its constituents, *v.* Fishborough and Esch *infra* 260, 314. It is called Evesham Hundred in P (1179–80, 80–1, 84–5).

In addition to these we may notice the fleeting division called *Kinefolka* in the Worcestershire Survey of c. 1150. This seems to have contained certain of the Bishop's and monks' manors, amounting in all to some 94 hides, which were not in Oswaldslow as constituted in 1086. An attempt seems to have been made to form them into an additional hundred instead of adding them to the 300 hides of the original Oswaldslow, but they were ultimately destined to swell that hundred. The name means 'royal folk.' As the land was not a royal holding it must presumably have been given because of the practically sovereign rights exercised over it by the Church of Worcester. As noted by Dr Round (VCH i. 244) we have a parallel for this use of *folc* in the old name for the people of county Durham, viz. *Haliweresfolc*. For this name cf. PN NbDu xiii.

Worcester

WORCESTER [ustə]

Ueeogorna civitate 691 (12th) BCS 75, 777 (12th) BCS 223, (*cæstre*) 789 (12th) ib. 256, 803 (12th) BCS 308, (*ceastre*) 889 ib. 560, c. 900 (11th) ib. 582

civitate Wegornensi c. 705 (12th) BCS 123

Uuegorna cestre 814 (11th) ib. 351

Wigranceastre c. 750 (11th) BCS 137

castrum Uueogernensis c. 736 (11th) BCS 156, (*æcclesiæ*) 780 BCS 234, 803 (11th) ib. 309, 814 (11th) ib. 350, n.d. (11th) ib. 368, 824 (11th) ib. 379

Uuigorna civitate c. 730 (11th) BCS 164

Uuegrinancæstir c. 730 (11th) BCS 166

Uuegernensi civitate c. 757 (11th) BCS 183, (*ecclesiam*) 780 BCS 238

Wigerna civitate 774 (11th) BCS 216

Uueogerna civitate 774 (11th) BCS 217, (*cestre*) c. 795 (11th) ib. 273, 849 (11th) ib. 455, 855 (11th) ib. 487, (*cæstre*) 855 ib. 490, (*cestre*) 875 (11th) ib. 540

Uuigrinnanceastre c. 760 (11th) BCS 220

Uuegerna civitate c. 760 (11th) BCS 205, 781 (11th) ib. 239, 240, 241, c. 802 (11th) ib. 304, 840 (11th) ib. 428, (*cæster*) 845 (11th) ib. 450

Weogerna Ceastre c. 775 (11th) BCS 226, (*cestre*) c. 790 (11th) ib. 283

Wigorcestrensis æcclesiæ 780 (11th) BCS 235

Wigorna ceastre 779 (11th) BCS 231, (*cestre*) 804 (11th) ib. 313, 851 (11th) ib. 462, 883 (11th) ib. 551, (*cestre*) 967 (11th) ib. 1201, 972 ib. 1284

Guigornensis æcclesiæ 779 (11th) BCS 233

Wegriñ civitate 794 (11th) BCS 269

Weogra ceastre c. 795 (12th) BCS 272

Wigornensem æcclesiam 802 (11th) BCS 307, 841 (11th) ib. 433

Wegoranensis civitatis 803 (11th) BCS 312

Wegernensis æcclesiæ 817 (11th) BCS 359, 360

Wiogoerna ceastre 825 BCS 386

Weogurnacestre 836 BCS 416

Uuigrecestre c. 872 (11th) BCS 537

Wigraceaster 904 (12th) BCS 608, (-*cæstre*) c. 1100 (959 F) ASC, (-*cestre*) c. 970 (12th) BCS 1184, c. 1050 (1033 D) ASC, (*cestre*) c. 1100 (1047 D) ASC, c. 1130 (1114 H) ASC

Weogreceastre 964 (12th) BCS 1135

Wiogorna ceastre 966 (11th) BCS 1180, 1181, 1182, 969 (11th) ib. 1236, 985 (11th) KCD 649

Wiogurna ceastre 969 (11th) BCS 1232, 987 (11th) KCD 661

Wiogerna ceastre 969 BCS 1233

Wigurna ceastre 969 (11th) BCS 1240, 974 (11th) ib. 1298

Wiornocensi æcclesiæ 1016 KCD 724

Wihgraceastre c. 1040 (11th) KCD 766

Wigeraceastre c. 1050 KCD 805, c. 1050 KCD 923

Wygracestre c. 1100 (1049 D) ASC

Wigeran-, Wigerna-ceastre n.d. (1298) KCD 898

Wihgeraceastre c. 1050 KCD 924

Wirecestre 1086 DB

Wircestre 1350 Pat and so to c. 1400

Worcetre 1396 *Bodl* 79 a

Wyrcettur, Wersyter 1459 Strat Gild, 1538 LP

Worcester al. *Wurcestre* 1487 Pat

Worcettur, Worssitour, Worcetur 1473 Strat Gild, 1491–8 Pat

Wiscettour, Wysseter 1538–40 LP

Professor Ekwall suggests that we should perhaps connect the first element in Worcester with Wyre Forest[1]. This is some miles to the north but may have occupied a larger area in former days. Wyre Forest appears as *Wira* in 1174 but behind it may well lie an earlier *Wigra*. There is a Gaulish stream-name *Vigora* (now *Voire, Viere, Vègre*) which may have been the original name of Dowles Brook, which runs through Wyre Forest, and the same river-name may be found in Wyre (La) used as a river-name. The only other example of *Wigor-* in English place-names is in Wereham (Nf) which is *Wigorham* in 1060 (Thorpe 591), DB *Wigreham*. No stream is marked here but the place lies in a little valley just off the fens through which a stream may once have run. The form *Wiogorna* suggests a tribal derivative of *Wigor*.

[1] Camden mooted the same idea (*Britain*, tr. Holland, 575), 'I dare not say of (i.e. from) Wire that woody forrest.'

The names of some of the Worcester streets are interesting. We may note:

The Bailey. *la Baillie* (13th WoCh), a common name for the outer defensive works of a castle.

Baker Street, now the Shambles. *Vicus pistorum* (13th WoCh), *Baxter-strete* (1302 ib.), *Baxters Street* al. *Backe Street* (1649 Surv), with substitution of *baker* for *baxter*, the common term for a baker in ME.

The Bar. *The Barr* (13th WoCh), *le Barregate* (1441 ib.). The name is self-explanatory. Cf. Above and Below *Bar* in Southampton and *le Barrestret* (1236) in Droitwich.

Bridport Street. *Bridiport* (1170 EHR xxxix. 82), *le Britteport* (13th WoCh), *Bridport* (1232 Ch, 1292 WoCh), *Breteport* (1299 *RBB*), *le Brideport* (1310 WoCh), *Brudeport* (14th AlmBk), *Briteportestrete* (1338 WoCh), *Byrtport, Birport* (1549 Pat). The etymology is obscure. The first part might possibly be 'Britons.' The second is *port*, 'gate,' but one cannot say where it led to, cf. *Birporte St* in Winchcombe (Gl), 1545 LP.

Broad Street. *Brodestrete* (c. 1230 *WoC*).

Copenhagen Street. This was *Cokestrete* (1395 WoCh), *Cokynstrete* (1402 ib.), *Cockenstrete* (1549 Pat), *Cooken Strete* (1649 Surv) in earlier days, and doubtless meant 'cooks' street.'

Cripplegate. *Crupelgate* (1218 *FF*, 1221 *Ass*), *Croepelgate* (c. 1230 *WoC*), *Crupplegate* (13th WoCh), *Crupelegate* (E1 BM), *Cripelgate* (1232 Ch). This has nothing to do with cripples. We have an OE *crypel-geat* (BCS 699) which corresponds to the dialectal *cripple-gate*, 'low opening in a fence or wall, to allow the passage of sheep from one field to another' (*v.* EDD) and doubtless the name came to be applied to any gate with a low passage to it. Cf. the well-known street of that name in London (Rawlings, *Streets of London*, 36). The first element is OE *crīepel, crȳpel*, 'burrow, drain.'

Dolday. *Dolday* (1272 Ipm, 1391 Pat). The etymology is unknown.

Edgar Street. This street is called *le Knowle End Street* in 1649 (Surv) and takes its name from the hill called *La Knolle* (1386, 1390 WoCh) and *Studemar Knoll* (1480 WoCh).

Eport. *Eport* (12th to 1535 WoCh), *Eporth, Aporth* (n.d. Ancient Rental WoPriory), *Ewport* (1549 Pat), *Eporte Strete* (1550 Pat), *Eport* al. *Newport* Street (1568 WoCh), *Eweport* al. *Neweport* (1649 Surv). The first element is OE *ea*, 'river,' and the name is descriptive of a gate by the river. The prefixing of *n* has many parallels in Wo and the turning of *Neport* into *Newport* is a piece of folk-etymology.

Fish Street. This is *Corviserstret* in the AlmBk (13th), from ME *corviser*, 'cordwainer' (*v.* NED s.v.).

Little Fish Street. This was formerly *Huxterstrate* (1232 Ch), 'petty trader street.'

Friars Street. *Frerenstret* (1402, 1429 WoCh), *Fryerstrete* (1613 WoCh), named from the house of the Franciscans.

Foregate. *Foryat* (13th WoCh) *For(e)gate* (ib.). Here, as in Shrewsbury, used of a tract of land in front of the city gate, called *Northgate* (1229 Ch). *Fordget* in 1170 (EHR *u.s.*) is either an error or contains *forð* for *fore*, cf. Forty Green *infra* 202.

Goose Lane (lost), now St Swithin's Lane. *Gosethrott* Lane (1326 St Swith), *Goose* Lane (c. 1741, Doherty's Plan). Presumably the name was given to the narrow lane from some fancied resemblance to a goose's throat.

High Street. This is variously known in the WoCh of the 12th and 13th cents. as *magno vico, alta placea, alto pavimento, la Haute ruwe.* It is *High Strete* in 1391 (Pat).

Key Street, The Quay. *The Key, Keyenstrete* (1480, 1552 WoCh), *Keynestrete* (1649 Surv). Self-explanatory. *Keyen* must be a plural form.

Lich Street. *Lichelone* (1316 WoCh), *Lychstrete* (1322–49 ib.), *Leech Street* (1649 Surv). The first element is OE *līc,* 'body.' The street is also called *Cadiferestret* in 1337 (WoCh) and it is clear that it is a 'corpse-bearing street' which led to the cemetery of the cathedral church.

Lydiate (lost). There was a *La Lidyate* (1343 WoCh) which was probably a gate into the forest of Ombersley from the Worcester-Droitwich road which bounded it on the east.

Mealcheapen Street. *Melechepyng* (1369 WoCh), i.e. meal-market.

New Street. This was formerly *Gloverstrete* (13th WoCh), *vicus cyrothecarum* (1328 WoCh).

Powick Lane (now Bank Street) took its name from the Powick family found in Worcester in 1275 and 1327 (SR).

Pump Street. This was formerly *Nedlerstrete* (1275 FF), *Nelderstrete* (1406 Pat), i.e. street of the needle-makers.

Queen Street. This was formerly *Forum bladi* (1249 WoCh) or *Cornchepyng* (13th WoCh), i.e. corn-market.

Risenbridge (lost). *Rysenbruge* (13th WoCh), *Rysyngbrugge* (ib.), *Rysnebrugge* (1275 SR). The first element would seem to be OE · *hrīsen,* 'made of brushwood' (cf. Risborough PN Bk 171), pointing perhaps to some peculiar feature in its construction. It may have been a brushwood causeway over swampy land. This may also be the origin of *Risbridge* Hundred (Sf), DB *Risebruge.* For such an extended use of *brycg,* cf. Laborde in EHR xl. 168–9.

Sidbury. *Sudebir'* (1170 EHR 39, 82), *Suthbire* (1221 *Ass*), *Suthbiri* 1232 Ch), *Suddiburistrete* (1302 WoCh), *Sidbury* (13th WoCh), *Sodbury Strete* (ib.), *Sudbury Yate* (1383 Pat), *Sidbury St.* (1649 Surv). This lies at the south-east corner of the city and must take its name from some ancient fortification at that point. The *burh* in question may well be that which Ethelred of Mercia and Ethelflæd are known to have made at Worcester (BCS 579).

Turkey. This is called *Tiebrigestrete* (1254 WoCh), *Tibrugge* (1396 Pat), *Tybruge* (1518 More), *Tidbridge* (1549 Pat), *Tybrugge* (1653

WoCh). Presumably the bridge was so called from the use of some particular type of *tie* in its building.

Wennall Street. *Wylenhalestret* (1306 StSwith), *Wullenhalestret* (1312 ib.), *Wollenhale Stret* (1348–50 StSwith), *Wynnelstret* (1473 ib.). This street would seem to take its name from some lost place called *Wyllanhealɛ* in Old English, a compound of a pers. name *Wylla* and *healh*.

There was also a *Wodestarstret* (1369 WoCh). This presumably led to what in *AOMB* 61 is called *la Wodestaþe, le Wodestathe* and in Dugd. ii. 422, *la Wodestack*. The *AOMB* form puts it beyond question that the right form of the second element is *stathe*. Mr Bloom (WoCh, xiii) identifies the street with Grope Lane which leads towards the river, where there was probably a *wood-stathe* or 'landing-place,' *v.* staith in NED.

For all questions connected with the streets of Worcester we are much indebted to Bloom's *Introduction to the Worcester Charters* (WoHS).

I. DODDINGTREE HUNDRED

Dodintret, Dodintreu, Dodentreu 1086 DB
Dudintree c. 1150 Surv, 1175 P
Dodintre 1276 RH

Doddingtree Hundred occupies the north-west of the county. It consisted in DB of 38 manors and was assessed at 120¾ hides. The hundred-court was held in Great Witley on the Abberley Hills, near the building known for two centuries as the Hundred House. The site is fixed for us by the statement of Heming (254) that certain land called *Rydmerlehge*, i.e. Redmarley in Great Witley, is '*juxta duddantreo sita*.' This gives us the earliest form of the name and shows that it is '*Dudda's* tree,' a pers. name found elsewhere in the Hundred in *Doddenham* and *Doddenhill infra* 46, 58. The naming of the hundred meeting-place from a tree is exceedingly common, cf. Wimburntree *infra* 87.

Abberley

ABBERLEY 81 A 8
Edboldelega 1086 DB
Albodeslega c. 1150 Surv
Haudebodeleya 1169 P
Albodelega 1180 (c. 1225) France
Abbedeslegh 1216 ClR

Albedeley 1275 SR, 1309, 1315 Ipm
Aubedeleye 1276 RH
Abbodeley 1327 SR, 1346 FA
Abbedeleye 1337 Ipm, 1349 Wigorn, 1400 IpmR
Ab(b)ot(t)(e)ley(e) 1346 Pat, 1433 IpmR, 1487 AD v, 1485 Pat
Abbudley 1399 Pat
Abboteslegh 1428 FA
Abburley 1478 Pat
Aberley 1480, 1484 Pat
Abbutley 1488, 1493 Pat
Abboteley al. *Abburley* 1499 Pat
Abbotsley 1637 QSR, 1663 D
Abberley 1649–1710 FF

'*Ealdbeald's* clearing,' *v.* leah. This p.n. has the same history as Abbotsley (PN BedsHu 252) with curiously similar fluctuation of forms.

BROOKEND

de Broke, atte Broke 1275, 1327 SR
Self-explanatory.

CRUNDELEND FM, UPPER AND LOWER (6″)

Crundel 1230 Pat (p), 1275 SR (p)
Cromdale 1316 Ipm (p)
Crondalend, Crundall End 1592 WillsP, 1598 QSR

v. crundel. Upper and Lower Crundelend Farms are from three-quarters of a mile to a mile south-east of Stockton. The *crundel* is in a steep bank to the south. The Crundels are on the Old Red Sandstone. There are several deserted quarries in the parish of Abberley, but none just hereabouts.

FIELD FARM (6″)

le Ffeild 1603 SR (p)
v. feld. Self-explanatory.

HAY OAK (lost)

de Heya, atte Heye 1275, 1327, 1332 SR
'Oak by the (ge)hæg or enclosure.'

NETHERTON FM

Netherton 1405 IpmR

NURTON'S FM

Overton 1221 *Ass,* (*atte*) 1327 SR, (*juxta Stanford*) 1376 IpmR, 1405 IpmR, 1663 FF
atte Noverton 1327 SR

These two names (*Over* meaning 'upper') are complementary, and descriptive of two farms, one of which is 250 ft. higher than the other. For the initial *n* we may compare Nash End *infra* 31 and other similar names with ME *atten*, 'at the,' prefixed to the significant word. The *s* is pseudo-manorial.

OLDYATES FM (6″)

Oldgate 1275 SR (p)

Self-explanatory. This may be manorial, i.e. Oldyate's.

ST CLAIR'S BARN (6″)

See under Syntley in Astley *infra* 37.

TOMKINS (Old 1″)

Robert Tomkyns contributed to the Lay Subsidy in 1332 in the vill of Abberley, so that this is a clear example of a place-name consisting of the possessive case of a pers. name pure and simple.

Acton Beauchamp[1]

ACTON BEAUCHAMP 81 F 5

Aactune 727 (c. 1200) BCS 146
Actune 972 (c. 1050) BCS 1282, 1086 DB

Other forms are without interest. The name means 'oak-farm,' *v.* ac, tun. It was called *Beauchamp* from the possession of the manor by that family from the 13th cent. onwards (VCH iv. 225). It was also known as *Acton ultra Tamedam* (ib. 224) from its situation on the far side of the Teme in relation to Worcester and in contrast to Acton in Ombersley[2]. The first form, with its archaic representation of *ā* by *aa*, is derived from one of the few OE Evesham charters which seem to have a genuine basis.

---

[1] Transferred to Herefordshire in 1897.
[2] In the bounds of Acton (BCS 1282) there is a *gislan forda*. This survived as part of a pers. name in the *Ilesford* of the 1275 Subsidy Roll. Initial palatal *g* is lost and common metathesis of *sl* to *ls* has taken place.

ACTON GREEN

atte Grene 1316 Ipm, 1332 SR   *Acton Green* 1640 QSR

Self-explanatory.

CRUISE HILL (local)

atte Cros(e) 1316 Ipm   *Cruise Hill* 1892 Kelly

This identification is not certain, but if correct suggests a curious corruption of LOE **cros**. Probably at some lost intermediate stage we have the influence of OFr *croise*, 'cross.' Cf. the Cross in Ombersley and Crossway Green in Hartlebury *infra* 243, 269.

HAGTREE FM

Yagetre, Yaggetre, Yaketre 1275 SR, 1316 Ipm, 1327 SR, all (p)

Eggtree 1789 Gough

This must contain the same pers. name *Geagga* which lies behind *Geaggantreow* in the bounds of Trescot (St) in KCD 650. It is also found in Yagland (D), 1311 *Ass Yaggalond*, in a lost Yagdon (Sa), now only surviving in Yagden's Lane (60 C 12)[1], DB *Iagedene*, Hy 3 Ipm *Jagedon*, and possible also in Yazor (He), *v.* forms in PN He 216. Such a pers. name might be a pet-form for OE *Geard-gār* or *Gearu-gār*, names not actually on record but formations such as we might expect.

HALFRIDGE FM

Heafocrycge 973 (c. 1050) BCS 1282   *Alfridge* c. 1830 O

If this identification is correct, the modern form is corrupt and the true name is 'hawk-ridge,' *v.* **heafoc, hrycg** and cf. Ockeridge *infra* 142. It is a very common place-name noted also in Berks, K, Sx.

KIDLEY'S FM

Kydele 1255 *Ass* (p)

Kydelow(e) 1275 SR, 1316 Ipm, 1327, 1332 SR, all (p).

This name is not as easy as it looks. The OE pers. name *Cydda* is not very likely as we should expect some ME forms with *u*. The first element may be ME *kide*, 'young goat,' though

---

[1] Information due to the kindness of Mr E. W. Bowcock.

as that word is a Scandinavian loan-word we should not expect to find it so early in the west country. Alternatively, the first element might be the obscure *kid(de)*, 'brushwood,' recorded in the NED s.n. *kid*, sb. 2. Either of these would suit the suffix hlaw, 'hill,' which seems early to have been confused with leah. It may be manorial, but no other place-name Kidley or Kidlow has been noted.

SEVINGTON FM

Selvintone 1275 SR (p)
Silvington 1777 Inscription in church
Sivington 1822 VCH iv. 225

No certainty can be attained with regard to this name. The first form refers to someone living in Hallow so it is possible it is not to be connected with this place at all. As there is a Silvington (Sa) it is very likely that the name is manorial and not original to this parish.

SINTONS END (6")

Suthinton, Sodinton 1275 SR, 1316 Ipm, both (p)

This 'end' is in the extreme south of the parish and we clearly have another example of the name discussed under Mamble *infra* 60.

WINTHILL (Old 1")

Wyndehull, Wynthull 1316 Ipm, 1327 SR, both (p)

If *t* is the correct consonant, then the first element in this name is the OE pers. name *Wintu*. If *d* is correct, then we have a parallel to Windhill (Y), meaning apparently 'wind-(swept)-hill.' Change from *d* to *t* would however be very difficult to account for.

WOOTON'S FM

la Wotton, Wotton 1316 Ipm, 1327 SR, both (p)

'Wood-farm,' *v.* wudu, tun. The *s* is probably only pseudo-manorial.

Alfrick

ALFRICK [ɔlfrik], [aˑfrik] 81 E 8

Alcredeswike 1204–34 AD ii
Alfrewike 1275 *Ass*
Albrich, Alfrich 1275, 1327 SR (p)
Aufurweke 1523 BM
Alferwick 1529 VCH iv. 357
Aufrick, Aufryke, Awfrycke 1577 Saxton, 17th Hab, 1649,
    1651 FF, 1675 Ogilvy, 1789 Gough
Alfricke 1649–1714 FF *passim*

The first identification is not absolutely certain but is highly probable. If correct the first element is the pers. name *Ealhrǣd*. For the *f* development cf. the history of Offerton *infra* 139. Note also Zachrisson, *AN Influence*, 107 ff. Hence 'wic of Ealhræd[1].'

BROOKPATCH FM (6″)

Brok(e)bache 1275 SR (p), 1552 Pat
'Brook-valley,' *v.* broc, bæc.

LUCKALLS FM. (6″).

Lockewelle, Lucwell, Locwell 1275 SR, 1289 Ipm, 1327 SR, all (p)

'Lucca's spring,' *v.* wielle. The only pre-Conquest evidence for an OE name *Luc(c)a* is found in *Lucan beorh* (BCS 1066), but Luckington (So, W) confirms the probability of its existence. It may well be a reduced form of the OE pers. name *Ludica*. The name is probably only pseudo-manorial in form.

OUGHTON WELLS (Old 1″)

Houton 1327, 1332 SR (p)

It is difficult to say if this is a genuine *hōh-tūn*, 'hill-farm' (*v.* hoh), or derives its name from someone bearing the name *Houghton* derived from some place elsewhere. It lies about a third of a mile south-south-west of Alfrick Church on the edge

---

[1] There is also in *WoC* a pers. name *Alkareswik, Alcchardewik* (c. 1250) belonging to a man who had a fee in Worcester. He probably came from Alfrick.

of a promontory enclosed by the 300 ft. contour, so that topographically the first solution is quite possible.

Yarringtons (6″)

This must take its name from a family coming from Yardhampton in Astley, of which the popular pronunciation was *Yarranton* or *Yarrington*. In 1649 (FF) William *Yarranton* bought an estate in Alfrick.

Areley Kings

Areley Kings [ɛ'əli] 71 J 9

> (*H*)*erneleia* c. 1138 BM
> *Ernele* 1156 (1266) Ch
> *Ernleʒe, Ernleie* c. 1200 and c. 1250 Layamon, A and B
> *Arneley* 1275 *Ass*
> *Alrelege* 1283 Wigorn
> *Arleye* 1291 Tax, 1428 FA
> *Ardley Regis, Kyngges Arley* 1405 Pat
> *Areley* 1453 Pat, 1535 VE, 1549 Pat

This place-name is clearly the same as that found in Upper *Arley infra* 30, though the places are too far apart for us to think that the same clearing is referred to in the two settlements. *Kings* because it was part of the royal manor of Martley. It was also known as *Nether* Areley in contrast to Upper or *Over* Arley and the curiously artificial modern spelling may have arisen from the same cause.

Dunley

> *Dunelege* 1221 *Ass*
> *Donesley* c. 1225 WoCh (p)
> *Dunley* 1275 Ipm, 1424 IpmR, 1527 LP, 1650 FF
> *Donneleye* 1327 SR (p)
> *Downeley* 1558 Wills

This is the 'clearing' (*v.* leah) of *Dunna* or *Dūn(a)*, though the existence of the last name (Redin 12) is not quite certain. *Donneleye* may be an error for *Douneleye*. The last form of all is probably an etymologising spelling.

Upper Arley[1]

UPPER ARLEY 71 F 8

Earnleie 996 Dugd vi. 1444
Ernlege 1086 DB, 1202 Cur
Erneslea 1166 P
Erlege, Erleia 1188, 1197 P, 1200 Cur
Arnlege, Arnleye 1276 Pat, 1316 FA, 1327 SR
Ar(e)leye 1332 SR, 1401, 1408 FA, 1465 Pat
Arneley vel *Arley* 1432 Pat

'Eagle-clearing' (*v.* earn, leah) or, possibly, 'Earna's clearing,'
that name being a pet-form for an OE name in *Earn-*. It should be
noted however that there is an OE river-name *Earn*, which may be
genuine, lying behind Earnshill (So), cf. *Muchelney Cartulary* 47.
There is a stream here coming down to the Severn, but, on the
other hand, compounds of *leah* with a river-name are not likely.
Earnley (Sx) is OE *Earnaleah* (BCS 1334), 'eagles' clearing,'
and it is possible that this is the original form here. It is also
known as *Over* Arley and Arley *de Port*, from the Port family
who were here from the 12th cent. They came from Port-en-
Bessin (VCH iii. 5). For *Over v.* Areley Kings *supra* 29.

BOWER (lost)

la Boure 1236, 1332 Fine (p), 1333 Cl
v. bur.

BROMLEY FM

Bromiley 1295, 1317 LyttCh (p)
'Broomy clearing,' *v.* bromig, leah.

COLDRIDGE WOOD

Colrugge E i LyttCh (p)
'Coal-ridge,' *v.* col, hrycg. We are on the coal measures here.

GOOD'S GREEN

From the pers. name *le Gode*, found in the 1327 and 1332
Subsidy Rolls for this vill, and again in a will of 1584.

[1] In Staffs till 1895.

HAWKBATCH (Old 1")

Auchebech a. 1172 Magnum Registrum Album (Salt. Soc. 1924)

Haukebache, Hawkebach 1360–1398 LyttCh, 1535 VE, 1547 Pat

Howkebaiche 1551 BM

OE *heafoca-bæc*, 'hawks' stream or valley,' *v.* heafoc, bæc.

HEXTONS FM

Hekstane 1227 LyttCh (p)
Heyston 1293 Salt. Soc. vii. 1, 172 (p)
Hexstan 1306 Salt. Soc. vi. 1, 217
Hexston 1312 Salt. Soc. ix. 43 (p)
Hex(s)ton 1313, 1486 FF (p)
Hekston 1520 FF

This is a difficult name. We probably have an OE significant name *hēah-stān*, 'high stone,' referring to some unknown rock or monument. For similar p.n. compounds without inflexion of the adj., cf. forms from OE charters collected by Ritter (139). The only other suggestion, for which we are indebted to Mr Bruce Dickins, is that the name was originally composed of two elements, a pers. name *Hēahstān*, which is well recorded, and a second element such as tun or stan, which had disappeared by the 13th cent. A parallel for such loss is to be found in Leystone (Herts), earlier *Lefstane cherche*, though there the loss is much later.

HILLHOUSE (Old 1")

la Hulle 1327, 1332 SR (p)
Self-explanatory.

KITLANDS COPPICE (6")

Kyttlondes 1456, 1481 LyttCh

This is probably derived from the Christian name *Kit*.

NASH END

le Nasshe Eynde c. 1330, 1412 LyttCh

One of the numerous examples of *Nash* for *Ash* with affixed *n* as in Nurton's *supra* 25.

PICKARD'S FM

Pykaslond, Pikarslond, le Pykards 1357, 1460, 1485 LyttCh

This is a genuine example of a name of the manorial type, for the family name *Picard* is found from 1276 (*Ass*) onwards.

SECKLEY WOOD[1]

Soegeslea (dat.) 866 (18th) BCS 513
Secceslea 866 (11th)BCS 514

'*Secg's* clearing' (*v.* leah) with the same unexpected phonological development which we find in Seckloe (PN Bk 16).

SHATTERFORD

Sciteresforda 996 Dugd vi. 1444
Sheteresford 1286 Duignan PN St 134

The same first element is found in *rivulus qui dicitur Scitere* or *sciteres stream* in So (BCS 476, 729), in *scyteres flodan*, *sciteres clif* in Ha and Berks respectively (BCS 1200, 932). The first-named stream lies behind Sherford in Wilton (So), 1353 Ch *Shiteresford*, and it is possible that a similar river-name lies behind Shitterton in Bere Regis (Do), DB *Scetre*, later *Scitereston*[2]. There can be no doubt that in each case we have OE *scītere*, a regularly formed agent-noun from *scītan*, 'cacare.' A ford across a tiny stream or the stream itself might clearly be so distinguished. *sciteres clif* probably owes its name to some incident or story now decently lost beyond recovery. That such an explanation is probable is shown by other evidence set forth in explanation of Skitterlyn (Nb) and Skitter Beck (L) in PN NbDu 128. Such a name is bound later to undergo corruption.

VALENTIA WOOD (Old 1″)

Viscount Valentia held Arley in the 18th cent. (VCH iii. 6.)

---

[1] The identification is not certain. Seckley Wood is on the right bank of the Severn, the place in the charter was in Wolverley. It is possible that the original Wolverley included Arley east of the Severn, but to include Seckley Wood we must believe that Wolverley crossed the Severn or else that the term *Secgeslea* described land on both sides of the Severn, cf. the use of Shelsley *infra* 76 as the name of manors on either side of the Teme.

[2] From Mr Gover's Devonshire collections we glean also Shutterton, which stands on a stream called *sciterlacu* in a charter of 1044, the place itself being called *Schiterton* in 1277 (*Ass*). Note also *Shitebrok* (1323) in Watlington (O).

WITNELLS END

Whytenhull, Wyntenhull, Whytehull 1295 LyttCh, 1325 Ipm, 1332 SR, all (p)

'White hill,' from OE (*æt þǣm*) *hwītan hylle, v.* hwit, hyll. The name is probably only pseudo-manorial in form.

WOODHOUSE FM

Woddus, le Wodehouse 1387, 1460 LyttCh

'House by the wood,' *v.* wudu, hus. This name is very common in old woodland areas.

Astley

ASTLEY 81 A 9

Æstlæh 11th Heming
Eslei 1086 DB
Estlege c. 1150 Surv

Forms in *Est-* and *Ast-* are equally common till c. 1430 after which those in *Ast-* prevail. *v.* east, leah. 'East' in relation perhaps to the 'ley' at Abberley and one of a group containing Sintley, Areley, Witley, Dunley, Shrawley, Shelsley.

BROOKHAMPTON

Brokhampton 1275 SR (p)

The hamtun by the brook, *v.* broc. The first of several *hamptons* in this parish. This is a very common place-name, cf. Brockhampton (Do, Gl, Ha, He, O), Brookhampton (Sa, Wa), and Brookhampton in Ombersley *infra* 269.

THE BURF

la Bergha 1212 Fees 140
Berewe, Berge 1327 SR (p)
Borough 17th Hab

v. beorg, cf. the well-known Abdon Burf (Sa). The VCH (iv. 234) says, 'the site of the manor of Berrow is not now to be identified, but it probably lay in the neighbourhood of the Burf.' As a matter of fact the names are the same, *Burf* from the nom. form, *Berrow* from the dat.

GLASSHAMPTON [glɑ·sən], [gleizəntən]

> *Glese* 1086 DB
> *Glyshampton* 1255 *Ass*
> *Glassehampton* 1260 Pat
> *Cles-, Clashampton* 1275 *Ass*
> *Glasne* 1275 *Ass*
> *Glashamton* 1327 SR
> *Glasshampton* 1342 FF, 1538 LP, 1595 BM

Glasshampton stands just above Dick Brook which, a little below, in Shrawley, is crossed by Glazen Bridge (Old 1″)[1], now known as Glasshampton Bridge, and there can be no doubt that we have here a hamtun taking its name from an old stream-name. From the DB reference and one of the 1275 ones it is clear that the place was at times simply named after the river alone without any suffix. Ekwall (PN La 94) shows that in Glazebrook and in Glaisdale (Y) we have a river-name of this type which has its parallel in the *Glasenbach* of the Salzburg district (10th *Glasa*), which Förstemann (ON i. 1065) derives from an adj. stem *glasa-* 'bright.' The forms with *e* and *a* suggest a derivative *glasjo*-stem for this stream. The form *Glasne* is interesting and it must be associated with the *on Glæsne* of KCD 699, which lies behind Glazenwood (Ess) in Bradwell next Coggeshall. Ekwall (PN La 171) calls attention to these names and their topography. If the *Glæsne* is a stream, it must be the small unnamed one which runs east from the wood and joins the Blackwater at Bradwell.

LARFORD

> *Leverford* 706 (12th) BCS 116
> *Lorford* 1327, 1332 SR (p)
> *Larford* 1663 FF

'Ford where the wild yellow iris grows,' *v.* læfer.

LONGMOREHILL FM

> *Langemere, Longmer* 1255 *Ass*, 1275 SR (p)

'Long-mere hill,' *v.* lang, mere.

---

[1] The bridge is still locally so called—*ex inf.* the Rev. R. A. Wilson.

OAKHAMPTON

Okhamton, Ockhampton 1275 SR, 1657 FF

'hamtun by the oak.' The vowel has been lengthened in modern times under the influence of the independent word.

POOL HOUSE

de Pola, atte Pole 1275, 1332 SR (p)
Pool House 1636 VCH iv. 231 n. 4

Self-explanatory.

REDSTONE ROCK

Reddestan 1181, 1184 P
Radestan c. 1200 Layamon, 1221 FineR, *Ass*, 1260 Pat
Radeston 1275 SR, 1277 WoCh, 1331 StSwith
Redstone 1658 FF

The name of a red sandstone cliff high above the Severn. There was a hermitage here. Simon the 'clerk' of Redstone is mentioned in 1181 and Layamon tells us that he dwelt at Areley Kings close by Redstone. Three miles higher upstream there was another hermitage at *Black*stone (*infra* 248).

SEVENHAMPTON (lost)

Sevinhampton 1255 *FF*
Sevenham(p)ton 1255 *Ass*, 1327 SR
Seveham(p)ton 1275 SR, 1332 SR (p)

This curious name must be taken with Sevenhampton (Gl), a place of the same name in Wilts, Seavington (So), DB *Sevvenumentone* and the *seofonhæmatun* of KCD 767. Grundy (*Arch. Journ.* lxxvii. 106) finds a difficulty in associating the bounds of this place with Sevenhampton (W), and suggests that the bounds may be those of the Gloucestershire place. There is no evidence however that they fit here and it may be pointed out that there is a *byde wil* in the bounds and this may contain the same stream-name as *Byde*mill Brook just by the Wiltshire Sevenhampton. Further, the estate in the Saxon Charter is one of 'x mansae.' In DB the Wiltshire manor is assessed at 10 hides, while the Gloucestershire one stands at 20 hides. However that may be, it is clear from the OE form that we have a compound of *seofon*, 'seven' and hæme and tun. The only possible interpretation of such a name would seem to be that it denoted a village which included at least seven homesteads (*v.* ham) and, from the frequency of the name, that there must have been some particular feature about a group of *seven* homesteads which led to their being given a distinctive name. The first hint we have in OE law and custom of the importance of the number *seven* is in the laws of Ine (§13). Up to the number of 7, thieves are reckoned as individuals, from 7 to 35 they form a *hloð* or band. With this statement should probably be linked the clause in the agreement between Aethelred II and Olaf Tryggvason which states that 'if eight men are slain, that makes a breach of the peace,' i.e. an act of war as distinct from an act of private violence (Liebermann, *A.S. Gesetze* i. 220). These passages at least suggest that some special significance was attached to the number *seven* in OE times. Later in actual date, but undoubtedly representing ancient custom, is a clause in the little custumal which introduces the DB description of Nottinghamshire. It states that a thegn who has more than *six* manors pays a relief of eight pounds to the king. A thegn with six or less pays three marks of silver to the sheriff. No doubt the *maneria* of this passage are very different from the *hams* under consideration. It nevertheless proves that in late OE law a person who possessed more than six units of property might be subject to far heavier payments to the king than a person who had six or less. The possibility therefore arises that, at the early date at which these names may be presumed to have arisen, a village which contained seven homesteads may have been assessed far more heavily to public burdens, such as the king's *feorm*, than a village which contained only six. No absolute certainty is possible but it is highly probable that the explanation of these difficult and interesting names should be sought along these lines.

SYNTLEY FM (6″)

Synteleye 1255 *Ass*, 1302 Ipm (p)
Cynteley, Cyntelegh 1322 Pat, 1346 FA, 1349 Pat, 1438 IpmR
Syntley 1637 VCH iv. 231 n. 5

This name presents difficulties. Heming (246) gives the bounds of Pensax. These bounds include a *sintlæges hyll*. The bounds are difficult to follow, as they certainly include a larger area than the present parish of Pensax, but *sintlæges hyll* may, with a good deal of probability, be identified with a ridge some 2 miles long, lying above the 500 ft. contour-line, which runs north-north-west from Abberley Park. Just by is *St Clairs* Barn and the first part of this name may be a corruption of *sintlæge*, closely similar to that of the curious St Chloe (Gl), identified by Mr Baddeley (PN Gl 136) with the *Sengedleag*, *Sengetlege* of BCS 164, 574. This name appears later as *Seintley*, *Sencle*, *Senckley*.

The existence of a *sintlæge* so near Syntley and yet not identical with it is curious, but seems certain. As to the etymology of it the only suggestion that can be made is that, as with a good many other names in the same bounds, Heming has here given us a post-Conquest form for an earlier *sengetlæge*. With reference to that name we may note that Middendorff (*Flurnamenbuch* 115) assumes that the first element here and in *sænget hryg* (BCS 506) and *sænget þorn* (BCS 629) is the past part. of OE *sengean*, 'burn,' or '*singe*,' but the persistent *t* in these names and in *senet hricg* (BCS 1282), *sænget hyrst* (BCS 1198) and *sænget den* (BCS 396) suggests that the first element is really a noun *sænget* denoting the action of burning, an exact parallel to OE *bærnet*, which gives us The Barnets *infra* 83.

WOODHAMPTON HO

Wodehampton 1347 WoCh

'The hamtun by the wood.'

WORDLEY FM[1] (6")

Wordisley 1425 IpmR, 1591 BM

The forms are too late for interpretation to be certain, but it is probable that we have the OE pers. name *Weorð* found in Woodsfield *infra* 226.

YARHAMPTON[2] [jærən]

Yarranton 1558 Wills   *Yallington* 1667 FF

---

[1] In the VCH (iv. 234) forms for Worsley in Rock are assigned to this place.

[2] There is a form *Sardhamtone* in the 1275 Subsidy Roll, which may possibly be a blunder for *Yardhampton* or it may refer to *Sandhampton*, not found on the map but recorded in Kelly's Directory (1892).

F

Bayton

BAYTON 71 H 6

Beitone 1080 France
Betune 1086 DB
Beton 1230 Pat
Beytune 1275 SR
Bayton 1327 SR

'Beage's farm,' the pers. name *Bēage* being found in OE as
the name of the daughter of a Gloucestershire ealdorman of the
8th cent. whose name actually survives in Bibury (Gl), which
was granted to her and her father. This name, or the masc.
Bǣga, is also found in Bayworth (Berks), BCS 535 *Beganwurð*,
Baywell *infra* 121 and in many other place-names[1].

CARTON FM[2]

Carletune 1086 DB
Carkedon, Karkedon 1211 RBE, 1249 *FF*, 1287 Ipm, 1318
   Pat, 1346, 1431 FA
Karketon 1235 Fees 527
Karkeden 1242 Fees 960
Kardunn c. 1250 Fees 610
Karledon 1415 FF
Carton 17th Hab

In considering the etymology of this name we may note that
there was also a *Carkemor* in Mamble (1327 SR), that in BCS
120 and 125 we have *Carcadic* in the bounds of Abbots Morton
and *Carkeford* in Harvington by Evesham, and that there is a
Cartland in Alwington (D), *Carkelond* 1330 *Ass. Carkeford* is a
ford over the *Fulanbroc* in the bounds of Norton and Harvington,
while *Carcadic*, some nine miles away in a different watershed, on
the bounds of Abbots Morton and Rous Lench, may be either
a 'dyke' or a 'ditch.' It is difficult to identify it exactly.
Professor Ekwall points out that in the Carton by Mamble
we are in very hilly ground and similarly, though at a good

---

[1] In the 1275 Subsidy Roll we have in Bayton a pers. name derived
from a place called *Solneye*. This would seem to be a trace of the *solnhæma
broc* found in the metes of an enlarged Pensax given by Heming (246).
[2] Formerly in Mamble.

deal lower level, the ground is very hilly and broken in the neighbourhood of Abbots Morton and Harvington. Cartland is also in much-broken ground. He suggests that the first element should be connected with OWelsh *carrec*, 'cliff, rock,' which may be found in Cark and High Cark (PN La 197, 199).

CLOWS TOP

Cluse 1275 SR (p)
Clouse 1294 Ipm (p)
la Clouse 1328 Ch
Cloes 1448 BM
Clowes Toppe 1663 QSR

This is clearly, as Professor Zachrisson has pointed out to us, the OE *clūse*, which lies behind Clowes in Blean (K), *Cluse* in FA (1346), found also in the Wickhambreux charter (BCS 869) as *Cluse*, and in a lost *atte Cluse* in Warnham (Sx) in 1332. As a matter of fact the second form almost certainly refers to Clowes itself, for it is not one of the bounds of Wickhambreux but of one of the *denns* in Blean Wood which belonged to it. *Cluse* is named as one of the western boundaries and would fit in exactly with the site of Clowes Farm. Professor Zachrisson notes in addition the unidentified *Shettinge* (BCS 407), also near Canterbury, which seems to be the pure English equivalent (cf. PN in -ing 6) of this loan-word from Latin, which also denotes an 'enclosed place.' The other sense which this word has in OE, viz. 'narrow pass,' does not seem to suit the topography of either the Kentish or the Worcestershire place very well, though the cluse in this Wo case might possibly be the valley on the side of which Clows Fm stands.

CULVERNESS HO (6″)

Coluernest 1255 *Ass* (p)
Culuernest 1305 FF (p)
Culverness 1892 Kelly

'Dove-nest,' *v.* culfre, cf. Crowneast *infra* 91.

NORGROVESEND FM (6″)

Northgrave 1275, 1332 SR, 1316 Imp, all (p)
Norgroves 1615 Wills P
Though all the early examples of this name are personal it is probably not manorial. The grove lies at the north end of the parish.

SHAKENHURST [ʃækənhəːst]

Shakenhurst, Sakehurst 1255 *Ass*
Shekenhull, She(c)kenhurste 1275 *Ass*, 1302 *FF* (p), 1304 Pat (p), 1327 SR (p), 1330 *FF* (p), 1622 Wills (p), 1673 FF
'Scæcca's wooded hill,' *v* hyrst. The pers. name *Scæcca* is not on independent record in OE but is found in *scæccan halh* in Grimley (Wo), BCS 1139, and is cognate with OGer *Scacca* (Förstemann PN 1303), ON *Skakki*.

THORNSGATE (Old 1″)

Thornesyate 1327 SR (p)   *Thorngate* 1789 Gough
'Gate of (or by) the thornbush,' a clear example of the somewhat rare place-name compound of the genitival type. *v.* geat.

TIMBERLAKE (lost)

Tymberlacke 1316 BM
Timberlake, Tymberlake 1425 IpmR, 17th Hab
'Wooded stream,' *v.* timber, lacu.

Bewdley

BEWDLEY 71 G 9

This place-name is found in its original French form as *Beuleu, Beauleu, Beaulieu* from 1275 SR to 1424 Ipm and also Latinised as *Bellum Locum*, as in 1308 Pat. The Anglicised forms are as follows:

Buleye 1316 Ipm
Beudle 1335 Ipm, Orig
Beudeley 1349 Pat
Beaudeley 1381 IpmR, 1465 Pat
Bewdeley 1547 Pat

A well-known type of French place-name. The nearest

parallel to this Anglicising that has been noted is Beadlow (PN BedsHu 147).

'Worthily so called for the Beautifull site thereof' (Camden's *Britain*, tr. Holland, 573). Leland (*Itinerary* ii. 87–8) waxes even more eloquent, culminating in the statement that 'at the rysynge of the sunne from este the hole towne gliterithe being all of new buyldynge, as it wer of gold.'

TICKENHILL[1]

Tykenhull 1399 Cl, 1424 IpmR
Tyknyll, Tyknell 1455, 1460 Pat

'Kid-hill,' *v.* ticcen, hyll, and cf. Ticknall (Db), *Ticcenheal(l)e*, KCD 710, 1298.

Bockleton

BOCKLETON 81 C 3

Boclintun 1086 DB
Bockintona c. 1086 (1190) *EveB*
Boclinton 1175 P, c. 1225 *Bodl* 3, 1274 Cl, 1275 SR, 1316 Cl
Bokelinton(a) 1217 Bracton, 1327, 1332 SR, 1340 NI
Bockleton 1535 VE
Borkulton, Borkleton 1621, 1808 Marr

OE *Boccelingtun,* 'Boccel's farm,' *v.* ingtun. The name *Boccel* is not on record in OE but is a regular diminutive formation from the name which lies behind Bocking (Ess), *v.* PN in -ing 9. Cf. Bockleton (Sa).

LITTLE BIRCHES (6″)

Burches 1439 Kyre

Self-explanatory.

BIRCHLEY FM

Bercheleg, Birchele(ye) 1235 *FF*, 1275 SR, *FF* (p), (*in Boclinton*) 1283 *FF*

'Birch-clearing,' *v.* leah.

---

[1] Saxton (1577) and Speed (1610) have *Tychnell* and *Tichnell*. The *ch* s probably an error for *ck*.

GETTES ASHBED (6″)

Probably to be explained from a surname *Gette* found locally, as in John *Gette* of Holt (1642 QSR). For Ashbed *v.* Hollybed *infra* 214.

GRAFTON

la Grafton 1251 Ipm (p)   *Graphne* 1674 Kyre
'Grove-farm,' *v.* graf, tun.

HILL FM

la Hulle 1275, 1327 SR (p)   *Hull* 1626 WillsP
Self-explanatory.

QUINTON

Quenton 1221 *Ass*, 1243 Ch, 1251 Ipm
Quinton 1275 SR (p)
Queynton 1665 FF

The history of this name is probably the same as that of Quainton (PN Bk 109) and Quinton (PN Gl 126), which seem to go back to OE *Cwēningtūn*, 'farm of *Cwēna*,' the latter being a pet-form of one of the OE pers. names in *Cwēn-*, *v.* ingtun.

SALLINGS COMMON

la Saline 1275 SR (p)
Salynes 1324 Ch
atte Salye 1332 SR
Salen c. 1830 O

The earliest forms present difficulties, and Professor Ekwall suggests that we may have an OE *salegn*, a derivative of *sealh*, with the same suffix *egn* that we have in OE *holegn*, *ifegn*, 'holly,' 'ivy.' The third form would then show the same loss of *n* as in *holly* from *holegn*. The form *Sallings* is probably a vulgarism, cf. *kitching* for *kitchen*, and Holling Fm *infra* 63.

WESTON FM

la Weston 1275 SR (p)

The farm lies near the western border of the parish. There was apparently a *Middleton* in the parish at one time, to judge by a surname in the 1275 Subsidy Roll.

Clifton-on-Teme

CLIFTON-ON-TEME [klifn] 81 C 7

Cliftun ultra Tamedam 934 (11th) BCS 700
Clistune 1086 DB

'Cliff-farm,' from its situation on high ground overlooking the Teme. *Ultra* or 'beyond' Teme, in relation to Worcester and to distinguish it from Clifton 'on Severn' *infra* 227, cf. Acton Beauchamp, *supra* 25.

AYNGSTREE FM (6")

Anestie 1275 SR (p)
Annstyns, Hansties, Hangsties n.d. *Deeds*[1]
Angstrey c. 1830 O

v. anstig. Ayngstree Farm lies at the top of a hill nearly 500 ft. above the Teme, with a steep track leading up to it, evidently part of an old way from the Teme itself. It was a veritable stronghold. The modern form is corrupt.

BUTTFIELD

This probably takes its name from the family of *Botte* mentioned in deeds of 1359 and 1365.

GATLEY (6")

Catteley 1275, 1327 SR (p)   *Gatley* c. 1830 O

Probably this was originally '*Catta's* clearing' (*v.* leah) with the pers. name which can be inferred from *Cattaneg* (BCS 1176), though it might also contain the animal name catt(e). Later arose confusion of initial *c* and *g* which has similarly established itself in Glendon (Nth), DB *Clendone*, Glenfield (Lei), DB *Clanefeld*, from OE clæne (see further IPN 114 and Gurnox *infra* 47).

HAMCASTLE FM

Homme 11th Heming, 1086 DB, 1274 Ipm, 1327 SR (p), 1382 IpmR, 1455 Pat
Hamme 1255 *Ass* (p), 1315 Ipm, (Castell) 1346 FA, 1402 Pat
Overhamme 1465 Pat

---

[1] For the *Deeds* and *Tithe Apportionment* referred to in this parish we are indebted to the kindness of the Rev. R. G. Griffiths, F.S.A.

v. **hamm.** The place clearly takes its name from the wide 'ham' in the course of the Teme here. *Over* because on higher ground than Ham Fm.

HAM FM

Parva Hamme, Luttle Hamme 1275 *Ass*
Chapel Home, Nether Home 1462, 1466 IpmR
Holme Fm c. 1830 O

Ham Fm is in the next lower bend to Hamcastle and is *Nether* and *Little* in relation to it.

HOLLANDS MILL (6″)

Huggesbrig mylne 1436 *Deed*
Huddesbrige 1496 VCH iv. 252
Hugsbrook or *Hugburg Mill* 1680 ib.
Hugh Batch Mill 1843 *Tithe Apportionment*

The modern name is quite distinct in origin but the sites are identical. The original name was probably 'Hud's bridge,' from the OE pers. name *Hudd*, found in *Huddesig* (BCS 801). We may also note the tradition that *Hudde*, Earl of Gloucester (temp. Edw. Conf.) gave the land on which Malvern Priory stands. The development from *ds* to *gg* is common, cf. *Mod. Lang. Rev.* xiv. 342.

INDHOUSE COPPICE (6″)

atte Ynde 1332–3 SR (p)

It is possible that *ynde* is here a variant form of *ende*, representing the dialectal pron. *ind*, noted by Wright (EDG) in Oxfordshire and Berkshire. The Coppice lies near the border of the parish.

LITTALS (local)

Luttlewale 1348 *Deeds*

'Little spring,' *v.* **wielle, lytel.**

MAIL ST (local)

In a deed of c. 1330 we have mention of land called *Mayele* in Clifton, which seems to be the source of this street-name. The street appears as *Maile* or *Mayle* Street c. 1700. The name looks as if it were from OE *Mægan-lēage*, 'Mæga's clearing,' *v*. leah, but the forms are too scanty for certainty. The forms forbid our considering it more than a coincidence that the street leads from the village cross (*v*. mæl)[1].

MOORFIELDS FM (6")

Mora 1275 SR (p)

Self-explanatory.

SALFORD COURT FM [sɔ·lfəl]

Schalcwelle 1221 *Ass* (p)
Salecwell 1235 *FF*
Salewill, Shalwell 1242 P
Salk(e)well 1242 P (p), 1291 Tax
Salinchwell 1255 *Ass* (p)
Salwell 1255 *FF*, 1290 Heref
Salewelle 1255 *FF*
Sal Wall 1275 SR (p)
Salwall 1510 IpmR
Salford 1541 Ipm

'Willow-spring,' *v*. sealh, wielle, with AN *c*, *k* for *h*. The later forms show a curious corruption of the suffix. The change may, in part at least, be due to phonological causes, cf. the frequent confusion of *worth* and *ford* in unstressed positions as illustrated in PN NbDu 268.

WOODMANTON FM

Wodeminton 1255 *Ass*
Wodemonton, Wodemanton, Woddemunton 1275 SR (p), 1332
    Pat, 1333 Ipm

'Woodman-farm,' or, as there is earlier evidence for OE *wuduman* as a pers. name than as a common noun, it may be 'Wuduman's farm,' cf. Woodmancote *infra* 195.

---

[1] For the early forms and the topography we are indebted to the Rev. R. G. Griffiths.

Doddenham

DODDENHAM [dɔdnəm] 81 D 8

Dodhæma pull 779 (11th) BCS 233
Dodeham 1086 DB, 1291 Tax
Doddeham 1212 Fees 140
Dodham 1221 FF
Dudeham 1275 SR
Doddenham 1275 FF, 1327 SR, 1535 VE

'Dodda's homestead,' v. ham. In the first example, 'pool of the men of Doddenham,' we have the usual suffixing of hæmə to the first syllable of the name with no consideration of its logical division[1]. For this pers. name cf. Doddingtree Hundred itself and Doddenhill *infra* 58.

ANKERDINE HILL

Ancredham c. 1200 (c. 1240) WoC
Ancredeham, Aucredeham c. 1220 (c. 1240) WoC
Oncredam 1240 Wigorn (p), 1327 SR
Oncredeham 1240 Wigorn, 1275 SR, both (p)
Ankerdam, Onkerdam 1304, 1308 Ipm
Oncredenes 1312 AlmBk
Ankerden 1649 Surv

Professors Ekwall and Zachrisson agree in suggesting that this is a triple compound from OE *ancor*, 'anchorite,' hreod and hamm, hence 'reedy ham frequented by an anchorite.' The hill rises up from a big hamm in the course of the Teme. It should be noted that side by side with this place there was, close at hand, a place called *Brocredeham, Broccerdham, Brochardham.* This may have been another 'reedy ham' haunted by the brocc or badger. The *o*-forms show the common WCy *o* for *a* before nasals.

COLD HILL (6")

The first ed. of the 6" map has *Gold* Hill[2] and this hill perhaps takes its name from the *Golde* family found here in 1240 (WoP) and 1275 (SR).

---

[1] This interesting phenomenon was first noted and explained by Mr G. H. Wheeler in *Mod. Lang. Rev.* xi. 218–9.
[2] *Gold* Hill in the original name-book but altered to *Cold* Hill in 1902.

EASINGHOPE FM (6″) [i·zənhoup]

Esighope 1275 SR (p)
Esynghope 1327 SR (p), 1535 VE
Hesinghope, Esincote, Esincope 14th AlmBk (p)

'*Ēsi's* valley' (*v.* hop), the *ing* suffix being used in the same way as in ingtun names. It lies on the edge of a shallow valley. Cf. Isbourne, R. *supra* 12.

GURNOX (6″)

Curnockes 1649 Surv

This clearly takes its name from the pers. name *Curnock* which is found in Cropthorne in 1649 and survives elsewhere to this day.

MUNN'S GREEN

This takes its name from the pers. name *Mun(ne)* found in this parish in 1596, 1611 (Wills) and 1649 (Surv).

Dowles[1]

DOWLES 71 G 8

Dules 1217 Pat
Doules 1292 QW, 1312 *FF* (p)
Dowlys, Dowlyz 1535 VE
Dowles 1541 LP, 1549 Pat

This place is clearly named from the brook on which it stands[2]. *Dowles* Brook contains an old river-name preserved for us in Dalch R. (D), *Doflisc* in the first Crawford Charter, and in the place-name Dawlish (D), (*Doflisc* KCD 940) and Dowlish (So), *Douelish* in the Muchelney Cartulary, which like Dowles take their names from the streams on which they stand. Dawlish Water is still so-called; for Dowlish we have only Dowlish Ford on an unnamed river. See further IPN 24.

---

[1] In Salop till 1895.
[2] From a grant made in 1127 to Malvern Priory (Dugd. iii. 448) in which the land on the opposite side of the Severn from Northwood in Wribbenhall is called *Hakiesheia*, it is clear that this district had an alternative name of English origin. In an undated charter (Hy 1), inspeximus in Pat 1376, another form of the name is *Achiseia*. This is clearly the 'hay' (*v.* (ge)hæg) of a man named *Aecci* or *Ecci*; cf. Eckington *infra* 195.

Eastham

EASTHAM 71 J 5

Eastham 11th Heming
Estham 1086 DB, 1577 Saxton
Esthamme 1258 *FF*, 1276 RH, 1281 Ch

'East hamm or river-bend,' presumably in relation to Newnham in Knighton-on-Teme, just across the river (*v. infra* 55), though the forms of the latter suggest that it is really by origin a ham rather than a hamm.

BASTWOOD (lost)[1]

Bestwde 1086 DB
Hastwude (sic) 1255 *Ass*
Bastwode 1255 *Ass* (p), 1294 Ipm, 1303, 1330 *FF*, 1405 IpmR, 1409 *Hanley Charters*
Bastwood 1578 WillsP, 1653–5 FF

The most probable explanation of this name is that the full form of it was in OE *bī ēastan wuda*, 'east of the wood,' and that at a later date the preposition and noun were run together. That was certainly the case with other similar names. The district of Wells now known as East Wells was in early documents (*v. HMC Report on the MSS of Wells*, ii. 883) known as *Byestwalle, Bestwalles, Biestwalls* meaning really 'east of the walls,' and there is also a Bestwall in East Stoke (Do) which has early forms *Beastewelle* DB, *Byestewalle* 1316 FA, *Beestwall* 1431 FA and must have had a similar history[2]. Bestnover (Sx) is *Estenore* (1199 Cur), *Bestenor'* (1200 ib.).

CALLOW HILL (lost)

Callow Hill, Calloway Hill 1639–1818 *Eastham Parish Book*

'Bare hill,' *v.* **calu** and cf. Callow Hill in Feckenham *infra* 318.

---

[1] The site of the manor house was on that of the present Eastham Grange (VCH iv. 270).
[2] Heming (251) mentions a *Bufawudu* next to Eastham. This must be for OE *bufan-wuda*, 'above the wood,' and suggests that there were two places which took their name in relation to this wood, *Bastwood* and a lost *Bovewood*. Cf. also Southwood in Shelsley Beauchamp *infra* 76. Mr J. E. B. Gover provides a good parallel in Naithwood (D), *Bynethewode* in 1361 *Ass*.

COLDNALLS (lost)

Coldenhale 1275 SR (p), 1550 *Eastham Parish Book* (p)
Caldehale 1275 *Ass* (p)
Coldnalls 1739–1762 *Hanley Charters*

'Cold nook or corner,' *v.* healh, ceald. The *s* is pseudo-manorial.

HILLWOOD FM

la Hulle 1275 SR, 1311, 1328 *FF*, all (p)
The Hill al. *Hillwood* 1723 *Eastham Parish Book*

Self-explanatory.

HOCKERILLS FM

Okerhill 1786 *Tithe Terrier*
Ockerhill 1789, 1818 ib.

KNACKER'S HOLE (6″)

Nakers Hole, Knackers Hole c. 1770, 1843 *Tithe Terrier*[1]

Clearly a term of reproach, but in what sense *knacker* is used we cannot be sure. The NED gives us a choice of 'one who sings in a lively manner,' 'trickster,' 'deceiver,' 'harness-maker,' 'dealer in worn-out horses.' The last is the most likely.

MINTON (lost)

Moneton, Munton 1275, 1332 SR (p)

'Hill-farm or enclosure,' the first element being the same as the Shropshire *Mynd*, Welsh *mynydd*. Menutton in Clun, Minton, Myndtown and Mondaytown in Worthen (Sa) have the same history.

Edvin Loach[2]

EDVIN LOACH 81 D 5

Edevent 1086 DB
Yedefen 1182 P, 1211 RBE, 1332 SR
Iadefen 1212 Fees 140, 1400 *EcclVar*
Wedefen 1235 Fees 527

[1] The references to various unpublished local documents are due to the kindness of the Rev. E. E. Lea, rector of Eastham.
[2] Transferred to Herefordshire in 1893.

Ydefen Loges 1242 Fees 959, 1267 Wigorn, 1275 *Ass*, 1308 Ipm
Jeddefen 1287 Ipm, 1291 Tax, 1428 FA
Zedefen 1327 SR
Edfynloges 1535 VE
Edvin Loche, Loach 1652, 1668 FF[1]

'*Gedda's* marshy land,' *v.* fen. For such early loss of initial *g* cf. DB *Evestie* for OE *Geofanstige* (BCS 1074). This pers. name is also found in Yeading (Mx). Only the strong form *Geddi* is on independent record. John de *Loges* had a holding here in 1211 (RBE).

HOPE FM

de Hope 1275 SR

v. hop. It lies at the head of a valley.

Hanley Child

HANLEY CHILD 81 B 5

Hanlege 1086 DB
Cheldreshanle 1255 *Ass*
Chuldrenehanle 1265 Misc
Chylderne Henleye 1332 SR
Children Hanley 1348 *FF*, 1389 Pat
Nether hanley 1577 Saxton
Hanley Chylde 1581 Kyre

'High clearing,' *v.* heah, leah. Probably Hanley Child and Hanley William originally took their name from the same 'high clearing.' Later when separate settlements arose they were distinguished as 'Nether' and 'Over.' Nether Hanley was also distinguished as 'Children's' in which the exact sense of 'child' is uncertain. In Childerley (C), if we may judge by the entry in DB, it may be used of a sokeman. See further Mawer, *PN and History* 27. For Childwick (Herts) Mr Bruce Dickins notes the statement in the *Gesta Abbatum Mon. S. Albani* (Rolls Series i. 54) 'a pueris trahit locus vocabulum, quia ad alimenta Monachorum Juniorum lacticiniis alendorum, con-

---

[1] DB *Gedeven* and *Geddesfenna* from the Leominster Cartulary, for Edvin Ralph (He), an adjacent manor, may also be noted.

ferebatur: unde *Childewica* nuncupatur,' suggesting that it could be used of a young monk and a similar origin is given by that historian for *Childe Langeleya*, now King's Langley.

BROAD HEATH

> *Hanleyesheth* 1377 Pat   *Broad Heath* 1578 Kyre
> Self-explanatory.

CHEVERIDGE FM

> *Chaueru(g)ge* 13th Kyre, 1332 SR
> *Chaveryche* 1486 Kyre
> *Cheveridge* 1615 Kyre, 1669 FF
> *Chiefridge* c. 1830 O

'Chafer-ridge,' the first element being OE *ceafor*, '*chafer*, beetle.' For such a name cf. *ceaforleah* (BCS 622), *v.* **hrycg.** The history of Charingworth (Gl), DB *Chevringavrde* points however to the possibility of a pers. name of the same form.

THE FULLHAMS

> *Full(h)ams* 1486, 1513 Kyre   *The Fulhams* 1615–1675 Kyre
> Possibly 'foul enclosures,' *v.* **ful, hamm.**

HOLYWELL [hɔliwɔ·l]

> *Hollywell Field* 1673 Kyre   *Holly Wall* c. 1830 O
> 'Holy well,' *v.* **halig, wielle.** The old forms show the usual shortening of the vowel.

STRETCHES (6″)

> Hugo *Strech* is found in this vill in 1327 (SR), so that the name is manorial.

Hanley William

HANLEY WILLIAM 81 A 5

> *Hanlege* 1086 DB
> *Hanley Thome* 1242 Fees 961, *Williames Henle* 1275 *Ass*
> *Ouer hanley* 1577 Saxton

v. Hanley Child *supra* 50. *Thomas* de la Mare held the manor in 1212 (RBE), *William* in 1242.

Hillhampton

HILLHAMPTON [hiləntən] 81 A 8

Hilhamatone 1086 DB
Hullmanton 1255 *Ass*
Hulhamton 1240 WoP, 1275 SR, 1285 Wigorn, all (p)
Hullam(p)ton 1408 Pat (p), 1424 IpmR
Hillanton, Hillington 1605 QSR, 17th VCH iv. 293

OE *hyll-hǣma-tūn*, 'farm of the hill-dwellers,' *v*. hyll, hæme, tun.

STRUCTON'S HEATH

Tryxton 1265 Misc
Tro(c)keston 1275 SR (p), 1375 Wigorn
Truxton 1537 Wills
Thruxtons 1603 SR
Thruxton 1662, 1670, 1689 FF

There is some evidence for a pers. name Þrocc(*a*) in OE which seems to be found in Throcking (Herts), Throckley (Nb). It seems to have survived the Conquest in the form *Troke* (*Warden Cartulary* 11 b). Hence, 'Throcc's farm.' From early days there seems to have been the common confusion between initial *th* and *t*. The modern form is still more corrupt and has also been made pseudo-manorial.

WOOLSTAN S FM

Wolsiston, Wolsisdone, Wolstone 1275 SR, *Ass*, 1327, 1332 SR, all (p)

All the examples of early forms of this name are from pers. names. As there is a Woolstone (Gl), not so very far away, which comes from OE *Wulfsiges-tūn*, whose forms would agree with those of this family, it may well be that the name is manorial in origin.

Knighton-on-Teme

KNIGHTON-ON-TEME 71 J 4

Cnihtatun c. 957 (11th) BCS 1007
Cnistetone 1086 DB
Knyht(t)eton(e) 1230, 1275 FF

Knictetun 1240 WoP
Knython 1346 Heref
Knyghton 1550 Pat

OE *cnihtatūn*, 'farm of the *cnihts*.' For the use of this term in p.n.'s *v*. cniht. It may be not without significance in the early social history of Worcestershire that we have fairly close together this name and that of Hanley Child, in both of which we have a suggestion of some early holding in common by groups of men.

ASTON COURT

> *Tethenga de Estone* 1176 P
> *Estun* 1240 WoP
> *Astone* (*juxta Lindridge*) 1280 *FF*, 1327 SR (p)

'East farm,' *v*. east, tun. Why 'east' is not clear. It is perhaps in relation to Boraston (Sa) on the other side of the Corn Brook, which was also a manor of the Bishops of Worcester. *Tethenga* (OE *tēoþung*, 'a tenth') is the common word *tithing* (*v*. NED). *WoC* 75 (temp. E 3) distinguishes *Ouereastone* and *Netherastone*, corresponding probably to Aston Bank and Aston Court respectively.

BICKLEY

> *Bykelege, Bikele, Bykeley* 1240 WoP, 1275 *Ass*, SR, 1387 CompR
> *Bikerly* 1240 WoP
> *Byckley* 1554 Kyre

'*Bica's* clearing,' *v*. leah, unless we lay stress on the isolated form *Bikerly*. This might contain OE **bicere*, ME *bikere*, 'hive-keeper,' a word discussed by Miss Gilchrist in a letter to the *Times Literary Supplement* (Nov. 30, 1922), which may lie behind some of the English place-names in *Bicker-*, cf. *bycerafald* (BCS 1282) in the bounds of Acton Beauchamp [1].

CAINEY (6″)

> *Caweneie* c. 1230 (c. 1240) *WoC*   *Cawneysfield* 1550 Pat

The forms point to an OE pers. name *Caua* of uncertain

---

[1] This suggestion had been anticipated by the late Professor Earle in a MS note which has come into the hands of the editors through the kindness of Dr P. Haworth.

origin, but found in the early part of LVD. Cf. ME *Kaue* in a Norfolk Assize Roll (c. 1200). For this name *v.* Redin 88. The suffix is eg, used of low marshy ground. The form *Cainey* is irregular.

CLETHILL (6″)

Clethelde c. 1220 (c. 1240) WoC

The second element is hielde. The first is a plant-name, possibly 'burdock,' *v. Clethale infra* 313.

CORNWOOD (Old 1″)

Cornawude c. 957 (11th) BCS 1007
Cornewude Hy 2 HMC v, App. i. 301, c. 1220 (c. 1240) WoC
Cornwod(e) 1240 WoP, 1275 SR (p)
Cornwood 1649 Surv

In the bounds of Knighton (BCS 1007) we have 'from the Teme to *Corna broc*, along the brook up stream to *corna wudu*, from *corna wudu* to *corna lið* (probably for *hlið*), along the *lið* to the second *corna broc.*' The first three of these may be identified as Corn Brook, which here forms the county boundary, Cornwood just by it, and Coreley (Sa) a short way from the stream, on high ground which separates Corn Brook from a stream which is presumably the second Corn Brook of the charter. There is another Cornwood (D), DB *Cornehuda*. It is very difficult to be sure about these names, but for the present it is impossible to offer any other suggestion than that put forward in EPN, *s.v.* corn viz. that here we have a metathesised form (in the gen. pl.) of OE **cron* (*cran*), bearing in mind that that name is used dialectally of the common 'heron' as well as of the much rarer 'crane.'

DEPTCROFT (6″)

Depecroft c. 1208 (18th) Nash, c. 1220 (c. 1240) WoC
Deepcroft 1892 Kelly

'Deep croft,' i.e. in a hollow, *v.* deop croft.

FIELD FARM

de la Feld, atte Feld 1275, 1327 SR
'Open country,' *v.* feld.

MAYTHORN (6″)

Myethen 1586 Kyre

This is the name of the place where the Rea joins the Teme and there is no doubt that it really stands for OE (*æt þǣm*) *mȳðum*, '(at the) confluence(s),' *v.* myðe. The modern form is corrupt. Cf. The Mythe at Tewkesbury, at the junction of Severn and Avon, and Mitton *infra* 102, 254.

NEWNHAM

Neowanham c. 957 (11th) BCS 1007
Neoweham c. 1160 (c. 1240) *WoC*
Noweham 1206 (c. 1250) *WoC*
Newham 1240 WoP
Newenham 1240 WoP, 1392 Pat, 1535 VE
Nowenham 1542 LP

'New homestead,' *v.* niwe, ham, but cf. Eastham *supra* 48.

OXNALL FM (6″)

Oxenhale c. 1230 (c. 1240) *WoC*   *Oxenhall* c. 1600 Kyre
'Oxen-nook or corner of land,' *v.* healh and cf. Oxhall *infra* 76.

STONY CROSS (6″)

atte Cros 1327 SR   *Stoney Cross* 1582 Kyre

WOODGATES GREEN

Wodegate 1327 SR (p)   *Woodyates* 1655 WillsP
Both these names are self-explanatory.

Kyre Magna al. Kyre Wyard

KYRE MAGNA [ki·ər] 81 B 4

Cyr 11th Heming
Chure, Cuer 1086 DB
Cura, Cure c. 1086 (1190) *EveB*, 1210–2 RBE, 1287–1293 Ipm, (*Wyard*) 1323 Pat, 1431 FA
Cures 1235 FF
Cureward 1275 Ass
Cuyre 1308 Ipm, 1415 IpmR

Curwyard 1324, 1328 Ch
Keeres Common 1667 FF

There is no doubt that here we have a place-name derived from an old stream-name, for already in the 13th cent. (Kyre) we have 'the water-course called *Cura*' and the stream is to this day known as Kyre Brook. The manor was held by the *Wyard* family already in 1211 (RBE).

EASERFIELD COPPICE (6″)

Eswaldfield 1669 Kyre

The forms of this name are very late but it looks as if the first element were a pers. name *Ēswald*. Such names in *Ēs-* are not on record, but as we have, side by side in OE, pers. names *Ōsa* and *Oesa* with un-mutated and mutated vowels from the stem *Ōs-* so commonly found in OE pers. names, so there may have been such pairs of compound-names as *Ōswald, Ēswald*.

Little Kyre

LITTLE KYRE 81 B 4

Cures 1235 FF
Kettles Cure 1294 Ipm, (al. *Little Cure*) 1581 Kyre
Parva Cure 1295, 1305 Ipm

Henry *Ketel* held the estate in the 13th cent. (Kyre).

APPLE CROSS (6″)

de Cruce 1275 SR   *de la Crose* 1350 Kyre
Self-explanatory.

BANNALL'S FM

Banewelle 1305 Ipm (p), 1322 Pat (p)
Banwell 1327 SR (p)
Banwall 1332 SR (p), 1354 Kyre (p)
Banewall 1433 IpmR
The Banwalls, Bannoles, the Bannells 1575, 1585, 1704 Kyre

It is probable that this is a manorial name derived from a family which came from Banwell (So), for all the early forms except that for 1433 are from pers. names and there we have mention of *Banewall Manor*. Whether this be so or no, it is clear that the ultimate etymology of *Banewelle* is the same as that of the Somersetshire place-name which is found as *Bananwylle* (BCS 612, copy), *Banewyllan* (ib. 1149, copy), *Banawelle* (Earle 43, copy) and *Banuwille* (c. 1000 Asser). The common interpretation is 'slayer's spring or stream' from OE *bana*, 'slayer.' It may be however that *Bana* here is to be taken as a pers. name, the name which, in the expanded form *Bænisa* seems to lie behind Bensington (O), cf. IPN 172.

FLINT'S DINGLE (6″)

This takes its name from the family of Richard *Flint* who was in this vill in 1275 (SR). For *dingle* v. Field-names *infra* 390.

HULL FM

la Hull(e) 1275 SR, (*de Cure*) 1293 Ipm, both (p)

v. hyll. Noteworthy for the retention of the dialectal form hull as against StEng *hill*.

HURSLEY FM (6″)

Hurdesley 1275 SR, Kyre (p)   *Hertesle* 1327 SR (p)

OE *hierdes lēage* (dat.), 'shepherd's clearing,' v. leah.

Lindridge[1]

LINDRIDGE 71 J 5
Lynderycge 11th Heming
Lyndrug(g)e, Lindrugge 1125–50 (18th) Thomas, 1175 P, 1275 SR, 1360 LibPens
Lyndrygge, Lindrigghe 1240 WoP, 1275 *Ass*
Linderug 1240 WoP
Lyndrig 1355 Pat, 1535 VE
Lynderugge 1445 Pat
Lyndrich(e) 1445 Pat, 1509 AD vi
Linriche 1666 Marr

OE *linda-hrycg*, 'ridge of the lime-trees,' or *lind-hrycg*, 'lime-tree ridge,' v. lind, hrycg. Cf. Lindridge (K) (BCS 195 *lind-hrycg*) and (Lei).

[1] Wrongly identified as the *Linde* of DB in VCH i. 309. See Lindon in Rock *infra* 73. It is now in Oswaldslow Hundred, but since its constituent members Eardiston and Knighton are in Doddingtree Hundred in DB and according to Heming (309), it is here taken in that Hundred. It first appears in Oswaldslow in 1275 (SR).

CRUNDALL COPPICE (6″)

Crondal 1310 LibPens   *Cromdal* 1310 (18th) Nash

v. crundel. The local topography does not suggest any reason for the name.

DODDENHILL FMS

Doddenhulle 1240 WoP, 1275 *Ass*, SR, 1327 SR, all (p)
Doddenhill, Dodnell 1654, 1681 FF

'*Dodda's* hill,' *v.* hyll and cf. Doddenham and Doddingtree Hundred *supra* 46, 23.

EARDISTON [jəˑdistən]

Eard(g)ulfestun c. 957 (11th) BCS 1007
Eardulfestun c. 1050 (11th) KCD 952
Ardolvestone 1086 DB
Eardeluestuna c. 1085 (1190) *EveB*
Erdelvestun 1240 WoP
Erdeston 1275 SR (p)
Erdelstone 1295 Pat (p)
Adristone, Aderestone 1349 Heref
Yeardiston 1787 Cary

'Farm of *Eardwulf*,' *v.* tun. The same pers. name is found in Ardley (O), Addlethorpe (L, Y) and in Yessel Fm *infra* 106.

THE LOWE FM

apud Lawam 1240 WoP   *de la Lowe* 1275 *Ass*

v. hlaw. 'The hill.' Cf. the Lowe in Wolverley *infra* 259.

MEADOWS MILL (6″)

mol. de Medeweye 1240 WoP

Unless the old form is corrupt the original name for the mill was 'Meadway,' i.e. on the way to the 'mead' or 'meadow.' *v.* mæd.

MENITHWOOD

Menehey 1240 WoP
atte Meneheye 1315 AlmBk
Meneye 1327 Kyre (p)
Menney Wood 1649 Surv

There can be no doubt that this is a compound of OE (*ge*)*mǣne*, 'common,' and (ge)hæg, hence 'fenced enclosure in woodland, held in common.' From references in the charters (BCS 386, 1234) we find that mæd, feld, læs (i.e. open pasture), *yrðlond* (arable land), *wuduland*, could be described as *gemǣne* and the adjective is found compounded with gara, wielle, leah, denu, hyll, mor (BCS 390, 664, 1004, 1051, 1221). In 1240 (WoP) we have mention of a *mene medwe* in Lindridge. Cf. also Meneatt Fm *infra* 77, *Menewud* in Fineshade (Nth) (1227 Ch), Meanwood (Y) and *Menecroft* (LyttCh). Menith Wood was first enclosed in 1816 (VCH iii. 443).

MOOR FM

>*Mora* 1240 WoP   *Moore* 1649 Surv
>
>*v.* mor.

WOODSTON MANOR

>*Wdesinton'* 1200 (c. 1240) *WoC*
>*Wodesintun* 1240 WoP (p)
>*Wodeston* 1275 SR, 1315 AlmBk, 1327 SR, all (p)
>*Woodston* 1580 Kyre

The forms point to an OE *Wudesiging-tūn*, 'farm of Wude-sige.' For such a name we may compare *Wudeburgehlinc*, BCS 1066 (original) and Woodmanton *supra* 45. See also PN Bk 195 for a possible *Wudemund*.

Lulsley

LULSLEY 81 E 7

>*Lolleseie, Lulleseia* 12th VCH iv. 356
>*Lolles(s)eye* 1316 Ipm, 1364, 1369 Pat, 1656 FF
>*Lulsey* 1535 VE, 1649 FF, 1675 Ogilby, 1763 Bowen
>*Lullesey* 1649 FF

'Lull's eg.' *Lull* is a well-established OE name and eg is here used of low-lying land, partly surrounded by the windings of the Teme at this point. The modern form with a second *l* is corrupt.

Mamble

Mamble 71 J 6

Momela gemæra c. 957 (11th) BCS 1007
Mamele 1232 *FF*, 1255 *Ass*
Maumelegh 1275 *Ass*
Momele 1275 SR, 1304 *FF*, 1327 SR, 1411 Pat, 1425 IpmR,
    1428 FA
Momerle 1330 *FF*
Momulle 1431 FA
Momyll 1499 Ipm
Mamull, Momyll 1535 VE
Maumble 1577 Saxton
Momble al. *Momehill* 1591 BM
Mamble 1604 QSR

It is impossible to make any satisfactory suggestion with
regard to this name. It may be that we should associate it
(as does McClure, *British Place-names in their Historical
Setting* 268 n.) with *Mamilet* (He) and *Mamheilad* (Mon) in the
Liber Landavensis and with Mam Tor (Db) and Mamhead (D),
old hill-names, but beyond that it is difficult to go[1].

Moorend Fm

ate More de Momele 1340 NI
Self-explanatory.

Sodington Hall

Suðintun c. 957 (11th) BCS 1007, c. 1050 (11th) KCD 952
Sudtone 1086 DB
Sudinton(a) 1173 P, 1255 *Ass* (p)
Sutintone 1203 RBE, 1235 Fees 527
Suthington 1234 *FF* (p)
Sodintone, Sodynton 1275 SR, 1359 Ipm
Soudington 1305 Cl
Sodington 1327 SR, 1431 FA, 1458 BM
Sydynton, Syddington 1425 IpmR, 1499 Ipm
Shillington, Shellington 1547 Pat, 1551 Pat

---

[1] The *Cornbæce* of the bounds of an enlarged Pensax (Heming 246) must
be the same as the *Cornesbethe* (sic) in Mamble in SR.

Sodington al. *Syllington* 1591 BM
Sodington al. *Sullington* 1611 WillsP

The history of this name, together with that of Suddington in Ombersley, Sinton in Grimley, Leigh Sinton in Leigh, Sindon's Mill in Suckley *infra* 82, has already been given in PN BedsHu 109, where on the evidence of this and other names given by Mr Houghton it was shown that there was a common type of OE name *Sūðingatūn*, 'farm of the dwellers in the south,' which could readily be applied to a settlement in the south of any particular district. The form *Sydynton* has its parallel in the regular Siddington (Ch, Gl) from the same word, while for those with *l* we may compare those given for Sinton in Grimley *infra* 128. The DB form here, like the early form *Suðtun* (BCS 386) for Sinton, suggests that there was an alternative form for the name of the more usual type.

SPILSBURY HILL (6")

It is difficult to be sure if we have any early forms referring to this name. The form *Spelebury* quoted by Duignan (152) for 1275 belongs to a family in Elmley Castle and the *Spellesbury* of 1327 to one from Kempsey and Abberton, sufficiently far away, but as the name is not likely to have been a common one in place-names we should perhaps connect them with this place and believe that the family so called originally came from here. For Spilsbury (O) we have a form *Speolesbyrig* in BCS 1320 and this name may go back to the same OE form. This is presumably from a pers. name allied to the *Spila* found in the will of Bishop Alfwold of Crediton (*Crawford Charters*, no. x). Stevenson (132) connects this with the name *Spileman* found in Heming (291) and in the *Chester Cartulary* ed. Tait, i. 71. He notes the various names in *Spili-* to be found in Förstemann (1356). Hence '*Speol's* burh[1].'

WESTWOOD FM

Westwode 1275, 1332 SR (p)
So called in contrast to a lost *Suthwode* (1255) *Ass.*

[1] There was also a *Spilsberyslynge* in Ribbesford in the 16th cent., probably a 'linch' owned by a member of the Spilsbury family. Further, we may note a *Spellesberwe* in the 1408 extent of Bredon (*EcclVar*). It is probable however that this is from OE *spelles-beorg*, 'hill of speech,' used of some place of public assembly. *v.* spell.

WINDHILL FM

Wygenhull, Wynhull 1275, 1327 SR, both (p)

'*Wiga's* hill,' *v.* hyll. The same pers. name is found in Wyegate (Gl), *Uuiggangeat* (BCS 1282), DB *Wigheite* (Stevenson MSS). The *d* is a late intrusion.

WINRICKS WOOD (6")

Wynedwarwik, Wonewarik 1275, 1327 SR, both (p)

'The wic of *Wynwaru.*' This pers. name is not on record, but it may perhaps be inferred from *Winwareswik* (BCS 438). In that last case the form is late and the gender of the name has been forgotten. The *s* of *Winricks* is pseudo-manorial.

Martley

MARTLEY 81 C 8

Mertlega 11th Heming
Merlie, Mertelai 1086 DB
Merlega 1155–1192 P (*passim*)
Mardelega 1155 RBE
Mertlega 1178 P
Martelea 1184 P
Markleghe 1234 Cl
Marthley 1274 Ipm
Mertelee 1275 SR, 1300 Ch
Martleye 1327 SR
Mark(e)ley 16th Wills, 17th FF *passim*
Marteleye 1583 BM

This is probably a compound of OE *mearð,* 'marten-weasel,' and leah, the first part of the compound being either the nom. sg. or the gen. pl., hence 'weasel-clearing' or 'weasels' clearing'; cf. further Martley (Sf), DB *Mertlega, Martele* and Mardleybury (Herts), DB *Merdelai,* and we may note *mearðeshrycg* (BCS 455) in a Worcestershire charter. The change from *th* to *t* which is very common under Anglo-Norman influence may have been helped in this case by the existence of the common *martre,* the French name for the same animal. It should be added that there is some evidence for an OE pers. name derived from this animal name. See on this point PN NbDu (*s.n.* Mason) and add references to Marlingford (Nf), earlier *Marðingford* (Thorpe 592) which seems to contain a patronymic formation from this name and probably also the Germanic parallel of certain names set forth by Förstemann (PN 1098–9) though he is inclined to explain them otherwise.

BERROW HILL AND GREEN

de Berga, atte Berewe 1275, 1327 SR

v. beorg. Berrow *Hill* is pleonastic.

HIPSMOOR FM (6")

Hypesmor, Hipesmor c. 700 (11th) BCS 219

The forms are very scanty for anything to be done with them. Professor Zachrisson suggests that the first part may be a pers. name *Hyppi*, a pet-form for OE *Hygebeald* or *Hygebeorht* with unvoicing of *bb* to *pp* such as is often found in pet-names. Hence 'Hyppi's marshland,' *v.* mor.

HOCKHAM'S FM

Hockam 1570 (17th) Hab, 1603 SR

The forms are too late to do anything with except to note that apparently the name is pseudo-manorial in form.

HOLLING FMS

Holyne 1275 *Ass* (p), 1327 SR (p)
Holin 1275 SR (p)
Holynne 1332 SR (p)
Hollen 1773 T

The same name as Hollin *infra* 72 though it may be the dat. sg. rather than the plural.

HOLME (lost)

Holm(e) c. 1270 AD iii

This may contain the word *holm*, 'low-lying ground by a stream,' which is ultimately of Scand. origin but is hardly evidence of Scandinavian settlement. *v.* Addenda.

HOPEHOUSE FM

de Hope, atte Hope 1275, 1327 SR

The valley here is of the very shallowest so that hop must be used of a piece of enclosed land.

HORSHAM [hɔ·səm]

> Horsham 1271 Ipm, 1275 SR, Ipm, 1309 Ipm, all (p), 1527 LP

'Horse-farm,' cf. *horsham* (BCS 834).

LARKINS (6″)

This takes its name from the *Larkin* family, recorded in the vill in 1603 (SR).

THE NOAK

> Noke 1327 SR (p), *wood called the Nook* 1609 VCH iv. 290, n. 5

ME *atten oke* or *atte noke*, 'at the oak,' v. æt, ac.

PRICKLEY GREEN

> *Prikelege* 1221 Ass (p)
> *Prieleye, Prielea* 1275 SR
> *Preheleye* 1275 Ass
> *Pregele* 1289 Ipm (p)
> *Prighelege* 1308 Ipm
> *Prichel* 1332 SR (p)
> *Prykley* 1521 LP, 1537 Wills
> *Prickley* 1654 FF

Neither the OE *prica, price*, nor its derivative *pricel*, seems in OE to be used except of a prick or goad, or the action which results from such. If we take therefore the first element of this name to have anything to do with that word, the most probable solution is that the first element was some compound of *price*, such as *pric þorn* (BCS 945) and we must assume that the triple compound *pric þorn leage* has lost its middle element in the fashion demonstrated by Ritter (88 ff.). Numerous other compounds are possible, cf. *prickwillow, pricktimber*, etc. The variant ME spellings are probably due in part to an alternative palatalised form, for which cf. *pritch* (NED). It should be noted that a late pers. name *Price* is not entirely out of the question. Cf. that name as borne by a moneyer of Edward the Confessor. We may also note Prixford (D), *Pirkeworth* in 1238, *Pirkesworth* in 1330, *Prichescroft* in Bedwardine (14th), *Prickefeld* in Shurnock (1649 Surv). See also Prickshaw (PN La 60).

PUDFORD FM

Podeford 1275, 1327 SR (p)
Pudiford 1289 Ipm
Pudeford 1290 Pat
Pudford 1527, 1539 LP

'Ford of *Puda*.' This pers. name is very rare, but it occurs again in *Pudan mor* (printed *pudan mor*) in BCS 627, now Pudmore Pond in Thursley (Sr)[1].

RODGE HILL

la Rugge 1237 SR (p)   *Rodge Hill* 1676 FF
Ridge Hill c. 1830 O

v. hrycg. The nearest point for this dialectal development mentioned in EDD is north-west Oxfordshire.

Mathon[2]

MATHON [meiðən] 81 H 7

Matma 1086 DB
Mathine 1251 Ch, 1270–1300 Wigorn *passim*, 1275 SR
Madine 1275 Heref
Matheme 13th AD ii, 1332 SR, Pat (p), 1364 Wigorn (p)
Maham 1315 Ipm
Mathon 1332 SR, 1484 Pat, 1535 AD iii, 1542 LP
Matham 1467 Pat
Mathern 1577 Saxton, 1787 Cary

It is clear that the correct ME form for this name is *Mathme* or *Matheme*. The only parallel to this name that has been observed is in a 12th cent. Lincs charter (in the possession of Mr Langton of Langton) relating to Bulby, where certain lands abut *super Matheme ac Harepol*. The possibility presents itself that OE *maþ(þu)m*, 'treasure,' might have been applied to a piece of land. It is fruitless to speculate about the circumstances in which such a name might have arisen. Professor Ekwall suggests that OE *maþþum* may have originally meant 'gift,' like the Gothic cognate *maiþms*.

[1] *ex inf.* Mr J. E. B. Gover.
[2] Transferred (in great part) to Herefordshire in 1897. It is in Doddingtree Hundred in DB, but was later transferred to Pershore, cf. 1275 SR.

BAGBURROW WOOD (6")

grava de Baggebarwe 1275 *Ass*

'*Bagga's* wood,' *v.* bearu.

FARLEY (lost)

Farenlega c. 1250 (15th) *AOMB* 61
Farlege, Farley 1255 *Ass*, 1287 Abbr (p), 1327 SR (p), 1652 FF
Farnleye 1275, 1332 SR (p), (*juxta Mathern*) 1331 *FF*
Fareley 1316 *FF*

'Fern-clearing,' *v.* fearn, leah. Cf. Farley in Romsley *infra* 301.

HAM GREEN

angulus de la Homme c. 1275 (15th) *AOMB* 61
de la Homme, ithe Home, in the Home 1275, 1327, 1332 SR

There is no river hamm here, so the word must be used in the sense of 'enclosure.'

HOLLING'S HILL

This probably takes its name from the family of John *Holyn* mentioned in 1275 (SR).

THE LEYS (Old 1")

de la Lee, de la Lye 1275 SR, 1302 WoCh

v. leah.

MOOREND CROSS

de la Morend, atte More-ende 1275, 1332 SR

Self-explanatory.

SOUTH HYDE FM

la Suthide 13th (15th) *AOMB* 61, (*in Mathma*) ib.
Southyde de Mathine 1346 Heref

Self-explanatory. *v.* hid.

TOWN HOUSE (6")

de la Toune, atte Toune 1275, 1327 SR

'Town' must here be used in one of its older or dialectal meanings. *v.* tun in EPN.

WALMSPOUT COPPICE (6")

la Welme 1275 SR (p)

This is OE **wielm** (Anglian *wælm*) and a spring is marked on the map just to the north of the coppice.

Orleton

ORLETON 81 A 6

Ealretune 1023 (17th) KCD 738
Alretune 1086 DB
Alreton 1212 Fees 140
Holreton 1242 Fees 959
Olreton 1275 SR, (*super Temedam*) FF
Orleton 1357 Ipm

OE *alra-tun*, 'farm of the alders,' *v.* alor, tun. A similar metathesis is found in Orleton (Hc). The *ea* in the first form would seem to be an error.

Pensax

PENSAX[1] 71 J 7

Pensaxan (dat.) 11th Heming
Pensex 1231 (1303) AnnMon, 1240 WoP (p), 1355 Pat
Pen(e)sey 1255 Wigorn, 1275 SR
Pensax 1327 SR (p)

This name must remain an unsolved riddle.

BATCH (lost)

la Beche 13th WoCh, 1240 WoP (p)   *la Bache* 1275 SR (p)
v. bæc.

HAWKLEY FM

Hauekele, Hau(c)kele 1275 *Ass*, SR (p)

OE *heafoca-lēage*, 'hawks' clearing,' *v.* heafoc, leah.

HEATH FM (6")

Hethe 1240 WoP

Self-explanatory.

---

[1] The *hludi læge* of the bounds of an enlarged Pensax in Heming (246) survives in a pers. name *Lodeleye* found in Stockton-on-Teme (1275 SR).

PENN HALL

> *Penhyll* 11th Heming   *Penhull* 1240 WoP, c. 1830 O

Just to the north of Penn Hall there is a hill, rising to the spot-level of 623 ft. This is clearly the same as Pendle (La), a compound of Brit. *penn*, 'head, top,' and OE hyll.

WOODHOUSE (local)

> *atte Wodehouse* 1327 SR   *Woodhouse* 1892 Kelly

'House by the wood' rather than 'house of wood.'

Ribbesford

RIBBESFORD 71 H 9

> *Ribbedford* 1023 (17th) KCD 738
> *Ribetford* 11th Heming
> *Ribeford* 1086 DB, 1181 P (p), 1275 SR
> *Ribbefort* 1175 P
> *Ridelesford* 1179 P (p)
> *Redelesford* 1180 P
> *Ribbleford* 1188 P (p)
> *Rippesford* 1231 Pat (p)
> *Ribbesford* 1232 Cl (p)
> *Ripeford, Rypeford* 1236 Fees 527, 1253 *FF* (p)
> *Ribesford* 1316 Cl (p)
> *Rippeford* 1322 Cl (p)
> *Rybbesford, Rybbysford* 1431 FA, 1550 Pat
> *Ripsford* 1707 Marr

Mr Bruce Dickins suggests that the first element in this name is OE *ribbe*, 'ribwort,' 'hound's tongue.' He further suggests that the full original form was *ribbe-bedd-ford*, i.e. ford where there was a 'bed' or clump of ribwort (cf. Hollybed *infra* 214). This plant is not common and its occurrence at all abundantly in a particular locality might easily give rise to a place-name containing it. It is recorded from Wyre Forest by which Ribbesford lies. The *s* is pseudo-genitival and late.

HIGH OAK COPPICE (6″)

> *del Oke* 1275 SR

The identification is not certain.

Hook Barn (Old 1")

Hok 1275 SR (p)   *la Houke* 1328 Ch
Hoocke Wood 1588 AD v

v. hoc. It is not clear just what *hook* or corner of land is
referred to.

Trundalls Wood (Old 1")

Long Trentall 1595 AD v

Rochford [1]

Rochford 81 A 4

Recesford 1086 DB
Ræccesford 11th Heming
Rechesford c. 1230 (c. 1240) *WoC*
Rochesford 1249 Fees 1161
Racheford 1255 *Ass*, 1455 Pat, 1461 IpmR
Rachesford 1274, 1356, 1360 Ipm, 1366 Pat
Rachefford 1296 Pat, 1303 FA, 1455 Pat
Ratcheford 1316 FA
Rocheford 1322 Pat, 1535 VE
Reccheford 1388 IpmR
Recheford al. *Rocheford* 1538 LP

The form from Heming leaves little doubt that this name is
from OE *ræcces-ford*, 'ford of the *rache* or hunting dog.'
v. rache in NED. The development to *Roch-* is curious but has
an exact parallel in the history of Rochdale (PN La 54) with
earlier forms in *Rach-*. Presumably the common French *roche*
may have had its influence in both cases in replacing a ME
rache which was not readily understood.

Rock

Rock 71 J 7

del Ak 1224 *FF*
Ake, Aka 1253, 1259 *FF*, 1277 Heref, 1291 Tax, 1319, 1335,
    1338 Pat
Lake, Oke 1255 *Ass*
Rok(e) 1259 *FF*, 1308 Ipm, (*la*) 1332 Heref (p) and 1349,
    1351, 1377, 1550 Pat

[1] In Herefordshire till 1837.

H

Aca, Hake 1276, 1277 Heref
Rock(e), Rokke 1309 Cl, 1348 Pat, 1524 LP
Rook(e) (la) 1366 Cl, 1385, 1447, 1481 Pat, 1545 LP
Rok al. *Ak* 1381 Pat
Ak vel *Rook* 1385 Pat
Aka al. *Rocke* 1535 VE

OE *æt þǣre āce,* 'at the oak,' with later development to *at ther oke, at the roke.* The modern form should be *Roke* but it is clear that confusion with the common word *rock* has taken place. It should be noted that, ecclesiastically, forms without *r* were used to quite a late date. Rock in Washington (Sx) has the same history.

ALTON LODGE (6″)

Eanulfintun 1023 (17th) KCD 738
Alvinton(a) 1080 France, 1227 Pat, 1255, 1275 *Ass,* SR
Alvintune 1086 DB
Alveton 1319 *FF,* 1411 FF, 1431 FA
Alvington 1541, 1544 LP, 1547 Pat
Alton 1550 Pat, (al. *Alvington*) 1603 SR

'*Ēanwulf's* farm,' *v.* ingtun. This pers. name is also found in *Eanulfestun,* now Alveston (Wa), KCD 651, 666.

BARRETT'S FM (6″)

Named from the family of *Baret* found in this vill in 1275, 1327 (SR).

BLAKEMORE FM

Blakemere 1275, 1327 SR (p)

There are several pools near the farm so that probably this is a compound of blæc and mere, hence 'dark pool.'

BOWERCOURT FM

le Boure 16th VCH iv. 323
Bower in the Rock, in le Rocke 17th ib.

v. bur and cf. Bower in Upper Arley *supra* 30.

BROOK FM

Broke 1275 SR (p)
Self-explanatory.

BUCKRIDGE

Bokerugge 1275 SR (p)

This is probably a compound of OE *bōca* and hrycg, and we must translate it 'ridge of the beeches.' Cf. Lindridge *supra* 57.

BULLOCKHURST FM

Bolluchurst 1275 SR (p)

'Bullock wooded-hill,' *v.* hyrst.

CLAYBROOK BARN (6")

Cleybroke 1275, 1327 SR (p)

Self-explanatory.

CONNINGSWICK FM (6")

Colingwic 1086 DB
Colingwyke 1255 *Ass*, 1319 *FF*, 1332 SR
Collingwick 1275, 1327 SR (p)
Colingwych 1411 FF
Connisick 1643 Townsend
Coneyswick c. 1830 O

OE *Colingwīc*, 'Cola's dairy-farm,' *v.* ing, wic.

DEASELAND FM

Detheslond 1275 SR (p)   *Desland* 1603 SR (p)

Professor Ekwall and Mr Bruce Dickins agree in suggesting that the first element is OE *dēaþ*, used of 'a dead person, a departed spirit,' cf. B.T. Supplt *s.v.* The place was perhaps so named from being haunted.

FARMAN'S COURT

This contains the pers. name *Faremon* found in 1275 (SR) in this vill. This is from the Anglo-Scandinavian *Færeman* or *Farman*. Cf. the lost *Farmons* in King's Norton *infra* 353.

FERNHALLS FM (6")

Ferhale 1275 SR (p)   *Vernalls* 1613 VCH iv. 323

'Fern-grown nook,' *v.* fearn, healh. The *s* is probably pseudo-manorial.

FIELDHOUSE FM
> *Felde* 1275 SR (p)
> *v.* feld.

GORST HILL
> *Goorsteshull* 1550 Pat
> Originally a genitival compound, 'hill of gorse.'

HAZEL FM
> *Hasele* 1275, 1332 SR (p)
> Self-explanatory.

HEIGHTINGTON
> *Huythindone* 1325 Heref
> *Hutdynton* 1332 SR (p)
> *Hightyngton, Hightington* 1550 Pat, 1656 FF
> *Hitonton* 1588 Wills
> *Heightenton* 1599 WillsP
> *Hittington* 1592 QSR

This name seems to involve an early use of OE *hīehðu*, 'height,' with the sense 'high-place.' From this must have been formed a compound *hīehðinga-tūn*, 'farm of the dwellers on the high ground,' a name peculiarly suitable to this particular site. *v.* tun.

HILL FM (6″)
> *la Hull* 1275 SR (p)
> Self-explanatory.

HOLLIN FMS
> *to þam gemære æt þam holignan, of ðam holigena gemæra*
>   c. 957 (11th) BCS 1007
> *Hollim* 1086 DB
> *Holin, Holyn* 1275 Ass, 1389 IpmR, 1527, 1538 LP
> *Holine* 1275 SR, 1308 Ipm, 1327 SR, 1408 IpmR, all (p)
> *Holland* 1643 Townsend
> *Hollyn* 1649 FF

v. holegn. *holignan* is a late form of the dat. pl. *holegnum* and it is clear that this place was originally known as '(at the) hollies.' Cf. Holling Fm *supra* 63.

HURTLEHILL FM

Hortle 1275 SR, 1340 NI, both (p)   *ate Hurtle* 1332 SR

'Stag-clearing,' *v.* heorot, leah, a clear example of the reduction of final *ley* to syllabic *l*, cf. similarly Marcle (He).

LINDON (lost)[1]

Linde 1086 DB, 1169 P, c. 1225 France
Linda c. 1150 Surv
Lyndon, Lindon 1225 *Ass*, 1423 FF, 1596 Wills, 1835 Lewis
Lynden(e), Linden 1275 *Ass*, SR, 1327, 1332 SR, (*Coudray*)
    1328 Ch

v. lind. There would seem to have been alternative forms with dat. sg. *linde* and pl. *lindum* which would account for the later variations, hence 'at the lime(s).' *Coudray*, added to the name in 1328, is, in another document, used in the form *Coudree*, as an alternative name for Lindon (VCH iv. 323 n. 5). It is the OFr *coudraie*, 'hazel grove,' found also in Cowdray (Sx) and need not surprise us as a name in this well-wooded district.

NORCHARD FMS

le Orchard 1311 BM   *atte Norchard* 1327 SR
Norchard 1655 FF

v. orceard. For the prefixed *n* cf. Nurton's Fm *supra* 25.

OLDHALL FM (1")[2]

de la Oldehalle 1275 SR

Self-explanatory.

ROCK MOOR

More 1086 DB   (*la*) *More* 1210 RBE, 1275 *Ass*
Mora Hugonis c. 1150 Surv
Chenies More 16th VCH iv. 322
Cheany Moor 1786 ib. 323

v. mor. The *Hugo* of the Survey is unknown. The *Cheneys* are first definitely associated with the manor in the 16th cent. (VCH *loc. cit.*).

[1] In the 1275 Subsidy Roll Lindon is a separate vill and includes Deaseland, Farman's Court, Fernhall Fm, Hazel Fm, Hill Fm, Hurtle Hill. This makes it clear that the site of Lindon must be sought in the north-east of the parish. Local investigation has so far failed to find it.
[2] Lithographed ed., not on engraved ed.

SNEAD FM AND COMMON

Snede 1275 *Ass et passim*   *Snead* 1659 FF

v. snæd.

STILDON MANOR

Stilladun c. 957 (11th) BCS 1007
Stilledune 1086 DB
Stillindon 1275 SR (p)
Stildon 1332 SR (p), 1631 QSR

This is a difficult name and we can only explain it if we assume that *Stilladun* is a late OE form for *Stillandūn*, which would explain the later *Stillindon*. A pers. name *Stilla* is not found in OE but it would be a regular cognate to the names containing OGer **stilja* quoted by Förstemann (PN 1364), of which we have a derivative in the well-known Vandal name *Stil(l)ico*. The name must originally have been a nickname denoting the *still* or quiet one, cf. the OGer names *Stilla, Stillina* used of women. Hence 'Stilla's hill' (*v.* dun).

WILLETT'S FM (6")

This contains the family name *Wilotes* recorded in SR (1327), 'little Will's farm,' so to say.

WORSLEY FM

Worfesleahges gemæra c. 957 (11th) BCS 1007
Wermeslai 1086 DB
Werveslega c. 1150 Surv
Worvesle(ga) 1180 (c. 1225) France, 1275 SR (p)
Werueslea 1185 P (p)
Worwesle 1275 *Ass*
Werwesle 1327 SR (p)
Wornesleye (sic) 1332 SR
Wordesley 1424 IpmR
Worsley 1603 SR (p)
Wardisley 1613 WillsP

Just to the east of the farm there is a small stream running down into Dick Brook and probably the clearing (*v.* leah) takes its name from this stream, which must at one time have been called *Worf*. This stream-name is found elsewhere in the *uuorf*

(BCS 1093), *wurf* (BCS 788) which lies behind the name Wroughton (W). Hence, 'clearing of (or by) the Worf.'

Lower Sapey

LOWER SAPEY or SAPEY PICHARD[1] 81 C 6

æt Sapian 781 (11th) BCS 240
Sapie 1086 DB, 1221 FineR
Sapy 1212, 1235 Fees 140, 527
Sapi Pichard 1242 Fees 959
Nethersapi 1275 *Ass*, (*Parva*) 1362 IpmR

No suggestion can be made as to the etymology of this name. In 1212 (RBE) Miles *Pichard* held a knight's fee in Sapey.

BURTON COURT

Borton 1293 Ipm, 1327 SR, both (p)
Burton 1308 Ipm (p), 1650 Comp
Byrton 1431 FA
Bureton 1521 LP

v. burhtun.

HARPLEY

Hoppeleia 1222 FF
Harpele(y) 1275 SR (p), 1369 Pat (p), 1405 IpmR, 1611 QSR
Happeleye 1293 Ipm

The sequence of forms is not very clear but it is probable that we have the same first element which is found in Harptree (So), DB *Herpetreu, Harpetreu*, Harpley (Nf), DB *Herpelai*, Harpenden (Herts), 1285 (John Ch) *Harpendena*, Harpford (D), 1284 FA *Herpford*, perhaps also Harpswell (L), DB *Herpeswelle*, Lindsey Survey *Harpeswella*, and Harpsfield (Herts), 1303 FA *Herpesfeld*, and cf. *herpesford* in BCS 34 (late copy), now Harpsford (Sr). These would seem to go back in the case of the weak forms to an OE *hearpa*, 'harper,' as suggested by Skeat (PN Herts 21). This must early have been used as a pers. name. The frequent strong forms might be explained as from earlier and fuller *Herperes-*, from OE *hearperes* the genitive of an alternative form of the agent-noun. It should be added

---

[1] *vulgo* Pritchard.

however that both these suggestions alike leave untouched the disconcerting frequency of early *Herp*- rather than *Harp*-, the form which we should really have expected. Tentatively we may suggest that the name means 'clearing of *Hearpa*.' *v*. leah.

HATHOUSE FM, HATHITCH FM

> *de la Hatte* 1290 *Deed*[1]   *atte Hatte* 1327 SR
> *Hattsitch* 1602 WillsP

The first element in these names must be OE *hæt*, 'hat,' the place being so called from some fancied resemblance of the ground, or possibly of a building on it, to a hat, cf. Hett (PN NbDu 113) of similar origin and the parallels there given, also *Bedeleshattes* (? beadle's hats)[2], a field-name in Hanley Castle (VCH iv. 93). The modern *hitch* is apparently a corruption of *sitch* from OE sic, 'small stream.'

OXHALL

> *Oxen(e)well* 1222 *FF*, 1327 SR, both (p)
> *Oxenwall* 1275 SR (p)
> *Oxenhale* 1293 Ipm (p)
> *Oxewell* 1332 SR (p)
> *Oxhills* c. 1830 O

'Spring of the oxen,' *v*. **wielle**. For the *wall-* forms *v*. Introduction xxvii.

Shelsley Beauchamp

SHELSLEY BEAUCHAMP 81 B 7 [biˑtʃəm]

> *Celdeslai* 1086 DB
> *Sceldeslega* c. 1150 Surv
> *Scheldeleya* 1175 P
> *Seldeslei, Seldesley* 1194 Cur, P, 1275 SR
> *Sheldeslegh Beauchampe* 1255 *Ass*
> *Schellysley Becham* 1535 VE

For further forms, *v*. Shelsley Walsh *infra* 78. This name must be considered with the unidentified *sceldesheafod* (KCD 724, an 11th cent. original charter) in Wa, *sceldesford* (BCS 380,

---

[1] *v*. 43, note.
[2] Followed by *bedelleslond*.

a 9th cent. original charter) in Kent and probably with the two examples of *S(c)heldesput* in Bk, one of which now appears as Shelspit (PN Bk 57). All alike point to a pers. name *Sc(i)eld* in OE. This is the same as *Scyld*, who stands at the head of the Danish line in *Beowulf* and who appears in William of Malmesbury as *Sceldius* and in the West Saxon genealogies as *Sceldwa*. In the form *Scyld* his name is found in *scyldestreow* (BCS 917) in Wiltshire. The name must therefore be interpreted as 'Sceld's clearing,' *v.* leah.

Professor Zachrisson would prefer in all these names to find a lost OE *sceald* or (with *i*-mutation) *sc(i)eld*, a term for a shallow stream, cf. sceald as an adj. in EPN[1]. The Severn itself divides Shelsley Beauchamp from Shelsley Walsh but there is a small tributary of the Severn at Shelsley Beauchamp.

Shelsley Beauchamp, also known as Great Shelsley, was already in the possession of the Beauchamps in the 12th cent. (VCH iv. 332). Shelsley *Kings*, a hamlet in the parish, has always formed part of the royal manor of Martley.

Birch Fm

de Birche, atte Birche 1275, 1327 SR

Self-explanatory.

Brockhill

Brochulle 1274 Ipm, 1275, 1327, 1332 SR, all (p)

'Badger-hill,' *v.* brocc, hyll. Cf. Brockhill in Beoley and in Tardebigge *infra* 187, 362 and *brochyl* (BCS 154).

Meneatt Fm (6")

Meniate 1275 Ipm, 1327 SR, both (p)

This must have taken its name from some gate used in common. *v.* geat and *mǣne s.n.* Menithwood *supra* 58.

Southwood

Bisouthe 1274 Ipm   *Bisuthe* 1275 SR
Bysouthe 1315 *FF*, 1327 SR, both (p)

These forms show the presence of a family called 'By south' in this parish. One cannot say with certainty that they lived at Southwood. For such formations cf. *Bastwood supra* 48.

---

[1] ZONF, ii. 137 ff.

Shelsley Walsh

SHELSLEY WALSH 81 B 7

Sceldeslæhge 11th Heming
Caldeslei 1086 DB
Sholdesley Gilden a. 1189 (17th) Hab
Seldesle(ge) 1203 Cur, (*Waleys*) 1275 SR
Sildeley 1211 RBE
Seldelege 1235 Fees 527
Shellesley Gildon 1535 VE
Shelsley welsh 1577 Saxton
Gildons 1658 FF

For the etymology of this name *v.* Shelsley Beauchamp *supra* 76. This manor was held already in 1211 (RBE) by one Johannes *Walensis*, called *le Waleys* in 1235 (Fees). It is also known as *Little* Shelsley. For the mysterious *Gilden* or *Gildon*, see under *Ildeberg infra* 124.

Shrawley

SHRAWLEY 81 B 9

Screfleh, Scræfleh 804 (11th) BCS 313
Escreueleia c. 1150 Surv
Scrauele(ga) 1220 Fees 140, 1235 Fees 526, 1235 *FF*
Shreuele, Schreweley 1275 *FF*, SR
Shrou(e)legh 1297 Pat, 1346, 1428 FA
Schrauleye 1316 Ipm
Shrauele(ye) 1327 SR, 1344 Pat, 1349 Wigorn, 1361 Cl
Shrawley 1431 FA

It is difficult to avoid the belief that here we have a compound of OE *scræf*, 'cave, den, hovel,' in the form *scræfleah* or, with gen. pl. of the first element, *scræfaleah* (*v.* leah). An alternative possibility for the development of medial *e* in such compounds is explained in Zachrisson's *English PN and River-names* 30, n. 2. There can be no question of caves here but, near to the Severn, half a mile to the north-east of the church, there is a series of mounds known locally as 'Court-hills' or 'Oliver's mounds.' These do not seem to have been investigated but it is just possible that they might have been connected with pit-dwellings.

COOKS HOUSE (6″) and SANKYN'S GREEN

These probably take their names from families named *Cooke* and *Senkin* who appear in the Subsidy Roll of 1603.

DOLEHAM BRIDGE (6″)

Dolemylle 1488 VCH iv. 339

The first element in these two names, which may refer to the same site, for Doleham is on Shrawley Brook, is apparently OE *dal* and the reference may be to the *hamm* in the brook here and to a mill respectively in which various persons held *doles* or shares. Cf. Dallow (PN BedsHu 158).

Stanford-on-Teme

STANFORD-ON-TEME [1] 81 A 6

Stanforde 1086 DB, (*Esturmi*) 1242 Fees 960, (*upon Temede*) 1317 Cl, (*Wassebourn*) 1346 FA
Staunforde 1210 RBE

'Stony or rocky ford,' *v.* **stan, ford.** *Esturmi* from the holding of Johannes Sturmi in 1242, *Wassebourn* from the holding of the family of that name from Little Washbourne.

HILL COPSE (6″)

de la Hulle 1255 Ass (p)
Self-explanatory.

NOVERTON (6″)

Overton juxta Stanford 1305 Cl   *Noverton* 1431 FA

'Over or upper farm,' with the same history as Nurton's *supra* 25.

SOUTHSTONE ROCK

Sulstan 1214 ChronEve, 1308 Ipm (p)
Suleston 1214 ChronEve
Solestune 1278 FF (p)

---

[1] From information kindly given by the rector, the Rev. J. B. Hewitt, we may note that Busk Coppice takes its name from one *Busk*, the tenant of a neighbouring farm in 1631, Temple Dingle from a Greek Temple built there c. 1770, Beehive Coppice from the shape of the ground-plan, Furnace Fm from the charcoal burning, and Waste Hill Wood from the family of one Lewis *Waste*, a tenant here in 1631. All these are only on the 6′ map.

Soulston 1327 SR, 1544 LP, 1631 *Terrier*
Solughstone 1353 Heref
Sulston 1535 VE

This is the name of an isolated rock in the deep-cut valley of the Teme and there can be no doubt that the original name was a compound of OE *sulh*, 'furrow,' which came to be used in an enlarged topographical sense, and stan. A similar use of *sulh* is found in Souldrop (PN BedsHu 43). The modern form is corrupt.

Stockton-on-Teme

STOCKTON-ON-TEME 81 A 7

Stoctun c. 957 (11th) BCS 1007
Stotune 1086 DB
Stocton 1194 Cur *et passim*
Stocketon 1535 VE

'Enclosure made of *stocks* or stumps,' *v.* stocc.

Stoke Bliss

STOKE BLISS[1] 81 B 5

Stoch 1086 DB
Stoke de Blez 1242 Fees 806

After this the manorial addition appears as *Bles* (1277 Heref), *Blez* (1291 Tax), *Bleez, Bles* (1303–1431 FA), *Blys, Blisse* (1535 VE, 1544 LP).

v. stoc. The manor was held by William de *Bledis* in 1211–2 (RBE). The early forms of Blay (Calvados), Blies (Ain), Blé (Vienne) suggest that the family may have come from any one of these places. The first is the most probable.

GARMSLEY and GARMSLEY CAMP

Garmesley or *Wrathes* 1602–1700 Kyre

This is probably 'Garmund's leah' but the forms are too late for any certainty. Cf. the history of Gamsey (PN BedsHu 226). No explanation of *Wrathes* can be offered.

---

[1] In Herefordshire till 1897.

Hyde Fm

la Hyde 1329 Kyre

v. hid.

Perry Fm

la Pyrie, La Pirie 1303 Heref (p), 1322 Kyre
ate Pirie de Stoke Bles 1365 Heref
Perrie 1400
The Pyrry 1574 Kyre

v. pirige, 'pear-tree.'

Pool Cottage (6″)

Pole, the Poole 1442, 1649 Kyre

Self-explanatory.

Suckley

Suckley 81 F 7

Suchelei, Sucheleya 1086 DB, 1169 P
Succhele(ia) 1174 P, 1222 BM
Suggelega 1180, 1181, 1182, 1190 P
Secheli 1194 Cur, P, both (p)
Suckele, Sukkele(ya) 1242 P (ChancR), 1275 SR, 1280
   Wigorn, 1401–5 Pat
Sokele(y) 1288 Wigorn, 1335 Pat
Soukkeleye 1349 Heref
Sokkeleye 1351 Heref

This name can only be explained if we bear in mind the
confusion that arose in English from the existence of two verbs,
from different stems, *sūcan* and *sūgan*, both meaning 'to suck.'
There was an OE pers. name *Sucga* and a bird-name *sugga* or
sugge. Side by side with *Sucga* doubtless arose a form *Succa*,
with unvoiced consonant and this was probably the original
form of the first element in Suckley. Later, confusion with
Sucga took place, assisted by the common voicing of intervocalic consonants and gave rise to sporadic forms in *Sugge*,
cf. also *S(o)uggenhyde* in Droitwich AD iii.

BASTENHALL

> *Bastehale* 1275 SR (p)
> *Bastonhall* 1289 Ipm
> *Bastenhal(l)* 1327 SR (p), 1634 QSR

This name suggests the same pers. name which lies behind Bastwick (Nf). Dr Schram suggests that this pers. name *Basta* is that which we find in diminutive form in Basildon (Berks), earlier *Bestlesden* and in *Bæstlæsford* (BCS 565) which is close to Basildon. For this, Stenton and Skeat alike suggest a pers. name *Bæstel*. This may be a *t*-extension of the *Basa* found in Basing (Ha). Hence 'Basta's nook of land.' *v.* healh.

COLD GROVE (Old 1″), COLD PLACE[1] (6″)

> *Coll Grove* 1521 VCH iv. 358   *Colles Place* 17th Hab

Habington (i. 399) says that the estate took its name from the *Colles* family. They similarly gave their name to *Coles* Green in Leigh. *Cold* Place is also called *Coal* Place.

GROVE HILL

> *de la Grave* 1275 SR

Self-explanatory.

NORTON FM (6″)

> *Northinton* 1275, 1327, 1332 SR (p)

This stands in contrast to Sindon *infra*. For the formation cf. Sodington *supra* 60. It looks as if here, as in that name, there were alternative forms, with and without the formative *ing*.

PRIORY REDDING (6″)

This preserves a trace of the estate held here by the Priory of Little Malvern (1275 SR, 1322 Pat). *v.* hryding.

SINDON'S MILL (6″)

> *Suthitun* 1275 *Ass*
> *Suthinton, Suthyngton* 1275 SR, 1315 Ipm, both (p)
> *Sodynton* 1332 SR (p)
> *Sintons Mill* 1892 Kelly

---

[1] The latter place is in Lulsley.

So called in relation to Norton *supra* 82, cf. Sodington *supra* 60 and Sinton *infra* 128. The *s* is pseudo-manorial.

Tenbury

TENBURY 81 A 3

Temedebyrig 11th Heming
Tame(t)deberie 1086 DB
Tametbire c. 1086 (1190) *EveB*, 1212 Fees 140
Themettesbure c. 1236 Fees 610
Themedbire 1239 FF
Themedebiri 1273 Wigorn
Temedbury 1275, 1327 SR
Themedbury 1281 Heref
Temedebury 1287, 1308 Ipm, 1332 SR
Themedebure 1291 Tax
Themodebury 1430 Pat
Tenbury al. *Temodesbury* 1465 Pat
Ten(d)bury 1535 VE
Tembury 1543 LP
Tenbury 17th FF *passim*

'The burh by the Teme,' *v.* Teme, R. *supra* 15. The *burh* may be the mound known as Castle Tump which, though on the Shropshire side of the river, is included in the bounds of Tenbury. Here formerly stood Tenbury Castle (VCH iv. 426).

THE BARNETS (6")

le Barnet 1420 IpmR

v. bærnet. Stevenson, in illustration of this term, after citing Barnettwood (Sr), Barnet Wood (He), Barnetts Wood (Ha) and a lost *la Bernetewood* (Nth) from Cl (1309), quotes from a Merton College lease the clause (1303), 'arbores autem in gardino, sæpibus, vel in *Bernetto*.' We may add *le Barnet* near Clows Top (Wo), 1421 IpmR.

BERRINGTON GREEN

Beritune 1086 DB
Beriton 1255, 1275 *Ass*, 1291 Tax, 1509 AD iv
Biriton 1251 Ipm, 1275, 1327 SR
Berintona 1322 (1412) Pat
Beryngton 1535 VE

'Bera's farm,' *v.* ingtun. No OE pers. name *Bera* is on record but we have a rare OE name *Beruulf* and *Bera* may be a pet-form for this or some other such name. The corresponding name is fairly common in OGer (Förstemann PN 249 ff.), cf. Berrington (He).

BROOK FM (6″)

de Broka, atte Broke 1275, 1332 SR

Self-explanatory.

CINDERS WOOD and MILL

Sundre 1313 Pat   *Sondre* 1420 IpmR

In the first reference we have mention of houses at *Sundre* and in the second of the manor of *Sondre*. If the identification is correct we have here a wood and mill belonging to the manor. The name of this manor is clearly to be connected with OE *sundor*, 'apart.' This is not known elsewhere as a name by itself and it may be either the adj. used as a noun or a shortened form of such names as sunderland or *sundorwic* (*v.* **wic**) which are on record in Old English. The wood lies in a remote corner of the parish and this may have some bearing on the interpretation of the name. This view is rendered almost certain by two Wiltshire Charters (BCS 586 and KCD 585). The former gives the bounds of Chelworth and includes reference to *loco qui appellatur sunder* on the east side of Crudwell. The latter gives the bounds of Eastcourt, on the east side of Crudwell, and on the western boundary of Eastcourt we have reference to a *Sunderhamme* (KCD iii. 468). The two names, one with and the other without the suffix, must refer to the same spot. To complete the analogy it should be noted that *Sunderhamme* still survives in a field-name *Little Cindrams* in Chelworth (Akerman, *Possessions of the Abbey of Malmesbury* in Archaeologia xxxvii, 263, 268), cf. further *Sunderland* in Warndon *infra* 175.

FRITH FM (6″)

in the Frith 1275 SR

v. fyrhþ.

HAYES FM

de Haya, del Hay, in le Hey 1275 SR, 1302 Ipm
Heyswood al. *Beryton Haye* 1545 LP

v. (ge)hæg. These last two names remind us that we are in an old woodland area.

HILLTOP FM

de la Hulle 1275 SR
Self-explanatory.

KYREWOOD

Corewode 1275 *Ass* (p)   *Curewode* 1275, 1327, 1332 SR (p)
'Wood on Kyre Brook,' *v.* Kyre *supra* 55.

OLDWOOD COMMON

Oldwood 1545 LP
'Old' in contrast to a lost *Yongewood* (1545 LP).

PALMERS GATE (Old 1")

la Palmere and *le Palmer* are found as surnames in this vill in the Subsidy Roll of 1275, so that the first element is apparently a family name.

SPLASH BRIDGE (6")

Pla(y)ss(c)h 1306 *FF* (p), 1327, 1332 SR (p)
The modern name is apparently a corruption of an earlier 'Plash Bridge,' so called from a *plash* or pool, *v.* plæsc.

SUTTON

Sutton 1212 Fees 140, (*Sturmy*) 1405 IpmR
'South' farm, presumably in relation to Tenbury itself. Distinguished as Sutton *Sturmy* from the family of that name, who held $1\frac{1}{2}$ fees here in 1212.

TERRILLS FM (6")

Tirells 1542 LP
The *Tyrel* family is found in this vill in 1275 (SR).

I

Great Witley[1]

GREAT WITLEY 81 A 8

Whitele Major 1275 *Ass*
Wytleye 1290, 1307 Wigorn
Wyttel(ie), Wytteleye 1316 Ipm, 1340 NI, 1428 FA
Wyttlay 1535 VE

For further and earlier forms and for the etymology, *v.* Little Witley *infra* 183.

REDMARLEY

Ridmerlege, Redmerlei 1086 DB
Rudmerlege, -lighe, -leye c. 1150 Surv, (*juxta Dodintrou*) 1182
  (18th) *RBB*, 1275 SR, 1316 Ipm
Rumerle 1200 Cur
Ridmarlegh, Ridmareley 1296 Ipm, 1431 FA

The history of the name is clearly the same as that of Redmarley *infra* 156. It is the 'clearing by the reed-mere,' *v.* hreod, mere, leah. Within 500 yds of Redmarley there are five pools. It included two manors, viz. Redmarley Adam, which took its name from *Ada(m)* de Rudmarleg' who held it by a series of subinfeudations in 1242, and Redmarley Oliver, which took its name from Robert *Olifard*, who held Rudmarleg' *Olifar* in 1242 (Fees 961). For the description of it as 'by Dodintrou,' *v.* Doddingtree *supra* 23.

WALL HOUSE (6")

atewall 1340 NI

It is probable that this is OE weall, but why so called is not clear. OE wielle in the Anglian form wælla is not out of the question however.

WOODBURY HILL

de Oldbury, atte Oldbury 1275, 1327 SR

The sites, if not the names, of these places are probably identical. Woodbury Hill has a very fine hill-fort (VCH iv. 422). This was probably known in earlier days as the 'old' burh or fort.

[1] Great Witley was probably partly in Doddingtree and partly in Oswaldslow Hundred.

QUINZEHIDES (lost)

> *Quinzehides* 1275 *Ass*, 1313 Inq aqd, 1313 Orig
> *Quinsoludes* (sic) 1276 RH

This is a lost manor in Doddingtree Hundred. The parish is unknown but it is worthy of record as furnishing a parallel to the hybrid Trenthide (Do), 'thirty hides,' dealt with by Mawer, *PN and History* 22.

II. OSWALDSLOW HUNDRED

> *Oswaldeslaw, Oswoldeslau* 1086 DB
> *Oswaldeslawes Hundred* c. 1150 Surv
> *Oswaldestane* 1175 P
> *Oswoldeslowe* 1255 *Ass*
> *Osewaldesle* 1276 RH

This Hundred consisted of sixteen manors, all belonging to the Church of Worcester and assessed at 300 hides. It was made up of a compact area, roughly one-half, surrounding Worcester, and thirteen isolated areas of differing magnitudes lying to the south and east. It was a triple hundred which was supposed to have been constituted by King Edgar in a charter of 964 (BCS 1135) to the monks of Worcester in the days of Bishop Oswald. In that charter it is arranged that the three hundreds of *Wulfereslaw, Winburgetrowe* and *Cuðburgelawe* shall henceforth constitute one unit and meet at a place, henceforward to be called, in honour of Bishop Oswald, *Oswaldeslaw*. This place is mentioned in the bounds of Wolverton (KCD 612) and is to be identified with Low Hill in White Ladies Aston *infra* 88. Further light is thrown on this locality *s.n.* Stoulton, Spetchley, Swinesherd *infra* 165–6, 161.

The Hundred of Wimburntree, representing the *Winburgetrowe* of BCS 1135, is mentioned in the Hundred Rolls of 1276, where it included Blockley. The court of the triple hundred was then held there and the *curia de Wymeburnetre* is mentioned in a 1408 Survey of Blockley (*EcclVar*). It is also mentioned as *Wymburghtree* in 1376 IpmR.

Nothing further is known of the other two hundreds. Wimburntree and *Cuðburgelaw* took their names from women, called respectively *Wynburh* and *Cūðburh*, cf. *Rǣdburh* in Redbornstoke Hundred (PN BedsHu 67), *Wulfereslaw* from the man's name *Wulfhere*. The meeting-place of the hundred-court was not fixed. Swinesherd (*v. infra* 161) in its very name possibly records one of the meeting-places. Another was at a lost *Dryhurst*, near Worcester. In 1276 (RH) the Hundred of Oswaldslow met at *Druhurst*. In 1319 (Pat) we hear of the court of the Hundred of *Bruhurst* (sic) and this place is also mentioned in 1301 (Wigorn) as *Dryhurst*.

For the form *Oswaldestane*, cf. similar confusion under Redbornstoke and Wixamtree Hundreds in PN BedsHu 67, 87 and see under Stoulton *infra* 166.

Alstone[1]

ALSTONE 93 C I

Ælfsigestun 969 BCS 1233, 1046–60 (11th) KCD 805
Helsistona 1183 AC (p)
Alsiston 1221 *Ass, FF*, 1300 Wigorn, all (p)
Alseston 1240 WoP, 1349 CompR
Aleston 1255 *Ass*
Alston 1535 VE, 1649 Surv
Auls(t)on 17th Wills, 1763 Bowen

'Farm of *Aelfsige*,' *v.* tun. So also Alston (So), Alciston (Sx).

White Ladies Aston

WHITE LADIES ASTON 81 E/F 13

æt Eastune 977 (11th) KCD 615
Estun(e) 1086 DB, 1229 Ch
Estona, Estone c. 1086 (1190) *EveB*, 1221 *FF*, 1275 SR
Aston Episcopi 1247 FF, (under *Oswaldeslawe*) 1275 *Ass*,
    (*Brudely*) 1318 *FF*
Whitladyaston, -easton 1481 IpmR, 1577 Saxton

'East farm,' perhaps in relation to Low Hill or Oswaldslow. The manor belonged to the Bishop of Worcester. Part of it was held of him by the Cistercian nuns of Whitstones *infra* 115, hence *White Ladies*. The Bruleys, first mentioned as *Brusle* in

---

[1] Now in Gloucestershire.

the Pipe Roll of 1175–6 also held land here. Their name appears as *Bruille* in 1208 (Fees), *Bruyley* in 1262 (*For*). It is also known as Nether Aston (VCH iii. 560).

Low Hill

Oswaldes hlaw 977 (11th) KCD 612

This is the hill which gives its name to the Hundred (*v. supra* 87). It is an oval hill which lies astride the Worcester-Evesham road. *v.* hlaw.

St Johns in Bedwardine

BEDWARDINE [bedwədiˑn, bedwədin] 81 E 10/11

    Bedewordine 1235 FF
    Bedewrthin, Bedeworthin 1255 *Ass*, 1275 SR, 1317 Ipm
    Bedewurthyn 1323 LibAlb, 1337 WoCh
    Bed(e)wardyn 1327 SR, 1379 *FF*, 1392 Pat, 1501 BM

'*Bēda's* enclosure,' *v. worðign*[1]. There are forms *Bradewurthin* (1255 *Ass*) and *Bradewardyn* (1322 Cl (p)) which apparently refer to this place and may have been influenced by the neighbouring *Broadheath*[2].

Ambrose Fm (6″)

This clearly takes its name from the same *Ambrose* who owned the *molendinum Ambrosii* mentioned in 1240 (WoP). The mill still stands on the road from Worcester to Dines Green (VCH iii. 509).

[1] The etymology of Bedwardine has been the subject of interesting speculations. Habington (ii. 129) says, 'so called it may be from *Bedds* or lodgings in a Warde, as Bedford from Inns and Bedds at the ford, or of the Ward or Warden of Beades and devotion.' Nash (ii. 308) says, 'so called because it was allotted to supply the table of the monks with bread and provisions.' With reference to this last speculation it may be well, in view of its speciousness, to say (i) that the manor of Wick was the Bishop's and not the Prior and Convent's, (ii) that the refectory of the latter drew its revenue, not from Bedwardine but from Barbourne, Hillhampton, Twining, Powick and Tibberton.

[2] In the bounds of Bishop's and the other *wicks* in BCS 1139 we have a *streon(en) halh* with which may be compared the *streoneshalh* name which lies behind Strensall (Y) and the old name *Streanæshalch* given by Bede for the place afterwards called Whitby. For the name involved, cf. *Strēonberct* and *Strēonuulf* in LVD and *v.* Stevenson in the *Academy* for July 11, 1885.

ATCHEN HILL

> *ætinc weg, ættinc weg* 963 (11th) BCS 1106, 1107
> *ættingc gærstun* c. 970 (18th) BCS 1139
> *Estenhill* 1649 Surv

All these names alike would seem to contain the pers. name *Æti*, linked with **weg, gærstun** and **hyll** by the suffix **ing**, so that we have mention of a road, a grassy-enclosure and a hill associated with one *Æti*, that name being a pet-form of an OE name in *Ēad-*, possibly *Ēadsige*, as in the historical instance of the archbishop of that name who signs himself *Aeti* (KCD 784). The same pers. name lies behind Atcham (Sa) and *ætingden* in Kent (BCS 442) which is possibly to be identified with Etchden in Bethersden (1460 BM *Hacchesden*).

BIRCHEND FM

> *la Birche* 1182 (18th) *RBB* (p)
> Self-explanatory.

BIRCHEN GROVE (6″)

> *Birchenegrove* 1316 Ipm
> Self-explanatory.

BOUGHTON PARK

> *Boltone* 1275 SR (p), (*in Wyke*) 1309 Ch, 1346 *EcclVar*, 1502 Ipm
> *Bulton* 1494 Ipm (p)
> *Boulton* al. *Bulton* 1502 Ipm
> *Bowton, Boughton* 1562, 1587 Wills
> *Boulton* 1634 QSR, 1649 Surv, 1688, 1695 FF

This is not an easy name, but it may be suggested that it is a compound of **bold** and **tun**, the Midland equivalent of the common Northern **bōðltun**. The meaning is probably 'farm building with enclosure.' 'In Wyke,' i.e. in the Bishop's manor of *Wick*.

BROADHEATH, UPPER and LOWER

> *Hethe* 1240 WoP (p)   *le Brode* 1327 SR, 1418 *FF*
> *Broad Heath* 1646 Townsend
> Self-explanatory.

CLOPTON (lost), but lying in the south of the parish.

æt *Cloptune, Cloptune* 985 (11th) KCD 649, 1086 DB, c. 1086 (1190) *EveA*

Clopton(a) c. 1086 (1190) *EveB*, 1329 WoCh (p)

The first element in this name is fully discussed in PN BedsHu 22–3. There it is shown that it probably denotes something short and stumpy in character but whether a stump or a rock or what it may be we cannot say precisely and as the exact site of this manor is unknown it does not help us.

COLEWICK (lost)

Colewiche 1182 (18th) *RBB*

Colewic, Colewyk(e) 1232 Ch, 1238 *FF*, 1275 *Ass*, 13th WoCh (p), 1299 (18th) *RBB*, 1310 Pat, (*in manor of Wyke*) 1331 Pat, 1344 *FF*

'*Cola's* dairy-farm,' v. wic.

COMER GARDENS (6")

assart de Combire 1240 WoP

Comer in Temple Lawern 1316 Ipm

Colmore 1649 Surv

Little can be done with these forms. It looks as if the last form is an inverted spelling from names in which the *l* has become silent.

CROWNEAST COURT [krou nest]

Crow(e)neste c. 1250 Middleton, 1275, 1327 SR (p), 1343 Ipm, 1436 IpmR (p), 1672 FF

Craweneste, Craveneste 1255 *FF*, 1275 *Ass*, SR (p)

Crownyst 1546 Wills

'Crow-nest,' the place being in the highest part of the parish. For the name, cf. Crow's Nest Hill (Hu) and Crownest (Y) in PN S.W. Yorks 114. The modern form is a deliberate perversion.

CUTMILL (lost)

Cottemulne 1299 (18th) *RBB*

Cuttemulle 1408 *EcclVar*

Cuttemylle 1535 VE

Cottes or *Cutt Myll* 1544 LP

The presence of another Cutmill in Lindridge and of a Cutt Mill in Easington (O), with forms *Cuttydmylle*, *Cuttydemyll* (*Merton College Deeds*, 1420, 1450) shows that we must take the first element as a significant one. A 'cutted' mill may be one provided with a 'cut' or artificial channel carrying water to the wheel.

DINES GREEN

For this name we should probably compare *dina mor* (BCS 356) in the bounds of Hallow, for Dines Green is a mile south of the Hallow boundary. No suggestion can be offered as to the etymology of the name.

EARL'S COURT

This may be named after the family of *le Erl* recorded in this vill in 1275 SR.

THE ELMS

de la Helme 1182 (18th) *RBB*   *atten Elmes* 1299 (18th) *RBB*

Self-explanatory, the first form showing inorganic *h*.

GOLDENWICK (lost), now Upper Wick

Gold Hinewic, Goldine Wica, Goldinewyke 1182, 1299 (18th) *RBB*
Goldegynewyk c. 1240 WoP
Goldgivewik (bis), *Goldgivewyk* (bis) 1240 WoP
Goldenwick 1614 Kyre, 1649 Surv

The second element here is **wic**, the first is the OE woman's name *Goldgiefu*. The early *n*-forms are purely errors of transcription. When ME *Goldiuewik* had, by a natural sound-development, become *Goldiwick*, it seems to have been corrupted by a process of folk-etymology, or it is alternatively possible that a form *Goldinewick*, originally purely a scribal error, may have established itself as the correct form. For a similar confusion, which may in part at least be scribal, cf. Edington in Hungerford (Berks), DB *Eddeveton*, which clearly comes from OE *Ēadgifu* (*v*. Stenton, PN Berks 34)[1].

[1] The history of the corruption is made clear by the following forms, kindly supplied by Major Laffan: DB *Eddevetone*, 1166 P *Ediuetone*, 1195 FF *Edinton*, 1316 FA *Edyneton*, 1428 FA *Edyngtone*.

This explanation, at first advanced in tentative fashion, seems definitely to be established by the record (noticed afterwards) in the Domesday of the Bishop of Worcester (*RBB* fol. 16) in 1182, that in Bishop's Wick, " Goldiva holds *duas mansuras* which pay 11*s.* geld." This is almost certainly a reference to the tenant of Goldenwick herself.

HARDWICK'S SPRING[1] (6")

Hordewik 1240 WoP
Herdewik, Herdewic 1275 SR, 1365 Pat, 1535 VE
Hardwick 1649 Surv

v. heordewic and cf. Hardwick in Bredon *infra* 101.

KINGESHAM (lost)

Kingesham 1240 WoP, c. 1240 LibPens, 1292, 1321 CompR

This piece of land, always called a *pratum*, must be the same as that called *Kingesham* in the Worcester Cartulary (Cott. Vitellius C ix. f. 60) given by Hearne (p. 516). There it is said to have been given to Worcester by King Edgar, and to lie on the far side of the Severn, adjoining *Kyneswick*, i.e. one of the Wicks mentioned below. It looks as if the *ham* must have been a *hamm* by the river. It clearly took its name from its donor. It must be distinguished from Kinsham in Bredon *infra* 102.

LAUGHERN [lɔ·n]

æt Lawern 963 (11th) BCS 1108
Laure 1086 DB
Lawerne c. 1086 (1190) *EveA* & *B* (in *A* corrected from *Laure*)
La Warne 1255 *Ass*

This was a settlement on Laughern Brook (*v. supra* 12) named from it. In that settlement there developed various manors including

---

[1] In the Survey of 1649 Hardwick included Almoners Fm, Kitcheners Leasowe, Sextons Close, Croft and Neyte, all associated with officers of the Priory of Worcester. The *Neyte* is probably the islet (*v.* iggoþ) in Laughern Brook, a little west of St John's cemetery. For *Sexton's* cf. Sacriston Heugh (Du) in PN NbDu 171.

TEMPLE LAUGHERN

> *Lawern Willelmi* 1275 FF, *Tempull Lawarne* 1336 WoCh,
> *Temple Laughorne* (ib.)

This is the manor on Laughern Brook which belonged to one *William*, son of Miles, as early as 1236, and was sold to the Templars in 1249 (VCH iii. 505). Other manors were *Lawarne Dabitot* and *Bechameslawerne*, held by Urse D'Abitot in 1086 and afterwards held by John d'Abitot of the Beauchamps, and also *Lawerne Almoners* or *Elemosinary* belonging to Worcester Priory (ib. 505–6).

OLDBURY FM

> *Holebure* 1275 SR (p)
> *Holbury* 1316 Ipm, 1327 SR (p), 1518, 1557 Wills
> *Howbury, Howbery* 1550 Pat, 1610 QSR

This must be 'hollow burh,' but why so called it is impossible now to say. It lies on the spur of a hill.

PITMASTON HOUSE (6″)

> *Pectesmoneston* 1255 *Ass* (p)
> *Pydemanston*[1] 1255 *Ass* (p)
> *Pitemanston* 1299 (18th) *RBB*
> *Gt Pittmastons* 1665 FF

Behind this name must lie a lost OE pers. name *Peohtmann*. Both elements of that name are fairly common in OE pers. names. Hence 'Peohtman's farm,' *v.* tun.

PITTENSARYS FM (lost)

> *Pytenciarys Ferme, Pytensares Farm, Pyttensarys* 1608, 1616,
> 1638, 1661 WoCh

This was a small manor attached to the office of 'pittancer' in Worcester Priory.

RUSHWICK

> *Russewyk* 1275 *Ass*, 1275 SR (p)
> *Ruyschewyk* 1318 *Bodl* (52) (p)
> *Rushwyke* 1348 Pat, 1510 WoCh

---

[1] This is from the name of a man amerced in Pershore Hundred, but doubtless refers to this place.

Rushwyck, Rushwick 1540 Wills, 1684 FF
Rishwick 1669 Kyre
'Dairy farm by the rushes,' *v.* rysc, wic.

WICK EPISCOPI

Wican c. 760 (11th) BCS 219, *æt Wican* c. 970 (11th) BCS
    1139
Wiche 1086 DB, *Wike* c. 1086 (1190) *EveA*
Bisshopewike 1221 *FF*
Wyke Episcopi juxta Wigorn 1350 BM

The first form is really the dat. pl. of wic and suggests that
already there were two wicks, the later Upper and Lower
Wick. The land was granted to the Bishopric of Worcester in
the 8th cent.

UPPER WICK

The manor was granted in the 12th cent. to Osbert d'Abitot
and is known therefore as *Wyke Abitot* (*Wyke Abbetot* 1275 SR).
The manor, or part of it, is also named Goldenwick, *v. supra* 92
and *Sapynswyke* (14th VCH iii. 502), *Wike Sapey* (1420 Ipm)
and *Overwyke* (14th VCH ib.). The second derives from the
Sapy family who held land here in the 14th cent. (VCH *loc. cit.*).

LOWER WICK

This is called *Nether* Wick in 1649 (Surv).

Bengeworth[1]

BENGEWORTH [bendʒəˑd] 82 H 3
    Benigwrthia 709 (c. 1200) BCS 125
    Benincgurthe 714 (16th) BCS 130
    Benincwyrðe 780 (11th) BCS 235
    Bennincguuyrð 907 (11th) BCS 616
    Bynnyncgwyrðe 980 (11th) KCD 625
    Bennincwyrð 1003 (c. 1200) KCD 1299
    Benningeorde, Bennicworte c. 1086 DB
    Bennichwrth, Benningwrth c. 1086 (1190) *EveA* & *B*
    Beningworth 1251 Ch

    [1] Now in Blackenhurst Hundred.

Benychworth 1274 AD iii
Beningeworthe 1275 SR
Beningword 1275 Wigorn, 1280 Ch
Bengeworth(e) 1393 AD ii, 1535 VE
Benger 1692 Marr

'Enclosure of Be(o)nna,' the name *Beonna* or *Benna* being a pet-form of a pers. name in *Beorn-*, *v.* ing, worð. Cf. Benham (Berks), *Bennanham* in BCS 1055.

KNOWLE HILL (6")

Cnoll 1003 (c. 1200) KCD 1299

v. cnoll. Self-explanatory.

LONGDON HILL

Langendune 709 (c. 1200) BCS 125
Lang(a)dune c. 1010 (c. 1200) KCD 1358
Landon c. 1830 O

Self-explanatory.

PORT STREET (local)

le Portstrete 13th AD iii

Port is here used in its old sense of market-town, *v.* port and Portway *supra* 3.

Berrow

BERROW 92 B 9

la Berwe, la Berge 1190 (18th) Hearne's *Heming* 537

This is clearly from OE beorg. The reference must be to the western part of the parish, which rises to the top of the Malvern Hills. The place is sometimes spoken of as *La Berewe Geffrey* (1275 *Ass*) from one *Galfridus* de la Barue who held the manor. Sometimes it is described as *subtus Malvern* (VCH iii. 257), at others as *Netherberrowe* (Surv 1649) in contrast to Overbury, of which it was a chapelry (Heming *loc. cit.*).

CHASE END

The place is spoken of as *Keysende* as early as the 15th cent. (VCH iii. 258) and it is called *Keys* or *Case* End in the old 1" O.S. map and *Caisend* in Kelly's Directory of 1855. It must take its name from the *Keys* family mentioned in 1275 (SR). The modern form is doubtless due to the idea that the place was really the end of Malvern *Chase*.

RYE FM (6″) and STREET
> *atte Reye* 1327 SR   *Ryplace in Barow* 1437 Pat
> *Rie* 1473 IpmR   *la Rye* 1513 Ipm

Rye Farm is on land between two streams which was doubtless in old days spoken of as an **eg**. *Atte reye* is from earlier *at ther eye* and the place has the same history as The Rye (PN Bk 205).

UNDERHILL FM
> *Underhull* 1327 SR (p)

Self-explanatory.

Bishampton

BISHAMPTON [biʃəmtən] 82 F 2
> *Bisantune* 1086 DB
> *Bisshantune* c. 1086 (1190) *EveA* (*h* put in as a correction)
> *Bissamtona* c. 1086 (1190) *EveB*
> *Bishamtone, Byshamton* 11th Heming, 1346 FA, 1466 IpmR
> *Bihamtone* 1208 Fees 37
> *Bishampton, Byshampton* 1275, 1327 SR, 1291 Tax, 1415 IpmR, 1535 VE

The first element in this name is not clear. There is a river Biss in Wiltshire (*Bis* in BCS 1127, a ME copy) but Bishampton does not lie definitely on a stream. The northern end is half a mile from Whitsun Brook (*v. supra* 16) and it is just possible that *Bis* may have been the name of one of the small streams linked up with it at this point. Bisley (Gl) is *Bislege* in an equally late copy of a charter (BCS 574) and is *Biselege* in DB. This certainly does not lie on any stream. We should therefore probably take Bisley and Bishampton alike as containing the OE name *Bisi*, or, in a weak form, *Bisa*. In OGer this name is found in both strong and weak forms as *Bisi* and *Biso* (Förstemann PN 308). Hence 'Bisi's hamtun.'

Blockley

BLOCKLEY 93 B 7

Bloccanleah, Bloccanlea 855 (11th) BCS 489, 978 (11th) KCD 620

Blochelei 1086 DB

Blokesleia c. 1215 Giraldus Cambrensis (Opera iv. 106)[1]

(Further forms are without interest.)

'*Blocca's* clearing,' v. leah. This is the weak form of a pers. name *Blocc* found in Bloxham (O), Bloxholm (L), Bloxworth (Do) and Bloxwich (St). This name must be allied to the word *block*. If that is the case, the history of that name itself may be different from that suggested by the usual lexicographical material. It may be of OE origin and not a ME loan-word from some Germanic dialect, directly or indirectly.

ASTON MAGNA

Estona 1208 Fees 36, 1275, 1327 SR

Hangynde Aston 1282 FF

Honginde Aston, Hingyndaston 1292 FF, 1302 Wigorn, 1375 Pat

Aston juxta Blokeleye 1346 FA

Hanging Aston 1549 Pat

It lies *east* of Blockley and was described as 'hanging' because on the slope of a steep hill.

BRAN MILL (6")

Braundes Mill 16th VCH iii. 271

This mill must take its name from someone bearing the Anglo-Scandinavian name *Brand*.

DITCHFORD

Dicford c. 1050 (11th) KCD 804, 1086 DB

(Further forms are without interest.)

As the Fosse Way here crosses Paddle Brook, the dic must refer to that road and the name mean 'dyke-ford.' The name is interesting as showing that the Roman road could be described by the English word *dic* as well as by its Latin equivalent *fossa*.

---

[1] Stevenson MSS.

Similarly in the Ditcheat (So) Charter, *Dichesgate* in BCS 438, Dr Grundy points out that landmark no. 9 in the bounds, referring to a *dich* is either the agger of the Fosse Way or the ditch at the side of it.

DORN

> *Dorene* 964 (12th) BCS 1135, 1346 FA
> *Dorne* 11th Heming, 1190 *EveB*, 1208 Fees 35, 1275, 1327
>   SR, 1428 FA
> *Derne* 1182 (18th) *RBB*
> *Dorn* 1356 Pat
> *Doron* 1482 IpmR

Professor Ekwall suggests that this name should be connected with British *duro-*, 'fort, stronghold,' and for the vowel *o* for *u* of the first element, compares Dorchester (Do), British *Durnovaria*, *Dorvernum* for *Dur-*, the old name of Canterbury, and suggests that the name *Duronum* found in France (*v.* Holder *s.n.*) may provide a counterpart of Dorn. He notes that the place is on the Fosse Way and thus a place which may have had a Roman fort. In interesting confirmation of this suggestion it may be noted that there are Roman remains at Dorn Fm. Haverfield (VCH i. 221) discusses these but concludes 'without excavation we can hardly decide whether a villa with outbuildings stood here, or some wayside village connected with the Fosse.'

DRAYCOTT

> *Draicota*, *Draycote* 1208 Fees 38, 1275 SR

'Cottages by the dræg,' but it is impossible to say in what particular sense that word is used here. The hamlet lies on a small affluent of Knee Brook.

NORCOMBE WOOD (6″)

> *Northcumbe* 1299 (18th) *RBB*, c. 1300 *EcclVar*
> Self-explanatory.

NORTHWICK PARK

> *Norðwica* 964 (12th) BCS 1135
> *Norwyk juxta Blockele* 1254 *FF*
> *Northicke* 1577 Saxton

'North dairy-farm' (*v.* **wic**). It is north in relation to Blockley and is 'juxta Blockley' in contrast to Northwick in Claines.

PAXFORD

  Paxford 1208 Fees 38, 1275, 1327 SR, 1346 FA

We probably have here a lost pers. name *Pæcc* which lies also behind Packington (Ess, Wa), Patching (Sx). Hence '*Pæcc's* Ford,' *v.* ford. This place included a *Pakesheye* in 1299 (*RBB*). We should have expected *Patchford*, but there are many difficulties as yet unsolved in regard to names of this type, cf. Seckley *supra* 32 which one would have expected to appear as *Setchley* or *Sedgeley*. The explanation may be that *Pæcc* was influenced by a corresponding form *Paca (cf. Packington).

PYE MILL (6″)

  Peomull 1383 VCH iii. 271

There is an OE *pēo, pīe*, 'insect,' and it is just possible that in this name we have, as so often is the case, a mill-name of the nickname type, but no certainty is possible.

STAPENHILL FM

  Stapenhull c. 1300 *EcclVar*

This is probably for *stapol-hyll*, i.e. 'hill marked by a *staple* or post of some kind,' *v.* stapol, hyll[1]. For the *n* cf. IPN 106. From the form one might take this name for OE *steapan hylle* (dat.), 'steep hill,' but the topography puts this out of question. There are other examples of Stapenhill in Staffs, one two miles north-west of Stourbridge and the other in Burton-on-Trent, a mile to the south-east. Both of these are on well-marked hills and may well be 'steep hill.' Duignan (PN St 142) notes that the first of the Staffordshire Stapenhills is near the Staffordshire-Worcestershire boundary and takes the first element to be OE *stapol*. It may be noted that Stapenhill in Burton is similarly on the Staffordshire-Derbyshire border, but as we have a form *stapenh'* in BCS 773, it is unlikely that we have *stapol* here. The Worcestershire Stapenhill is on the boundary of the once independent vills of Paxford and Draycott in Blockley.

---

[1] This conjecture is strengthened by the existence of a *Stapulton Hulle* (probably the same site) in the 1408 Survey of Blockley (*EcclVar*).

UPTON WOLD FM

Huppetune 1182 (18th) *RBB*
Upton 1208 Fees 38 *Uptonwolde* c. 1300 *EcclVar*
Upton Old 1549 Pat

The district lies high in West Blockley and 'Old' is a common dialectal form of *wold* (*v.* weald).

Bredicot

BREDICOT [brediket] 81 E 13

Bradigcotan (dat. pl.) 840 (11th) BCS 428
Bradingccotan (dat. pl.) 978–92 (11th) KCD 683
Bradecote 1086 DB, c. 1086 (1190) *EveB*, 1187 P, 1317 BM
Bradicot(e) c. 1086 (1190) *EveA*, 1543 Wills
Brodecot 1275 SR (p)
Bredicot 16th Wills *passim*, 1649 Surv

'*Brāda's* cottages,' the pers. name being linked to the second element by the -*ing* found also in ingtun. There seems to be no reason for the development of the modern vowel.

Bredon

BREDON 92 A 13

Breodun in Huic̃ 775 (11th) BCS 209
Breadun, Breodun 780 BCS 234
Breodun in provincia Hwicciorum 780 (11th) BCS 236
Breodun 841 (11th) BCS 134, 1086 DB
Breoduninga gemære 984 Earle 208
Bridona c. 1086 (1190) *EveA*
Bredon 1208 Fees 37, 1295 Pat (*Herberd*)
Brudone 1299 (18th) *RBB*
Breudon 1302 Pat

For this hill-name *v.* IPN 25. It was distinguished from Breedon (Lei), also in Mercia, as 'Bredon among the *Hwicce*,' *v.* Introd. xv. The *Herberd* of the 1295 form is unknown.

BREDON'S HARDWICK

Herdwicke, Herdewyk in Bredon 1299 (18th) *RBB*, 1320 Pat
Breadon Hardwycke 1558 Wills

v. heordewic.

K

KINSHAM

Chelmesham 1182 (18th) *RBB*
Kelmesham 1208 Fees 37
Kilmesham 1275 *Ass*, 1299 (18th) *RBB*, 1327 SR, 1360, 1369
  Cl, 1433 IpmR
Kynsham, Kinsham 1535 VE, 1663–1700 FF

Kilmiston (Ha) is *Chenelmestun, Kenelmestun* in BCS 1077
and *Cylmestun* in BCS 1160. In DB it is *Chelmestune*, and
Kelmeston in 1254 (Pat). This shows that there was a pet-form
Celm or *Cilm* for *Cœnhelm* in OE. Cf. also *cylmes gemære* in the
bounds of Smite (Wo) in KCD 618. In Kinsham we have the
same name. Hence the ham of *Celm* or *Cylm*.

MITTON

Myttun 841 (11th) BCS 433
Muctun[1] 965 (11th) BCS 1166
Muttone 11th Heming
Mitune 1086 DB
Muttona c. 1086 (1190) *EveA & B*, 1208 Fees 37, 1227,
  1300 Ch
Muiton 1328 *FF*, 1360 Cl

v. (ge)myðe, tun. The hamlet takes its name from the 'mythe'
or junction of the Avon and the Carrant Brook. Similarly
Mitton (La) is at the junction of Ribble and Hodder, (Wa) of
Avon and Leam, Mytton (Sa) of Severn and Perry, Myton (Y)
of Swale and Ure, Upper and Lower Mitton *infra* 254, where
Severn and Stour meet.

MORETON'S FM (6″)

Mortun 990 (11th) KCD 674
Moretune 11th Heming
Morton juxta Bredon 1275 *FF*   *Morton Robert* 1275 *Ass*

'Marsh-farm,' *v.* mor, tun. In the 12th cent. a certain
Robert, son of Richard, held two hides in Moreton (Hab. i. 536).
The *s* is pseudo-manorial.

---

[1] *sic*, as kindly collated by Miss F. E. Harmer.

WESTMANCOTE

Westmonecote 1086 DB, 1275 SR, 1320 Pat
Westmenecote c. 1086 (1190) *EveA*
Westmanecote c. 1086 (1190) *EveB*, 1208 Fees 36
Westmecote 1327 SR
Westmancote 1340 *FF*
Westencote 1570 Wills, 17th *FF*

'Cottages of the western men,' probably so called because the hamlet lies on the west side of the parish, though the word may be used in a more general sense. Duignan (PN Wo 174) notes that *Wesman* (presumably for *Westman*) is found as a pers. name in DB.

Broadwas

BROADWAS¹ [brɑ·dəs], [brɔ·dəs] 81 E 8

Bradeuuesse, Bradewassan 779 (11th) BCS 233
Bradsetena gemære 961 (11th) BCS 1139
Bradewesham 1086 DB
Bradewas c. 1086 (1190) *EveB*, 1275 SR, 1291 Tax, 1327 SR
Bradewasse 1148 Thomas
Bradewesse 1182 (18th) *RBB*
Bradwas 1535 VE, 1577 Wills
Brodwas 1535–1611 Wills
Bradwaies, Bradwais 1577 Saxton, 1610 Speed
Braddis 1595 Wills

The suffix in this name is probably the same as that found in Alrewas, Hopwas (St) and Rotherwas, Sugwas (He), in all of which we have low-lying marshy ground. Zachrisson suggests (*English Place-names and River-names, etc.* 34 ff.) we have to do with OE *wāse*, 'mud, fen,' but the early forms in double *s*, the unvoiced final *s*, and the forms with -*wess*- offer a difficulty. Zachrisson would take these double *s*'s as late spellings which indicate the shortening of the unstressed syllable, but it is extremely doubtful if such are found in the Worcester Cartulary. See further on this point the discussion of Washbourne *infra* 176. The *e*-forms he would take to be due to the influence of OE

---

¹ In the case of Alrewas (St) we have a form of the year 1000, *Alrewæs* (O S. Facs. iii. Anglesey MSS, ii), which make *wāse* impossible.

wæsc, 'flooded place,' but while there is evidence for such confusion in Washbourne, there is no clear evidence for *sh*-forms in Broadwas. The DB form is probably a Latin accusative in *-am*, with inorganic *h* before it. In *Bradsetena* we have OE sæte added in the usual illogical fashion, straight on to the first element of the place-name, to denote the inhabitants of the place in question.

The normal development would have been to *Bradwas* or *Brodwas*, but here, as in Broadway *infra* 191, the influence of the independent word has been too strong[1].

Broad Green

de la Grene, atte Grene 1275 SR, 1304 Ipm, 1327 SR

Self-explanatory.

Cellers Grove (lost)

This is found in the 1649 Survey and denoted land used for the endowment of the office of cellarer in the Priory of Worcester.

Foxbatch (lost)

Foxbæce 779 (11th) BCS 233

Foxbach Hill 1649 Surv

'Fox-stream,' *v.* bæc.

Noxons Fm (6″)

This takes its name from the *Noxon* family, mentioned in More's Journal (1520) and in the Survey of 1649.

Bushley[2]

Bushley 92 B 12

Biselege 1086 DB

Bisselega, Bissele(y) c. 1086 (1190) *EveA* & *B*, 1159, 1190 P, 1221, *Ass, FF*

---

[1] In the 1649 Survey we have mention of 'land called *Cadur*' which must be connected with the *Kadera pull*, a stream mentioned in the bounds of Wick (BCS 219) and probably also with the Thomas le *Kadere* of the 1275 SR.

Lands called *Barretts* and *Hollway* in the same survey must contain the names of the families recorded as *Baret* and (*de*) *Holeweye* respectively in the same SR.

[2] Now in Pershore Hundred.

Busseleg', Busseleye 1212 Fees 139, 1261 Ipm, 1263 Pat
Bischeleye, Bishele, Byschele 1307, 1315 Ipm, 1344 Pat,
    1417 IpmR
Bussheley 1415 IpmR, 1575 Wills
'Bush-clearing,' *v.* bysc, leah. The woods of Bushley, which
were part of Malvern Chase, were formerly of great importance
(VCH iv. 46).

OXHEY FM (6")

    Oxehey Close 1610 VCH iv. 46
    'Ox-enclosure,' *v.* (ge)hæg.

PULL COURT

    Orices pul 972 (c. 1050) BCS 1282
    Lapule 1086 DB
    Lapulle, la Pulle 1212 Fees 139, 1222 *FF*, 1275 SR
    Le Pille 1275 *Ass*
    Pulla, Pulle 1284 Wigorn, 1327 SR, 1535 VE, 1585 Wills
    Poole in Bushley 1591 Wills

The pull here is the stream which feeds the Severn at this
point. In the earliest reference it appears as the possession of
one *Oric*, that probably being a pet-form for *Ordric* or *Ōsric*.

SARN HILL WOOD

    Saronhille 15th VCH iv. 46

The forms are too late for any satisfactory suggestion.

Charlton

CHARLTON 82 H 2

    Ceorletun 780 (11th) BCS 235, 11th Heming, 1086 DB
    Ceorlatuna 11th Heming
    Cherleton 1208 Fees 37, 1292 Ipm, (*apud Fladebury*) 1299
    (18th) *RBB*, 1431 FA
    Cherlinton 1346, 1428 FA
    Charlton 16th Wills

v. ceorl. The form *Cherlinton* possibly goes back to an
OE *ceorlena-tūn*, with weak gen. pl. such as we find in the
corresponding Scandinavianised *Carlenton*, which is fairly
common as an early form for *Carlton*. Cf. EPN 43. It may

however merely represent an irrational assimilation of the present name to the numerous *ingtun*-names in this county.

HASELOR HO

> *Haseloure* c. 1220 (c. 1240) *WoC*
> *Haseler Elm* 1649 Surv

'Hazel bank,' *v.* ofer and cf. Haselor (Wa) and Haselour (St).

RIDON HO

> *Rudun* c. 1220 (c. 1240) *WoC*
> *Ridon* 1649 Surv
> *Royden* 1820 G
> *Rowden* c. 1830 O

'Rye hill,' *v.* ryge, dun.

YESSEL FM

> *Erdulueshale* c. 1220 (c. 1240) *WoC*

'Eardulf's nook,' *v.* healh. For the development of initial *y*, cf. Eardiston *supra* 58 from the same pers. name.

Churchill

CHURCHILL 81 E 13

> *Circehille* 1086 DB
> *Chirchulle* c. 1086 (1190) *EveA* & *B*, (*juxta Aston Episcopi*) 1321 *FF*
> *Cherchull* 1208 Fees 36
> *Chirkhull, Chyrechull* 1275 *FF* (p), 1280 *FF*
> *Schercheshull, Schurchehull* 1280 *For*
> *Cershull-juxta-Humelbrok* 13th VCH iii. 297

This name and the Churchill in Clent Hundred *infra* 278 raise the whole question of the origin of Churchill and other allied names elsewhere. The evidence may be set forth as follows, dealing first with that which can be gleaned from the Saxon Charters:

(i) Birch no. 112[1] is a Glastonbury Charter, only preserved

---

[1] The details of this charter have been worked out and kindly placed at our disposal by Mr C. A. Seyler. It is to be taken with Birch no. 816 which deals with the bounds of North Wotton (121 D 2). In no. 112 he has identified *croppanhulle* with Crapnell Fm (121 C 3), *merkesburi* with Maesbury Castle (121 B 4), *than olden fosse* with Fosse Way, *pennard* with Pennard Hill (121 E 2/3). The references here and throughout are to the Popular 1″ O.S. map.

in a late copy, which gives the bounds of land on the river Doulting (So). This is not the village of Doulting but land near Dulcote (121 C 2), earlier *Dultingcote*, on the stream now called the River Sheppey but once known as *Doulting* as is shown by the presence of Doulting village near its source. In it there is *crichulle*, which can be identified with certainty as Church Hill (121 C 3). (ii) Birch no. 708 is a Shaftesbury Charter, only preserved in a comparatively late copy, dealing with lands at Tarrant (Do). As the lands belonged to Shaftesbury and are by the stream called *pimpernwelle*, which clearly gave its name to Pimperne (130 E 13), it is clear that it must be identified with Tarrant Hinton (130 D 14), of which the second name comes from OE *hīgna-tūn*, 'farm of the community,' a name commonly given to monastic possessions. In the charter we have reference to *Chircel ford* on the *wic herepaþ*. This is the point at which Week Street crosses the stream (131 D 1) on which, a little lower down, lie Long Crichel and More Crichel (131 E 2). These two places appear as *Circhel* in DB, *Churechel* in an Ipm of Hy 3, *Longa Kerechel, More Kerchulle* in FA 1285, and there can be little doubt that they take their name from the hill called Crichel Down which lies above them and that from the hill also came to be named the ford which lies at its foot[1]. (iii) Earle (432) prints, again from a late copy, the bounds of Compton Bishop (So). These include a reference to *cyrces gemære*, which must refer to the bounds of Christon (110 H 10) on the eastern spurs of Bleadon Hill[2]. This is *Cricheston* (1303 FA, 1381 BM) and *Crycheston* (1412 FA) in later documents. (iv) Birch no. 62 is a grant of land at *cructan* or *crycbeorh* on the Tone to Glastonbury, while no. 550 is a grant of land at *Cyricestun*. Examination of the bounds of this last charter tends to prove the identity of *crycbeorh* with the *cyric* which gave its name to *Cyricestun*, and these must be identified with Creechbarrow and Creech St Michael (So). Later forms for Creech St Michael are DB *Crice* and 1324 Ipm *Mighelis Church*. (v) Birch no. 1129 is a Peterborough grant preserved in a 12th cent. copy and includes reference to Churchfield in Oundle as *Ciricfeld*. From the remote situation of this place it is exceedingly unlikely that there was

[1] For this identification we are again indebted to Mr C. A. Seyler.
[2] Stevenson MSS.

ever a church here. (vi) There is an unidentified *cirichyll* in BCS 696, probably in Dorsetshire. (vii) There is an unidentified *cyrices hleawe* in BCS 1223, near the Cherwell in Wood or Water Eaton. This can hardly be OE *cirice*, 'church,' of which the genitive case was *ciricean*. (viii) There is a *cyric pæð* in the bounds of Newnham (Nth) in KCD 736 in which the form is *cyric* and not *cyrice*, and examination of the bounds as a whole makes it impossible to believe that there is a reference to a church. (ix) Heming (347) in the bounds of Shipston-on-Stour names a *cyric hyll* (*Cherchehull* in Pat 1320) which is the present Furze Hill, right away from any church. (x) In the bounds of Cotheridge we have a *cyrces pull* which, neither from its form nor from its topography, so far as it can be ascertained, can have anything to do with *cyrice*, 'church[1].'

From this evidence it is clear that there was a place-name element *cryc* in OE which can appear in OE itself as *cyrc*, *cyric*, later *church* and that this word when inflected is always given a strong masculine genitive and therefore is quite distinct from the ordinary word *cyrice*, 'church.' This OE *cryc*, as is shown by the famous passage in Birch no. 62, is the Old British *cruc* and denotes a hill or barrow. This, as noted by Ekwall (IPN 25) appears in various forms as Creech, Crich, Crick and Crutch (see further *infra* 281). When the English came, hills once called *cruc* often had the English word *beorg* added to them. *Crycbeorg* appears as Creechbarrow Hill (So) and Crookbarrow Hill (Wo) *infra* 178. Alternatively *hyll* might be added and hence we get Crichels and Churchills as shown above[2]. Churchill is a very common place-name. There are two in Worcestershire, another in Somersetshire beside that already noted, one in Oxfordshire and three or four in Devonshire. When we only have post-Conquest evidence it may be argued that these are really compounds of the common word 'church,' but it should be noted that (i) in some of the Devonshire examples there can never have been a church and that in the case of Churchill (So) and Churchill in Clent Hundred the church is in the valley and not on the hill so that it is unlikely that it enters into the

---

[1] There is also a prominent Church Hill in Bayton. Unfortunately we have no early forms, but it may be noted that it is away from any church.
[2] Cf. also Crook Hill in Ashopton (Db), 1250 Ch *Cruchull*.

place-name at all, and (ii), in many ways more striking, it is impossible to get by the fact that, apart from these Churchills, compounds of *church* in place-names are exceedingly rare. If we take the names in Bartholomew's *Gazetteer* the only ones for which we have early evidence are Churcham (Gl), Churchstowe (D) and the Churchfield (Nth) dealt with above. The natural inference must be that there is real connexion between *church* and *hill* when they are so frequently found together.

The only difficulty about this suggestion is that the proper metathetical derivative of *cryc* would be *kirch* rather than *church* (to use modern forms to represent the sound changes involved). It is clear that confusion must have taken place at an early date. By a process of popular etymologising OE *cyr(i)c* with initial *k* and final *ch* was readily confused with OE *cyrice* with initial and final *ch*. That this was the case is clearly shown by the evidence set forth above and in the additional note appended[1].

THE MARSHES (6″)

Le Mershe n.d. VCH iii. 298

Self-explanatory.

[1] Further examples of what seem clear cases of place-names with a first element consisting of a gen. sg. *cyrices* are provided by Churchdown (Gl), Sarsden (O). The first is *Circesdune* in DB, *Schurchesdon*, *Churchesdon* in FA, with persistent medial *s* which has been preserved in the local pronunciation of the name of the hill as *Chosen*. Sarsden appears in the form *Cercendene*, *Cerchesdene*, *Cherchesden* in the Eynsham Cartulary (PN O 179). It lies opposite Churchill (O), across a small valley, each standing on a hill, with several tumuli marked in the neighbourhood. No satisfactory pers. name can be suggested for the first element, the stream-name *Sars* is clearly only a back-formation, and it certainly looks as if Sarsden also contains the gen. of *ciric* rather than *cyrice*. The forms for *Churchfield* Hundred (now Reigate Hundred) given by Hopwood, PN Sr 38, afford excellent examples of the confusion of *church* and *crich*. They are *Chirchefeld*, *Cherchefelle* (DB), *Crichesfeld* (1159 P), *Chircfeld* (1159 P), *Crechesfeld* (1164–99 Dugd vi. 172). Cruchfield (Berks) provides a further example of genitival forms in *es* and, what is more important, there is no *church*, while there is a well-marked *crich* or hill. Early forms, all of the 13th cent., are *Cruchesfeld* (Fees), *Curchesfeld* (Ass), *Crichefeld* (Ch), together with *Cherchesfeld* (1310 Cl). As an example of metathesis we may note Creech (Do) which appears as *Chirce* in DB and finally we may note that the *Cyrichburh* of the ASC (s.a. 915 Cl) is almost certainly Chirbury (Sa) and is far more likely to have taken its name from the prominent hill on which it stands than from its church.

North Claines

CLAINES 81 C 11

Cleinesse 11th Heming

Cleines, Cleynes 1234 (c. 1240) *WoC*, 1269 Wigorn, 1275 SR (p), 1291 Tax

Claynes 1283 Wigorn, 1428 FA

Clynes 1293 Wigorn

Cleynesse 1299 (18th) *RBB*

Cleynis 1327 SR (p)

Claynis 1558 Wills

Claynche, Clainch 1577 Saxton, 1675 Ogilby

There can be little doubt that this is a compound of OE clæg and næss. The church stands on a very slight headland formed in the 100 ft. contour, which may have stood out more markedly before trees, hedges, etc. concealed it. This name tends to confirm the explanation of Haynes in PN BedsHu 152. Hence 'clay-headland.'

ASTWOOD

Estwode 1182 (18th) *RBB*   *Astwode in Wyston* 1392 Pat

'East' wood, probably in relation to *Wyston* or Whitstones itself, *v. infra* 115.

ATTERBURN BROOK (Old 1″)

(in) Oterburnan 1038 Earle 239

'Otter-stream,' *v.* oter, burna.

BARBOURNE

Beferburna 904 (11th) BCS 608

Bevreburna 1208 Fees 36

Beverb(o)urne 1240 WoP, 1275 *Ass*, 1315 *FF*

Bereb(o)urn(e) 13th AD ii (p)

Berbourne 1392 Pat

Barborn 1445 IpmR

Barborne, Barbours Brook, Barbon Brook 1535 VE, 1543 LP, 1649 Surv

'Beaver-stream,' *v.* beofor, burna.

BEVERE ISLAND [bevəri]

Beverege insula c. 1150 FW
Bevere(ye) 1240 WoP, 1275 SR, both (p)
Bevery 1542 LP

'Beaver-island,' *v.* beofor, eg. Cf. *beferig* in BCS 802.

BILFORD (6")

Byltford 1275 SR (p)
Bileford 1321 Pat
Balford 1327 SR (p)

The material is insufficient for any safe conclusion to be attempted, but as there is an isolated hill here, parallel to the river, it is just possible that we have an OE *bylte*, 'hill,' for which *v.* Bouts *infra* 325. If so, the name means 'ford by the hill.'

THE BLANQUETTES (6")

The *Blanket* family held land here from the 13th cent. (VCH iii. 304) and are mentioned in 1275 SR, 1293 Pat, AlmBk, 1327 SR. The estate is called *The Blancketts* in 1607 (Wills).

ELBURY HILL

grava q. v. Elebury 1299 (18th) *RBB*

This perhaps contained a pers. name *Ela*, allied to OE *Eli*, *Elesa*, *Elsa*, which are on record. Hence 'Ela's stronghold,' *v.* burh.

FERNHILL HEATH [fə·nəl]

Fernhull 1275, 1327 SR (p), 1299 (18th) *RBB*
Fernall Heath c. 1830 O

Self-explanatory.

HOLY CLAINES FM (6")

Hallow Claines 1327 (17th) Hab   *Holly Claines* 1892 Kelly

Habington (ii. 38) says that this division of Claines was so called because it contained the church (*v.* halig).

LINACRES FM (6")

Linaceran wege 1038 Earle 239   *Lynacres* 1612 QSR

The form in the charter-bounds probably represents a late weak gen. pl., 'road of (i.e. to) Linacres,' i.e. 'flax-fields,' *v.* lin, æcer. Cf. Linacre (K, La) and *Linacre* in Halesowen (LyttCh).

LOWESMOOR (6")

Losmare 1232 Ch
Losemere c. 1270 (15th) *AOMB* 61, 1275 *Ass*
Losomere (sic) 1299 (18th) *RBB*
Losmere, Losmerestrete 1293 WoCh, 1316 Ipm, 1549 Pat

This is probably from OE *hlōse-mere*, 'pool with a pigstye by it,' *v.* hlose, mere. The first form would suggest a second element mære, but it is difficult to see what the sense of such a name could be. Cf. Lowe's Wood (PN BedsHu 144).

MERRIMAN'S HILL

This must take its name from the family of *Merimon, Merriman*, mentioned in Wills (1544, 1613).

MILDENHAM MILL (6")

Moldenhome 1182 (18th) *RBB*
Muldenham 1240 WoP, 1299 (18th) *RBB*
Mulderham 1242 FF
Mildenham 1291 CompR, 1299 (18th) *RBB*
Mildenhall 1649 Surv

This name presents difficulties. The second element would seem to be OE hamm. If the first is a pers. name it would seem that it must have been an OE *Mylda*, though *Molda* or *Mulda* is just possible, as we do occasionally find, especially before point-consonants, *u* becoming *i*. The only English parallel for such a name that has been noted is in Mouldsworth (Ch), for which, between 1167 and 1302 we have forms with *Molde-, Moldes-* and *Mulde-* for the first element. The only Germanic parallel that has been noted is the rare Norse name *Moldi* (m.) or *Molda* (f.). The only other possible alternative seems to be to take the first element as a lost OE *molder* or *mulder*, a cognate of the element *molder* found by Jellinghaus in certain Westphalian names (*Die Westfälische ON*, s.n. *molt, molder*). This would be a derivative of OE *molde* itself, and we should have to interpret the name as 'hamm by, near, or marked by the presence of *molder*,' which would probably mean something like 'loose earth.' In that case we should have to assume that the *n* forms were AN corruptions of earlier *r*. In the other case, that the single *r* form was a corruption of the usual *n*, cf. IPN 106.

NORTHWICK [nɔˑðik]

Norwiche 1086 DB, c. 1086 (1190) *EveA*
Northewike c. 1150 Surv
Northwyk juxta Wygorniam 1346 FA

'North dairy-farm,' north in relation to Worcester and ' by Worcester' in contrast to Northwick in Blockley *supra* 99.

OVER (lost)

Oure 1221 FF
Ouera, Overe 1225 Wulst (p), 1275 SR (p), 1300 Pat
le Oeure in the manor of Northwyke 1332 Wulst
v. ofer.

PERDISWELL HALL [pəˑdzəl]

Perdeswell 1182 (18th) *RBB*, c. 1305 *Bodl* 57 *a* (p), 1308 *FF*
Perdiswell 1309 Ipm, 1340 NI, 1552 Wills, all (p)
Perdeswall 1333 *Bodl* 58
Persewell 16th VCH iii. 303
Peardswall 1658 FF

Cf. Pardshaw (Cu), *Perdeshau* (1203) and *Perdeley* (1300 Wigorn), also *Pirdiswelle* (W) in BCS 672. It is possible there was a pers. name *Perd(i)* a pet-form for *Peohtræd*. If so, the name may mean 'Perdi's stream,' *v.* wielle.

PITCHCROFT

Prichcroft 1375, 1473 CompR
Prichecroft 1479 LyttCh, 1542 LP, 1549 Pat
Prechecroft 1509 WoCh
Pichecroft 1533 WoCh, 1535 VE

The pers. name *Prych* is found in 1215 (WoCh) and 1275 (SR) and this croft doubtless took its name from a man of that name. For the possible origin of such a pers. name, cf. *pritch* (NED).

PORTEFIELDS FM (6″)

> *le Portfeld* 1408 (18th) *RBB*

This name, like Portmeadow in Oxford, refers to the port or town open fields.

PORTERSHILL FM and PORTER'S MILL (6″)

These doubtless take their names from a pers. name. Cf. Alditha *La Porter* in 1275 (SR) and *le Porter* in 1327 (SR) in this parish.

SPELLIS FM (6″)

> *Spellys in Hallow Claines* 1327 (17th) Hab

This takes its name from the family of *Spelli* mentioned in the Subsidy Rolls of 1275, 1327, 1332.

TAPENHALL FM (6″)

> *Tapanhalan* 957 (11th) BCS 993
> *Tapen halan* 1038 Earle 239
> *Tapenhale* 1230 WoP, 1269, 1295 Wigorn, 1321 Pat
> *Tepenhalle* 1275 *Ass*

'The nook of *Tapa*,' the form *halan* probably being a late dat. pl. of healh. For the name *Tapa*, *v.* Taplow (PN Bk 230) and cf. *Tappantreo* (BCS 778). The form *Tepenhalle* seems to show the influence of the allied name *Tæppa* found in Taplow (Bk).

TOLLADINE FMS

> *Tolewardin* 1182 (18th) *RBB*
> *Tolwardyn, Tolwardin(e)* 1229 WoCh (p), 1314 StSwith (p),
>   1315 *FF*, 1327 SR (p), 1361 WoCh
> *Tolewurthin* 1262 *Ass* (p)
> *Tolleworthone* 1299 (18th) *RBB*
> *Talardyn* 1546 Wills
> *Taladine, Tollardine* 1633 QSR
> *Tollerdine* c. 1830 O

It may be suggested that the first element in this name is the late OE *Tole*, a pers. name of Scandinavian origin. Thus there was a *Toli* in North Piddle in DB (TRE). There is no difficulty in compounding this with *worthine* from OE *worðign*, for this element was still living at a late date (*v. infra* 393). It should be added that an OE *Tolla*, a pet-form for such a name as *Torhtlāf*, is not out of the question.

TUTNALL (6")

> *Totenhulle* 1275, 1327 SR (p), 1299 (18th) *RBB* (p)
> '*Tota's* hill,' *v.* hyll.

WHITSTONES (not on map)[1]

> *Witstan, Wytstan* c. 1160 (c. 1240) *WoC*, 1182 (18th) *RBB*
> *Wystan* 1255 *Ass*, 1299 (18th) *RBB*
> *Wyston* 1286 Wigorn, (*in Northwick*) 1321, 1392 Pat
> *Wytston* 1295 Wigorn
> *Whitston* 1300 Pat
> *Whiston* 1330, 1393, 1406 Pat, 1535 VE, 1549 Pat

'White stone,' *v.* hwit, stan. There is no likelihood of any prominent natural stone or rock here and the reference must be to some lost artificial monument, a boundary stone or the like. Nash (i. 209) says that it was so called from a white stone or cross erected here. In William the Conqueror's time this stone was pulled down and used to build a lavatory for the monks of St Mary, and he quotes Heming as his authority, though there does not seem to be any confirmatory evidence in Heming so far as can be discovered. For the name we may compare Whiston (La, Y), Whitestone (D), Whitstone Hundred (Gl) and Whitestone Hundred (So) and *huitan stan* in Aston Fields (BCS 203)[2].

Conderton

CONDERTON 93 A 1

> *Cantuaretun* 875 (11th) BCS 541
> *Cantertun* c. 1170 (c. 1250) *WoC*
> *Canterton, Kanterton* 1201 Cur, 1220 Bracton, 1227, 1258 *FF*
> *Conterton* 1269 *FF*, 1322 Pat, (*juxta Overbury*) 1233 *FF*, 1327 SR

[1] The Tything of *Whitstones* is a civil parish and so mentioned in Kelly's Directory for 1892. The site is now known as White Ladies (6").
[2] In the 1649 Survey we have field-names *Frenches* and *Pallfrey Stile* which go back to the pers. names *le Franceis* and *Palefre* recorded in 1275 SR.

Canderton 1577 Saxton
Conderton 16th and 17th Wills *passim*

In view of the first form quoted here it seems almost impossible to avoid the conclusion that this name is from OE *Cantwara-tūn*, 'farm of the men of Kent,' and that the settlement must have been established by some migrants from that county[1]. Cf. Exton (Ha) which was a settlement by men from Essex. *v.* Mawer *PN and History* 10. The only other possibility is to take the first element as an unrecorded fem. pers. name *Cæntwaru*, parallels to which are found in *Centwine* and *Centweald*.

SYMONDFORD BROOK (lost)[2]

Simæresford 875 (11th) BCS 541
Simonds Foord 1649 Surv   *Symonford brook* 1772 T

'Ford of *Sigemǣr*,' *v.* ford. A similar corruption has taken place in Edmondthorpe (Lei), which really contains the pers. name *Ēadmǣr*.

Cotheridge[3]

COTHERIDGE 81 E 9

æt Coddan hrycce, Coddanhrycge 963 (11th) BCS 1106
Codrie 1086 DB
Codere c. 1150 Surv
Codderegge c. 1086 (1190) *EveB*
Cod(d)erug(ge) 1208 Fees 37, 1240 WoP, 1250 Ipm, 1275 SR
Codrugg 1274 Ipm
Codrigg 1287 Cl
Coterich 1474 IpmR
Coderych, Coderich 1539 LP
Cotridge 1549 Pat
Cotheridge al. *Cotteridge* c. 1760 Bowen

'Codda's ridge,' *v.* hrycg. The pers. name *Cod(d)* or *Codda* is not found on independent record in OE but may safely be

---

[1] It can only be a coincidence, but it is a curious one, that in a Fine of 1258, a Hugo de *Kent* is mentioned in connexion with Conderton. We may note also that *Kent* was very common as a surname in North Wo in the 13th cent. See further Introd. xix.

[2] It formed part of the boundary with Beckford and flowed into the Carrant Brook.

[3] Now in Doddingtree Hundred.

inferred from this name. It probably forms the first element in Codnor (Db), cf. also Codford (W), BCS 595 *Codanford*. For *d* becoming *th* before *r* in the next syllable, cf. the history of Etherley, Gatherick and other names in PN NbDu 260, and Potheridge (D), DB *Porriga*, 1183 P *Puderigge*. The loss of intervocalic *g* in the DB and Survey forms is curious.

HOWSEN

Huweleston 1259 Ipm
Huleston 1274 Ipm
Holeweston, Houlston 1275 *Ass*
Howelineston 1299 (18th) *RBB*
Houleston 1304 Ipm, 1310 Kyre
Hulleston, Hulston 1466 IpmR, 1492 Kyre
Howson 1669–1699 Kyre

The first element is probably the Welsh pers. name which appears as *Huwal* in ASC s.a. 926 D and as *Howæl* in the signature to OE charters as the name of a Welsh sub-regulus. *Hoel* is a horse's name in *Lib. Albus* (ed. Wilson, p. 60) in 1306. The form *Howelineston* is probably due to confusion with the OGer *Huglin*, OFr *Hugelin*, which sometimes appears in ME as *Huwelin*, cf. Forssner 157, but as this form may be as early as any of the others it is quite possible that *Hugelin* was the original pers. name and that the forms without *in* are later ones derived from it, with loss of *in* in the polysyllabic word.

LIGHTWOOD

Lugtewod 1275 SR (p)   *Lyghtwood* 1466 IpmR
Self-explanatory.

OTHERTON FM (6″) [ɔðətən]

Otherton 1240 WoP (p), 1275 *Ass*, SR (p), 1316 Ipm, 1386
      FF, (*juxta Coderugge*) 1409 *FF*, 1423 Kyre, 1649 Surv
Oterton, Otortons, Otterton 1412 Pat, 1466 IpmR, 1549 Pat

This must be, as Duignan suggests (PN Wo 123), OE (*se*) *ōðer tūn*, 'the other or second farm,' in relation to some previous settlement. Cf. Otherton (St), DB *Orretone*, 1166 P

L

Odertona. Professor Tait aptly notes the parallel usage whereby DB speaks of a vill thrown off as an offshoot of another vill as *alia villa* (IPN 123).

Earls Croome

EARLS CROOME [krʌm] 81 J 11

    Cromman, (æt) cromban 969 (11th) BCS 1235
    Crumbe 1086 DB, c. 1086 (1190) *EveA*
    Cromba c. 1086 (1190) *EveB*
    Crombe Adam 1255 *Ass*, *(Simon)* 1275, 1327 SR, 1275 *Ass*
    Crumb Adam 1340 NI, 1291 Tax
    Symondis Crombe 1310 *FF*, 1348 *Wigorn*, 1397 Pat
    Cromb Symond 1462 Wigorn
    Erles Crome 1495 Pat
    Crome Symondes al. *Erles Grove* al. *Erles Crome* 1547 LP

It is tempting to take this name as a derivative of OE *crumb*, 'crooked,' used perhaps as a noun (cf. Duignan PN Wo 46) but the sense is not clear. There are great curves of the Severn here and the whole district may once have been called '*æt þǣm crumbum.*' The Croomes do not actually border on the Severn, but we must remember that they were carved out of the manor of Ripple which lies along that river. The manorial history is that the manor was granted to one *Adam* (c. 1100), *Simon* held it in 1182 (P), other Simons and Adams followed and, before 1369, it passed into the hands of the *Earls* of Warwick (cf. VCH iii. 316–7).

SMITHMOOR COMMON

    Smeathmore 1649 Surv
    'Smooth marshy land,' *v.* smeðe.

Hill Croome

HILL CROOME 81 J 12

    Hylcromba 1038 (18th) KCD 760
    Hilcrumbe 1086 DB
    Hulcrumba, Hulcromba c. 1086 (1190) *EveA* & *B*

Later forms are without interest except that *Hul(le)* is persistent till 1406 (Pat). The place stands on a steepish hill.

BAUGHTON

Bocctun 1038 (18th) KCD 760
Bocton(a) 1208 Fees 37, 1255 *Ass*, 1275 SR, 1310 *FF*
Boketon 1319 *FF*
Boughton 1397 Pat, 1419 IpmR, 1598 Wills
Boghton 1406 Pat
Baughton 1619 Wills, 1674–91 FF
'Beech-tree farm,' *v.* boc, tun.

BAUGHTON HILL

de Hulle 1275, 1327 SR
Self-explanatory.

Croome d'Abitot

CROOME D'ABITOT 81 H 12

Molde Crombe 1182 (18th) *RBB*, 1340 NI
Crumba 1208 Fees 36
Crombe Dabetoth 1275 SR
Crombe Osbern 1349 Wigorn
Abbots Crome 1535 VE
Clares Crome 1584 VCH iii. 314

The d'Abitots held the manor of the Beauchamps from c. 1150 to c. 1450. From the Beauchamp holding it came perhaps to be called *Srreve Crombe* (VCH iii. 313 n. 11), i.e. Sheriff Crombe, the Beauchamps being hereditary Sheriffs of Worcestershire. *Osbern* is probably an error for *Osbert*, who held the manor in 1182, *Molde* is from *Maud* de Crombe who held 5 hides here in 1182 (VCH iii. 313 n. 11). *Abbots* is an etymologising form for *Abitots*. *Clares* is from the *Clare* family who held the manor in the 16th cent.

Cropthorne

CROPTHORNE 82 H 2

Cropponþorn 780 (11th) BCS 235
Croppeþorne 780 (11th) BCS 235
Croppanþorn 841 (11th) BCS 432
Cropetorn 1086 DB
Croptorna, Croppetorna c. 1086 (1190) *EveA & B*
Croppethorne 1305, 1335 Pat, 1428 FA

It would seem that the first element in this name is an otherwise unknown pers. name *Croppa*, found also near here in *Croppedune* (*WoC*), possibly originally a nickname from OE *cropp*, 'sprout, bunch.' It must also lie behind Cropredy (O) and Crapnell Fm (So), BCS 112 *Croppanhull*[1]. Hence 'Croppa's thornbush,' *v.* þorn.

The element *Crop* must have been current in OE nomenclature at a very early date for in Berkshire and Oxfordshire documents there is evidence of a mutated derivative *Crypsa*, formed with a diminutive suffix *s* which passed out of use before the time of written records; cf. *crypsan hylle* (BCS 216) and *crypsan dic* (BCS 789).

PERRYFORD (lost)

Piriforda (dat.) 972 (c. 1050) BCS 1282   *Peryford* 1536 LP

'Pear-tree ford,' *v.* pirige, ford. The combined evidence of the two passages in which this ford is referred to proves that it was on the common bounds of Cropthorne and Bricklehampton where they meet the Avon. Salters Lane (almost a continuation of the Droitwich, Martin Hussingtree, Pinvin road, which passes over Oswaldslow) now comes to a dead end in Fladbury parish within 200 yards of the Avon just when it is heading direct for the suggested site of the ford. Beyond the crossing it goes rather to the east of the present road, and near Elmley Castle it is marked as 'Saltway' and has on it a Salters Barn. It is an important point as it stands first in the boundary-points of the *tunlanda* of Pershore.

Cutsdean

CUTSDEAN 93 C 5

   Codestun 977 (11th) BCS 1299, 987 (11th) KCD 660, 1086 DB, c. 1086 (1190) *EveB*, 1240 WoP
   Chodestun c. 1155 (c. 1240) *WoC*
   Cotteston 1242 P
   Cotestone 1255 *Ass*, 1275 SR, 1291 Ipm, Wigorn
   Cotesdon 1330 Ch, 1428 FA
   Coteston 1346 FA
   Kutsyn, Cutson 1535 VE, 1650 FF

For this identification we are indebted to Mr C. A. Seyler.

Cudston 1540 LP
Codiston 1549 Wills
Cuttesdon 1610 Speed
Cudson 1653 FF
Cutsdean 1676 FF

'Codd's farm,' *v.* tun. For this pers. name cf. Coddimoor (PN Bk 74). The name is found also in *Codesuuellan, Codeswelle* (BCS 236, 430) in this parish, and cf. Cotheridge *supra* 116. For its possible further significance *v.* Cotswolds *supra* 1. The *Cot-, Cut-* forms are probably due to anticipation of the *t* of the suffix.

Daylesford

DAYLESFORD 93 E 10

Dæglesford 718 (11th) BCS 139, 841 (11th) BCS 436, 875 (11th) BCS 541, 979 (11th) KCD 623
Deilesford 777 (14th) BCS 222, c. 1050 (c. 1200) KCD 963, c. 1150 Surv
Dæiglæsford 914 (12th) BCS 1135
Degilesford 979 (11th) KCD 623
Dagelesford c. 1050 (c. 1200) KCD 963
Eilesford 1086 DB
Aleford (corrected to *Dailesford*) c. 1086 (1190) EveA
(Other forms are without interest.)

'Dægel's ford.' *Dægel* is not on record, but would be a regular diminutive of *Dæga*, a pet-form of one of the numerous OE names in *Dæg*. It has its parallel in OGer *Dagalo* and other names cited by Förstemann (PN 391–2).

BAYWELL WOOD[1] (6")

Bæganwellan (dat.) 718 (11th) BCS 139
Bægenwelle 979 (11th) KCD 623
Beaganwylle c. 1050 (c. 1200) KCD 963
Beiwelle n.d. (c. 1200) KCD 1367

The stream of *Bēaga* or *Bǣga*. In the first charter land is granted at Daylesford to a servant of God named *Bægia* for the

---

[1] The wood is across the boundary, in Adlestrop (Gl), but the stream itself forms the boundary.

founding of a monastery and it seems safe to assume that he is the same person as the one who gave his name to *Bæganwelle* named in the bounds of the land in question[1].

Elmley Castle

ELMLEY CASTLE 82 J 1

> *Elmlege* (dat.) 780 (11th) BCS 235
> *Elmlæh* 1042 (18th) KCD 764
> *Elmelege* 11th Heming, c. 1150 Surv, 1208 Fees 36, (*Beauchamp*) 1275 *Ass*
> *Halmelega* c. 1086 (1190) *EveA*
> *Aumele*(*gh*) 1234 Cl, 1259 Ch, 1265 Pat, 1298 Ipm
> *Almelege, Almeley* c. 1270 Gerv, (*sub Castellum*) 1313 Wigorn
> *Castel Elmeleye* 1327 SR

'Elm-clearing,' *v.* elm, leah and cf. Elmley Lovett *infra* 240. The Beauchamp family held land here from the 12th cent. (VCH iii. 341). The *Castle* is not the present house so called, but the ancient Castle of Elmley which stood on the northern slopes of Bredon Hill, half a mile to the south. Hence the phrase 'sub castellum.'

KERSOE

> *Criddesho, Cryddesho* 780 (11th) BCS 235, 1401 IpmR
> *Crideshoth* (sic) 1182 (18th) *RBB*
> *Crydesho, Crideshoe, Crydeshoo* 1275 *Ass*, SR (p), 1423 *FF*, 1439 Pat, 1445 IpmR
> *Griddesho* 1275 *Ass* (p)
> *Cryeso, Crisso* 1544 LP, 1548 Pat
> *Kersowe, Kirsoe* 1588, 1635 Wills
> *Cridshow* 1708 FF

Kersoe stands on a well-marked hoh or spur of land. The first element would seem to be the otherwise unknown pers. name *Criddi* which it is difficult to dissociate from the name *Crioda* found in the early Mercian genealogies, which apparently appears as *Crida* in the ASC s.a. 593. Cf. also *creodanac* (BCS 455) in Cofton (Wo).

---

[1] Hearne in his edition of Heming (642–3) has an interesting note in which, on the information of a correspondent, he tells us that the brook on the east side of Daylesford was still called Baywell Brook and that there were three springs called by that name (Stevenson MSS).

Evenlode

EVENLODE [emlou·d] 93 D 9

æt Euulangelade, æt Eulangelade 772 (16th, 12th) BCS 209, 210

Eunelade 777 (14th) BCS 222

Eownilade 779 (c. 1200) BCS 229

Eowengelad 784 (11th) BCS 244

Eowenland (sic) 964 (12th) BCS 1135

Eowlangelade 969 (11th) BCS 1238

Eowniglade c. 957 (12th) BCS 1317

Eunelade c. 1050 (c. 1200) KCD 912, 1221 *Ass*

Eunilade 1086 DB, c. 1086 (1190) *EveB*

Eunelode n.d. (c. 1200) KCD 1367, 1308 Wigorn

Eunilate c. 1086 (1190) *EveA*

Evenlade 1185 P, 1275 Wigorn

Heuneslode 1275 SR

Ewenelod 1291 Tax

Evenelod 1369, 1395 Wigorn

Emlod 1549 Pat, 1538–1599 Wills (*passim*)

Evenlode 1649–85 Wills (*passim*)

Emload 1649–85 Wills (*passim*), 1705 Marr

Evilod 1649–85 Wills (*passim*)

Evenlode stands on a stream of that name, but we know that the proper name of that stream is *Bladen* (*v. supra* 11) and its use as a river-name is an example of back-formation of a river-from a village-name. With regard to the village-name, if we take the modern pronunciation to be a genuine development from the early forms of the name, it is clear that we must take the first element to be the gen. sg. of a pers. name *Eofla*, a weak diminutive formation from the pers. name *Eof* which lies behind the not very distant Evesham (cf. *Evlengrave* in Claines in 1182 (*RBB*)). We must then suppose that at a later date *Evlenlade* became *Evnenlade*, and so *Evne-* or *Even-lade*, by the very common process of interchange of *l* and *n* (cf. IPN 106 ff.). The only difficulty about this explanation is the number of early forms which seem to show *w* rather than *u* and the absence of any forms with *f* such as we must assume to lie behind the *Eul-*, *Eun-* forms. An alternative which, in view of the earliest form, is more likely, is to start from the pers. name *Eowa* and take the first element to be a pet-diminutive *Eowla* formed from it. *Ewlenlade* would become *Ewnenlade*, *Ewnilade* or *Eunilade* by the same process as is suggested above. We should then have to take it that the *u* was misunderstood as having the consonantal rather than the vocalic value and that a spelling pronunciation arose which ultimately affected the whole history of the name. Such a change would be helped by the influence of the adjective *even*. Similar spelling pronunciations are occasionally found, cf. Goldenwick *supra* 92 and Harvington *infra* 238. For the possibility of confusion and uncertainty with regard to a pers. name in early times we may note that Florence of Worcester in giving the genealogy of the West Saxon kings (256) gives in error *Eawa* for *Eafa* or *Eaua*, cf. Redin 93.

The second element in this name also offers difficulty. It is clearly OE gelad. It has been suggested that this refers to a short cut across a bend in the river but there is none nearer than Daylesford and it can hardly have given its name to Evenlode. The question of the exact character of the 'lode' owned by *Eofla* or *Eowla*, and whether it was a water or a land-track, must therefore remain open.

For the *Emlode*, cf. Chaucer's *emcristene* from *evencristne*, 'fellow-christians.'

Four Shire Stone

This stone stands where the shires of Worcester, Warwick, Gloucester and Oxford meet. In BCS 1238, a 12th cent. copy of a charter of 969, we find that the bounds of Evenlode, at one point of their circuit, run from one stone to another stone and then to a third and then to a fourth. So that in those days there must actually have been four stones at this point.

Ildeberg (lost)

In the text of Domesday (VCH i. 307) Abbot Walter is said to have proved his right to certain land in Bengeworth in a court of four shires held at *Ildeberga*. In the account of this suit given in the *Chronicle of Evesham* (97) the place is called *Gildeneberga*[1], and Dr Round is doubtless right in identifying the place with

[1] The form is *Gildenberga* in a 12th cent. document quoted *ib*. Introd. xlviii.

the *Gildbeorh* (969) of the bounds of Evenlode (BCS 1238) where, aptly enough, it is mentioned just before the four stones which preceded the present Four Shire Stone. From the context in which this name is found and from its alternative forms there is no doubt that we must take the first element as the OE *gild*, 'guild, association,' in the one case, and as *gildena*, gen. pl. of *gilda*, 'a member of a guild,' in the other. Other pre-Conquest examples of this element are to be found in *Gildenebrigge* in 1045 (Thorpe 572), now Ealing Bridge in Harlow (Ess), a lost *Gildenebrige* in Hodsock (Nt)[1] and a lost *Gildeneburgh* in Wilts or Dorset (BCS 664, late copy). The Nf hundred of Guiltcross, DB *Gildecros*, is a further example of the association between guild and hundred. Found only in post-Conquest documents we have Gilcote (So), DB *Gildenecote*, Gilmorton (Lei), DB *Mortone*, E 1 Ipm *Guldenemorton*, 1344 Ch *Gildemorton*, Moreton Pinkney (Nth), DB *Mortone*, E 2 Ipm *Gildenemorton*, Guilden Morden (C), DB *Mordune*, 1205 P, 1255 BM *Geldenemordon*, 1284 FA *Gylden Mordene*, 1317 BM *Guldemorden*, 1377 Ch *Gildenmordene*, Guilden Sutton (Ch), DB *Sudtone*, 1303 Chamberlain's Accts *Guldunsutton* (p), n.d. AD vi *Guldensutton*, an unidentified *Ildenebrugge* in the 1275 SR for Little Witley (Wo) and *Gildwelle* in Mathon (*AOMB* 61). It is impossible now to determine just what the relation of these guildsmen was to the place in which their name is found[2]. In some cases, as in that with which we are now primarily dealing, it must refer to an actual meeting of such at the place in question. In others, and this applies specially to those which are of comparatively late origin, it probably denotes that the guild or its members had certain beneficiary interests in the land so named or had constructed the bridge in question. Of this latter type doubtless is the suffix *Gilden* or *Gildon* found added at times to the forms for Shelsley Walsh in this county (*v. supra* 78). This must refer to the interest of some guild in the manor[3].

[1] Reference from Thoroton's *Hist. of Notts* 407 b, found in Stevenson MSS.

[2] For the wide prevalence of gilds among the Anglo-Saxons see Liebermann, *Gesetze der Angelsachsen*, ii. 1, 445 s.v. *genossenschaft* and Gross, *Gild Merchant*, i. 174 f.

[3] We are indebted to Mr Bruce Dickins for calling our attention in the first instance to the significance of the Cambridge and Leicestershire names and to Professor Tait for some of the examples.

The variant forms of the initial sound of names with this element are explained in the NED *s.v. guild*. There was a variation between forms with initial *g* and initial *y*.

HEATH END FM

> *la Hethe* 1275 *Ass*
> Self-explanatory.

Fladbury

FLADBURY 82 G 2

> *Fledanburg* 691 (18th) BCS 76, *Flædanburh* 691 (c. 1000) Middleton 200
> *Fladeburg* 709 (12th) BCS 125
> *Flædanbyrg* (dat.) 779 (18th) BCS 238
> *Fledanburh* 820 (11th) BCS 238, *Flædanburh* 820 (c. 1000) Middleton 204
> *Fledebiri(e)* 1086 DB, 1208 Fees 37
> *Fladebury, Fladebure* c. 1086 (1190) *EveA*, 1275 SR, 1291 Tax
> *Fladebyrya, Fladebiri* c. 1086 (1190) *EveB*, 1229–1255 Ch

'*Flǣde's burh*.' The name is not found independently in OE but is a regular formation from OE women's names in -*flǣd* (e.g. *Ēanflǣd*), cf. Fledborough (Nt), DB *Fladeburg*.

CRAYCOMBE HILL

> *Craucumbe* 1268 Pat, 1275 SR (p)
> *Crowecombe* 1275 SR (p)
> *Crawecombe* 1299 (18th) *RBB*, 1378 Ipm
> *Cracumb* 1617 QSR

'Crow-valley,' *v.* **crawe, cumb.**

Grimley

GRIMLEY[1] 81 C 10

> *Grimanlea(ge), Grimanlæge* 851 (11th) BCS 462, 964 (12th) ib. 1135
> *Grimsetene gemære* 969 (11th) BCS 1242
> *Grimanleh* 1086 DB
> *Grimeleia, Grimeleg(a)* c. 1086 (1190) *EveA* & *B*, 1240 WoP

[1] The *sceacan healh* of the bounds of Grimley (BCS 462) survives in the *Sechenhale* of WoP (1240). Cf. Shakenhurst *supra* 40.

Grimeslea 1186 P (p)
Grimley, Gryndley 1542, 1546 LP

The pers. name *Grim* as commonly found in 10th cent. documents and in numerous place-names in Scandinavian England is commonly and rightly taken to be a loan-word from the Scand. name *Grímr*. It is however a little difficult to think that we have that pers. name in the well-known Grim's Dyke (W), *grimes dic* in BCS 934, or in this name or in the neighbouring Greenhill in Hallow *infra* 131, which clearly contains the same pers. name *Grīm(a)* as this one does, and must indeed be named from the same man[1]. Grimley and Greenhill and a lost *Grimenhille* in Alvechurch (*FF* 1244) point clearly to the existence in OE itself of a pers. name *Grīm(a)*, which is the cognate of the Scand. name and of OGer *Grim(o)* (cf. Förstemann PN 669). This name itself is the OE *grīma*, 'spectre, goblin[2].' For *Grimsetene v.* Broadwas *supra* 103.

BIRCHALL GREEN (6″)

Bircholt 1240 WoP

'Birch-wood,' *v.* bierce, holt. Cf. Oakhall Green *infra* 128.

GUMBORN FM (6″)

Gunburnus 1240 WoP

This name must contain the Scand. name *Gunnbiörn*, and the name be really 'Gunbiorn's.' The loss of the second element in this name would be helped by the fact that the pers. name itself sounded like an English name in -*burn*. The existence of this Anglo-Scandinavian name in this area is shown by a *Gunb'n* in Hallow in 1275 (SR) and a *Gumbar* in Warndon in 1327 (SR), a few miles away on the other side of the Severn.

MONK WOOD

Monckewod 1240 WoP   *Monekeswode* 1275 SR

---

[1] In BCS 356 the boundary is said to run *betweonan Griman and Halheogan.* If we accept this as correct we must take *griman* as some significant word of unknown meaning, but probably it is simply a careless shortening of the full name *Grimanleage.*

[2] In *WoC* (19 b) we have *Werlegesmora* and in WoP (42 b) we have *Werle,* both in Grimley. These must be the *Wærlega* of the bounds of Hallow (BCS 356). The *Sifurdeleyam* of *WoC* (61 b) must also contain the stream-name *sih(t)ferð* in the bounds of Grimley (BCS 462).

Grimley belonged to the Priory of Worcester and the wood was held in demesne in the 13th cent. (WoP 47 *a*).

MOSELEY

Moseleage, Mosleage 816 (17th) BCS 357, 851 (11th) BCS 462
Mossetena gemære 851 (11th) BCS 462
æt Mosleage c. 965 (11th) BCS 1139

'Moss or bog-clearing,' *v.* mos, leah. For *Mossetena* cf. Broadwas *supra* 103.

NOKEN FM (6″)

This is clearly one of the numerous examples of ME *oke* becoming *noke*. The 'oak' may be that referred to in the pers. name *de Ack, de Ake* (1240 WoP, 1327 SR). The relation of the name to the 15th cent. form *Nokenham* given by Duignan (PN Wo 116) is not clear.

NORTHINGTOWN FM

Northinton, Norinton 1240 WoP, 1275 SR, both (p)

So called in contrast to Sinton *infra* and in the same fashion as Norton in Suckley *supra* 82.

OAKHALL GREEN

Ocholt, Hocholt 1240 WoP, 13th AlmBk

'Oak-wood,' *v.* ac, holt and cf. Birchall *supra* 127.

SINTON

Suptun 825 (18th) BCS 386
Suthintun 1240 WoP (p)
Sudintun 1240 WoP, 1255 *Ass*, 1275 SR, all (p)
Synton 1483 CompR, 1522 More
Syllington 1521 More, 1614 QSR

So called in contrast to Northingtown *supra*. For the name cf. Sodington in Mamble and Sinton in Leigh and in Suckley.

THORNGROVE

Thorngrava 1240 WoP
Self-explanatory.

Hallow

HALLOW[1] [hɔlou] 81 D 10

Heallingan, halhagan (wudes), heallinga (weallan), (of) hal-
hegan, (æt) halheogan, hallinga (homm) 816 (11th) BCS 356
Hallege 964 (12th) BCS 1135, c. 1086 (1190) *EveB*
Halhegan 1086 DB
Hallaga, Hallage c. 1150 (c. 1240) *WoC*, 1240 WoP
Halh c. 1240 *WoC*
Hallauwe 1240–50 (c. 1250) *WoC* (ter), 1275 SR, 1298 BM
Hallowe 1291 Tax, 1327 SR
Hallewe 1428 FA

The history of this name seems clear in spite of the somewhat
bewildering variety of forms. The first element is the OE healh
and the second is **haga** with occasional variants containing the
closely allied **hege**. Cf. *kyninges hagan* in Grimley (BCS 462).
Thus the name means 'enclosure on the nook or corner of land.'
This will account for most of the forms, including those like
Hallege, Hallage which show early loss of *h*, while the latest
forms are due to ready confusion with ME *lawe, lowe, lewe* from
OE **hlaw, hlæw**. From the *healh* on which this 'haw' or 'hay'
stood, the people themselves could be spoken of as the *Healh-*
ingas (v. ingas), which would readily become *Heallingas*.

EASTBURY MANOR (6″)

Earesbyrig 11th Heming
Eresbyrie 1086 DB
Heresbyria c. 1086 (1190) *EveB*
Alesberga c. 1086 (1190) *EveA*
Esebyre, Esebire 1240 WoP, 1275 *Ass*
Eselbyre 1240 WoP
Eylesbyri 1255 *Ass*
Estebury 1270 LibPens
Esbire 1275 *FF*
Essburi, Esburie 1316 Ipm, 1616 QSR
Esbury al. *Estbury* al. *Aylesbury* 1486 Pat, 1497 Ipm
Eastbury 1656 FF

[1] The *cisburn* of the bounds of Hallow (BCS 356) survives as *chiseburn* in
WoP (1240). It means 'gravel-stream,' *v.* cis.

The explanation of this name is difficult. From the first form and from the lost *Earesbroca* in Arley (Dugd. vi. 1445) it would seem that there may have been an OE pers. name *Ēar* or *Ēare*, which may possibly be the source of the OE *Ere* found as that of a moneyer of Athelstan, though it is more likely that this last is a pet-form of such a name as *Erewine*. The possibility of *Ear-* (from earlier Germanic *Aur-*) as a pers. name element is made probable by names in Germany and Scandinavia. Förstemann (PN 210–1) gives several names in *Aur-*, *Or-*, which he does not seriously attempt to explain. Amongst them perhaps the most important is the well-established OGer pers. name *Aurivandal*. This corresponds to the ON mythological name *Ǫrvandill* and possibly to the OE *ēarendel*, used, not as a pers. name, but of a 'ray of light, dawn.' In Old Norse there are several mythological names beginning with *Aur-*, but it does not seem ever to be used as an element in names given to historical personages. Tacitus (*Germania* c. 8) also gives *Aurinnia* as the name of a German prophetess[1]. This may be a derivative of the same stem, and indeed, considering the mythological associations of many of these names and words in *Aur-*, *Ear-* such a suggestion seems very probable. This element may be the same as the ON *Aurr*, a mythological name for Earth itself (originally meaning 'wet clay, loam') and OE *ear*, the name of one of the Runic letters in the OE alphabet, which probably denotes 'earth' (cf. Earith in PN BedsHu 205). Professor Tolkien, taking into consideration the use of OE *ēarendel* as a personification for Lucifer, and the sense of ON *Ǫrvandils tá*, suggests that the first element should rather be associated with IndoGer *aus-*, 'light.' It is even possible that at an early date this element was used to form compound pers. names in England. The early charters of Abingdon Abbey refer to a place rendered in different documents *Æaromundeslee*, *Earmundeslea*, *Earmundeslæh*, *Ærmundelea*. In the last, a charter of 942, which is probably genuine, it is stated that the name of the place was *æt Æppeltune*. It is now Appleton in North Berkshire. The earlier charters are all spurious as they stand but may in part be founded upon early material. They are all derived from the *Historia Monasterii de Abingdon* (12th cent. MS). See further, Introd. xxi.

[1] v.l. *Albrinnia*. Cf. Schönfeld, *s.n.*

Assuming the existence of such a name in OE, probably of great antiquity, we can explain the later history of the name as follows. *Eares* would become *Æres*, *Eres*. Then alternative forms arose. On the one hand, by a common process of dissimilation (cf. IPN 106), *Eresbiry* became *Elesbiry* or, with occasional metathesis, *Eselbiry*. On the other hand, the *r* was often lost from the consonant group *rsb* giving rise to a form *Es(e)biry*. By a natural process of folk-etymology this was associated with ME *este* or 'east.' Hence 'burh of Ear(e).'

The Elms

Helme 1240 WoP, 1275 SR, both (p)

This is probably the ordinary tree-name, with inorganic *h* in the ME forms. Habington (i. 499) thinks, from the phrase in an early document 'In Elemes Wm. de Winchester holds ½ yard-land,' that the real name of this place was 'in Elemosinam,' and that the name refers to the tenure!

Fieldy Fm (6″)

de Felde, de la Felde 1240 WoP, 1275, 1327 SR

v. feld. The added *y* is curious and unexplained.

Greenhill Fm (6″)

Grimeshyll 816 (11th) BCS 356
Grimanhyll 957 (11th) BCS 993
Gremanhil 1086 DB
Grimhelle, Grimhull c. 1086 (1190) EveA & B, 1208 Fees 36
Grimenhulle, Grymenhull 1240 WoP, 1275 Ass, SR, 1284
   Wigorn, 1300 Pat (p), 1316 Ipm (p)
Grymehull 1316 WoCh, 1374 Wigorn, 1502 WoCh
Grymhylle 1549 Pat
Grynhill 1655 FF

For the history of this name *v.* Grimley *supra* 126. At a late stage it has undergone wanton corruption.

Greenstreet Fm

Grenanwege 816 (11th) BCS 356, 963 (11th) BCS 1108
la Grenestrete 1316 Ipm

'The green road,' *v.* grene, weg.

HALLOW HEATH
>   *Hethe* 1327 SR (p)
>   Self-explanatory.

HENWICK [henik]
>   *Higna gemære* 851 (11th) BCS 462
>   *Hinewic, Hinewyk, Hynewike* 1180 P (p), 1240 WoP, 1249 *FF*,
>   1352 CompR
>   *Henewic* 1181, 1182 P (p)
>   *Hyndewyke* 13th WoCh
>   *Hynwyche, Hynwick* 1518 More, 1547 LP, Pat, 1558 Wills
>   *Henwicke* 1651 FF
>   'Dairy farm of the monks' or of their servants. OE *hiwan*
> might be applied to a community of either, *v.* higna, wic. In
> the first reference mention is made of the bounds of this pro-
> perty.

HILL FM
>   *de Monte* 1240 WoP, 1327 SR
>   Self-explanatory.

HYLTON (lost)[1]
>   *Hultone* c. 1200 (c. 1240) *WoC*
>   *Hultune* 1240 WoP
>   *Hultenestre'* 1299 (18th) *RBB*
>   *Hultonestrete* Hy 3 StSwith
>   *Hylton Strete* 1521 AcctsWo
>   *Hylton St* 1855 Kelly
>   The 'hill farm' to which this street or road led must have
> been on the ridge which separates Laughern Brook from the
> Severn. The ridge is referred to as *la Hulle versus Lawerne* in
> *AOMB* 61.

PARTRIDGE FM
>   This is probably derived from the family name *Partrich* found
> in the Subsidy Roll of 1275.

---

[1] The present Hylton Rd must in part at least be identical with Hylton
Street. The site of Hylton must now lie within South Hallow in the city of
Worcester.

PEACHLEY

Peceslea(ge) 11th Heming
Pec(c)hesle(ye), *Peccheslega* 1240 WoP, 1241 *FF*, E 1 BM,
    1345, 1355 Pat
Pechilege 1250 *FF*
Pechulle 1275 *Ass*
Peachley 1632 Kyre

Professors Ekwall and Zachrisson agree in suggesting that the
first element in this name is a pers. name *Pecci*, an *i*-derivative
of the pers. name *Pæcc* which must lie behind Patching (Sx).
This should have developed to *Petchley*. The modern form
with a long vowel is probably due to etymologising association
with the common word *peach*.

SHOULTON

Selgeton c. 1220 (c. 1240) *WoC*, c. 1250 ib.
Scolegeton c. 1220 (c. 1240) *WoC*, c. 1250 ib.
Soultone 1327 SR (p)
Shelton 1518 More
Shewton, *Shelton* 1571 Wills
Shoulton 1649 Surv

The first element in this name is OE sceolh, 'awry, twisted.'
The exact significance of this element as applied to tun is not
clear. The cognate German *scheel* is also used in the sense
'sloping, slanting.' This would describe the site of Shoulton.
For its use in place-names, cf. Förstemann (PN 771) who gives
examples of it compounded with *flet*, *husen*, *horn* and *dorf*.

WOODHALL FM

Wodehalle 1240 WoP, 1275 SR, 1291 Tax

'Hall by the wood,' cf. Wood Hall in Norton-juxta-Kempsey
infra 151.

Great and Little Hampton[1]

GREAT and LITTLE HAMPTON   82 H 3

Hamtona 709 (c. 1200) BCS 125
Heantun 780 (11th) BCS 235
Hantun 714 (16th) BCS 130, 1086 DB

[1] Now in Blackenhurst Hundred.

M

Heamtun 988 (c. 1200) KCD 662
Hamtun 988 (c. 1200) KCD 662
Hamton c. 1086 (1190) *EveA* & *B*, 1275 SR
Hampton 1327 SR

OE (*æt þæm*) *hēan tūne*, 'high farm,' the village rises up from the stream and is definitely higher than the corresponding part of Evesham on the opposite bank.

Harvington

HARVINGTON 82 G 4

Herverton 709 (12th) BCS 125, 1275 SR
Hereford 799 (11th) BCS 295, 804 (11th) BCS 307
Herefordtun juxta Avene 964 (12th) BCS 1135
Herferthun 1086 DB
Hervertona c. 1086 (1190) *EveB*
Herwerton 1227 FF
Hervorditun 1240 WoP
Herfertun 1240 WoP *passim*
Herfortun 1249 FF, 1311 Pat, 1334 BM, 1535 VE
Hervington 1508 Pat
Herforton al. *Hervington* 1542 LP
Harvington 16th Wills

'Army-ford' originally (*v.* here, ford) and then, when a settlement was made near it, the suffix tun was added. The village is a good half-mile from the ford, cf. Harford (D) DB *Hereforda* and Hartford (PN BedsHu 208). 'By the Avon' in distinction from Hereford on the Wye (He). In Saxon times the names were identical.

HARVINGTON HILL

la Hulle 1275 SR (p)
Self-explanatory.

WIBURGESTOKE (lost)

In DB *Wiburgestoke* is held along with Harvington in Oswaldslow and the same manor is referred to as *Wiburga Stoke* in the 1150 Survey. It cannot now be identified. It is a compound of the OE woman's name *Wigburh* and stoc.

Hill and Moor

HILL AND MOOR 82 G 1

Hylle c. 1050 KCD 923
More et Hylle 1086 DB
Hulle juxta Fladebury 1346 FA, *Mora juxta Fladebure*
    1306 AD ii
Hulle and More 1375 Cl, 1431 FA

Self-explanatory, but the name is interesting as indicating the contrast between the 'hill' and the low-lying 'moor' or swamp.

Himbleton[1]

HIMBLETON 81 D 14

Hymeltun 816 (11th) BCS 256, 884 (18th) BCS 552, c. 972
    (11th) KCD 680
Himeltun 1086 DB
Humeltuna c. 1086 (1190) *EveB*
Humelton(e) 1240 WoP, 1275 SR, 1291 Tax, 1346 FA, 1389
    Pat
Hemelton 1320 Pat
Hymulton 1535 VE
Humulton 1549 Wills
Himbulton 1564 Wills
Himbleton 1570 Wills

The first element in this name is clearly the same as that found in the old name *Hymelbroc* for the Bow Brook (*v. supra* 10) on which it stands. That stream is mentioned in the bounds of Crowle, Peopleton and Grafton Flyford, some miles to the south in those of Himbleton itself, and in those of Phepson to the north of Himbleton. It is however more likely that the *tun* and the *broc* were named independently than that the one took its name from the other. The same element is found in *hymelmor* in Wolverley (KCD 645) and also in Himley (St). It is probable that in all alike the reference is to some plant but we cannot be sure to what. The wild hop has been suggested but it is very doubtful whether it is a native plant. More probably it is used here as in some of the OE vocabularies,

---

[1] Partly in Esch Hundred.

of either bryony or bindweed, and the whole name would then refer to the frequency of the plant here.

BLACKPIT LANE (6″)

blacan pyt (acc.) 884 (18th) BCS 552
Black Pitt Corner 1649 Surv
The name is self-explanatory. Cf. *blakeput* in Broadwas (*WoC* 11 *b*).

DEAN BROOK

Denebrigge 1275 *Ass*   *pontem de la Dene* 13th (18th) *Pat*
The reference is to a bridge over the present Dean Brook, *v.* denu. It should be noted that the brook itself certainly does not form a 'dene' if we think of any deep-cut or well-marked valley.

DUNHAMPSTEAD[1]

Dunhamstyde 814 (11th) BCS 349
Dunhæmstede c. 972 (11th) KCD 680
Dunhamstede 11th Heming, (*juxta Crowele*) 1280 *For*
Dunhamstud 1148 (c. 1240) *WoC*, 1240 WoP, c. 1245 *Bodl* 15
Donhamstede 1300 *Pat*
Donamstude 1310 *FF*, 1327 SR, both (p)
Dunnamsteed 1649 Surv

'The hamstede on the hill,' *v.* dun. The hill is only a slight slope.

EARL'S COMMON

This probably dates from the time when the earls of Hereford held the manor of Himbleton (VCH iii. 392–3).

FOREDRAUGHT LANE

the Vardroe 1649 Surv, 1820 G, c. 1830 O
Foredrove 1786 Map of Worc. Canal
For this name see EDD *s.v.* It is a very common term in

---

[1] The field called Great *Charsleys* in the Survey of 1650 is probably the same piece of land that is referred to as *cyranleage* in the bounds of Dunhampstead in Himbleton (BCS 349). The *Winsty* Meadow of the same document must be the same as the *wynna stigele* in the bounds of Himbleton in Heming (356).

Wa and Wo for a lane or path for the purposes of draught from a farm to the main road.

HARMAN'S HILL

Armon Hyll 1549 Pat

Harman is a well-established Worcestershire name (Wills, FF).

HORNHILL WOOD (6")

Harnell 1649 Surv   *Harnil Wood* 1884 6" O.S.

KING'S WOOD (6")

Kingeswode 1275 SR (p)

Self-explanatory.

NEIGHT HILL

Neyte Hill 1649 Surv

This seems to be ME *eyte*, from OE **iggoð**, with the common prefixing of *n* from the inflected definite article *then*. The situation is not quite what one would have looked for, but as the hill lies between two stream-valleys and slopes up fairly sharply from one, it may have been thought of as an island-hill. For the form *neight*, cf. the piece of ground called the 'neite encompassed by the River of Severne on all sides' in Bewdley (*Surv.* 1650). Note also *neight* as a field-name in a Defford terrier (1714). Cf. Comberton Aits *infra* 194.

PHEPSON[1]

Fepsetnatun 956 (11th) BCS 937
Fepsetenatun 1086 DB
Fepsintuna, -tune c. 1086 (1190) *EveB*, c. 1150 Surv, 1240 WoP
Vespinton 1255 *Ass*
Fepsinton 1275 SR, 1276 RH, 1304–5 Wigorn
Vepsenthone 1280 *For*
Phepsynton, Phepsington 1302, 1305 Wigorn
Fepson 1583, 1589 Wills
Phepston, Fepston 1649 Surv, 1679 FF

This is a difficult name. It seems probable that we should

---

[1] In Esch Hundred. On the 6" map the fuller form *Fepsinton* is preserved in the name of a farm in Phepson; cf. Suddington *infra* 271.

bring it into relation to the district in Middle Anglia which Bede (i. 271) calls *in Feppingum*. It cannot actually be identified with Phepson, for Himbleton is definitely out of Middle Anglia, though not far from what must have been its southern border (cf. Mawer, *PN and History* 11). We have seen above (*s.n.* Broadwas) how the inhabitants of a place might be named by taking the first element in its name and tacking on to it in quite illogical fashion the element sæte. It is possible that there may have been a migration of people from the district of the *Feppingas* into Himbleton. These migrants might well be called *Fepsæte* and their new home *Fepsetenatun*, 'farm of the Fepsæte.' For the etymology of *Feppingas v.* Ekwall, *PN in -ing* 112, n. 1, where it is suggested that this is from a pers. name connected with OHG *Faffo, Faffilo*[1]. See further Introd. xviii.

SALDON WOOD (6")

Saulden Head, Soulden Yate 1649 Surv
Saldings c. 1830 O   *Saldens* 1892 Kelly
'Willow-valley,' *v.* sealh, denu.

SALEWAY

la Sale 1255 *Ass* (p), 1262 *For*, 1327 SR (p)
'(at the) willow,' with later addition of *way, v.* sealh.

SHELL[2]

Scylfweg 956 (11th) BCS 937
Scelves 1086 DB
Shelue, Scelue, Schelve, Shelve 1221 *Ass*, 1256 Ipm, 1269 *FF*, 1275, 1327 SR, (*juxta Hambury*) 1325 *FF*, 1346, 1428 FA, (*juxta Temple Brocton*) 1355 *FF*, 1394 Pat, 1535 VE, 1582 Wills
Shell 1596 Wills
Shelves, Shell-bridge 1549 Surv

The *scylfweg* of the first reference simply means 'the road which runs to *Scylf* or Shell' and is apparently the road from the north of Phepson to Shell. The exact sense of *scylf* here,

---

[1] For this etymology of Phepson we are in part indebted to criticisms and suggestions by Ekwall (*loc. cit.*) upon a previous suggestion made by Mawer (*loc. cit.*).

[2] In Esch Hundred.

as always, is difficult to determine. The place lies down by a stream.

SHERNAL GREEN

Shurnall 1649 Surv

Hindlip

HINDLIP 81 D 12

Hindehlep 966 (11th) BCS 1180

Hindelep, Hyndelepe 1086 DB, c. 1086 (1190) *EveA & B*, 1208 Fees 36, 1276 RH, 1300 *Pat*, 1316 Ipm, 1327 SR

Hindeslepa 1191 P (p)

Hyndelupe, Hindelupe c. 1250 *Bodl* 14, c. 1270 ib. 9, 1316 Ipm

Henlype 1577 Saxton

This may refer to some famous 'hind-leap' as there is some fairly steep ground, but more probably the reference is simply to the existence of a 'leap-gate' for hinds, *v.* Leapgate *infra* 243. *v.* hind, hlyp(e).

OFFERTON FM

Alhðretune 978 (11th) KCD 618

Alðryðetune c. 1040 (18th) Hickes ii. 299[1]

Alcrintun 1086 DB, 1275 SR

Alcrinton(a), Alcrynton c. 1086 (1190) *EveA & B*, 1182 (18th) *RBB*, 1280 *For*, 1288 Ipm

Alchrinton c. 1200 (c. 1250) *WoC*

Alreton in Hindelep 1232 Ch

Alcretun c. 1235 Wulst

Alfverton 1275 SR

Alcrentone 1280 *For*

Alfreton 1535 VE, 1546 Wills

Auferton 1559 Wills

OE *Ealhðrÿðe-tūn*, 'farm of a woman called *Ealhthryth*,' with an alternative form in which the two elements were linked together by ing, *v.* ingtun. The final development of the *Alf-, Auf-* forms is not easy to explain. Were there earlier pronunciations

---

[1] The identification is not certain but Hickes gives this as the name of a place granted by Bishop Lyfing (3 hides), in a charter which was at Worcester in the time of Dugdale, and it is difficult to suggest what other place can be referred to.

in which the spirant *h* (= χ) in *Alh-* had become *f* or was the development a sheer accident? The SR form is in favour of the former suggestion. Note also the history of Alfrick *supra* 28, where we have further evidence for an early *f* from *h*.

SMITE HILL[1], SMITE FM[2] (6")

> *æt Smitan* 978 (11th) KCD 618
> *Smita Archid* 1167 P
> *Smite* 1271 Ipm, 1275 SR

The first reference is from the grant of a single hide at Smite. In the boundaries that follow we have the phrases *to Smitan, of ðære Smitan* which suggest that the place took its name from a stream. The same stream-name is found in Wanborough (W) in the *Smitan* of BCS 477, 479, in Olveston (Gl) in an unidentified *Smita pull*, BCS 936, in Smite (Wa), DB *Smitham*, on Smite Brook. There is also a stream of this name in Lei and Nt. In 1167 Godfrey the Archdeacon held half a hide here.

Holdfast

HOLDFAST HALL (6") 92 A 11

> *Holanfæstene* (dat.), *Holenfesten* (dat.) 967 (11th) BCS 1205
> *Holefæst* 11th Heming
> *(H)olefest* 1086 DB, 1221 *Ass*
> *Holeuestre* c. 1086 (1190) *EveA*
> *Oleuest* c. 1086 (1190) *EveB*
> *Holevast* 1182 (18th) *RBB*
> *Holefast* 1299 (18th) *RBB*
> *Holfast* 1315 *FF*, 1328 Ch, 1537 BM
> *Holvestre* 1471 IpmR

'(At the) hollow stronghold' (*v.* holh, fæsten), though the appropriateness of the description is not now apparent. The forms with *r* are interesting. It is clear that there was in OE a word *fæstern*, 'strong house' (*v.* ærn) which gave rise to Vasterne (W)[3] and which has influenced, if it does not itself actually form the first element in, such forms as *fæstergeat, festergeweorc*

---

[1] Formerly in Claines.
[2] Formerly in Warndon.
[3] Note also *le Vasterne* (1278), *Fasterne* (1282) in Halesowen.

found side by side with the usual forms in *fæsten*. So common was the confusion that, quite illogically, we find *fæstern* actually used for the word *fæsten*, 'fasting,' both by itself in the derivative *fæsternlic* (BT *s.n.n.*) and in Scots *Fastern's E'en* for Shrove Tuesday. It may be that we have such confusion here. Buckfast (D) is *Bucfæsten* in KCD 1334, DB *Bucfestre*, with later persistent *r*. This may be in part an AN spelling, but it is probably also due to a confusion similar to that just noted.

BARLEY HOUSE (6″)

Burgelege 1086 DB
Burlega, Burlege, Burlegh c. 1086 (1190) *EveB*, 1165 P (p), 1182 (18th) *RBB*, 1208 Fees 35, 1299 (18th) *RBB*
Burleye 1347 Pat
'Clearing marked by a burh' (*v.* leah). Possibly there was once a stronghold here commanding the passage of the Severn. The modern form is corrupt.

THE REDDINGS (6″)

In the 15th cent. there was a *Bastrudyng* in Longdon (VCH iv. 112). *Reddings* is just over the eastern border of Longdon and *Bastrudyng* is probably to be interpreted as 'east of the *rudyng.*' In any case the name is clearly from OE hryding and denotes a clearing. The plural form may point to some of the other *rudyngs* mentioned in VCH (*loc. cit.*). For *Bast-* cf. Bastwood *supra* 48.

Holt

HOLT 81 B 10

Holte 1086 DB
v. holt.

BALL MILL (6″)

This preserves the original name of Grimley Brook on which it stands, viz. *Bæle. v.* Grimley Brook *supra* 11.

BENTLEY FM

Beonotsetena gemære, Beonetsetnægemære 851 (11th) BCS 462, c. 965 (11th) BCS 1139

Beonetlege, Beonetlæ(a)ge 855 (11th) BCS 487, 862 (11th) BCS 1087

Beonetleah 1017 KCD 1313

A common type of place-name, for which *v.* beonet, leah. For sæte cf. Broadwas *supra* 103.

HURST FM

de Hurste, atte Hurste 1275, 1327 SR

'Wooded hill,' *v.* hyrst.

OCKERIDGE WOOD

Heafuchrycg[1] 962 (11th) BCS 1087
Hauekerugge 1275 *Ass*
Hawkerydge Hy 8 VCH iii. 401
Haucridge 1633 QSR

'Hawk-ridge,' *v.* heafoc, hrycg, cf. Halfridge *supra* 26 and Hawridge (PN Bk 95).

Huddington

HUDDINGTON[2] 81 D 14

Hudigtuna gemæra c. 840 (11th) BCS 428
Hudintune 1086 DB, c. 1086 (1190) *EveB*
Hodintona 1173 P
Hodingthone, Hodyngton 1182 (18th) *RBB*, 1280 *For*, 1396 Pat, 1431 FA, 16th Wills
Hudinton, Hudenthon, Hudynthon 1232 Ch, 1280 *For*
Hodyngton 1332 SR, 1340 NI, 1428 FA
Huddington 16th Wills

'*Hūd(a)'s* farm,' *v.* ingtun. It may be something more than a coincidence that *Hodes ac* is found on the boundary of Huddington (BCS 1282). Cf. Hudnall (PN Bk 94).

BOSSIL WOOD (6")

Bawsall 1649 Surv

---

[1] Miss F. E. Harmer has kindly collated the MS and says that the reading here is as given and as found in Kemble. Birch's *Heafnehrycg* is a misprint.

[2] In the bounds of Himbleton (BCS 542) we have an *uffanleage*. This survives as Uffeley Coppice in the *Parliamentary Survey* (1650) of Huddington. For the pers. name involved, *v.* Offenham *infra* 266.

MAYBRIDGE CLOSES (lost)

mægidna brycg 840 (11th) BCS 428
Maybridge Closes 1650 *Surv*

'Maidens' bridge,' *v.* Medbury (PN BedsHu 71) for names of
this type. The bridge was across the Bow Brook, on the bounds
of Huddington and Crowle.

SALE GREEN

This is found as *Sale Greene* in the 1650 *Survey* of this parish.
The first element is probably the same as that found in the pers.
name Christina *atte Sale* in the adjacent Himbleton in 1327.
This means '(at) the willow,' *v.* sealh.

TRENCH LANE (6") and WOOD

Trunchet 1240 WoP   *Trench* 1327 SR (p) (*in Oldberrow*)
highway called the Trench 1650 *Surv*

The earliest form is probably corrupt and the origin is OF
trenche, 'cutting.' The word is evidently used in the first sense
given in the NED, viz. path or track cut through a wood or
forest. Trench Lane is part of a road from Droitwich through
Huddington to Stratford, probably a saltway. It forms the
north-east boundary of Trench Wood. The original route may
have been through the wood itself for there is a track passing
through the wood, parallel to the road and it forms a parish
boundary[1].

Church Iccomb [2]

ICCOMB 93 F 5

Icancumb, Iccacumb 781 (11th) BCS 240
Iccacumb 964 (12th) BCS 1135
Iccecumb 11th Heming
Iacumbe 1086 DB

[1] Trench Fm in Wem (Sa) may furnish a parallel. It is *le Trench* in
1300 (Ipm). From local enquiries kindly made by Mr E. W. Bowcock it
appears that the *trench* can be one of three things : (*a*) the trench of the ancient
camp here, (*b*) a sunk road which preceded the present made-up road leading
to Trench Hall, (*c*) the ravine known as the Drumble, to the west of Upper
Trench Hall.

[2] Entirely in Gloucestershire since 1844. Till then Church Iccomb was
always in Worcestershire, and the rest of the present parish in Gloucestershire.

la Cumbe c. 1086 (1190) *EveB*
Ikcumbe 1221 FineR
Iccombe 1316 FA

The existence of an OE pers. name *Icca* is demonstrated under *Ickford* (PN Bk 124) and there is no doubt that we have it here. The *cumb* may be the small and narrow valley which lies at the foot of the church or its more marked eastward extension a mile away. In the same charter (BCS 240) there is an *Icangæt*.

Kempsey

KEMPSEY 81 F 11

Kemesei 799 (11th) BCS 295
Cymesig 977 (11th) KCD 612
Kymesei, Chemeshege, Kemesige 11th Heming
Chemesege 1086 DB
Camesi, Cameseia c. 1086 (1190) *EveA* & B
Kemeseia, Kemeseye 1208 Fees 37, 1235 BM, 1255 Ch, 1291 Tax
Kemsey 1615 Ogilby

The suffix **eg** is probably descriptive of the 'island' of higher ground on which the church and camp stand.

For the first part of the name we may compare the forms for Kempston (Nf). These are *Kemestun* DB, *Camestone* c. 1100 (c. 1300), *Harl* 2110, *Kamestona* (ib.), *Chemestune* c. 1145 ib., *Chemest'* Hy 2 BM. Professor Zachrisson suggests that in both these names we have an OE pet-name *Cemmi* for *Cēnmǣr*. The formation is a regular one. The *a*-forms represent AN spellings with *a* for *e*, while the *y* is for *i*, showing the common raising of *e* to *i* before front consonants, cf. especially the spelling *Bynnyncgwyrðe* for Bengeworth *supra* 95 and *Bynsincgtune* for Bensington (O) in KCD 625, BCS 547 from the same Cartulary as the *Cyme-* forms for Kempsey. Hence 'Cemmi's well-watered land.' The discovery of these names and their probable solution suggests that we may also have this pers. name in Kempston (Beds) and that this may furnish a better solution of that name than the one offered in PN BedsHu 75.

---

[1] *ex inf*. Dr O. K. Schram.

Ashmoor Common

East mor 972 (c. 1050) BCS 1282   *Astmore* c. 1830 O

This is the 'eastern' marsh-land in contrast to Normoor Common in the same parish. It should be noted however that Ashmoor is to the west of Normoor so that they must have been named from different centres, Ashmoor perhaps from Clifton, Normoor from Kerswell. For *Ash* cf. Ashbrook (Gl), DB *Estbroce*.

Baynhall

Beynhale 1275 SR (p)   *Baynold* 1593 Wills

This is probably from OE *Bǣganhēale* (dat.) *v.* healh and contains the same pers. name as Bayton *supra* 38 and Baywell *supra* 121.

Brook End

le Broke 1182 (18th) *RBB   de la Brok, atte Brok* 1275, 1327 SR   *Brook End* 1613 QSR

Self-explanatory.

Broomhall Fms

Bromhale 1275 SR, 1320 Pat   *Bromehale* 1544 LP, 1665 FF
Broome Hall 1620 WillsP   *Bromhall* 1649 Surv

'Broom-covered healh.'

Clerkenleap

Clerkenlip 1542, 1545 LP   *Clerkenleape* 1544 LP
Clerconleppe 1548 Pat   *Clerkenlippe* 1634 QSR

Clearly 'clerks' leap.' The place lies on a slight slope, but it is impossible to reconstruct the story of these venturesome clerics. Cf. similarly *presta hlype*, 'priests' leap,' in KCD 813.

Draycott

Draycote, Draycott 1275 SR, 1548 Pat, 1590 Wills
Dreycote 1303 Wigorn
Dra(y)cott 1649 Surv

v. dræg, cot. This place lies on gently rising ground, away from water, cf. Draycott in Blockley *supra* 99.

HOLDINGS FM (6")

> *Houdene* 1320 Pat (p)
> *Houdon* 1327 SR (p)
> *Howdens* 1444 HMC x, App. iv. 445
> *Holden* c. 1830 O

This is apparently a purely manorial name. It takes its rise from a grant by the Bishop of Worcester (c. 1305) to one Adam of *Howeden*. The modern form is in part an inverted spelling, due to the common development of *old* to *owd*, and in part a vulgarism such as is dealt with by Wyld, *Colloquial English* 290.

KERSWELL GREEN

> *Chirswell* 1182 (18th) *RBB*
> *Kereswell* 1208 Fees 37, (*juxta Kemeseye*) 1309 *FF*, 1347 Pat,
>   1419 IpmR, 1548 Pat
> *Kers(e)well* 1275 SR, *Ass*, 1613 QSR, 1649 Surv
> *Keyreswell* 1471 IpmR
> *Caswell* 1772 T, 1789 Gough

'Cress-grown spring,' *v.* cærse, wielle.

NAPLETON

> *Lepeltone, Apelton* 1182, 1299 (18th) *RBB*
> *de Appletone, atte Appelton* 1275, 1327 SR
> *Napleton, Nappleton* 1593 Wills, 1649 Surv

'Orchard,' *v.* æppeltun. One of the numerous examples of affixed *n* in this county.

THE NASH

> *Esse* 1182 (18th) *RBB* (p)
> *de Fraxino* 1255, 1275 *Ass*, 1275 SR, 1338 Pat
> *Asshe* 1301 (18th) *RBB*

'Ash,' *v.* æsc and cf. Napleton *supra*.

STONEHALL [stʌnǝl]

> *Stonhale* 1275 SR, *Ass*, 1299 (18th) *RBB*
> *Stonhall* 1580 Wills   *Stonnal* 1628 QSR

'Stony healh.' The form has probably been influenced by Woodhall Fm.

WOODHALL FMS

de Wodewelle 1275 SR, 1299 (18th) *RBB*
Woodhall 1581 Wills, 1649 Surv
'Spring by the wood,' *v.* **wudu, wielle.**

Kenswick

KENSWICK 81 D 9

Checinwich(e) 1086 DB, c. 1086 (1190) *EveA*
Kekinwiche c. 1086 (1190) *EveB*
Kekingwik(e) 1208 Fees 36, 1240 WoP, 1270 Wigorn, 1275 SR
Kinstwick 1221 *FF*
Kekenwic 1242 P (p)
Keckingewyke 1275 *Ass, FF*
Ketelingwyche 1275 *Ass*
Kelyngwych 1411 FF
Kelonwyche al. *Kekonwyche* al. *Kenchewhiche* 1497 IpmR
Kengewick 1535 VE, 1577 Saxton
Kenswike 1560 Wills

The clue to this name is provided by the field-name *Kekes Ruding* which occurs in a charter of c. 1230 (*WoC* 39 *b*). There is also an Osbert *le Keke* in 1275 (SR). This discovery confirms Ritter's suggestion (132) that we have to do with an OE *Cēcingwīc* formed from a pers. name found also in Kesgrave (Sf), earlier *Kekesgrave*. Ritter points out that we should have expected ME forms in *Kech-* rather than *Kek-*, but it is clear that some unexplained cause prevented the normal development of this pers. name from *Cēc* to *Keche*. The ME and early ModE evidence prove an *-inge* pronunciation, suggesting OE *Cēcingawīc* rather than *Cēcingwīc*. The same pers. name is probably found in Keckwick (Ch), 1281 Plea Roll *Kecwyke* (p),1329 Ch *Kekwic*. From this place-name, at some stage in its history, must have been thrown off the pers. name *Kekewich*.

Knightwick

KNIGHTWICK 81 E 7

Cnihtawic 964 (12th) BCS 1135
Cnihtewican (dat.) 1023 (17th) KCD 738
Cnihtewic 1086 DB

(Later forms are without interest.) The name means wic or dairy farm of the *cnihts*, *v.* cniht and cf. Knighton *supra* 52.

MAPNORS (lost)

> *Mappenor(e)* c. 1220 (c. 1240) *WoC*, 1275, 1327 SR (p)
> *Mappenouer* 1340 NI (p)
> *Mapnors* 1556 VCH iii. 440

The first entry is definitely that of a place-name, though it is not clear to what part of Wo (if any) it refers. If it refers to this, then the name is pseudo-manorial and the name is a compound of a pers. name *Mappa*, otherwise unknown, and ofer, 'bank.'

PITHOUSE (lost)

> *de la Putte* 12th Coll. Top. et Gen. iv. 238–40
> *Pytehouse* 1544 LP

Self-explanatory.

Abbots Lench

ABBOTS[1] LENCH 82 F 2

> *Abeleng* 1086 DB
> *Hebbelenz, Hebbelench* c. 1086 (1190) *EveA* &ͮ*B*
> *Abbelench* 1227 FF
> *Habbelench* 1273 *FF*, 1275 SR, 1297 Pat, 1340 NI, 1346, 1428 FA
> *Habelinge* 1275 *Ass*
> *Ab(e)lench* 1316 Ipm, 1431 FA, 1544 Wills
> *Hablenche* 1477 IpmR, 1492 Ipm
> *Hoblench* 16th, 17th Wills *passim*
> *Abs Lench* 1704 Marr

The *Lench* of this name, Rous Lench *infra* 149 in the same hundred, and of Church Lench, Atch Lench and Sheriffs Lench in Esch Hundred *infra* 330 and of Lenchwick in Fishborough Hundred *infra* 264 is an unsolved problem. The OE form would seem to have been *Lenc*. The late W. H. Stevenson in a letter to the *Times Literary Supplement* (Nov. 9, 1922) called attention to this group of names and suggested that perhaps it was the name of a stream, now lost. Examination

---

[1] This is the form now used on the maps, but it has no historical justification.

of the topography of the places in question shows however that they cannot be named from any single stream, and indeed tend to be rather away from streams. They cover an area some 5 miles long and 2 miles broad, and *lenc* would seem rather to have been the name of a district, most of the places which take their names from it tending to be on relatively high ground. We may note also that somewhere in the Lench area there was a *lencdun* (BCS 124).

The name must be the same as the Lench discussed by Ekwall in PN La 65. The forms of that name are very late but he suggests that it is the same as the dialectal *lench* used in Cheshire of 'a seam of rock-salt,' and in Derbyshire of 'a ledge of rock' (*v.* EDD *s.v.*) and that it is connected with OE *hlinc*, 'ridge.'

It must be formed from another grade **hlank* of the same stem. *h* before *l* is lost already at times in Old English itself (cf. Sievers, *A. S. Gramm.* 217, n. 2) as in *lið* for *hlið* in the quotation *s.n.* Cornwood *supra* 54. There is evidence for such a place-name element in the *lanke*, 'seite,' in Westphalia (Jellinghaus, *Die Westfälischen ON* 126) and possibly in one or two other place-names given by Förstemann (ON ii. 35, *s.v. lank*). The relation of the two words is similar to that of OE *hlinc*, 'link, bond,' and *hlence*, 'link-armour.'

Abbots Lench was first distinguished from the other Lenches by the prefixing of the pers. name *Aebba* or an unrecorded *Hæbba*, a pet-form of such an OE name as *Hēahbeorht* (cf. Ab Kettleby (Lei) for a similar addition). This was corrupted to *Hob* and last of all to *Abbot*.

Rous Lench[1]

ROUS LENCH 82 E 2

æt Lenc 983 (11th) KCD 637
Lenc 11th Heming
Biscopesleng 1086 DB
Lenz c. 1086 (1190) *EveA*
Bissopes Lench c. 1086 (1190) *EveB*
Lelenz Rand 1167 P

[1] For Church Lench *v.* Esch Hundred.

N

Lens 1176 P (p)
Lench Randolf 1230 *FF* to 1431 FA
Rous Lench 1445 VCH iii. 498, 1535 VE

This manor was held by the Bishop of Worcester in DB.
It was held by one *Randolf* in the time of Hy 2 and passed into
the hands of the *Rous* family in the 14th cent. (VCH iii. 498).

RADFORD

Radeford c. 1230 (15th) *AOMB* 61, 1255 *Ass*, 1275 *FF*, SR
Radford 1271 *For*, 1535 VE

'Red ford,' *v.* read, ford.

STAKENFORD BRIDGE (6″)

Stakumford Bridge c. 1830 O

We have no old forms for this name, but the first element is
probably the word *stakyng* found in the Red Book of the Bishop
of Worcester. There a certain *cottarius* holds a *stakynge juxta
Temede*, i.e. by the Teme, and we have reference to the rent of
six shillings derived from the pools (*gurgites*) and *stakyngorum
per aquas de Temede Sabrine*, i.e. on the Teme and Severn.
These *stakings*, though the word is not on record in the NED,
were doubtless 'staked' grounds of some kind for fishing. The
ford may have been by such ground or it may be that the name
simply denotes a ford marked out by stakes, cf. *Stakynbroke* in
Hagley (AD i) which is near the present hamlet of Stakenbridge.

Little Malvern

LITTLE MALVERN 81 G 9

parve Malvernie, minor Malvernie, la petite Maluerne 1232 Cl,
1275 SR, *Ass*

v. Great Malvern *infra* 210.

Netherton

NETHERTON 82 J 2

Neoðeretun 780 (11th) BCS 235
Neoðerehæma gemære 1042 (18th) KCD 764
Neotheretune 1086 DB

Nudertona c. 1086 (1190) *EveB*
Netherton 1240 WoP
Noþerton 1256 *WoC*
'Lower farm,' probably because it lies at the foot of the
northern slope of Bredon Hill.

Norton-juxta-Kempsey

NORTON 81 F 12

Norðtun 989 (11th) KCD 671   *Nortona* 1208 Fees 37,
    (*juxta Wadeberwe*) 1275 *Ass*, (*juxta Kemeseye*) 1346 FA
'North farm.' It lies to the north-east of Kempsey and was
a chapelry of it.

BOTANY BAY (6")

Botenaysse 1299 (18th) *RBB*
If this identification is right, and the similarity of forms not
a mere coincidence, the true meaning of the name is '*Bōta's*
ashtree,' *v.* æsc. The modern form of the name is doubtless due
to the fact that it is in a remote corner of the parish.

HATFIELD

Hadfeld 1182 (18th) *RBB*   *Hathfeld* 1275 SR
Hatfeld 1275 *Ass*, 1321 Pat
'Heath-covered open land,' *v.* hæð, feld.

NEWLANDS FM

Newland 1220 *Ass* (p), 1612, 1654 WillsP
Self-explanatory.

WOOD HALL

Wodehall 1302 Wigorn, 1324 Ch, 1411 *FF*
Woodhall neere Norton 1655 WillsP
'Hall by the wood,' cf. Woodhall in Hallow *supra* 133.

Bredons Norton

BREDONS NORTON 92 A 13

Nortune 1086 DB   *Northton in Bredon* 1320 Pat
The village is north of Bredon.

CLATTSMORE (6″)

Clottesmor 972 (c. 1050) BCS 1282

The first element in this name would seem to be OE *clott*, used significantly or else as a pers. name. The word *clott*, denoting a clot or lump, seems occasionally, at least in alliterative poetry, to have been used of a heap or hill, and it is conceivable that here we have it used in a genitival compound, 'marshland of or marked by a hillock,' but more probably we have the word used as a pers. name, by origin a nickname, and that the name means '*Clott's* marshy ground.' For a similar pers. name cf. Cladswell *infra* 325.

HALL COURT (lost)

en la Hale 1275 SR   *Hall Court* 1649 FF, Comp, 1679 FF

v. healh. The name shows common confusion of *hale* and *hall* if, as seems probable, the first identification is correct.

Oddingley

ODDINGLEY 81 C 13

Oddingalea 816 (11th) BCS 256, 840 (11th) BCS 428
Odduncalea, Oddunggalea 963 (11th) BCS 1108
Oddunclei 11th Heming, 1086 DB
Oddingelega, Oddingeleye c. 1086 (1190) *EveA*, 1275 SR
Odungeleie c. 1086 (1190) *EveB*
Odigile 1182 (18th) *RBB*
Oddingesle 1255 *Ass*
Oddinghulle 1275 *Ass*
Oddyngley 1327 SR, 1535 VE
Odingley 1540–4 LP

'Clearing of the people of Odda,' *v.* leah. The existence of a compound like this makes it quite certain that Redin's doubts about an OE pers. name *Odda* are unfounded. It is a natural hypocoristic formation from an OE name in *Ord-*. The variant forms in *ung* rather than *ing* are noteworthy. Similar variation between patronymic derivatives in *ing* and *ung* is found in OGer, cf. Förstemann, PN 959.

FOLEYS WOOD (Old 1″)

This takes its name from Thomas *Foley*, who held the manor in 1661 (VCH iii. 459).

Overbury

OVERBURY 93 A 1

Uferebreodun vel Uferebiri 875 (11th) BCS 541
Uuera Breodun 964 (12th) BCS 1135
Oureberie 1086 DB
Ouerberga, Ouerberia c. 1086 (1190) *EveA & B*
Uuerbyre 1240 WoP
Overebure 1291 Tax, 1355 Pat

'Upper burh,' here probably referring to some old earthwork, perhaps the camp in North Conderton, which was a chapelry of Overbury, *v.* ufera, burh. 'Upper' because it lies some 200 ft. higher than Bredon.

EMMOTS (lost)[1]

This field-name survived in the 19th cent. and clearly corresponds to the *eomot sic* and *eomodes poll* of the bounds of Overbury (BCS 541). *Eomot sic* is a small stream running into the Carrant Brook (*v. sic*) and *eomot* is doubtless an error for ea-mot, 'river-meet.' *eomodes poll* would seem to be for *eamotes-pull*, 'pool or stream of (or by) the river-meet.'

MERECOMBE (local)

Mærcumb 875 (11th) BCS 541
Upper and Lower Mercu 1649 Surv

'Boundary valley,' *v.* (ge)mære, cumb.

PIGEON LANE (local)

This lane runs from the top of Overbury across to Conderton (*ex inf.* Mr Holland Martin) and must be connected with the '*Pigeon* House called *Hide*' of the 1649 Survey, and that in its turn with the 'Bursarius de *Hyda*' of the 1275 Subsidy Roll.

RUMBLESMORE (local)

This is a bit of black marshy land (*v.* mor) on the Kemerton

---

[1] For information with regard to this name and to Merecombe, Pigeon Lane and Rumblesmore we are indebted to Mr Holland Martin, F.S.A., Lord of the manor of Overbury.

boundary (*ex inf.* Mr Holland Martin). It corresponds to the *Rumballs Moore* of the 1649 Survey. That is almost certainly the *Rumwoldes mor* of BCS 541, which is on the bounds of Overbury, with lost intervening forms *Rumold-*, *Rumbold-*. There is also a *Romells Moore* in the 1649 Survey which would suit the OE form even better, but we do not know its site.

Pendock

PENDOCK 92 C 9

> *Peonedoc, Penedoc* 875 (11th) BCS 541-2
> *Penedoc* 967 (11th) BCS 1208, c. 1086 (1190) *EveA*
> *Pe(o)nedoc* 1086 DB
> *Penedoch* c. 1086 (1190) *EveB*
> *Penedo(c)k* 1275 SR
> *Pendoke* 1327 SR

It is difficult to make any suggestion with reference to this name. If the first element contains the Welsh *pen*, head, Professor Ekwall would parallel the curious forms *Peonnan*, *Peonnum* for Pen Selwood and *Peonho* for Pinhoe in the ASC, as examples of the same OE *eo* for *e*.

CLEEVE HOUSE

> *de la Clive, atte Clive* 1275 *Ass*, 1322 Ipm

> *v.* clif. The place stands on gently rising ground. Cf. Cleeve Prior *infra* 314.

CROMER GREEN

> *v.* Cromer Fm in Eldersfield *infra* 197.

PENDOCK MOOR

> *de Mora, atte More* 1275, 1327 SR (p)

> *v.* mor. Significant of the sense of this word in place-names is the fact that on the old 1″ map it is called Pendock *Marsh*.

PRIORS COURT (6″)

> The Prior of Little Malvern is mentioned in the Subsidy Rolls of 1275 and 1327 as having property here.

Wyre Piddle

WYRE PIDDLE 82 G 1

Pidele 1086 DB
Wyre Pidele 1208 Fees 36
Wirre 1349 Pat
Wyrepedell 1478 IpmR
Weripedell 1487 AD ii
Wyrepedyll al. *Werepedall* 1487 Pat
Wyerpedille 1495 Pat
Werepedill 1550 Pat

Wyre Piddle, like North Piddle, stands on Piddle Brook (*supra* 14) and takes its name from it. No suggestion can be offered with regard to the first element.

Queenhill

QUEENHILL [kwinəl] 92 A 11

Cunhill[1], *Chonhelme* 1086 DB
Cumhille, with *Cynhylle* written above 11th Heming
Cuhill 1175 P
Queinhull 1209 Fees 25
Kuhull 1210 RBE, (*Cuhull*) 1212 Fees 139
Kunhulle, Kinhulle 1221 *Ass*
Qwenhulle 1275 SR, *Ass*
Quenild 1299 Ipm (p), 1327 SR
Quenhull 1316 Ipm, 1423 IpmR
Quenehull 1329 Pat, 1535 VE
Queenhull Hy 6 IpmR
Quynhylle 1544 Marr
Quenehull al. *Quinhull* 1547 Pat

Professor Ekwall would take the first element to be OE *cyne*, 'royal.' Professor Zachrisson suggests that the name was OE *cūna-hyll, cȳna-hyll*, 'cows' hill,' with an alternative form *cū-hyll*, 'cow-hill.' Whatever the ultimate history of the name it is clear that at a later stage the name underwent corruption, but whether that was purely phonological, or due to some folk-etymologising process, whereby the name was associated with

---

[1] *Cumhille* is a possible reading.

'queen,' we cannot say. For a similar compound of OE *cȳna*, cf. Keynor (Sx) as explained by Zachrisson in *Mélanges de Philologie offerts à M. Johan Vising* (194)[1].

Redmarley D'Abitot

REDMARLEY D'ABITOT [ridmɑ·li] 92 C 8

Reodemæreleage 963 (11th) BCS 1109
Rydemæreleage 978 (11th) KCD 619
Ridmerlege, Ridmarleye, Rydmereleye 1086 DB, 1323 BM, 1327 SR
Rudmerlege, Rudmerley, Rudmarleye c. 1086 (1190) *EveA* & B, 1322 BM, (*Dabitot*) 1345 BM

This is clearly a compound of OE **hreod** and **mere** and **leah**, the whole name denoting 'clearing by the reed-mere,' cf. Redmarley *supra* 86. The feudal addition is derived from the family of Urse *d'Abitot* of whom, already in DB, two hides were held. The name *Abitot* probably derives from *Abbetot* in Normandy, a compound of NFr *tot* (= toft) and the pers. name *Api* or the common word *æble*, 'apple.' For *mære*, cf. the same form for *mere* in Layamon.

BLACKFORD MILL (6″)

Blacanmoresford 972 (c. 1050) BCS 1282

'Ford of the black marshy land,' an example of the genitival compound place-name and of the dropping of the middle element in a triple compound, as noted by Ritter (88, 155).

BURY COURT and MILL (6″)

Buristude 1275 SR (p)   *Bery House & Mill* 1521 LP
Bury Mill 1545 LP

All these names contain 'bury' used in the manorial sense (*v.* burh), and *Buristude* must refer to the site of the manorial house (*v.* stede). This may also lie behind *Berr* Ends (6″), half a mile to the east, on the Pendock boundary.

---

[1] This can only be true if we reject the identification of Keynor with the *Cymenesora* of the ASC (s.a. 477) and the *Cumenesora* of BCS 64. The site of the latter was probably a mile or two west of Keynor, and the medieval forms of Keynor itself are also against the identification.

CARPENTER'S FM (6")

The family of *Carpenter* is found in this parish in 1608, 1625 (QSR).

CHURCHES FM

Church Heyes 1549 Pat

'The hays or enclosures (*v.* gehæg) belonging to the church.'

GRIMER'S FM

The family of *Grimer* is found in the parish in 1275 (SR).

HOLFORD (lost)

Holeford 1221 *Ass*, 1275 SR, both (p)

'Hollow ford.'

INNERSTONE (6")

Inardeston(e) 1230 *FF*, 1275 SR (p), *et passim* to 1416 Ipm

Hynarston juxta Redmarley 1376 *FF*

Inardestone al. *In(n)arstone* 1380 BM

There can be no doubt that this is the farm of one *Isnard*, a name of continental origin derived from OGer *Isenhard*. This name was borne by an historic personage in Worcestershire, called variously *Isnardus* and *Inard*, who dates from about 1135 (VCH i. 330), and is associated with Himbleton and Hampton by Evesham. Whether he also had interests in Redmarley we cannot say.

KING'S GREEN

This probably takes its name from the family of *le King* recorded in 1275 (SR).

MURRELL'S END

Moreheldende, Morellynde 1502 BM

Murrowes End 1662 FF

This may contain the pers. name *Morel(le)* which is fairly common in Wo in the 15th and 16th cents., but no certainty is possible. It lies in a remote corner of the parish.

PAYFORD BRIDGE

Paiford, Payford 1221 *Ass* (p), 1413 BM

'Pæga's ford,' *v. Pæga* in Redin (106).

PLAYLEY GREEN

Pleyleye 1275 SR (p)

This may be 'play-clearing' (*v.* plega). It might also be *Pleganleage* (dat.), 'Plega's clearing,' *Plega* not being on actual record but a regular formation from one of the OE names in *Pleg-*, cf. Plealey (Sa).

Ripple

RIPPLE 92 A 11

Rippell 780 (12th) BCS 551, 1208 Fees 37
Rippel, Ryppel 1086 DB, c. 1086 (1190) *EveA & B*, 1275 SR, 1291 Tax, 1549 Pat
Repell 1255 Ch
Rippull 1408 *EcclVar*
Ripell 1549 Pat

Professor Ekwall explains this as from OE *rippel*, well attested in the charters and explained in B.T. Supplt. as 'coppice,' cf. EDD *s.v. ripple*. The root-idea is however 'strip,' as in Norw *ripel*, 'strip,' only later 'strip of wood, coppice.' As Ripple is on a tongue of land the earlier sense is more probable here. Ripple (K) similarly lies on a projecting spit of land.

HOLLY GREEN

atte Grene, de la Grene 1275, 1327 SR
Holly Green 1619 QSR

Self-explanatory.

NAUNTON

Newentone c. 1120 (17th) Hab, 1299 (18th) *RBB*
Nounton 1182 (18th) *RBB*
Newyntone 1275 SR, 1375 Wigorn
Newton 1373 Wigorn
Nawnton 1548 Pat

'New farm,' cf. Naunton Beauchamp *infra* 215 and Naunton in Severn Stoke *infra* 228.

RYALL

Ruyhale 1182 (17th) Hab, 1299 (18th) *RBB*, 1407 IpmR, 1431 FA
Ruhale 1221 *Ass*, 1275 SR, *Ass*, 1332 SR

Ryhale, Rihale 1239 *FF*, 1299 (18th) *RBB*
Rughale 1346 FA, 1407 BM
Ryall 1456 Pat, 1608 QSR, 1656 FF
'Rye-healh,' i.e. where rye grows.

SAXON'S LODE

Cestrelade 12th (17th) Hab, 1299 (18th) *RBB*
Cestraneslede 1202 P (p)
Sesterlade 1255 FF (p)
Sesteneslod 1270 Wigorn
Sistonlade 1298 Wigorn (p)
Cestaneslade 1298 Wigorn (p)
Sextaneslade 1299 (18th) *RBB*
Cesterneslade 1303 Wigorn (p)
Sestaneslade 1319 Pat (p)
la lode de Rippul 1347 Pat (p)
Sextons Loade 1636 VCH iii. 491

It is difficult to attain any certainty with regard to this name.
The suffix is OE (ge)lad and the reference is to the passage of
the Severn at this point, but the first element is less certain.
It is probable that it is really the OFr *Segrestein, Secrestein,*
'sacristan, sexton,' and that the passage in question was so called
from its use by some such person. The word, as we might
expect, assumes a bewildering variety of forms in ME (*v.* NED
s.v. *sexton*) which would serve largely to explain the ME forms
of the place-name. If this etymology is correct the history of
the word *sexton* is carried back some 150 years earlier than the
examples of it quoted in the NED[1].

Professor Zachrisson points out that folk-etymology may have
had its part in the history of this word through association with
the common O and ME *sester*, 'jar, measure for beer.'

SOUTHLEY (lost)

Suthlega 1176 P (p)   *Sutheley* 1275 SR   *Sudleye* 1327
SR (p)   *Southleye* 1332 SR, 1347 *FF* (p)
Self-explanatory.

---

[1] It is perhaps worthy of note that the sacrist of the Priory of Worcester
(WoP 110 b) drew revenues from a meadow by the Severn and, just before,
we hear that he drew revenues from Ripple. It may well be that the 'lode'
took its name from this land of the sacrist(an) on the Severn.

STRATFORD

Stretford 1182 (18th) *RBB*, 1319, 1347 Pat, 1649 Surv
'Road-ford.' This carries the Saltway or Worcester-Tewkesbury road over Ripple Brook. *v.* stræt, ford.

UCKINGHALL [ʌkindʒəl]

Ugginchalan 11th Heming
Ogginhale 1182, 1299 (18th) *RBB*
Uginhale, Ugynhale 1221 *FF*, 1286 Wigorn
Ukinghale 1241 *FF*
Hugungehale 1275 SR
Okynhale c. 1300 *EcclVar*
Hokynghale 1309 *FF*
Okyngealles 1548 Pat
Uckingale 1654 WillsP
Uckingell, Uckingill 1675 Ogilby, 1692 *FF*
Uckingshaw c. 1830 O

We should probably start from an OE *Ucca*, presumably a pet-form of OE *Ūhtred*. Such a name seems to lie behind *ucking echer* (BCS 300), *ucincg ford* (ib. 727), and *ucing cumb* (ib. 960), Uckington (Sa), DB *Uchintune*, and Uckfield (Sx). In that case we must take the *g* to be due to the common voicing of *k* to *g* between vowels illustrated *s.n.* Eggington (PN BedsHu 121). If we take the *Ugg-* forms to be the original ones then we must compare Ugford (W), BCS 1030 *ucganford*, which seems to contain a pers. name *Ucga*. The change from *Ugg-* to *Uck-* would however be very difficult to account for.

St Martins without Worcester

CUDLEY COURT

æt Cudinclea 974 (11th) BCS 1298
Cudelei 1086 DB, c. 1086 (1190) *EveB*
Cudelega, Cudele c. 1086 (1190) *EveA*, 1276 RH
Codeley(a) c. 1225 WoCh (p), 1275, 1327 SR, (*juxta Speches-leye*) 1312 *FF*
Cudley 1610 QSR

'*Cūda*'s clearing,' *v.* leah. The pers. name and the second element are connected by the same use of ing as in the ingtun names.

LEOPARD GRANGE[1]

Lipperd 969 (11th) BCS 1240, c. 972 (11th) KCD 681, c. 1020 BM Facs iv. 13

Lippard, Lyppard 1240 WoP, 1248 Pat, 1275 SR, 1300 (18th) Nash, 1535 VE

Leppart 1293 CompR

Lippards 1601 QSR, (al. *Leopards*) 1667 WoCh

Leppards 1651 WoCh

NUNNERY WOOD

This is on land once belonging to the nuns of Whiston.

PERRY WOOD (6″)

(*æt þære*) *pirian* 969 (11th) BCS 1240   *Pyriae*, c. 1020 BM Facs iv. 13

Pyrya, Pirya, Pirie c. 1086 (1190) *EveA* & *B*, (*juxta Wygorn*) 1307 *FF*

Pirywode 1370 Wulst

'Wood by the pear-tree,' *v.* **pyrige**. This is the last remains of the important manor of *Pirie*.

RONKSWOOD

This name is found in similar form in 1610 (QSR). It points to a pers. name (or nickname) derived from OE *ranc*, 'proud.'

SPARROW FIELDS FM (6″)

This may be the same as the *Sparwecroft* (c. 1255) of *RBB*, possibly from a person of that name. It is found as a pers. name in Stoulton and in Upton-on-Severn (1275 SR).

SWINESHERD[2] [swenzhəd]

Swinesheafde, Swynesheafdan 974 (11th) BCS 1298, 989 (11th) KCD 670

Swinesheved 13th (18th) Nash

Swineshead 1649 Surv, 1793 Cary

'Swine's head.' For this name and others of its type, cf. PN BedsHu 21. It is worthy of note in connexion with Bradley's

---

[1] The form *Lappewrte* in DB is an error, due to a curious confusion with Lapworth (Wa).

[2] This form is clearly a corrupt one, first found in Greenwood (1820), but has been accepted by the O.S. on local authority.

interpretation of names such as this, that one of the leets for Oswaldslow Hundred was held here (VCH iii. 516), cf. also Swineshead Hundred (Gl). Schröder has an interesting article on German names with this suffix in NoB xii. 110 ff. and quotes parallels such as *Hundshaupt, Mannshaupt, Rosshaupt*. English names of this type do not however lend support to his theory that in all these cases we have reference to a 'head' of a stream.

St Peters without Worcester

BARNESHALL FM

> *La Neweberne* 1327 Dugd i. 614   *Bernes* 1376 CompR
> *le Bernys* 1535 VE   *Barnes* 1545 LP, 1606 QSR, 1636 Wills
> *Barns Hall* 1789 Gough

v. bern. 'The barns.' In the cellarer's expenses (1376 CompR) there is an entry of a payment for looking after *boviculos* at *le Bernes*.

BATTENHALL FMS (6″)

> *Batenhale* 969 (11th) BCS 1240, 1295 *Bodl* 49, 1304 *FF*, 1335 Pat
> *Oldebatenhale* 1365 BM
> *Bathenhull* 1542 LP
> *Batenhall* 1545 LP
> *Batnold* 1557 Wills

'Bata's nook,' *v.* healh. The pers. name *Bata* is only recorded as a nickname in OE and in Batcombe (So), *Batancumb* (BCS 1174) and probably in Batton (D), *Bateton* 1254 *Ass*. For *Batnold* cf. Cakebole *infra* 236.

CHERRY ORCHARD

> *Shirreves Orchard* 1327 Pat

'Sheriff's orchard,' a curious corruption.

DIGLIS LOCKS [digli]

> *Dudeley* 1299 (18th) *RBB*
> *Dudleg, Dudley(a), Dudleye* 1232 Ch, c. 1275 WoCh, 1284, 1288 Wigorn, 1327 Pat, 1349 CompR

Duydeley 1375 CompR
Digley 1483 Pat
meadow called *Dudley* 1490 WoCh
Dydeley 1518 More, 1535 VE
Digeley, Dudeley 1546 LP
Diglis 1640–1663 Townsend
Dougleys al. *Diglis* 1649 Surv
Dugleys al. *Digleys* 1669 WoCh

This is the clearing (*v.* leah) of either *Dudda* or *Dydda*. In the former case we have the same curious phonetic development that is found in Dinnington (Nb), Dinton (Bk, W), which all go back to OE *Dunna*. For the change from *Didley* to *Digley* we may compare *Bignam* for Biddenham (PN BedsHu 26), where we have a similar change from *d* to *g* before a liquid. This place has naturally been much confused by indexers and editors with Dudley in the same county.

RED HILL

Redhill 1303 Wigorn, 1532 More   *Redehull* 1327 Pat

Self-explanatory. This was close to, if not identical with, the *readan ofre*, 'red bank,' of BCS 1240. The *readan wege* of KCD 670 ran eastwards from Redhill and is referred to as *Raddeweye* in 1255 (*For*). All take their name from the colour of the soil. In this neighbourhood also lay the *Rodeleah* of DB, *Radleie* in EveB, *Radeleya* in 1182 (18th) RBB. This also is the 'red' leah and the DB form must be an error.

TIMBERDINE FM

Timberden, Tymberden, Timberdene 1150 (c. 1240) *WoC*,
    1240 WoP, 1243 HMC v, App. 1, 302, 1275 SR, *Ass*,
    1292 Pat, 1299, 1307 Wigorn
Thimberdene c. 1250 WoCh
Tymberdenne 1260–1313 WoCh

'Timber-valley' (*v.* denu) or, as there is no distinctive valley here, perhaps we should lay stress on the *denne* form and take the second element to be OE *denn*, 'woodland pasture.'

Sedgeberrow

SEDGEBERROW[1] 93 A 3 [sedʒiberou]

Segcgesbearuue 777 (11th) BCS 223
Secgesbearuwe 964 (12th) BCS 1135
Secghæma gemære 1042 (18th) KCD 764
Seggesbarue 1086 DB
Sechesberga c. 1086 (1190) *EveA*
Segesberga c. 1086 (1190) *EveB*
Segesberewe c. 1150 Surv
Sekeberga, Secheberhe 1221 *Ass*
Seggesberwe 1275 SR, 1291 Tax, 1327 SR
Seggeburg 1284 Wigorn
Seggesburwe 1285 Wigorn
Seggebarowe 1420 Pat
Seg(e)barow 1535 VE
Sedgeberrowe 1649 Surv

'The grove of *Secg*' (*v.* bearu) with later corruption of the suffix through confusion with beorg. This seems the most probable interpretation, though in the bounds of Dumbleton (Gl) mention is made of a *Secgmere* (BCS 667) which looks like 'sedge-mere.' It is not easy to see how 'sedge' could be compounded with *bearu*, especially in a genitival compound, and the most likely explanation of the form is that *secgmere* is really a blunder for *secghæma gemære*, the form used in KCD 764 to denote 'bounds of the men of Sedgeberrow.'

Shipston-on-Stour

SHIPSTON-ON-STOUR[2] 82 J 10

Scepuuæisctune (also *vadum nomine Scepesuuasce*) c. 770 (11th) BCS 205
Scepwæsctun 964 (12th) BCS 1135
Scepwestun 1086 DB

---

[1] In the 1649 Survey we have *Bachlers* and a close and croft called respectively *Palmer* and *Wells*. These go back to the pers. names *le Bachiler*, *le Palmer* of the 1275 SR and *atte Welle* of the 1327 SR. There was also a *Batchelers* in Overbury, similarly going back to *la Bacheler* in 1275 SR.

[2] In the 1649 Survey we have a curtilage and a pasture called respectively *Mogg* and *Boggies*. These must take their name from the families of Robert *Mogge* in Armscott hard by (1275 SR) and Will. *Bogy* (1327 SR).

Scepwastona, Schepwastona c. 1086 (1190) *EveA* & *B*
Sepwestun 1240 WoP
Sip(p)estone 1275 SR, *Ass*
Chepston 1291 Tax
Schepestone 1299 (18th) *RBB*
Shepeston 1355 Pat
Shipston 1542 LP

'Farm by the sheep-wash,' *v.* sceap, wæsce, tun.

WADDON HILL (6")

Hwætedun 757 (11th) BCS 183
Hwætdune 11th Heming
Odden Hill 1649 Surv
Walden Hill c. 1830 O

'Wheat hill,' *v.* hwæte, dun. Cf. Whaddon (Bk) and Waddon (Sr).

Spetchley

SPETCHLEY 81 E 12

Spæcleahtun 816 (11th) BCS 356
Speacleahtun 816 (11th) BCS 357
æt Speclea 967 (18th) BCS 1204, 1086 DB
æt Spæclea 967 (11th) BCS 1205
Swæchæme gemære (sic) 978–92 (11th) KCD 683
Spechlega, Spechleie, Spechelegh c. 1086 (1190) *EveA* & *B*,
    1173 P, c. 1225 *Bodl* (p), 1246 *FF*
Spechesle(ye) 1271 Ch, 1275 SR, 1346 FA, 1446 BM
Spechestley 1327 SR
Specthesleye 1329 *FF*
Spechisley 1440 BM
Specheley, Spechley, Spetchley 1561–1627 Wills

There can be no doubt that Duignan (PN Wo 152) was right in associating this place with the proximity of Low Hill (*supra* 89) in Aston, which was the meeting-place of Oswaldslow Hundred on the borders of Spetchley parish, and interpreting the name as from late OE *spǽc*, 'speech' and leah. It is the open space where the speeches at the Hundred-meetings were made. The names stand in much the same relation to one another as Skirmett and Fingest (PN Bk 178, 180) and

Landmoth and Fingay Hill in the North Riding. Dr A. H. Smith has recently shown that these latter names are from OE *land-gemōt*, 'land-meeting place,' and ON *þinghaugr*, 'hill of assembly.'[1]

SNEACHILL

fnætes-wyllan (*sic*) 977 (11th) KCD 612

The *f* here is almost certainly an error for *s*. It may be noted, in the absence of any intermediate forms for the identification of this name, that *ts* would very probably appear later as *ch* and that in the unstressed syllable *wyll* might easily be reduced to *ill*. In favour of the identification is the fact that *snæteswyllan* is on the bounds of Wolverton and that Sneachill is near the Spetchley-Wolverton border. The first element is the pers. name found in Snettisham (Nf), DB *Snet(t)esham*. This is unknown elsewhere in England, but may be allied to the pers. names *Snato*, *Snazi* given by Förstemann (PN 1350).

Stock-and-Bradley

BRADLEY 82 C 2

Bradanlæh c. 730 (11th) BCS 153
Bradanlæg(e) 789 (11th) BCS 256, 962 (11th) BCS 1087
Bradanleage (dat.) 803 (11th) BCS 308
Bradinleah 11th Heming
Bradelege 1086 DB
Bradeleye juxta Feckeham 1275 FF
Other forms are without interest till
Bradeley et Stokke 1376 Pat   *Stoke Bradley* 1418 FF

'Broad clearing,' *v.* brad, leah and stocc. Stock Wood is in the neighbouring parish of Inkberrow.

Stoulton

STOULTON [stoutən] 81 F 12

Stoltun 840 (11th) BCS 430, 1086 DB
Stolton(a) c. 1086 (1190) EveB, 1208 Fees 36, 1275 SR, (*juxta Watberg*') 1276 FF, 1454 AD iii

---

[1] In the Assize Roll of 1275 appears a vill named *Spechull* in association with Whittington and Bredicote. These are by Spetchley and there can be little doubt that this is an alternative name for it. So also we have in *RBB* in the 1299 Survey, mention of a Thomas de *Spechehull* who held half a virgate of land in Kempsey, equally close to Spetchley.

Stowelton 1535 VE
Stulton 1532, 1554 Wills
Stoulton 16th Wills *passim*
Stowton, Stouton 1577 Saxton, 1675 Ogilby

The first element is clearly OE *stōl*, 'seat, throne,' but the sense of the compound is not clear. There can be but little doubt that this curious and otherwise unparalleled compound must be associated with the close neighbourhood of Low Hill or Oswaldslow (*supra* 89) and with Spetchley and *Spechull supra* 165–6 and Swinesherd *supra* 161, all of which have to do with the Hundred-courts of Oswaldslow. The stol must have been some such seat of authority as the Hurstingstone or Abbot's Chair in Huntingdonshire (PN BedsHu 203). 'juxta Watberg' from its position near Wadborough.

HAWBRIDGE

Haubruggestrete 13th (15th) *AOMB* 61
Hawbridge Green 1625 (18th) Nash

v. haga. 'Bridge by the hedge' or 'by the enclosure,' cf. Hawford *infra* 270. As the bridge is on the Stoulton-Pershore boundary the *haga* may be a boundary hedge. The *strete* is the Pershore-Worcester road.

MUCKNELL FM

Mucenhil 1086 DB
Mucheulla c. 1086 (1190) *EveA*
Mukehulla c. 1086 (1190) *EveB*
Mukenhull 1208 Fees 36, 1255 *Ass*, 1316 Ipm
Mokenhulle 1275, 1327 SR, 1346 FA
Mucknill 1649 Surv
Muckenhill 1892 Kelly

'Mucca's hill,' *v.* hyll.

STONEBOW and STONEBOW BRIDGE (6″)

Stonebow 1574 Pat

This is the name given to the bridge over the *Hymelbroc*. Later the name of the stream was altered to fit the bridge and it is now called *Bow* Brook. *Stonebow* for an arch of stone is

similarly used in the name of one of the gates of Lincoln.
Cf. also *Stanbowe* in Halesowen Ct Rolls (1282). *v.* Bow Brook
supra 10.

WOLVERTON, UPPER and LOWER

Wulfrincgtun 977 (11th) KCD 612
Wulfrin(g)tun 984 (11th) KCD 645
Ulfrintun 1086 DB
Wlfrintona c. 1086 (1190) *EveA & B*, 1221 *FF*
Wulūton 1175 P (p)
Wolfrintona, Wolfrynton 1208 Fees 36, 1316 Ipm, 1346,
    1428 FA
Wulurinton 1221 *Ass*
Wolferton 1275 SR, 1332 Ipm
Ouer and *Nether Wolfreton* 1318 *FF*
Wollerton 16th VCH iii. 534
'*Wulfhere's* farm,' *v.* ingtun.

Teddington[1]

TEDDINGTON 93 B 1

Teottingtun 780 (11th) BCS 286
Teotingtun 780 (c. 1000) Middleton 202
Teotintun 964 (12th) BCS 1135, 1086 DB
Teottincgtun 969 BCS 1233
Teodintun, Tidingctun 977 (11th) KCD 617
Teothintun, Theotinctun 11th Heming
Tetintona c. 1086 (1190) *EveA*
Tedintona c. 1086 (1190) *EveB*, 1201 Cur, 1275, 1327 SR,
    1535 VE
Totinton 1202 Cur
Todinton 1203 Cur
Tedington 1246 *FF*
Thedinton 1355 Pat

'Teotta's farm,' *v.* ingtun, cf. Tettenhall (St), *Teotanheale*
ASC s.a. 910. The name *Tēotta* is not on record, but we have

---

[1] There has been much confusion between Teddington and Alstone (Wo)
and Tiddington and Alveston (Wa), which were also estates belonging to
the Bishops of Worcester. This was not confined to modern editors. The
form in the second reference is altered from an earlier *Tidingtun*.

Teoda and (in place-names) its diminutive *Teodec*. These last are clearly pet-forms from names in *þēod-*. There must have been another pet-form with *t* for *d*, and indeed the forms of this place-name suggest that both were in use here. Such alternative forms with voiced and unvoiced consonants respectively are not uncommon.

BARHAM (lost)

Bereham al. *Bergham* 1291 Tax
Barham 1772 T, 1789 Gough

'Homestead by the hill,' *v.* beorg, ham. Cf. Barham (PN BedsHu 233).

Throckmorton

THROCKMORTON 82 F 1

Throcmortune 11th (18th) Hickes ii. 299
Trotemertona (sic) 1175 P
Trochemerton 1176 P
Trokemerton 1176 P, 1208 Fees 37, 1254 *FF*
Trocmaretona 1227 Bracton
Throkemerton 1227 *FF*, 1275 SR
Trokemareton 1229 Ch
Trochmarton 1233 *FF*
Trokemertun 1240 WoP
Trokemarton 1255 *Ass*
Throkemarton 1325 Ipm, 1396 *Bodl* 78, 1415 Pat (p)
Throgmerton, Throgmarton, Throkmorton 1436–51 Pat
Throgmarton 1577 Saxton
Frogmorton 1696 Marr

This is a difficult name. If, as seems probable, we ought to take the first part to be *throcmer(e)*, it is probably more than a coincidence that there is a place called *þrocmere* (BCS 508), with variant forms *þorcmere, þorocmere* (BCS 1080), now Rockmoor Pond (Ha). This is a pond, and by Throckmorton there are two old moated areas. If so, it would seem that the whole name must mean 'farm by the *þroc*-mere.' The exact sense of this word is uncertain, but the late Henry Bradley suggested to Dr G. B. Grundy (*Arch. Journ.* lxxvi. 186) that the word was connected with the dialectal *thurrock* and meant drain. This is found apparently by itself in Thurrock (Ess), DB *Thurruca*, *Turroc*.

It is of course possible that the first element was really *þrocmor* later weakened to *Throcmer-*. The element *þroc*, in the sense suggested, would be equally appropriate with mor. Note also Drockbridge (Ha), *þrocbrigg* in BCS 393 and *Throkbach* (*v.* bæc) in Alvechurch (*RBB*).

TILESFORD FM

Tuwelesbrugge 1229 Ch   *Tylesford* 1634 QSR
Tiles Hall 1892 Kelly

There is very little to go upon here, but comparison with the forms of Tilsworth (PN BedsHu 133) suggests that the original name was *þȳfeles-brycg*, 'the bridge of one Thyfel,' a name the existence of which can well be assumed from the evidence set forth for Tilsworth.

Tibberton

TIBBERTON 81 D 12

Tidbrihtincgtun 978–92 (11th) KCD 683
Tidbertun 1086 DB
Tibertonie c. 1086 (1190) *EveB*
Titbrictune c. 1105 (18th) Thomas
Tibrittune, Thibrictun 1240 WoP
Thibrithon, Tibryton 1243 Cl, 1275 SR
Tiburtone 1248 Pat
Tybrichton 1255 *Ass*
Tybresthone 1280 *For*
Tibrinton 1283 Wigorn
Tyberton, Tiberton 1535 VE, 1542 LP

There were probably two forms of this name, *Tīdbeorht-tūn*, 'Tidberht-farm,' and, with connecting ing, *Tīdberhting-tūn*, cf. Wolverton (PN Bk 27). The same name is found in Tibberton (Gl) and Tyberton (He).

EVELENCH FM

Yveling, Iueling 1146–89 (c. 1240) *WoC*, 1240 WoP, 1262 *For*, 1280 *For* (p), 1327 SR (p)

Heveling 1221 *Ass* (p)
Eveling 1340 NI (p)

There are also names *Diveling* and *Deueling* in 1275, 1327 (SR) which are probably for *d'Eveling* or *d'Iveling*. If we compare the forms for this name with those given for Whitlinge *infra* 246 it is clear that the final element is really OE hlinc. This suits the site of Evelench, which is on a small hill. The first part is probably the OE pers. name *Eofa*, hence 'Eofa's hill,' cf. Evesham *infra* 262.

MOOR END

de Mora 1240 WoP   *Moore End* 1649 Surv

'Marshy land,' *v.* mor.

RAVENSHILL FM

Ræfneshyl 816 (11th) BCS 356
Reueneshell 1167 P
Revenshull 1240 WoP, 1257 FF (p), 1266 Pat (p)
Reven(e)shull 1257 FF (p), 1292 Wigorn, 1327 SR, both (p)
Raueneshull 1280 *For*
Ravenshill 1689 D

Probably 'hill of Hræfn' rather than 'raven's hill.' The pers. name *Hræfn* was certainly native English as well as a common loan-name from Scandinavian. Cf. PN Bk 61.

Tidmington

TIDMINGTON 93 A 10

æt Tidelminctune 977 (11th) KCD 614
Tidelminton, Tydelminton 11th Heming, c. 1086 (1190) *EveB*, 1208 Fees 37, 1255 *Ass*, 1428 Pat
Tidelmintun 1086 DB
Tidelintun 11th Heming
Tydaminton 1252 Ch
Tydelington 1327 SR
Tydylmynton 1431 FA, 1535 VE
Tidmington 16th Wills
Tidillmington 1685 FF

'Tidhelm's farm,' *v.* ingtun.

Tredington

TREDINGTON 82 H 10

> *Tredin(c)gtun* 757 (11th) BCS 183, n.d. (12th) BCS 1320
> *Tyrdintun* 964 (12th) BCS 1135
> *Tredinctun* 978 (11th) KCD 620, 1086 DB
> *Tredintun* 991 (11th) KCD 676, 1203–12 (c. 1250) *WoC*
> *Tredinton* c. 1086 (1190) *EveA* & *B*, 1208 Fees 38, 1275 SR

'Tyrdda's farm,' *v.* ingtun. This would seem to be made clear by the statement in BCS 183 that the land had the same boundaries as the land held before by 'comes Tyrdda.' The relation of the *Tyrd-* and *Tred-* forms is not however clear. *Tyrd-* should have yielded later *Tryd-*, *Trud-* rather than *Tred-*, and it may be that the form *Tyrdintun* is really an alternative for the usual *Tredington*, due to the fact that the estate was associated with one *Tyrdda* at one stage in its history. On the other hand, it should be noted that, apart from the OE pers. name *Tredewudu*, there is no evidence of the possibility of such a name as *Treda* in OE except in the not very distant Tredington (Gl). It may be that the forms of that name have influenced those of the Worcestershire name[1].

ARMSCOTT

> *Eadmundescote* 1042 BM Facs iv. 23
> *Edmundescote* 1166 RBE *et passim* to 1428 FA
> *Admundescote* 1323 Pat, 1327 *FF*, 1332 Misc
> *Admyscote* 1366 Pat, 1535 VE
> *Armscote* 1544 LP

'*Ēadmund's* cottage(s),' *v.* cot.

BLACKWELL

> *Blacwælle* 964 (12th) BCS 1135
> *æt Blace Wellan* 978 (11th) KCD 620
> *Blacawella* 11th Heming, 1159–81 (c. 1250) *WoC*
> *Blachewelle* 1086 DB

'Black stream or spring,' *v.* blæc, wielle.

---

[1] In the bounds of Shipston-on-Stour in Heming (347), where they begin to be common to Shipston and Tredington, there is a reference to *Tordeland*. It is tempting to think that there is some etymological connexion with *Tyrdintun* which is quite possible if we take *Torde* to be an 11th cent. spelling for *Turde* from *Tyrdan*.

DARLINGSCOTT

Derlingiscote 1272 Ipm
Derlingescote 1275, 1327 SR, 1273 Ipm, 1284 Wigorn, 1331 BM
Dorlingescote 1283 *FF*
Dorlyngscote 1323 Pat, 1535 VE, 1549 Pat
Darlingscot 16th Wills
Durlingscot 1724 Marr

'*Dēorling's* cottages,' *v*. cot. This name is not on record in OE, but there was a moneyer of Henry 1 named *Derling*, and a certain *Derling* had property in Lincoln in the reign of John. The present place-name may have arisen after the Conquest.

LONGDON FM

æt Longandune 969 (11th) BCS 1243
Langandun ib.
Longedun 1086 DB
Langedun 11th Heming
Langeton 1255 *Ass*
Longedon 1275, 1327 SR, 1297 Wigorn, 1535 VE
Longdon Travers 1398 Pat, 1654 FF

'Long hill,' *v*. lang, dun. The Travers family were here in 1166 (RBE). Also called Longdon *Parva* in the 17th cent. (VCH iii. 546) in distinction from the Pershore manor of Longdon, not far distant (*v. infra* 208).

NEWBOLD-ON-STOUR [noubəld]

Nioweboldan (dat.) 991 (11th) KCD 676
Neubold 1208 Fees 38
Newebold super Stoure 1364, 1392 Pat
Nobold 1695 Marr

The *an* of the first form must represent the dat. pl., so the name must be 'at the new buildings,' *v*. niwe, bold.

TALTON FM

Tætlintun 991 (11th) KCD 676
Tadlington, Tadlynton 1175 P (p), 1327 SR, 1346, 1428 FA
Tatlinton, Tattlynton 1208 Fees 38, 1227 *FF*, 1272 Ipm (p), 1275 SR, 1304 Orig, 1332 SR, 1364 Pat

Tatleston 1275 *Ass*
Tadlington, Tadlyngton 1311 Cl, 1535 VE
Talton al. *Tadlington* 1702 FF

'Farm of *Tǣtel*,' *v.* ingtun. The name *Tatel* is on record, a regular diminutive of OE *Tāta*, perhaps for *Tātol*. *Tǣtel* shows an alternative diminutive suffix causing mutation of the stem vowel. Cf. the name *Tǣtica* which is on record with a different diminutive suffix.

Upton-on-Severn[1]

Upton 81 J 11

Uptun 897 (11th) BCS 575, 962 (11th) BCS 1088
Upentona c. 1086 (1190) *EveB*
Optun 1189 (c. 1240) *WoC*
Upton super Sabrinam 1327 SR

'Farm (further) up the Severn,' in relation to Ripple, of which it once formed part.

Buryfield (6″)

Buryfeld 1416 IpmR

The 'bury' is perhaps an earthwork marked on the 6″ map.

Longdon Heath

atte Hethende 1327 SR

Southend Fm

de Suthende 1275 SR

Self-explanatory. There was once a *Northende* (1275 SR).

Tiltridge Fm (6″)

Telderugg, Teldruge 1275 *Ass*, SR (p)
Tylkcrege, Tyltryge 16th VCH iv. 215
Teteridge 1892 Kelly

There can be little doubt that the first element is OE *teld*, 'tent, pavilion,' possibly in the gen. pl. In *Sir Gawayne and the Greene Knight* (l. 11) the word is used in the wider sense of habitations. What dwellings may be referred to it is impossible to say. The only alternative would be to take it as OE *Teolta*,

---

[1] In Pershore Hundred since 1760 (VCH iii. 240).

a pers. name only evidenced from the place-name *teoltan-ford* (BCS 699).

Warndon

WARNDON 81 D 12

> *Wermedun* 1086 DB
> *Warmindone* c. 1086 (1190) *EveA*
> *Warmendone* c. 1086 (1190) *EveB*, 1240 WoP
> *Warmentone* 1182 (18th) *RBB*
> *Warmedon(e)* 1208 Fees 36, 1275 SR, c. 1285 *Bodl* 13, 1374 Wigorn
> *Warmyndon* 1262 *For*
> *Warminthone* 1280 *For*
> *Warmydone* 1327 SR
> *Warrenton* 1577 Saxton, (or *Wardon*) 1763 Bowen
> *Warndon* 16th Wills *passim*

This is probably from *Wǣrman-dun* or *Wǣrming-dun* with a pers. name *Wǣrma*, a pet-form for *Wǣrmund*, an ancient Mercian name found also in *Wǣrmundingford* in Clopton in St Johns (KCD 649). Cf. further *wǣrman dene* (BCS 1282) in the bounds of Powick.

SUNDERLAND (lost)

In the bounds of Cudley (BCS 1298), the boundary goes along a *strǣt*, which is the original Worcester-Stratford-on-Avon road, thence to a spring and then *on sunderlond*. There can be no doubt that this is the curious peninsula-like projection of Warndon parish into the estate of Cudley. It practically touches the above-mentioned road. This then is 'separate land,' *v.* sundor and cf. Cinders Wood *supra* 84.

TROTSHILL

> *Trotte(s)well* c. 1086 (1190) *EveB*, 1240 WoP, 1262, 1280 *For* (p), 1552 Wills, 1667 WoCh
> *Croteswelle* (sic) 1182 (18th) *RBB*
> *Trottuswelle* 1332 *SR* (p)[1]

---

[1] This appears as *Croccuswelle* in the printed edition, but Miss Scroggs has collated it with the original MS, and the form here given is the correct one and disposes of any suggestion to associate this with Crowle as is done by Duignan (PN Wo 47).

Trotsall, Trotswell 1649 Surv
Trots Hall c. 1830 O

This is a compound of **wielle** and the pers. name *Trott* found in *Trottesclif* (BCS 253) now Trotterscliffe (K) and Trotsworth in Egham (Sr). It may be a pet-form for an OE name in *Torht-*.

Little Washbourne[1]

LITTLE WASHBOURNE 93 B 2

æt Wassanburnan 780 (11th) BCS 236
æt Wasseburne 780 (c. 1000) Middleton 202
UUassanburna 840 (11th) BCS 430
Wassaburna 840 (c. 1000) Middleton 207
Wasseburne 977 (11th) KCD 616, 1203 Cur, 1240 WoP, 1259 Ipm, 1275 SR, 1284 Wigorn
Waseburne 1086 DB
Wassebourne 1286, 1295 Wigorn, 1327 SR, 1346 FA, 1347 Cl, 1428 FA
Wasshebourn 1340 NI
Wasshburn 1348 Cl
Knyghts Wassheborne 1492 Ipm

Professor Zachrisson would explain this name (*English PN and River-Names*, etc. 37–8) as containing the genitive of OE *wāse*, 'mud,' explaining the double *s* as a variant of single *s* after the Anglo-Norman fashion, or as a device to show that the long vowel has been shortened, such as is found in OE texts from the transition period. This cannot be true of Washbourne, for spellings are found with double *s* in a MS which is definitely of the end of the 10th cent. in the forms from the fragmentary Worcester cartulary, while the others come from a cartulary in which it is very doubtful if spellings of the kind postulated by Zachrisson are to be found. For this name we must therefore still turn to a pers. name *Wassa*. For the possibility of such a pers. name reference may be made to the evidence quoted *s.n.* Washingley (PN BedsHu 200) and to the *wassandun* of BCS 520 which was the name of a down in Hants. We may add further that while the *wassam* (sic) *hamme* of BCS 762 may have to be associated with *wāse* or *wæsce* as

---

[1] Transferred to Gloucestershire in 1844.

denoting low-lying well-watered land, such an explanation seems very improbable for *wassandun* (BCS 389, 520).

It is clear that at a later stage in its history the first element in Washbourne was confused with the common *wash* and re-fashioned accordingly.

Welland

WELLAND 81 J 9

Wenelond 1182 (18th) *RBB*
Weneland 1190 (1335) Ch, 1233 Cl
Wenland c. 1197 (18th) Thomas, 1649 FF
Wentland 1275 SR
Wennelond 1299 (18th) *RBB*
Wenlond(e) 1326 SR, 1428 FA, 1535 VE
Wenlone 1328 *FF*

No definite suggestion can be made with regard to this name. There is evidence for OE pers. names in *Wēn-* (*v.* Searle), and there may have been a pet-form *Wen(n)a* formed from such (cf. *Wennanstan* BCS 476). This would suggest interpreting the name as '*Wēna's* land,' *v.* land. On the other hand it may be more than a coincidence that the Welland Brook and the Wynd-brook (*v. supra* 17), earlier *Wenbroc*, join one another and flow into the Severn, in which case we probably have to do with some non-English element.

DAUNCIES (lost)

Dauncies 1463 Cl

Nothing is known of the origin of this name, but it looks as if it were manorial and derived from someone taking his name from Dauntsey (W), or it may be for *Daunce's* and derived from the common Worcestershire name *Daunce*.

HOOK FM

wood called *le Hooke* 1545 LP

The wood was doubtless so called from its shape.

THE LOVELLS

This is named from the family of Thomas *Lovell* mentioned in 1627 and 1633 (QSR).

MUTLOWS (not on map)

William *Mucklow* bought the manor of Dauncies in 1515 (VCH iii. 555) and his name is preserved here. Interchange of *t* and *k* is common, cf. Nackington (K) earlier *Natindun.* The Mucklow family took their name from Mucklow in Halesowen *infra* 297. The name is preserved in Kelly's Directory for 1892, but is not on the map.

Whittington

WHITTINGTON 81 E 12 [hwitəntən]

 Hu(u)itingtun 816 (11th) BCS 357
 Hwitintune 989 (11th) KCD 670
 Widintun 1086 DB
 Witintona, Wytinton c. 1086 (1190) *EveA,* c. 1235 *Bodl*
     18 *b,* c. 1245 ib. 19, c. 1255 ib. 28
 Whitenton, Whytinton, Whytyntone 1227 *FF,* 1327 SR,
     1333 *Bodl* 58, 1365 BM
 Wiþindon c. 1240 *WoC*

'*Hwita's* farm,' *v.* ingtun. DB and *WoC* are curiously in agreement in going astray over this name.

CROOKBARROW HILL

 Cruchulle 1182 (18th) *RBB*
 Crokeberewe, Crokeberghe, Crokberewe c. 1225 Wulst, 1275
     Ass, 1314 *FF,* 1330 Ch
 Cruckebire c. 1255 Ipm
 Crickeboreg, Cricheboreg 13th Wulst
 Crokkeberew, Crokkeberow c. 1245 *Bodl* 19 (p), 1275 SR,
     1306 Wigorn, 1328 WoCh
 Crikkeberewe 1329 *FF*
 Crok(e)barwe 1330 Ch, 1453 IpmR
 Cruckberwe 1330 Pat
 Crokebarow 1527 More

There is no doubt that here we have OE beorg suffixed to the British **crouka* (Welsh *crug*), both alike meaning 'barrow.' Crookbarrow Hill is described in VCH (iii. 514) as 'a very large elliptical mound with an artificial top reputed to be sepulchral.' That is doubtless what is referred to in the name. *Cruchulle* is an interesting variant. Cf. Churchill *supra* 106.

ERSFIELD FM

In the bounds of Wolverton-Pershore (KCD 612 and BCS 1282) we have a stream-name *yrse*. There is a stream which flows south through Spetchley Park, past Ersfield Fm and ultimately forms part of the boundary between Stoulton (Wolverton) and Pershore Holy Cross. It is clear therefore that Ersfield is the 'open-land by the *Yrse*-stream' (*v.* feld). *v.* Erse, R., *supra* 11.

Wichenford

WICHENFORD 81 C 9

Wiceneford 11th Heming
Wicheneford, Wycheneford 1208 Fees 37, 1235 *FF*, 1240 WoP,
   c. 1270 *Bodl* 41, 1288 Wigorn, 1291 Tax
Wychenford 1340 NI, 1346 FA
W(h)ichingford 1594 VCH iii. 562, 1675 Ogilby
Winchingfford 1569 VisitWo

This is probably from OE *Hwiccena-ford*, 'ford of the *Hwicce*,' with the common gen. pl. form in *-ena* found in tribal-names. For this people *v.* Introduction xv. Why the name of the people should have been attached to so unimportant a ford it is difficult to say. The only suggestion that can be made is that at an early time it was the first ford in *Hwiccan* territory reached by a traveller from the territory of the *Magasætan* (the present Herefordshire).

ABBINTON'S FM (6")

Abyndon 1316 Ipm, 1327, 1332 SR, 1340 NI, all (p)
Abington 1651 FF (p)

This may be a true name of the manorial type deriving from a family which ultimately came from Abingdon (Berks), but there is no certainty. The family of the Worcestershire historian Habington belonged here. They claimed association with Abington in Cambridgeshire, but as it is clear that there was a family of *Abyndon* in Wichenford from the 13th cent. onwards and Abington (C) is a *-ton* and not a *-don* name, the genealogy claimed is very doubtful.

ARUNDLE'S FM (6")

Arundel, Arondel 1275, 1327 SR (p)   *Arundels* 1616 Terrier

This is almost certainly of the manorial type, from a family deriving their name from Arundel (Sx).

BIRCHEND FM (6")

at Byrethe (sic) 1299 (18th) *RBB*   *atte Birche* 1327 SR

Self-explanatory.

BURYENDBUSH FM (6")

la Buriende 13th VCH iii. 564

BURYEND TOWN

atte Burrytown 1332 SR   *Burying Town* 1820 G, c. 1830 O

These two *bury*-ends may mark the two 'ends' of the north part of the *bury* or manor of Wichenford.

COBHOUSE FM

This takes its name from the family of *Cobbe* who appear in the Subsidy Roll of 1327.

COCKSHOOT FM

Cocscute c. 1230 (c. 1240) *WoC*

Cf. Cockshot in Cakemore *infra* 293, and *Cocscute* in Knighton (*WoC*). In both these cases we have the obsolete word *cocksho(o)t*, explained in the NED as 'glade in a wood through which woodcocks etc. might dart or "shoot," so as to be caught by nets stretched across the opening.' This name appears in various forms as *Cockshot(t)*, *Cockshut(e)*, *Cockshutt* in some thirteen Worcestershire parishes on the present-day map. It is also common in Gl, He (cf. PN Gl 46, PN He 46). In addition to the forms for Cockshoot and Cockshot we have in the Kyre Park Charters an unidentified *Cokkesheotefeld* in Kyre, in the 13th cent. These forms carry back the history of the word some 250 years further than the forms in the NED and tend to show that the proper form of the suffix was OE *scēot*.

After this article was written, an article by Professor Zachrisson appeared in ZONF ii. 146, which demonstrates the existence, side by side with the familiar sceat in place-names, of a second form *sciete*, with much the same sense. He shows, on the same lines as those in our article, that derivation from *shoot* will not explain the early forms of *Cockshoot* and suggests that the name was originally *coc-scīete*, 'corner into which the cocks were driven,' or the like. *scīete* would explain the later forms equally well with *scēot*, and it is difficult to suggest a sense for the latter.

Mr St Clair Baddeley tells us of a Cockshoot Wood under Longridge in Painswick (Gl). This land was held (c. 1420) by the rent of two woodcocks from Lord Talbot, by the then vicar of Painswick. This is an interesting proof that the *cocks* in such names were really *woodcocks*.

COLKETT'S FM (6″)

Coldecote 1275, 1327 SR (p)   *Coldcot* c. 1830 O
Calketts 1892 Kelly

'Cold or exposed cottages,' *v.* **ceald, cot**. Almost certainly only pseudo-manorial.

HORSAGE FM

Ossage 1884 VCH iii. 562

Nothing can be done with this name, but we may compare Ossage Lane (Sa), earlier *Hosage*, for which Professor Zachrisson (*English PN and River-Names*, etc. 15) hazards a possible association with *wāse*, 'mud.'

KING'S GREEN

This probably contains the family name (*le*) *King* found in 1275 (SR).

MALLENDER'S COTTAGE (6″)

In the Collecta Caleyana in the Birmingham Reference Library there is a form *The Mallinder* for this property, taken from a 16th cent. terrier in the Worcester Consistory Court. In Davenport's *Washbourne Family* 187 there is a lease in which it is spoken of as 'The two Malenders.' It is clear from these forms that the possessive form is an error and that the name contains the word *malender, mallander*, usually used in the plural, the name of a horse-disease. Presumably the ground was so called from some outbreak of it.

P

POOLFIELDS (6″)

Pull, pulles heofod (sic) 779 (11th) BCS 233
terra de Pulle 1240 WoP   *la Pulle* 1275 SR (p)
Poole Field 1649 Surv

The pull is the stream which forms the boundary of Doddenham and Wichenford parish and afterwards of Broadwas and
Wichenford. It is probably the same as the *Kaderapull* of
BCS 319, in the bounds of Wick which then seems to have
included Cotheridge, Wichenford, Little Witley and Holt.

RUGG'S PLACE (6″)

Rugge, de la Rugge, othe Rugge, atte Rugge 1208 Fees 37, 1275,
    1327 SR
le Rughal 1343 Ipm, 1346 FA
Ruggehalle 1390 Cl
Rugehale 1436 Ct
Ridge Hall 1556 IpmR

If, as seems probable, this identification is correct, the modern
form is corrupt and the name should really be *Rudge* place. In
earlier days it was apparently first 'ridge,' then 'ridge nook'
(*v.* healh), and then with the common confusion of *hale* and *hall*,
'ridge-hall.' Ridgend Fm to the SE of Rugg's Place probably
marks the end of the 'ridge' estate and preserves a more usual
form of this name.

WOODEND FM

There was a Peter de *Bosco* here in 1275 and Habington
(i, 503) quotes a deed of 1471 relating to the Manor of *Wood-
hend*. Nash calls the farm 'the Wooden farm' (ii. 458).

WOODHALL FM and WYATS COPSE (6″)

Wodehalle 1256 (c. 1300) WoC
Wyardswodehalle 1486 WoCh

This estate, 'the hall by the wood,' was in the possession of
the widow of John *Wyard* in 1299 (VCH iii. 563). *Wyats* is
a corruption of earlier *Wvards*.

Little Witley

LITTLE WITLEY 81 B 9

Wittlæg 964 (12th) BCS 1135
Witleah, Witleag 969 (11th) BCS 1242, c. 972 (11th) KCD
682
Wihtlega 11th Heming
Witlege 1086 DB
Wit(er)lega c. 1086 (1190) *EveA*
Widelega 1187 P (p)
(Parva) Wyttelege 1249 *FF*
Wytele Minor 1275 *Ass, Litelwytele* 1388 IpmR
Little Whytley 1550 Pat

The early forms of this name and Great Witley *supra* 86 make it certain that the first element is not the adjective hwit, for we should have had that adjective in the weak oblique case, *hwitan*. The form quoted from Heming suggests very strongly that the first element is OE *wiht*. For this element in OE place-names, cf. Great Whyte (PN BedsHu 216) and the evidence there, and ib. xli. It is there suggested that the word *wiht* may in OE have been used of a 'curve or bend in a stream.' Shrawley Brook as it runs up from Little to Great Witley has a somewhat sinuous course, and it may well be that the whole leah or clearing originally took its distinctive first element from one or other of these well-marked bends in the stream which goes through it. Wetmoor (St), whose early forms suggest a similar first element (Duignan PN St 170) lies in a bend of the Trent. Whitehall Fm in Tackley (O), KCD 709 *Wihthull*, lies in a well-curved hollow at the foot of a hill.

III. HUNDRED OF PERSHORE

This hundred was assessed at 298 hides and consisted of 5 manors with a hidage of 100 belonging to Pershore Abbey, and 21 manors, with 1 hide at Droitwich, total hidage 198, belonging to the Abbey of Westminster. These last originally belonged to Pershore, but were taken by Edward the Confessor for the founding of the Abbey of Westminster. The hundred as such is not mentioned in DB, the land being assessed as 'the land of St Mary of Pershore' and of 'St Peter of Westminster.' The hundred-courts were held in Pershore itself, at Rhydd Green and at Pinvin (*v.* VCH iv. 3).

The greater part of this Hundred was continuous, stretching from Pershore to the Hereford boundary on the Malvern Hills, but there were seven isolated areas belonging to it. There seems to be no record of an original division into three hundreds.

Abberton

ABBERTON 82 E 2

Eadbrihtincgtun 972 (c. 1030) BCS 1282
Edbretintune 1086 DB
Edbritone, Edbrytthone, Edbryton 1086 DB, 1280 *For*, 1290 Wigorn
Eadbrithtona c. 1086 (1190) *EveA*
Edbricton c. 1215 (15th) *AOMB* 61
Edbristone 1275 SR
Eadburiton 1283 (15th) *AOMB* 61
Ebrightone, Ebrihton 1291 Tax, 1305 Wigorn
Adbrighton, Adbryton 1297, 1377 Pat, 1340 NI
Abburton 1535 VE
Abryton vel *Abburton* 1544 LP

'*Ēadbeorht's* farm' (*v.* ingtun). The same pers. name is found in Ebberston (Y), Ebrington (Gl).

KETCHES FM (6″)

Kedges Fm 1892 Kelly

This may contain the pers. name *Keche* recorded in Old Swinford (1327 SR) and in Tewkesbury (1509 Wills).

Alderminster

ALDERMINSTER 82 G 9

Aldermanneston 1169 P, 1226 *FF*, 1255 *FF*, *Ass*
Audremaneston 1251 Ch
Aldermonnston, Aldremonston 1255 *Ass*, 1275 SR, 1291 Tax
Aldremeston, Aldremuston, Aldermeston 1327 SR, 1338 Wigorn, 1340 NI, 1344 AD iv, 1432 Ct
Alderminster, Aldermynster 1450–1650 Wills, 1535 VE
Aldermaston 16th, 17th Wills *passim*, 1765 Ogilby, 1787 Cary

'Farm of the *ealdormann*,' *v*. tun and cf. Aldermaston (Berks) and Aldermanbury (PN BedsHu 11). Later the name underwent a curious corruption.

BARN HILL COPPICE (6″)

Bernewelle 13th AD iii

As both these are by Goldicote, they perhaps took their name from the same barn (*v.* bern) or from the same man named *Beorna*, or the *Barnhill* may be a corruption of *Barnwell* after it was reduced to *Barnell*.

COOMBE FM

Longecumb 1312 AD iii   *Coumbes Hull* 1326 AD iii

v. cumb. Self-explanatory.

GOLDICOTE HO

Goldicote 1212 Fees 139, RBE, 1226 *FF*, 1235 Fees 526, 1248 (15th) *AOMB* 61, 1275 *Ass* 1327 SR, 14th AD *passim*, 1644 Townsend
Caldecote 1275 SR
Caldicote 1249 *FF*
Golddikote 1254 *FF*
Coldicote 1275 *Ass*
Coldecote 1334 *FF*
Goldecote 1445 IpmR
Collicote 1644 QSR

Confusion of initial *c* and *g* is not uncommon (*v.* Gatley *supra* 43). It is difficult to say which is the original here. In favour of *g* is the large preponderance of such forms. If that is correct the first element must be OE *Golding-*, and we have to do with the same pers. name as in Goldington (PN BedsHu 59), *v.* ing. On the other hand the early *Cald-* forms are not likely to have developed from an original *Gold-*, though they might possibly have been substituted for *Cold-*, if that form is really older than the evidence suggests, by someone who was conscious of the relation of the *Cald-*, *Cold-* names. The alternative is to take the original name as one of the common *Caldecott* or 'cold cottages' type, which would not be unsuited to its site, and to believe that *Cald-* became *Cold-* under the influence of the independent word and was commonly corrupted to *Gold-*. Very definitely adverse to this theory is the persistent medial *i* which is not commonly if ever found in the *Caldecott* names, at least at an early date.

KNAVENHILL

Knaveslade 1322 AD ii   *Knavene Slade* 1326 AD ii
Knove Hull 1490 VCH iv. 7

OE *cnafan-* or *cnafena-slæd*, 'boy(s)' valley' or 'hill,' *v.* slæd. Cf. Nanhurst (Sr), 1304 BM *Knavenhurst*.

UPTHORPE FM (6″)

Uppthrop 990 (11th) KCD 674
Hupthorp 1275 *Ass*
Upthrop 1275 SR, 13th AD vi, 1431 FA
Upthorp 1275 *Ass*, 1356 Ipm

'Upper village,' *v.* þorp, so called because it is a mile higher up the Stour than the parent-settlement at Alderminster.

Beoley[1]

BEOLEY [bi·li] 72 J 4

Beoleah 972 (c. 1050) BCS 1282
Beolege 1086 DB
Bielege c. 1086 (1190) *EveA*
Buelega 1175 P (ChancR, *Belega*)
Beleg(e), *Beleye* 1220 Bracton (p), 1221 *Ass*, 1275, 1327 SR
Buleg, *Buley* 1244 Ch, 1285 Wigorn, 1304 Pat, 1316 Ipm, 1428 FA
Beeley 1346 FA, 1481 Pat, 1741 Marr
Beoley 1431 FA, 1445 IpmR

'Bee-clearing,' i.e. where they often swarm, cf. Boehill (D), *byohyll* in BCS 1027, *beodun* (BCS 797) and *beocumb* (BCS 633)[2].

---

[1] Often confused with Beeley (Gl), as in Fine Rolls (vol. iii) and elsewhere. See *Brist. and Glouc. Trans.* xvii. 134, 185. Note also that Close Rolls wrongly identify *Bello Loco* (1331) with Beoley instead of Bewdley *supra* 40 and *Weleye* (1280) with Beoley instead of Weoley in Northfield *infra* 350.

[2] In the bounds of Beoley (BCS 1282) we have a *Beardyncgford*. This doubtless takes its name from the same man *Bearda* from whom *Berdemedwe* in Beoley (1316 Ipm) is named.

BALSFORD HALL (lost)

Baltesford 1316, 1482 Ipm   *Balsford Hall* 1517 Ipm

Little can be done with this name. Possibly the OE form was *Bealdesford*, from the pers. name *Beald* found in *Bealdes-sol*, BCS 797. There is a Baltington (Do), but the earliest form that has been noted is identical with the present in 1428 (FA).

BROCKHILL FM (6″)

Brokhull, Brochulle 1275, 1327 SR (p)

'Badger-hill,' *v.* brocc, hyll and cf. Brockhill in Shelsley Beauchamp *supra* 77 and in Tardebigge *infra* 362.

GORCOTT HILL

Gorcote 1183 P, *Gorcote Hull* c. 1470 AD iv

'Muddy cottage(s),' *v.* gor, cot.

Besford

BESFORD 81 H 13

Bettesford 972 (c. 1050) BCS 1282

Beford 1086 DB

Bezford c. 1086 (1190) *EveA* & *B*, a. 1198 (15th) *AOMB* 61, 1231 Pat (p)

Bezeford 1176, 1181 P, 1230 Pat (p)

Bezcefort 1176 P (p)

Bezfort 1212 Fees 139

Bestfordia, Bestforde 1227 Bracton (p), 1640 Marr

Besceford 1230 FF

Beseford 1275 SR

Besse-, Bisse-, Bosseford 1275 *Ass*

Besseford 1322 Cl

Besforde 1327 SR

'*Betti's* ford,' *v.* ford. Cf. Besford and Beslow (Sa) with the same pers. name.

BUCKNELL WOOD (lost)

Buckenhull c. 1225, 1249, c. 1260 (15th) *AOMB* 61

Bucknells 1544 LP

'Bucca's hill,' *v.* hyll. This must be associated with the *Bokindona* of *EveA*, which is the 1 hide of Walter Ponther in DB.

RAMSDEN

Romlesdun a. 1234 *AOMB* 61, a. 1250 ib., 1249 AD iii
Rommesdun, Romesdon, Ramesdune 1249 ib.
Rommesdon 1263 ib.

It is difficult to be certain about this name. The *l* may be an intrusive *l* which we sometimes find in ME spellings. If so, the name is probably 'ram's down,' *v.* ramm, dun.

Birlingham

BIRLINGHAM 81 H 13

Byrlingahamme (dat.) 972 (c. 1050) BCS 1282
Berlingeham 1086 DB, 1330, 1334 Pat
Burlingeham c. 1086 (1190) *EveA & B,* a. 1148 (15th) *AOMB*
  61, c. 1150 Surv, 1241 *FF* (p), 1245 Cl
Burlingham, Birlingham 1212 Fees 139, c. 1320 Ch
Berlingham 1420 IpmR

This seems clearly to point to a patronymic derived from an OE pers. name *Byrle*, which (with Duignan) must be identified with OE *byrle*, 'cupbearer.' Hence 'hamm of Byrle's people.' Birlingham lies in a great bend of the Avon.

ASHAM COMMON (lost)

Hessehom c. 1240 (15th) *AOMB* 26 d   *Asshames* 1545 LP
Asham Common 1773 VCH iv. 24, n. 4
'Ash-tree hamm.'

THE MOORS (6″)

More Hall 1471 IpmR
Self-explanatory. *v.* mor.

NAFFORD

Nadford 1086 DB   *Nasford* c. 1220 (15th) *AOMB* 61 (p)
Nafford 1290 Wigorn

The paucity of forms makes this name difficult to interpret. It is impossible to do anything with a first element *Nad-*, but it is possible that the *d* is an AN spelling for *t* (cf. IPN 109, n. 2) and the original OE form may have been *Natanford*, later *Nateford*. If this is correct the first element may be the pers.

name *Nata* which can be inferred from OE *Natangrafas* (BCS 165), now Notgrove (Gl) and *Natanleaga* (ASC s.a. 508), now Nateley (Ha). Forms like *Nategrave* in DB and in FA down to 1316 and the whole development of Nateley suggest that the vowel here must be short. The name may be cognate with the OGer names *Nat(o)*, *Nazo* found in Förstemann (PN 1154), but if so Förstemann's explanation of these names as allied to ON *náð* must be rejected. Rather the name must be related to the stem which lies behind OE *nett* (from *năt-*).

Professor Ekwall suggests with much probability that the OE name was really *nēatford*, 'cattle-ford,' *v*. neat. For the *d*-form cf. DB *Stradford* for Stratford (PN Bk 49).

Bransford

BRANSFORD[1] 81 E 9

> *Branesforde* 716 (14th) BCS 134, c. 1086 (1190) *EveA*, 1215 (13th) ChronEve, 1316 Ipm
> *Bregnesford* 963 (11th) BCS 1106
> *Bradnesford* 1086 DB
> *Berneford* c. 1086 (1190) *EveA*
> *Brantesford* 1255 *Ass*
> *Brannesford* 1270 *FF*
> *Bransford* 1275, 1327 SR
> *Braunceford*, *Braunsford* 1308 Wigorn (p), 1420 IpmR, 1675 Ogilby

In dealing with this name we must also take into account the *Bragenmonna broc* of BCS 1107, which seems to flow into the Teme opposite to Bransford. The phonology of the various forms is difficult, and the meaning of the first element uncertain. It is possible that it is also found in Brayfield (Bk, Nth), cf. PN Bk 4. Professor Ekwall suggests that in both we have OE *brægen*, **bragen*, 'brain,' but used also of the crown of the head, as appears from the use of *brægn* to translate Latin *verticem* in the 'fall on his own pate' of the Psalms. There is a hill-spur at Bransford, rising some 60 ft. above the Teme. The Brayfields lie on high ground above the valley of the Ouse.

---

[1] *Warewykesiche* in Bransford (*AOMB* 61, c. 1260) is not found elsewhere. The Beauchamp Earls of *Warwick* were lords of Bransford.

BRACE'S LEIGH

Lega Ricardi c. 1150 Surv   *Bracy Legh* 1328 Ch
This is the manor in Leigh (*v. infra* 204) held by the *Bracy* family from the 13th cent. onwards (VCH iv. 104). The *Ricardus* of the Survey cannot be identified.

BROOK FM

atte Broke 1327, 1332 SR

HALL FM

de Aula, atte Hall 1275, 1327 SR
Both self-explanatory.

Bricklehampton

BRICKLEHAMPTON[1] [brikləm] 82 A 1

Bricstelmestune 1086 DB
Brichtthelmentona, Brichtelmentona c. 1086 (1190) *EveA* & *B*
Bricchthelinton a. 1198 *AOMB* 61
Brihtellemeton 1204 AD iii
Brysthampton 1275 SR
Brithampton 1275 *Ass*, 1327 SR
Britelhampton 1327 SR
Briklanton, Bricklanton 1340 *FF*, 1577 Saxton
Brightlampton, Brythelampton   (*juxta Elmeleye*) 1332 *FF*,
     1397 Pat, 1407 BM
Brytlahamton 1440 BM
Brykelampton, Bryghtlampton 1535 VE
Bricklehampton 16th Wills *passim*

'Beorhthelm's farm,' *v.* ingtun. For the phonetic development cf. Brightlingsea (Ess), pronounced *Bricklesea*. The same pers. name is found in Brickworth (W), Brighthampton (O), and Brighton (Sx).

---

[1] In the Edgar charter to Pershore the first manor mentioned is *Brihtulfingtun*, which is followed by Comberton and then by Pensham. Bricklehampton, the Combertons, and Pensham lie in topographical succession, and it is difficult not to believe that *Brihtulfingtun* and Bricklehampton are identical. If that is the case, the manor must first have been named from one *Beorhtwulf* and then re-named from some successor, probably of the same family, bearing the name *Beorhthelm* with the same first element.

Broadway

BROADWAY 93 A 5

Bradsetena gemere c. 860 (c. 1200) KCD 289 (iii, 396)
Bradanuuege (dat.) 972 (c. 1050) BCS 1282
Bradeweia, Bradewega, Bradeweye 1086 DB, c. 1086 (1190)
    EveA, 1183 AC, 1275 SR
Bradwey, Bradway 1535 VE, 1675 Ogilby
Brodwey 1554 Marr

'Broad road,' but probably not the one familiar to all visitors to Broadway, running east and west, but the older road running north and south past the old church and up the valley. Cf. *Birm. Arch. Scc.* xliv. 126 ff. The modern form is due to the influence of the independent word *broad*, cf. Bradway (Db) and Broadway (Herts, So). For *Bradsetena* cf. *s.n.* Broadwas *supra* 104.

BURHILL[1]

Wadbeorhe 972 (c. 1050) BCS 1282   *Burrell Hill* c. 1830 O

This name is a compound of **beorg** and **hyll**, the old 1″ O.S. name recording a curious triplication of the hill-idea. Working out the bounds of Broadway as found in the great Pershore charter it is clear that the *wadbeorh* or 'woad-hill' of that charter is to be identified with the *beorh* of Burhill.

HAYWAY FM[2]

Hegeweie, Hegewege 709 (12th) BCS 125, n.d. KCD 1368
Heigweig 854 (12th) BCS 482
Highway 1820 G

'Hay-road,' *v.* **heg, weg**. There was another *Heiweie* in Charlton, c. 1220 (*WoC*), *Hayway* 1649 (Surv).

NO MAN'S LAND (local)

nanesmonnes land 972 (c. 1050) BCS 1282

This interesting field-name, for whose identification we are indebted to Mr C. A. Seyler, lies S.E. of the Fish Inn and is a remarkable case of long survival. Cf. *Nonemanneslonde* in

---

[1] Partly in Buckland (Gl).
[2] This identification is due to the kindness of Mr C. A. Seyler.

Pershore (AD iii) *Mommonelond* (sic) in Bishampton (Nash), *Nanesmanneslande* in the DB for Middlesex, *Nomansland* in Droitwich (1456), *Nanesmonnes land* in Cleeve (Gl), BCS 246.

PEASEBROOK FM

> *Pesbroc* 972 (c. 1050) BCS 1282

WEST MEADOW (local)

> *West mæduwan, medwan* 972 (c. 1050) BCS 1282

Mr C. A. Seyler informs us that this name still survives in a field-name in Peasebrook Farm. It is named also in the Enclosure Award of 1767.

Broughton Hackett

BROUGHTON HACKETT 81 E 13

> *Broctun* 972 (c. 1050) BCS 1282
> *Broctune* 1086 DB, c. 1086 (1190) *EveB*
> *Brochtona* c. 1086 (1190) *EveA*
> *Brocton Inardi* c. 1150 Surv
> *Broctone* 1212 Fees 139, (*Haket*) 1275 SR, (*Beuchamp*) 1316 Ipm
> *Broghton* 1265 Pat
> *Browghton* 1514 LP
> *Haggetts Broughton* 1544 VCH iv. 44

'Brook-farm,' *v.* broc, tun. *Inardi* from the *Isnardus* who held several of the Beauchamp manors (VCH i. 330), cf. Innerstone *supra* 157. The Hackett family were here before the end of the 12th cent. (ib. iv. 44).

Chaceley

CHACELEY 92 C 11

> *Ceatewesleah* 972 (c. 1050) BCS 1282
> *Chaddeslega, Chaddesleia, -leye* c. 1086 (1190) *EveA*, c. 1150 Surv, (*juxta Longedon*) 1316 *FF*, 1346, 1428 FA
> *Cheddeslega* Hy 2 BM
> *Chaseleia* 1185 AC (p)
> *Cadeslega* 1190 P
> *Chadesleg'* 1212 Fees 139, (*juxta Seuarne*) 1358 *FF*
> *Chasteley, Chattisley, Chatysley* 1535 VE, 1596 Marr

Apart from the first form one would take the first element to be the pers. name *Ceatta* or *Ceadda* in a strong form. For these two forms *v.* Redin (88). It is difficult however to overlook the first form, especially as the same name, in a weak form, seems to lie behind the *ceatwanbeorge* of BCS 526, a Shaftesbury charter relating to Dorset[1]. Further, we must note that there is evidence for other OE names with an extension in -*wa*. There is the *Sceldwea* or *Scyldwa* of the genealogies (Redin 78) and *Tætwa*, also found in the genealogies. For the possible history of this difficult suffix *v.* Kögel in *Zeitschrift f. deutsches Alt.* 37, 271, n. 1 and Björkman in *Englische Studien*, 52, 150, n. 1.

The modern *Chaceley* in place of *Chatsley* or *Chadsley*, such as we should expect, may well be due to a conscious attempt to distinguish it from Chaddesley Corbett. *v.* Introd. xx.

CUMBERWOOD[2]

Cumbranweorð 972 (c. 1050) BCS 1282

'Cumbra's enclosure,' *v.* weorð. The pers. name *Cumbra* is found also in *Cumbranwylle* in Salwarpe and in Comberton *infra.* Cf. also Comberworth (L).

HAWKER'S FM (6″)

Haukeres place 1397 Pat

HILLEND

de Monte 1275 SR   *Hillend* 1673 FF

CHACELEY STOCK

de la Stokk 1275 SR

All three are self-explanatory, *v.* hyll, stocc.

Great and Little Comberton

GREAT COMBERTON 82 H/J 1

Cumbrincgtun 972 (c. 1050) BCS 1282
Cumbrintune 1086 DB, c. 1086 (1190) *EveB*
Cumbritun(e) 1086 DB
Cumbrinton(a) c. 1086 (1190) *EveA*, 1227 Ch

---

[1] There is a pers. name *Cetwa* in Florence of Worcester, but this seems to be simply an error for *Tetwa* or *Tætwa* (Redin 70).
[2] In Gloucestershire.

Cumbreton 1198 Cur
Cumbrenton 1201 Cur
Cumbirton 1268 Wigorn
Cumbrington, Combrington 1270 Ch
Combreton, Cumberton 1316 Ipm
Comberton, Magna et Parva 1428 FA
Commerton 1577 Saxton, 1669 Marr

'Cumbra's farm,' *v.* ingtun. For the pers. name cf. Cumberwood in Chaceley *supra* 193 and Comberton *infra* 249.

COMBERTON AITS (6″)

These islands in the Avon are probably those spoken of as
lez Neytes in 1544 (LP) in a grant of Elmley Castle, *v.* iggoð.
The form *Neytes* shows the common prefixed *n*, cf. Neight
supra 137.

Defford

DEFFORD 81 H 13

Deopanforda (dat.) 972 (c. 1050) BCS 1282
Depeford 1086 DB, c. 1086 (1190) *EveB*
Depford c. 1086 (1190) *EveA*
Dufford 1299 (18th) *RBB* (p), 1320 Cl (p)
Defforde 1327 SR
Desseforde sur le Bourne 1393 Pat

'Deep ford,' *v.* deop, ford.

BOURNE BANK FM and BROOK (6″)

winterburne 769 (11th) BCS 1235
la Burne a. 1264 (15th) *AOMB* 61   *le Bourne* 1393 Pat

v. burna. The first reference is from the boundaries of Croome
and it is clearly the stream which first forms the bounds between
Croome d'Abitot and Defford and afterwards between Defford
and Strensham.

COPPINS COURT (lost)

First mentioned in 1562 (FF), it must take its name from the
family of *Copyn* found in Birlingham in 1275 (SR).

WOODMANCOTE

Wodemannecote a. 1198 (15th) *AOMB* 61
Wudemancote 1227 *FF*
Wodemancote 1275 *Ass*, 1287 Wigorn, 1431 FA
Wodemoncote 1329 *FF*
Woddyncote, Woddencote 1557, 1568 Wills
'Woodmen's cottages' (*v.* cot), cf. Woodmanton *supra* 45.

Dormston

DORMSTON 82 D 2

Deormodes ealdtun 972 (c. 1050) BCS 1282
Dormestun 1086 DB, 1221 *FF*, 1230 Cl
Dormeston 1226 ClR, 1255 *Ass*, 1275 SR, 1535 VE
Doramstone 1392 *Wigorn*
Dormyston 1431 FA, 1544 LP
Darmston 1724 Marr

'*Dēormod's* farm' (*v.* tun), with the interesting additional description of it as the 'old' farm or enclosure in the first mention of it. In the Dormston-Inkberrow boundary we have mention of a *Deorelmes-dic* (BCS 1110). It is possible that *Dēorhelm* and *Dēormod* belonged to the same family, which favoured the element *Dēor-* in their pers. names, cf. Bricklehampton *supra* 190 n. The same pers. name is found in Darmsden (Sf) and Dormers Well in Southall (Mx).

Eckington

ECKINGTON 81 J 13

Eccyncgtun 972 (c. 1050) BCS 1282
Aichintune 1086 DB
Hekintona c. 1086 (1190) *EveA & B*, c. 1150 Surv
Achinton 1176 P
Ekinton, Ekynton 1233 Cl, 1275 SR, 1279 Wigorn, (*Poer*)
    1297 Cl
Equinton 1312 *FF*
Ekkyngton 1542 LP

'*Ecci's* farm' or *Ecca's* farm, *v.* tun.
The oldest spelling and the modern form suggest derivation from a pers. name *Ecca* compounded again in Eckington (Db),

Earle 220 *Eccingtun*, and (Sx). The DB and Pipe Roll forms (like DB *Achintone* for the Sx name) cannot stand against the weight of evidence for initial *e* as against *æ*. For the DB *ai*, cf. DB *Ailetone* for Elton (Nt) which always elsewhere has initial *e*. The *a* of the Pipe Roll form is AN *a* for *e*.

BANBURY STONE

Bænintèsburg 778 (18th) BCS 232
Bænincgesbyrig 972 (c. 1050) BCS 1282

The burh is the ancient camp, of which Banbury Stone, a great mass of rock on the summit of Bredon Hill, forms the nucleus. It is spoken of as an *urbs* in the first of the above charters. The first element is an unrecorded pers. name *Bænincg*, allied to that found in Bannall's (*supra* 56) and in Bensington (O), *Bænesingtun* (ASC). Its bearer was presumably the owner of the site at some time in its history. The *t* of the first form is due to the not uncommon confusion of *c* and *t* in Old English script. See further Introd. xxi.

WOOLLASHILL

Wullaueshulla 1176 P
Wllauesella c. 1190 *EveA*
Wllaueshulle 1194 (15th) *AOMB* 61
Willaueshale 1201 Cur
Wullafeshull 13th HMC v, App. 1, 301 (p)
Wolaueshulle 1235 *FF*, 1275 SR
Wullaueshull 1256 Pat
Wolweshulle 1275 *Ass*
Woloshulle 1301 Ipm (p)
Wollarshull 1346 FA
Wolashulle 1366 Pat
Wollashull 1431 FA, 1586 Wills

'*Wulflāf's* hill,' *v.* hyll. In the adjacent Woollas *Hall*, the suffix has undergone corruption. The same pers. name is found in Wollaston (Nth), Woollaston (St) and in Wollaston in Old Swinford *infra* 311.

Eldersfield

ELDERSFIELD 92 C 9

Yldresfeld 972 (c. 1050) BCS 1282
Edresfelle 1086 DB
Heldresfelde c. 1086 (1190) *EveA*, 1167 P
Hederefeld, Ederefeld, Ederesfeld, Æderesfeld 1183, 1185
1190 P
Eldrefeld(ia) 1220 Bracton, 1221 *FF*
Eldresfeld 1262 Ipm, 1275 SR, 1291 Tax, 1394 IpmR
Elde(s)feld 1327 SR, 1362 *FF*
Ellesfeld 1431 FA
Eldresfeld al. *Elsfeld* 1493 Ipm

It is impossible to explain the first element in this name
without assuming some kind of irregular development. OE
Yldres- could not in this district, if we assume the *y* to be
original, yield post-Conquest *e* and *æ*. It is possible to associate
yld-, *eld-* and *æld-* forms if we take *y* to be LWS for *ie*, but no
pers. name which could yield in WS *Ieldres-* or in Mercian
Aeldres- is known. The suggestion may be hazarded that the
first element is really the OE pers. name *Ealdhere* but that this
was confused with the comparative form *ældra* (WS *ieldra*)
derived from *eald* and that the name became *Aeldresfeld* and
even *Yldresfeld*. In many of the early forms the first *l* of the
whole name has been lost by a process of dissimilation. Hence
'Ealdhere's open land,' *v.* feld.

BRADFORD (lost)

vill de Bradeforde 1221 *Ass*   *Bradeford* 1275, 1327 SR (p)

The meaning is clear. The place may perhaps be identified
with the *bradan ford* of BCS 1282.

CORSE LAWN[1]

Cors 1210 RBE, 1275 *Ass* (p), 1317 *FF* (p), 1327 SR (p),
1340 NI (p)
Corys 1384 Pat
Corse Lawnde 1478 Pat
Croslawnde, Crosselaunde 1486, 1495 Pat, 1535 VE

[1] Largely in Gloucestershire.

Q

This is the name of an ancient forest which was an appendix to that of Malvern (VCH ii. 317). The ground is low-lying and this name is clearly the Welsh *cors*, 'marsh.' Cf. Gauze Brook (W), BCS 922 *Corsbrok*. For the suffix *v.* launde.

CROMER FM (6")

> *Cranmere* 875 (11th) BCS 542, 967 (11th) BCS 1208
> *Cronmere* 963 (11th) BCS 1109
> *Cronemere* 1275 SR (p)

'Crane pool' or possibly 'heron pool,' for the term *crane* is used locally of such, *v.* cran, mere. Cf. *cranmere* in Pershore, BCS 542.

DRINKERS-END (6")

Named from the family of *le Drynkar* mentioned in 1297 Cl, 1327 SR.

GADBURY BANK

> *atte Berewe* 1327 SR

GADFIELD ELM

> *Gatefeld* 1275, 1327 SR (p)

These places are within a quarter of a mile of one another and should probably be associated. The second is clearly OE *gāta-feld*, 'open land of the goats' (*v.* gat, feld). Gadbury Bank is a conspicuous hill and may be the *Berewe* (*v.* beorg) of the first quotation. The full form of the name may have been OE *gāta-beorg*, ME *gate-berewe*, or it may simply have been influenced by the neighbouring place-name.

HARDWICK GREEN

> *Herdewiche* 1183, 1185 P   *Ordewike* 1210–2 RBE
> *v.* heordewic.

HILL FM

> *super montem* 1275 SR
> Self-explanatory.

MARSH COURT

> *de Marisco, atte Merch* 1275, 1327 SR   *le Mersh* 1431 FA
> Self-explanatory.

NASH END

de Fraxino 1275 SR

v. æsc and cf. Nash End *supra* 31.

TUTS HILL (6″)

Toteshill 1549 Pat

This may be a corruption of the familiar *Tote-* or *Toot*-hill, 'look-out hill,' or a new compound in which the first element is the same word *tote*, which is sometimes used of the watch-tower itself, hence 'hill of the look-out place.'

Flyford Flavell

FLYFORD FLAVELL 82 E 1

Fleferth 930 (13th) BCS 667

Flæferð 972 (c. 1050) BCS 1282

æt Fleferht 1002 (13th) KCD 1295

Flavel 1190 *EveB*, 1212 Fees 139, RBE, 1269 Wigorn, 1315 Ipm, 1428 FA

Flefrith 1316 *FF*, 1317 Pat

Fleford 1420 IpmR

Fleford Flavell, Fleford Fluvell 16th, 17th VCH iv. 83

This place and Grafton Flyford *infra* 200 are about a mile apart on either side of the Piddle Brook, just a little way to the south and north of it respectively. We clearly have reference to the two settlements in the *locis...silvaticis ad Fleferth dextra lævaque illius rivuli qui vulgariter Piduella vocitatur* (BCS 667) and in the *locis siluaticis in utraque parte rivuli qui Piduella appellatur, huiusque agnomen loci æt Fleferht dicitur* (KCD 1295). *Fleferth* or *Flæferð* is the name therefore of an old wooded district (cf. *foresta de Flavel RBB*, fo. 69) but why so-called it is not clear. The analogy of the lost *Wenferth* (*supra* 16) would suggest that it was a stream-name rather than a woodland-name. If so, it must be another name for Piddle Brook. It may be added that the phraseology of BCS 937 which, in giving the bounds of Phepson, speaks of them as running from Dean Brook 'on *fleferð*,' tends to support this view, for in a list of bounds of this kind we should not be likely to have the name of a large district introduced. The ultimate etymology of the name must however remain obscure[1].

The name Flyford Flavell is of a type that is probably without parallel. Anglo-Norman scribes and speakers, finding a difficulty in dealing with the name *Flaferth* or *Fleferth* turned it into *Flavel* (cf. IPN 106 ff.). In the meantime the word had undergone another corruption due to folk-etymology. The suffix *-ferth*, *-verth*, *-varth* was changed to the more familiar *-ford*[2] and thus the two forms *Flavell* and *Fleford* (and possibly also *Flaford*) were evolved as names of the same place, and the place now known as Grafton Flyford could be called alternatively *Grafton-under-Flavell*, *Grafton Flavell*, or *Grafton Fleford*. In the meantime the necessity arose for distinguishing the village on the south of the stream from that on the north and this was done by adding *Flavell* to *Fleford* (or *vice-versa*, for we cannot be sure which way the business was done) and so creating a pseudo-manorial name in which the two halves were really identical.

It should be added that Flyford Flavell probably also had its English name, for there is good reason for identifying it with the *Ælflædetun*, i.e. the farm of a woman called *Ælflæd*, in BCS 1282.

Grafton Flyford

Grafton Flyford 82 D 1

> *Graftun* 884 (18th) BCS 552, 972 (c. 1050) BCS 1282
> *Fleferð* 956 (11th) BCS 937, 972 (c. 1050) BCS 1282
> *Flæferð* 972 (c. 1050) BCS 1282

---

[1] On the other hand the phrases *sub Fleuarth, under Flavel* in the 13th and 14th cents. (*v.* Grafton Flyford) tend to show that by this time it was thought of as a district pure and simple.

[2] An interesting parallel to such confusion is afforded by certain names in Do and So. Winford (So) is *Wunfrod* in KCD 694 and appears as *Wenfre, Wynford, Wynfreth* and *Wyndfrith*. Winford Eagle (Do) appears as *Winford, Wynfrid*, while Winfrith Newburgh (Do) similarly appears as *Winfrode, Wynfred*. All alike probably take their name from a lost stream-name (*v.* Bradley in *Essays and Studies*, i. 32) whose last element is identical with the name of the Froome. Winfrith Newburgh indeed lies on the upper waters of the Froome. Another example is the stream noted by Ritter (131), variously called *Sihtferð, Sihtforð, Sihtfyrð, Sihferð* (BCS 462, 1087, 1139, 1242) on the bounds of Grimley, Bentley and Witley, and another stream of unknown locality called *Sehford, Sehfrod* (KCD 770).

Garstune 1086 DB

Grafton(a) c. 1086 (c. 1190) *EveA* & *B*, (*Ebraudi*[1]) c. 1150
Surv, (*juxta Flavell*) 1285 *FF*, (*sub Fleuarth*) 1317 FF,
(*souz Flavell*) 1350 LyttCh, (*Flevarth*) 1397 Pat, (*Flevorell*)
1400 IpmR, (*Flevord*) 1439 IpmR, (*Fleford*) 1509–38 LP,
1550 Pat

'Grove-farm,' *v.* graf, tun, an apt enough name in this *locus
silvaticus* (*v. supra* 199 for this and for the suffixed *Flyford*).
This place, like Flyford Flavell, seems to have had two names,
an English and an earlier Celtic one. The *Ebraudus* of the Survey
cannot be identified.

HILL COURT

Hull 1203 ChR, 1327 SR (p)
Hulleplace 1446, 1478 IpmR, 1447 Pat
Hulplace 1487 AD v
Hilcourt 1630 Wills, 1651 FF

v. hyll. Self-explanatory.

LIBBERY

Hleobyri (dat.) 972 (c. 1050) BCS 1282
Leobury 1327 SR, 1337 WoCh
Lebbery 1506 StratGild
Liberyfeld in Grafton Flyford 1550 Pat
Leoberie 1591 Wills

'Protecting earth-work' or the like, a compound of OE
hleo and burh.

WOODHOUSE END FM (6")

Wodehus 1203 ChR

Cf. Woodhouse in Upper Arley and Pensax *supra* 33, 68.

Hanley Castle

HANLEY 81 J 10

Hanlie, Hanlege 1086 DB
Heanlega 1181 P (p)

---

[1] The printed text has *Ebrandi*, but this must be an error for *Ebraudi*,
the latter being a Latinised form of OGer *Ebrald, Eberolt*.

Hanley 1314 *FF* (*subtus Maluerne*), 1344 FA (*juxta M.*),
   1535 VE (*Castrum*)
Potters Handley 1633 QSR

OE (*æt ðæm*) *hēan lēage*, 'at the high clearing,' *v.* heah, leah.
The castle goes back to King John (VCH iv. 93). From VCH
(iv. 89, n. 1) we find that potters were among the customary
tenants in 1296. They are mentioned again in 1307 and in the
16th cent. Cf. Potterspury (Nth), called also from the same
trade.

BLACKMORE PARK

Blakemore c. 1200 (c. 1250) *WoC*, 1261 Ipm

Other forms are without interest and the meaning is clear.
v. mor.

CLIFFEY WOOD and CLIFFEY FM (6″)

Clifheye 1308 Wigorn, 1315, 1359 Ipm, all (p)
Cliffhey 1545 LP

'Enclosure of woodland by the cliff,' *v.* clif, (ge)hæg. It lies
just above the Severn.

FORTY GREEN (lost)

Fort(h)ey is very common as a place-name (or as part of a
pers. name) in early Worcestershire records, but this Forty
Green and another in Redmarley d'Abitot (6″) are the only
ones of which we know the site, and the former is now no longer
recorded on our maps. In the map in Gough's *Camden* (1789)
it is half a mile east of Hanley Swan. The site is a peninsula
which pushes out into low-lying land below the 100 ft. contour,
and in the immediate neighbourhood there are several little
islands of land surrounded by that contour line. The other
Forty Green is in somewhat broken ground pushing out into
low-lying valleys. Elsewhere we know the exact site of Forty
Hall in Enfield (Mx), which is called (*atte*) *Fortey* (E iii)[1]. It
lies on an isolated hill of which the eastern end thrusts itself
out into the low-lying district of Enfield Wash. There is also a
Fortheye[1] in Little Stanmore (1320 AD ii) which is said to lie

---

[1] Forms kindly furnished by Mr J. E. B. Gover.

between Grim's Ditch and the high road to Watford. This points clearly to the hill marked with a spot-level of 506 ft., from which the ground falls away fairly steeply on three sides and more gradually on the fourth[1]. There was a *le Forthei* or *le Fortheye* in Wick by Pershore (1360, 1419 AD ii) which must have been part of the long island-like hill which here bounds the great bend of the Avon at its southern end, also a street called *le Forthei* (which may have been the same place) in Pershore itself in the 14th cent. (VCH iv. 154). There was a *la Fortheye* in Grimley (1240 WoP), found also in pers. names in the same vill (1275, 1327 SR). This may be the island of land marked by the 200 ft. contour in the neighbourhood of Oldhill Fm and Elm Hill, or it may be one of the numerous projections of higher ground into the valley of the Severn itself that are to be found near here. In the Kyre Park Charters we have *Forteys* in Cotheridge. This may be the peninsula at the south-east corner of the ridge which gives its name to Cotheridge, or it may be the peninsula which faces it in the south-east corner of the parish. In the 1299 Survey of Ripple (*RBB*) we have a pers. name *atte Fortheye*, found also in the SR for 1275, 1327 and 1332. The man bearing it belonged to Ryall and the *forthey* was probably the long peninsula (marked by the 100 ft. contour) which projects itself down to a point north-east of Ryall Court. The same pers. name is found in Lenchwick (1275 SR) where there is an island of land (200 ft. contour) just to the east of the village, in Timberdine (1292 Ipm), where there is a tiny island (100 ft. contour) just to the north-east of the farm, in Severn Stoke (1256 Ipm), where there are several islands of land (50 ft. contours) near the Severn.

From the general topography of the places in question it is clear that we have to do with a compound of OE *forð*, 'in front,' and eg, 'island or peninsula.' Cf. Furtho (Nth) which is a specially prominent hoh. They are all islands or peninsulas of land standing well out from surrounding marshy or, at least, comparatively low-lying ground. For similar compounds of this type with the more usual *fore*, v. Fairfield and Forhill *infra* 275, 333. Initial *Forth-* became *Fort-* under Anglo-Norman influence and doubt-

---

[1] There is also a Forty Fm in Wembley, for which no early forms have been noted. It stands at the foot of a well-marked isolated hill.

less the *fort-* forms were strengthened by popular etymological associations with *forty*[1].

GILBERT'S END

This must take its name from *Gilbert* de Hanley who in 1210 (RBE) held 1 virgate as keeper of the Forest of Malvern.

HILL'S FM (6″)

del Hulle, atte Hulle 1275 SR, 1307 Ipm

Self-explanatory. The form is pseudo-manorial.

NORTHEND FM

Northend 1275 *Ass*

Self-explanatory.

ROBERT'S END (6″)

This takes its name from either father or son in the *Robert fil.* *Robert* de Hanley, mentioned in 1234 (VCH iv. 97, n. 77). It appears as Robertson Street in Gough (1789).

SEVERN END

Persons named *de Sabrina* and *de Seuarne* are mentioned in 1275 and 1327 (SR) and clearly lived at this end of the parish, which is by the Severn.

Leigh

LEIGH[2] [lai] 81 E 9

Beornothesleah, Beornoðesleah 972 (c. 1050) BCS 1282
Lege, Lega 1086 DB, c. 1086 (1190) *EveA*, c. 1150 Surv, 1291 Tax

---

[1] This etymology will not explain Forty Green (Bk). Unluckily we have no early forms. It stands on a knoll of ground with the land falling away on most sides (the ground as a whole is much broken) but it is well away from streams of any kind and could hardly be called an eg at all. Possibly the name is of entirely different origin, possibly it may have been named from another *Forty* elsewhere, the isolated hill bearing some vague resemblance to it.

The term was also used in Berks, for we have a John *de la* (or *atte*) *Forteye*, *Fòrtheie* (1318 Cl, 1323 Pat), who is associated with Wallingford and the neighbouring Crowmarsh (O).

[2] In the bounds of Powick (BCS 1282) we have the bound running *on codran ford ondlang codran*, in those of the adjacent Leigh (*ib.*) the bounds run *on codran of codran*. This is apparently a stream-name and it survives in the following names found in Leigh later on: *campus vocatus Codere*

Leya 1251 BM, 1275 SR
Lye juxta magnam Maluerniam 1389 FF
Ly3gh 1535 VE
Leight, Lyeth, Lyght 16th Wills
Lye 1646 (18th) Nash, 1675 Ogilby

v. leah. Originally this clearing was distinguished by the prefixing of the pers. name *Beornnōð*, later as 'near Malvern.'

BARTON (lost)

Bertone 1226 *FF*, 1275 SR (p)

v. beretun.

BENSTOKEN COPPICE (6")

In Ancient Deeds (vol. ii) we have mention in 1338 and c. 1275 of *Denestocking* and *Menestocking* (*Menstocking* in *AOMB* 61), 'clearing in the valley' and 'clearing held in common,' cf. Menithwood *supra* 58. There is also a *la Fenstocking* (c. 1270) in *AOMB* 61. Possibly this name is a corruption of one of these.

BROCKAMIN

Brockham End 1571 D   *Broken End, Brockamend* 1596 Wills

This is probably from OE broc-hamm, the place lying fairly steeply above a hamm stretching to Leigh *Brook* and the Teme.

CASTLE GREEN

Casteleye 1275 *Ass*
Castellygh(e) 1384 AD i, 1392 Pat, 1393 AD iii

v. leah. This is the 'clearing' distinguished by a 'castle,' probably that of the Pembridge family, and still surviving as a moated mound. This would seem to be one of the cases where final leah is reduced to *le*, cf. Crowle *infra* 315.

CHERKENHILL FM[1] (6") [tʃɔknəl]

Chokenhull 1359 Pat, 1374 Wigorn, 1558 Wills

campus de Coder (13th *AOMB* 61), *Thos. de Coder*, 1275 SR. On the opposite bank of the Teme is Cotheridge, but if *codra* is a stream-name it would seem that the similarity of name can only be a coincidence.

We may note also a field in *AOMB* 61 (13th cent.) called *la Muthe, Mutha in la Homme de Lega*. This myðe must have lain between Leigh Brook and the Teme. There is a broad hamm by the junction.

[1] The form in the 6" O.S. map is *Clerkenhill*. This has now been noted by the O.S. as an error to be corrected.

Chokynhall 1434 Wigorn
Chokynhyll, Chockenell 1535 VE

There is an OE pers. name *Cēoc(a)* dealt with by Redin (28), found perhaps also in *ceokan eg* (BCS 82) and *chekewell* (BCS 1313). This pers. name may have developed to either *Cheke* or *Choke* in ME, cf. *choke*, sb. 2 in NED. This would make the name 'Ceoca's hill,' *v.* hyll.

COLES GREEN

After the Dissolution the Pershore manor of Leigh was in the hands of the *Colles* family (VCH iv. 103).

COWLEIGH PARK

Kaulege 1251 Ch
Cowleigh 1287 Duncombe's *Herefordshire* (p), 1351 AD iii, 1453 BM
Couleghe c. 1300 (15th) *AOMB* 61 (p)
Couley(e) 1351 AD vi, 1360 Pat, (*juxta Malverne*) 1384 FF

It is possible that the first form is corrupt and that the name is what it appears to be, viz. a compound of cu and leah. If it has to stand we must take the first element to be OE *cawel*, col from Lat. *caulis*, used especially of rape. Hence 'clearing where cole grows.' *v. cole*, sb. 1 in NED, of which the various ME forms would explain those given here.

HOPTON COURT

Hopton 1308 FF, 1327, 1332 SR, 1338 AD ii, all (p)

It is impossible to say if this is a place-name or a manorial name derived from one of the other West Country *Hoptons*. In favour of the latter view is the fact that in 1297 there was a *Hoptonsbrugg* near Sandlin Fm (*v. infra* 207), VCH iv. 102, n. 8, as also the name Ricardus *de Hopton de Leigh* (1308 FF).

HOWSELL, UPPER and LOWER

Howeshulle c. 1230 AD iii
Houselle 1262 (15th) *AOMB* 61
Housel(e) 1279 Ipm, 1312 FF (p), 1383 FF
Neotherhousel in Leyghe 1354 FF
Howeshell n.d. AD iii
Howsell 1558–92 Wills, 1592 QSR, 1664 FF

Professor Zachrisson suggests that in this name the first element is the OFr pers. name *Hugo(n)* which appears in the 13th cent. in English as *Huwe, Howe, Hewe.* Hence 'Hugh's hill,' *v.* hyll.

LINK COMMON, MALVERN LINK

Link, la Lynke, atte Lynkes 1215 Cl, 13th VCH iv. 102, n. 9, 1327 SR
Linche, la Lynche 1215 Cl, 1275 SR, 13th VCH ib.
Malvern Link, the Link 1608 QSR, 1776 Enclosure Act
v. hlinc. The reference is to the lower slopes of the Malverns.

SANDLIN FM

Sondlinge 12th Dugd ii. 422
Sollyng, Sonlyng, Sondlyng 1380–7 Ct
Sandelyng 1558 Wills
Sandling 1619 QSR, 1682 FF
This is 'sand-ridge,' *v.* sand, hlinc and Link Common *supra,* cf. also Sandling (K) in Ekwall, PN in *-ing* 29 and (*to*) *sandhlincan* (KCD 1363).

SHERRIDGE HO

Surigge c. 1275 (15th) *AOMB* 61
Sharugge 1332 SR (p)
Shurugges 15th VCH iv. 103
Sherydge 1558 Wills
Sherridge 1619 QSR
Professor Zachrisson suggests that this difficult name may be for OE scīene-hrycg, 'fair' or 'bright ridge.' For early loss of *n* before *r* we may compare OE *mīre, āre* for *mīnre, ānre* (Sievers, *A.S. Gramm,* § 188, n. 4).

LEIGH SINTON, SINTON END

Sothyntone in Lega c. 1275 AD ii
Suthin(g)ton 1275 SR, 1316 Ipm, both (p)
Sodyngton, Lye Sinton al. *Syddington* 14th–16th VCH iv. 105
This is in the south end of the parish. For the history cf. Sodington *supra* 60.

STURT COPPICE (6″)

The first element may be the same as that found in the pers. name *Steruthale* in Leigh (1275). *v.* steort. Cf. further *Sterteshale* in Great Comberton in *AOMB* 61.

Longdon

LONGDON 92 A 10

(into) langan dune 952 (c. 1050) BCS 1282
Langedune, Longedune 1086 DB
Langeduna Osmundi c. 1150 Surv
Langentona c. 1086 (1190) *EveA*
Langedon, Langedun c. 1086 (1190) *EveB*, 1235 Ch
Longedon, Longdon subtus malverne 1327 SR, 1378 IpmR

'Long hill,' *v.* lang, dun and cf. Longdon in Tredington *supra* 173. The *Osmund* is unknown.

AGGBERROW WOOD (6″)

Akeberg 13th VCH iv. 112
Acberge 1275 SR (p), in Holdfast

'Oak-hill,' *v.* ac, beorg, cf. Aggborough in Kidderminster *infra* 248.

BUCKBURY

Buccebur c. 1200 VCH iv. 115
Buckbire c. 1200 BM
Buckeb' 1291 Tax
Bugbury 1312 Pat, 1535 VE, 1538 BM
Buckbury, Buckbery 1555 BM, 1582 Wills

This is probably 'Bucca's burh.'

CHAMBERS COURT

The place is called *Chambers* in 1711 (FF) and must take its name from the family referred to as *de Camera* in 1275 (SR), *de la Chambre* in 1347 (FA). Presumably they were originally servants of the king's household or of some great lord's. Cf. Chequers (2) and Wardrobes (PN Bk 150, 174, 194).

DRINKWATER'S FM

This derives from the family of *Drinckwater* recorded in 1694 (Wills).

EASTINGTON HALL

Estinton 1255 *Ass*   *Estington* 1658, 1674 FF

This would seem to be a compound of east of the same type as the numerous compounds of *sūð* noted under Sodington, Sinton *supra* 60, 207. The place lies to the north of the parish now, but when Longdon included, as it once did, Castle Morton, and the parish extended a good three miles further west, Eastington would have been definitely on its eastern side.

GUNNICE

The name *Gunny* is found in this vill in 1275 (SR); the place must have been called *Gunny's* and appears in the old 1″ map as *Gunnis*.

HILL HO

de Monte 1327 SR   *atte Hulle* 1340 NI   *Hulcourte* 1668 FF
Self-explanatory.

LONGDON MARSH, MARSHEND

Wildres Mareys Joh Abbr.
de Marisco, in le Mersshe 1275 SR, 1340 NI
Wildres Mershe 1350 Pat

Self-explanatory. The first and last forms may be from OE *wildor*, 'wild animal,' hence 'marsh of the wild animals,' cf. also *Wildesmor* in this parish (Hy 3 BM). It was a likely haunt for such, for originally the marsh was some 10,000 acres in extent, the last remains of the great tidal estuary of the Severn above Gloucester (VCH iv. 111). Cf. Wildersmoor and Wilderswood (PN La 44).

Madresfield

MADRESFIELD [mædəzfiˑld] 81 G 9

Madresfeld c. 1086 (1190) *EveA*, 1275, 1327 SR *et passim*
Medeleffeld c. 1150 Surv
Metheresfeld 1192 P
Mederefelde, Mederesfeude 1196 *FF*, 1210 RBE
Matheresfeud, Mathersfeld 1255 *Ass*, 1369 Pat
Mader(e)sfeld(e) 1328 Ch, 1332 AD vi, 1392 Pat
Matysfyld 1522 More

Madresfyld, Maddersfield 1535 VE, 1748 Marr
Matchfield 1597 Wills

'*Mǣðhere's* open land,' *v.* feld. The same pers. name is found in Mattersey (Nt), Matson (Gl) and Methersham (Sx).

AGGBOROUGH (lost)

Acberge, Acberugh 1196, 1227 *FF*
Akberwe 1275 SR
Agbarwe, Ackebarwe 1312 *FF*, 1322 Ipm

'Oak-hill,' *v.* ac, beorg, cf. Aggberrow in Longdon *supra* 208.

HAYSWOOD FM (6″)

Heyeswode 1326 AD vi

'Wood of the *hey* or forest-enclosure,' *v.* (ge)hæg.

Great Malvern

GT MALVERN [mɔlvə·n], [mɔ·və·n] 81 H 9

Malferna 1086 DB
Maluern(i)a 1156 P, (*major*) 1233 Cl, 1275 SR, 1535 VE
Moche Malv'ne 1521 VCH iv. 188
Malborne 1536 LP

Professor Ekwall in IPN 25 suggests that the first element in this name is the Welsh *moel*, 'bare,' while the second shows a mutated form of the Welsh *bryn* (OBret *bren*), 'hill.' This would suit the hills[1].

BALDENHALL (lost)[2]

Baldehalle 1086 DB
Baldehalle 1192 P (p), 1221 *Ass*, 1275 SR
Baldenhale 1201 Cur, 1280 Wigorn, 1324 *FF*, 1413 AD vi
Baudehale 1249 *FF*, 1255 *Ass*

---

[1] One may note as a curiosity William of Malmesbury's etymology of this name (*Gesta Pontificum* 296): 'Malvernense monasterium quod mihi per antifrasin videtur sortitum esse vocabulum. Non enim ibi *male*, sed bene et pulcherrime religio *vernat*.'

[2] *Baldenhall* must have occupied approximately the area of the present ecclesiastical parish of Guarlford. There was also a *Baldegate* (RH 1276) where the lords of Hanley Castle had a gallows. It is clear from the early documents quoted by Nash (Introd. lxxi) that this *Baldegate* or *Baldeyate* (his form) was on the top of Malvern Hill. The places almost certainly take

Badnall 1541 LP
Baldenhall 1562–73 Wills
'Bealda's nook or corner,' *v.* healh.

BARNARDS GREEN

This is probably named from the family of *Bernard* mentioned in 1275 (SR), the place being called Bernards Green in 1789 (Gough).

GUARLFORD [gɔ·lfəd]

Garlford 1275 SR (p)
Garleford 1291 Tax, 1535 VE, 1541 LP
Galvert 1820 G   *Galfords Court* c. 1830 O

There is a name *Gerling* found in DB, which Forssner (108) suggests may be a derivative of the name *Gerlo*, of continental origin. This continental name would explain *Guarlford* if it is of post-Conquest origin. On the other hand, there is evidence for OE names in *Gǣr-*, as in *Geruald* and *Geruini* in LVD. There may have been an OE *Gǣrla*, a pet-formation from such names. So the name might be pre-Conquest in origin, hence 'ford of *Gerlo* or of *Gǣrla*.' One of these names must lie behind Garliford (D), 1333 SR *Gerlaford*.

HERIOTS FM (6″)

This perhaps takes its name from the family of Philip *Hariot* mentioned in SR (1327) under Newland, but the place is apparently referred to as *Haryett* in the 16th cent. (VCH iv. 125) and this looks as if, after all, it might not be manorial in origin. It may be a shortened form of OE *heregeat-land* (Thorpe 546), 'heriot-land.' The latter is certainly found in *Haryetfeld* in Ripple (1408 *EcclVar*).

their name from the same person. The grant of the site of Malvern Priory (1283 Wigorn) speaks of the land as including the wood as far as *Baldeyate*.

In the bounds of Powick (BCS 1282) there are mentioned *Baldangeat* and *Baldanhrycg*. These places seem to be on the southern boundary of Powick, which then included Madresfield. The two *Baldangeats* cannot be the same, but it is clear that the places on the Powick boundaries are only further examples of places derived from the same pers. name and presumably from the same individual owner.

Moat Court

Grange de la Motte 1535 VE   *Mote Court* 1541 LP

OFr *mote, motte* was used of a mound, hillock, or embankment and may already in Normandy have come to develop its later English sense of *moat* or ditch. There is still a moat here.

North Hill

Northull 1275 SR (p)

Pool Brook

de la Pulle, atte Pulle 1275, 1327 SR
Poole End 1558 Wills   *Pool Brook* 1634 QSR
Both self-explanatory, *v.* hyll, pull.

Rhydd Green

la Ridde 1241 FF, 1276 RH
The Rid Green, Ridd Green 1725 BiblWo, 1772 T

This is probably simply 'the cleared land,' cf. ridde in EPN. *Rhydd* is on the Severn and the modern spelling is an artificial one due to an attempt to connect the name with the Welsh *rhyd*, 'ford,' cf. Rhydd Covert in Kidderminster *infra* 252. The lords of Hanley Castle had gallows here and a trace of this remains in *Hangman* Lane just to the south.

Sherrard's Green

Shyrrold 16th VCH iv. 125   *Sherolls Green* 1597 Wills

The surname *de la Schirholte* is found in *Baldenhale* in Malvern in 1275, so that possibly there was a scir-holt or 'bright wood' from which they took their name and this wood may have left its name in the later *Shyrrold*. If so, the modern form is pseudo-manorial. No certainty is possible. For this name cf. Sherholt (St) of the same origin.

Shire Ditch

in trenchato Hereford' 1164–79 (c. 1250) WoC
in Haro Hereford' c. 1180 (c. 1240) ib.

This would suggest that there was a shire ditch 100 years before Gilbert de Clare made a ditch (c. 1287) separating his lands from those of the Bishop of Hereford (cf. VCH iv. 93).

Martin Hussingtree

MARTIN HUSSINGTREE 81 C 12

HUSSINGTREE [hʌsəntri·]

(to) *Husantreo* 972 (c. 1050) BCS 1282
Husentre 1086 DB
Hossintre Abbatis 1167 P
Hosintre, Hosyntre 1255, 1275 *Ass* (p), 1356 Pat, 1525 WoCh
Husinton 1271 Wigorn

MARTIN

Meretun 972 (c. 1050) BCS 1282
Merton 1271 Wigorn, 1256, 1392 Pat, 1428 FA

MARTIN HUSSINGTREE

Marten Hosentre 1535 VE
Martin Hosyngtre, Howsingtree, Hussingtree 1545–1600 Wills
Merter Nosyntre, Marten Nosyntre 1546 Marr

There were originally two separate vills, later merged into one. The first is 'Husa's tree,' the OE pers. name *Hūsa* being well established. The second is probably *mere-tun*, 'farm by the mere,' though it is just possible that it is for *mǣre-tun*, 'farm by the boundary,' for the parish is on the borders of Oswaldslow and Pershore Hundreds. *mǣre* appears as *mere* in the same document in the name *Dydimeretun*. Both were manors of the Abbot of Westminster.

Birtsmorton

BIRTSMORTON 92 B 9

Morton le Bret 1241 *FF*   *Brittes Morton* 1250 *FF*
Morton Bret 1275 SR   *Brettes Morton* 1275 *Ass*
Morton Brut 1291 NI, 1301 Wigorn, 1322 BM
Bruttes Morton 1346 FA, 1408 Ipm   *Morton Brid* 1431 FA
Birch Morton 16th and 17th cent. *passim*
Burchmorton 1577 Saxton

This place, like the neighbouring Castle Morton *infra* 214, lies on the edge of a low-lying mor. It owes its distinctive appellation to the family of *le Bret* or *Brut* to whom it was granted

R

in 1166 (P). The family came from Brittany, as their name indicates.

MILLER'S COURT (6")

This may take its name from the family of the *molendinarius* mentioned in 1275 (SR).

Castle Morton

CASTLE MORTON 92 A 9

Mortun 1235 Ch
Morton Folet 1275 SR
Castell Morton 1346, 1428 FA

'Farm on the mor.' The castle was probably erected in the reign of Stephen (VCH iv. 49) by the *Folliott* family who were certainly here early in the 13th cent.

HILLEND COURT

We have pers. names *de Monte* (1239 *FF*, 1275, 1327 SR, 1428 FA) and *Hill* (1384 Pat) in this vill and they doubtless belonged here. The place is itself called *Hullonde* (1275 *Ass*) and *Hullplace* (1593 FF).

HOLLYBED COMMON

Holibed Hy 3 BM   *Holybet* 1378 IpmR
Holybedde 1535 VE

Compounds of *bedd* with a plant- or tree-name are common. The first element is holegn, 'holly,' cf. *holenbedde, holnebedde* followed soon by *wiþibedde* or 'withy-bed' in BCS 910, *þyrnbedd* or 'thorn-bed' in KCD 705, *riscbedd* or 'rush-bed' in BCS 687, *æsc-bedd* or 'ash-tree-bed' in BCS 552, cf. Gettes Ashbed *supra* 42 and Nettlebed (O).

KEYSES FM

This must take its name from the family of *Keyse* who were well established in Longdon, of which Castle Morton is a chapelry. They are found in Wills of 1584, 1592, 1628 and 1642 in Longdon and of 1631, 1633 in Castle Morton. They were doubtless ultimately the same family as that which gave its name to Chase End *supra* 96.

PEWTRICE FM (6″)

The pers. name *Pewtris* (1630 Wills), *Pewtress* (1699) is found in this parish. This is the fem. of the occupational name *Pewterer* (*v.* Bardsley *s.n.*).

Naunton Beauchamp

NAUNTON BEAUCHAMP 82 E 1

Niwantune (dat.) 972 (c. 1050) BCS 1282
Newentune 1086 DB
Niwenton 1166 P
Neuuintona, Newintone, Newyntone c. 1086 (1190) *EveA*,
    1212 Fees 139, 1275, 1327 SR, 1309 BM, 1346, 1428 FA
Neuentona, Newenthone, Newenton c. 1086 (1190) *EveB*,
    1280 *For*, 1291 Tax, 1298, 1324 Ipm, (*Beauchamp*) 1370 BM
Neuneton c. 1285 *Bodl* 38
Newynton al. *Nawnton* 1545 LP
Naunton Becham 1563 Wills
Nawington, Newington 1666, 1667 FF

'New farm,' *v.* niwe, tun. The *Beauchamps* held the manor from the end of the 11th cent. It is said to have been called *Dirty* Naunton at one time (VCH iv. 143).

SHERIFFS NAUNTON (lost)

Shirrevesnewenton 1431 FA   *Shyreves Nauntton* 1500 Ipm

A manor now merged in Naunton Beauchamp. The Beauchamps were hereditary sheriffs of Worcestershire.

Newland

NEWLAND 81 G 9

Nova Terra 1127 (1321) Ch
Nova Landa 1232 Ch (p), c. 1245 *Bodl* 5 (p), 1255 *Ass*
Newelond 1327 SR

Descriptive of land newly acquired by the Priory of Malvern from the gift of Gilbert Crispin of Westminster (cf. VCH iv. 126).

LIMBERROW COTTAGES (6″)

Limberg(a) 1127 (1321) Ch, 1376 Pat

This probably has the same history as Limber (L), *Lind-*

beorhg in KCD 953, DB *Linberga*, 12th cent. Danelaw Charters *Limbergia*. The meaning is 'lime-tree hill,' *v.* lind, beorg.

PIN'S GREEN

This is probably the same as *Pynnesfeld* in AD ii (1338), named from its possessor. *Pynnesfeld* is in the adjacent parish of Leigh. The name *Pin* is found in Great Malvern in 1275 (SR).

Peopleton

PEOPLETON [pipəltən] 81 F 14

Piplincgtun 972 (c. 1050) BCS 1282
Piplintune 1086 DB
Piplintona c. 1086 (1190) *EveA* & *B*, 1166, 1210 RBE, 1195 P, 1291 Tax, CompR
Pupplynton, Pupplinton 1240 WoP, 1266 Pat, 1272 Ipm, *FF*, 1275 SR, 1428 FA
Puplanton 1273 Cl
Pupellenthone, Pubblinthon 1280 *For*
Puppleton 1328 Ch, 1397 Pat
Publynton 1349 *Wigorn*
Pupilton 1373, 1438 IpmR
Pipplington 1382 IpmR
Pipulton 1401 Pat
Pepilton 1431 FA, 1653 FF
Puplyngton 1541 LP
Pippleton 1577 Saxton
Pepleton, Pepulton 16th, 17th Wills
Pibbleton 1615 Marr
Peopleton 17th FF *passim*
Pebbleton 1677 Marr

'Pyppel's farm,' *v.* ingtun. This pers. name is a diminutive of the pers. name discussed above under Pepwell and Pepper Wood *infra* 245, 277.

Pershore Holy Cross

PERSHORE[1] [pɑ·ʃər] 81 G/H 14

Perscoran 972 (c. 1050) BCS 1282, (acc.) 1066 (13th) KCD 824

Persceoran (dat.) c. 1055 (18th) KCD 804

'*Persore* 1086 DB, c. 1086 (1190) *EveA & B*

Perschora 14th BM

Percior 1456 Pat

Parshior, Parshore 1464 Pat, 1484 AD i, 1610 Speed, 1675 Ogilby

Pershore and Portsmouth 1542 LP

As suggested by Ritter (133) this must be from a lost OE word which lies behind ME *persche*, 'osier, twig.' It is definitely a West Country word and still survives in Gloucestershire *persh* used in the same sense. OE *persoc*, 'peach,' would have developed to *Persk-* and not to *Persh-*. The second element is ora. Hence 'osier-bank.' *Portmote* was the part of the town which belonged to Westminster Abbey, cf. *Portmot* in a pers. name in 1185 P. Through the forms *Porchmouth, Portysmouth* it was finally corrupted to *Portsmouth* (VCH iv. 153). *Portmote* is 'town-meeting' (*v.* port).

ALLESBOROUGH HILL

Ellesberge c. 1240 (15th) *AOMB* 61

Alesbergh 1377 Pat

Allesbaruwe, Allesborowe, Allesborough 1418 AD iii, 1535 VE, 1547 Pat

Alesborough 1675 Ogilby

'The hill of *Aelli*,' *v.* beorg.

BINHOLME (not on map)

Binham, Bynham 13th AD i, c. 1255 (15th) *AOMB* 61

Binnehomesfeld 1317 (15th) *AOMB* 61

[1] Apart from the obvious High, Bridge, Broad, Head St we may note that there were once: *Lich(e)stret* (AD iii. 13th), 'body' street, because it led to a cemetery (cf. the same street-name in Worcester *supra* 22), *Chepyngstret* (13th) and *le Rotherchepyng* (AD iii. 1476), 'cattle market' (*v.* hryðer), *Taddelon* (AD iii. c. 1280), 'Tad(d)a's lane,' *la Lode* (*v.* (ge)lad), from the High St to the river.

Bynholme, Binholme 1535 VE, 1536, 1542 LP, 1711 BM,
1892 Kelly
Bynehomme 1555 Pat

This may be OE binnan hamm, i.e. within the *hamm* or bend
of the river. The actual site of the manor-house was 600 yards
north-west of the abbey, but the land of the manor may have
extended a good way to the south.

BLAYTHORN FM[1]

Blakethorne 1255 *Ass* (p)   *Blakethurne* 1316 Ipm
Blackthorne 1327 SR (p)
Self-explanatory.

DRAKE'S BROUGHTON

Broctun, Broctune 972 (c. 1050) BCS 1282, 1086 DB, c. 1086
(1190) *EveA*
Broctone 1275 SR
Brakebroghton (sic) 1329 *FF*

'Brook-farm,' distinguished from Broughton Hackett, also
held by Pershore, by the name of the *Drake* family, found here
in 1275 (SR).

CADDECROFT FM

Cadycroft, Cadicroft 1541 LP, 1623 BM
Catticroft 1820 G, c. 1830 O

Probably this is for OE *Cadan-croft*, 'Cada's croft.' For the
preservation of the inflexional syllable, cf. Body Brook *supra* 9.

CALDEWELL

caldan wyllan (acc.) 972 (c. 1050) BCS 1282
Caldewelle a. 1198 (15th) *AOMB* 61, 1275 SR, 1318 Ipm,
1391 AD i, 1392 Pat
Caud Hill 1772 T
Self-explanatory.

CALLANS WOOD (6")

Challing Coppice 1544 LP   *Calians Wood* c. 1830 O

There is little doubt that this is the same name as Calling-

---

[1] Blackthorn in the original O.S. name-book but altered to the present
form in 1903.

wood (St) which Duignan (PN St 31) shows to be a compound of *wood* and the element *calenge* or *chalenge*, the variant forms being respectively the AFr and Central French forms. The name means 'wood whose ownership is in dispute.' Cf. Threapwood (Ch), Threepwood (Nb), which have the same sense, but use a native English prefix.

Chevington Fm (6″)

Civincgtune 972 (c. 1050) BCS 1282
Civintone 1086 DB
Chiuinton, Chyvinton c. 1086 (1190) *EveB*, 1275 *Ass*, SR (p)
Civington 1255 *Ass*
Chevyngton, Chevington 1535 VE, 1539 Wills, 1544 LP

'Cifa's farm,' *v*. ingtun. The pers. name *Cifa* may also be inferred from Chieveley (Berks), *Cifanlea* in BCS 892, Chevington (Sr) and Chivenore (D). See further Introd. xxi.

Deerfold Wood

Derfolde 1316 Ipm   *la Derfaud* 14th VCH iv. 155
Durfold 1820 G   *Durford* c. 1830 O

Self-explanatory.

Harley (lost)

Harlege, Harley 1241 *FF*, 1275 SR (p), 1374, 1376, 1392, 1393 AD i
Hareley 1275 SR (p), 13th (15th) *AOMB* 61, 1322 Pat
Harley Court 1547 Pat

The site of this manor is unknown, so speculation as to the meaning of the first element is more than usually difficult. It may be OE hara or har.

Hermitage Fm

Hermitorium de Wadberg c. 1230 (15th) *AOMB* 61
Armitage 15th VCH iv. 158
Le Hermitage 1541 LP, 1623 BM

The second form represents the usual popular development of the word.

HURST FM

la Hurste c. 1240 (15th) *AOMB* 61
v. hyrst.

HYDE FM (Lithog 1″)

terra voc. la Hide 1248 (15th) *AOMB* 61, 1249 AD iii
v. hid.

MYTHE (lost)

prat. voc. Muta, la Mutha c. 1230 (15th) *AOMB* 61
Wood of la Mue 1229 Ch, c. 1240 (15th) *AOMB* 61
v. myðe. This 'mythe' is the narrow tongue of land where the Piddle flows into the Avon.

NEWLANDS (6″)[1], locally NEWLAND

la Newelande 13th AD ii, c. 1250 (15th) *AOMB* 61
The Abbot of Pershore's part of the borough was divided into Oldland and Newland, the latter being an extension of the borough south-west from the High Street (VCH iv. 153).

THORNDON FM (6″)

Torendune c. 1150 Surv
Thorindon a. 1198 (15th) *AOMB* 61
Thorndon(e) 1255 *Ass*, 1275 SR (p), *et passim*
Thorendone 1275 *Ass*
Thorundon 1445 IpmR
Thornton c. 1830 O

'Thorn-hill,' from some conspicuous thorn-tree or bush. Working out the bounds of the *tunland* of Pershore as given in BCS 1282 it would seem that the thorn-bush in question is what is called *lusporn* in those bounds.

WADBOROUGH

Wadbeorgas (pl.) *Uuadbeorhan* (dat. pl.) 972 (c. 1050) BCS 1282
Wadberg(e) 1086 DB, c. 1086 (1190) *EveA*, 1220 Bracton, 1324 Ipm
Watberg(e) a. 1198 (15th) *AOMB* 61, 1276 *FF*
Wauberg 1251 Ch, 1298 Ipm

---

[1] Now the name of a street.

Wadbarewe 1454 AD iii
Wadborough 1628 QSR

'Woad-hill' or 'hills,' for the form (twice repeated) in the OE charter is in the plural. Cf. *wadbeorh* (BCS 1299) in Cutsdean, *wadbeorgas* (BCS 183) in Tredington, *wadlond* in Hallow (BCS 356), *wadleage* (Heming 356), *wadleahe* (BCS 1222), *waddene* (ib. 1068), Odell (Beds), Woodhill (W) and Waddicar (La), all with the same first element.

These names, apart from those for which we have only post-Conquest forms, would point to the cultivation of woad in OE times, at least in Worcestershire, Berkshire and Hampshire[1].

WALCOT

Walecote c. 1150 Surv, 1275 SR, 1327 SR (p)
Walcote 1391 AD i

'Cottage(s) of the Britons' or 'of the serfs,' *v.* wealh. This is another example of the fairly common occurrence of Waltons and Walcots in the neighbourhood of important settlements.

Pershore St Andrew

CALVECROFT (lost)

Calcroft 1418 VCH iv. 14, n. 20   *Calvecroft* 1690 ib.
'Calves' croft,' *v.* cealf, croft.

PENSHAM

Pedneshamme (dat.) 972 (c. 1050) BCS 1282
Pendesham 1086 DB, 1190 P, 1327 SR
Pednesham a. 1198 (15th) *AOMB* 61
Pennesham 1231 Pat
Pensham, Pensam 16th Wills *passim*

Ritter (192, n. 3) has shown that in this name we have a pers. name *Peden*, an *n*-derivative of a pers. name *Peda* found in *pedan-hrycg* (BCS 820), now Pettridge (K). To the examples of such derivatives collected there we may add from the Stevenson MSS, *Berhteningleag* (BCS 442), *Cægineshamm* (Ethelweard),

---

[1] We have evidence of the cultivation of woad in the 16th cent. in Hampshire from the archives of the Borough of Southampton. It is repeatedly found in several localities in Britain (including Lincolnshire and Norfolk) but is scarcely fully naturalised, except near Tewkesbury, where it appears to be indigenous. In England, as elsewhere, it was ousted by the introduction of indigo. (Information kindly supplied by Professor J. Maclean Thompson.)

now Keynsham (So) from *Cæg* (PN BedsHu 15), and possibly *Motenesoran* (BCS 699) and *Drocenesford* (BCS 393), now Droxford (Ha). From post-Conquest material we have DB *Edenestou* now Edwinstowe (Nt). See further Introd. xxiii.

The hamm refers to a bend in the Avon.

TIDDESLEY WOOD

> *Tiddesle* (*boscus de*) 1218 *FF*
> *Tedelee* 1233 Bracton (p)
> *Tydesle(ge)* 1243 Cl, 1276 RH
> *Tydele* 1275 *Ass*
> *Tidsley* 1637 QSR

'*Tidi's* clearing,' *v.* leah and for the pers. name Redin (124).

North Piddle

NORTH PIDDLE 82 E 1

> *Pidelet* 1086 DB (bis), c. 1086 (1190) *EveA* & *B*, (*Radilfi*)
>   c. 1150 Surv, 1175 P (p)
> *Pydele* 1234 *FF*   *Northpidele* 1271 *For*
> *Norpidel* 1290 Wigorn
> *Northpedeley* 1461 IpmR
> *North Pedyll* 1492 Ipm

This village takes its name from the stream on which it stands (*v. supra* 14) and is called North in contrast to Wyre Piddle *supra* 155. The -*et* suffix in the earliest forms is the Norman diminutive, dealt with by Zachrisson in IPN 94. This village was perhaps 'little' in contrast with Wyre Piddle. In addition to this name derived from the stream there seems to have been an alternative English one derived from an English settler, for the boundaries suggest that it should be identified with the *Wihtlafestun* of BCS 1282, i.e. farm of *Wihtlāf*.

ENNICK FORD (6″)

> *Hennuc* 972 (c. 1050) BCS 1282   *Ennekesford* 1255 *Ass*

Hennuc is a stream-name in the list of bounds in which it is found[1]. The 13th cent. form is a good example of a genitival

---

[1] For this identification we are indebted to the kindness of Dr G. B. Grundy. We may add that the *Enedeford* (1229 Ch) of the bounds of Horwell Forest almost certainly refers to this place and seems to be a blunder for *Enekeford*.

compound. For a possible parallel to this stream-name *v.*
Inkford Brook *supra* 12 and Inkford in King's Norton *infra* 354.

Pinvin

PINVIN 82 F 1

Pendefen 1275 SR   *Piendefen* 1416 AD iv
Pyndeven 1493 IpmR   *Pennefynne* 1542 LP
Penfin 1571 BM   *Pendfin* 1597, 1606 Wills
Pynfen, Pynvin 16th, 17th Wills

OE *Pendan-fen*, 'fen or marsh of Penda,' *v.* fenn. The same
pers. name is found in Pinbury (Gl) and Pinley (Wa) and
Pendiford in King's Norton (1240 WoP). Apart from its
occurrence in place-names the only example of the name is
Penda, king of the Mercians. *Pendræd, Pendweald* and *Pendwulf*
are recorded and *Penda* is no doubt a shortened form of such
names as these.

Pirton

PIRTON 81 G 12

Pyritune 972 (c. 1050) BCS 1282
Peritune 1086 DB
Piritune 1086 (c. 1190) *EveB*
Perintona c. 1086 (1190) *EveA*
Periton(a) 1175 P, 1275 SR
Pyriton, Piriton Power 1327 SR, 1333 *Bodl* 38, 1352 Ch,
    1411 IpmR
Puriton, Puryton 1316 Ipm, 1482 IpmR
Pyrton 1523 BM

'Pear-tree farm,' *v.* pyrige, tun. This estate was held by
Walter *Ponther* in DB and by Hugh *Puher* in 1176 (RBE).

CROOME PERRY WOOD

Pyrie 1327 SR (p)   *Perywode* 15th VCH iv. 181
'Pear-tree wood,' *v.* pyrige.

Powick

POWICK [pɔik] 81 F 10

Poincguuic 972 (c. 1050) BCS 1282
Poiwic(h)(a) 1086 DB, c. 1086 (1190) *EveA & B*

Poyswyke 1275 SR
Poywy(c)k, Poywik 1212 Fees 139, 1249 Ch, *FF*, 1291 Tax
et passim
Puwyk 1300 Ch
Powyck 1535 VE

There is considerable likelihood of an OE name *Pohha* (Redin 77) both independently and in the Berkshire *pohanlæh* (BCS 366) and in Poughill (D). Stevenson (MS note) suggested that the full form of this name was *Pohingwic,* i.e. 'Poha's wic,' *v.* ing. The later forms perhaps come from an alternative *Pohanwic* rather than from *Pohingwic.*

BASTONFORD

Berstanesford 1275 SR (p)   *Bestanesford* 1347 *FF*
Bastingford 1787 Cary

'The ford of either *Beorhtstān* or *Beornstān,*' the forms being consistent with either. Barston (Wa) is from *Beorhtstānestūn.*

BEAUCHAMP COURT

Poiwica Willelmi de Bellocampo c. 1150 Surv

This manor represents the holding of William de *Beauchamp* in Powick in the time of Stephen (VCH iv. 186).

BOSWORTH'S FM

This is probably from the family of *Bosworth* mentioned in 1662 *FF.*

CALLOW END

This may possibly contain the pers. name *le Calewe* found in the Subsidy Roll of 1275. The place-name appears as *Callaway* in 1820 (G).

CLEVELODE

Clivelade, Clyuelade c. 1086 (1190) *EveA*, 1237 Wigorn,
   1275 SR (p)
Clivelode 1275, 1332 SR (p)

The lad is clearly the ferry across the Severn to Clifton, but the 'cleve' (*v.* clif) is probably that at Clevelode itself rather than the one at Clifton.

COLLETT'S GREEN

Collicke 17th Wills (p)   *Cholic* 1820 G

This place presents difficulties of identification. We have numerous references to a lost Colewick (*supra* 91) which, on the whole of the evidence, would seem to have been in the parish of St John's in Bedwardine, the most definite passage being one in which, in the Register of Worcester Priory, we hear of the monks holding land at *Colewyk*. On the other hand, in the Survey of Wick Episcopi, mention is made of a *campus versus Colewyke* (*RBB*), then of a *Homme* and then of *Colewyke Homfeld*. As we have a place *Collicke* or *Cholic* just across the river it is difficult to believe that they have no connexion, but it is impossible to make a definite choice between the two difficulties, on the one hand of believing in the existence so close together of two places of the same name, on the other of believing that Worcester Priory could hold pasturage in a Westminster manor. Another possibility is that a migrant from Colewick may have settled in Powick and given his name to the estate. The name of the place means 'Cola's dairy-farm,' *v*. **wic**. The form is probably pseudo-manorial and for the final *-ett* we may compare the history of Collett (PN Bk 141).

DAWS HILL

This is *Daws End* in Greenwood's map (1820) and embodies the pers. name *Dawe* found in the SR of 1275.

KINGS END

This name is found in 1613 (QSR) and must come from the family name *le Kynge* recorded in 1327 (SR).

PIXHAM

Picresham, Pykresham c. 1086 (1190) *EveA*, 1275 SR (p)
Pikeresham, Pykeresham 1221 *Ass*, 1243 *FF*, 1255 *Ass*, 1294
    Wigorn, WoCh (p)
Pykereshamm 1276 RH
Pyxam, Pixham 1535 VE, 1549 Pat
Pukesham 1576 Wills

This place-name, certainly in its first element, and possibly in its second also, is a duplicate of the *Picereshamm* (KCD 289),

Picereshomm (ib. 1368) which Mr C. A. Seyler has identified as a meadow still named Pickersom, on the Avon in Littleton, *v. infra* 266. Searle (p. 571) suggests a pers. name *Pichere*, but there is no authority for such a compound. More probably it is a pers. name *Pīcer*, an *r*-derivative of the OE pers. name *Pīc*, which we have good grounds for assuming. This name is found in Pickering (Y) and further notice of the likelihood of such names will be found in PN Bk 110 *s.n. Doddershall*. The name is therefore probably either Picer's hamm or his ham. It is to be regretted that we have no earlier forms than *Pyckersled* (VCH iv. 123 n. 27) for Pickersleigh in Great Malvern (Wo) which seems to contain the same first element. *v.* Introd. xxiii.

Pole Elm

de la Pole, atte Pole 1275, 1332 SR

This seems to contain OE *pāl*, 'pole, stake,' cf. the use of Staple (K, So, W) as a place-name.

Pursers Fm

This must contain the family name *Purser* recorded in Wills (1565–1619) and QSR (1607).

Stanbrook

Stanbroc, Stanbroke 1275, 1327 SR (p)

'Stone-brook,' i.e. stony, *v.* stan, broc.

Woodsfield

Wrdesfelda Hy 1 (1377) Pat, 1251 *FF*
Wordefeud, Wordfeld 1249 *FF*, 1291 Tax
Wordesfeld 1275 SR, 1417 AD vi
Wodisfield, Woodsfield 1541 LP, 1628 QSR

Here, as in Wordley *supra* 37 we seem to have an OE pers. name *W(e)orð*. Hence, 'Weorth's open land,' *v.* feld.

Staunton

Staunton 92 D 9

Stantun 972 (c. 1050) BCS 1282, 978 (11th) KCD 619
Stanton 1275 SR
Staunton 1327 SR, 1346 FA

v. stan, tun, and for spelling *v.* IPN 105. This was sometimes distinguished from the other Stauntons as Staunton in Corse, or near Corse (*v.* Habington i. 374–5, Nash ii. 372), cf. Corse Lawn in Eldersfield 197 *supra*.

HETHELPIT CROSS, HETHELPIT GATE

Heath Myll Pytt 1633 QSR

The exact sense is not clear. By a curious coincidence we have in SR (1275) in succession, Will. de *Cruce*, Reginaldus *Molendinarius* and Lenota *de la Putte*.

SNIG'S END

Snygges-place 1493 Ipm

This probably embodies the pers. name *Snygge*, *Snyge* found in 1349 in Dudley and in 1275 (SR) in Birlingham and Cleeve Prior.

Severn Stoke

SEVERN STOKE 81 H 11

Stoc 972 (c. 1050) BCS 1282
Stoche 1086 DB
Stokes c. 1086 (1190) *EveB* and (*Roberti*) *EveA*
Savarnestoke, Savernestok' 1212 Fees 139, 1232 Cl, c. 1245
  Bodl 5, 1272 *FF*
Severnestok 1275 SR
Syuernestoke 1350 *FF*

'The stoc by the Severn.' The *Robertus* is unknown.

BIRCH FM (6″)

del Birche 1275 SR

Self-explanatory.

CLIFTON

Clifton 1256 Ipm, (*juxta Sauernestoke*) 1319 *FF*, (*on Severn*) 1633 QSR

The *cliff* is a very gentle rise from about 40 ft. on the Severn to about 55 ft., a good illustration of what a clif might be in OE.

CLIFTON ARLES (6")

This is *Orls* in the first ed. of the 6" map and is clearly the local form of OE alor, cf. Orleton *supra* 67.

THE HILL

de Monte 1275 SR, *Ass*, 1327 SR

Self-explanatory.

HORWELL (lost)

Horwylle 972 (c. 1050) BCS 1282
Hor(e)well 1229 Ch, 1291 Tax, 1322 Pat, 1327 SR, 1535 VE
Horwelwodd, Horwellwood in Defford 1401 Pat, 1542 LP

'Dirty stream' (*v.* horh, wielle), the reference probably being to the stream which divides Severn Stoke from Defford.

KINNERSLEY

Kinardesle(ge), Kynardesle 1221 *Ass*, 1232 Ch (p), 1256 Ipm (p), 1275 *Ass*
Kynerslege, Kynersly 1314 Ipm, 1591 Wills
Kynnersley 1650 FF

'Cyneheard's clearing,' *v.* leah, cf. Kinnerley (Sa) and Kinnersley (He).

NAUNTON

Newinton 1275 SR, 1340 NI, 1408 IpmR, all (p)
Newetone 1275 *Ass*
Neuton 1315 *FF*
Naunton, Nawnton 1545, 1579 Wills

'New farm,' also known as *Black* Naunton to distinguish it from Naunton *Beauchamp*. It was so called from Robert le *Blake* or *Blac* who had a holding here (1180–2 P). We have also a Robert le *Neir* and Reginald le *Blake* in 1332 (SR), a good example of a second name which early seems to have become practically a surname.

NORTHAL (lost)

Northal 1232 Ch   *Northale* 13th Wulst
v. healh.

SANDFORD

Sandford, Saunford, Sondford, Sanford 1275 SR, *Ass,* 1314,
 1316 Ipm, all (p)
San(d)ford 1655, 1681 FF
Self-explanatory.

Strensham

STRENSHAM [strensəm] 81 J 13

Strengesho 972 (c. 1050) BCS 1282
Strenchesham c. 1086 (1190) *EveA,* 1275 *Ass*
Strengesham a. 1198 *AOMB* 61, 1210 RBE, 1212 Fees 139,
 1275 SR, 1291 Tax, 1346 FA, 1349 Wigorn, 1428 FA
Strenesham 1214 Ipm
Strongesham 1227 *FF*
Stringesham, Stryngesham 1328 Ch, 1397 Pat
Streynsham, Streinsham 1431 FA, 1547 Pat
Straynsham 1471 Pat
Strensham 16th Wills *passim*

There would seem to have been an OE pers. name *Streng* to
judge from this name and from Stringston (So), *Strengestune*
DB, *Strengesburna* in the bounds of Pensax in Heming (246)
and an unidentified *Strengesburieles* (BCS 458)[1], but no parallel
has been noted in the other Germanic languages. It is presumably OE *strenge,* 'strong,' and must originally have been
a nickname. The name therefore means 'Strong's homestead,'
v. ham. In the first form the suffix is OE hoh and the
reference is to the cliff above the Severn on which Strensham
stands.

LEY FM

de la Lee, atte Lee 1275 SR, 1340 NI
v. leah.

MOGSTOCKING (6")

Moggestokyng 1332 (15th) *AOMB* 61
The clearing made by the family of *Mogg,* recorded in South
Worcestershire in 1327, 1332 SR and 1240 WoP, *v.* stocking.

---

[1] Stevenson MSS.

s

Upton Snodsbury

UPTON SNODSBURY [snɔdʒbəri] 81 E 14

Snoddesbyri 972 (c. 1050) BCS 1282
Snodesbyrie 1086 DB
Snodesbery c. 1086 (1190) *EveA*
Snodesbiry c. 1086 (1190) *EveB*
Snodesbury, Snodesbure 1275 SR, 1280 *For*, 1282 *FF*
Snodisbury 1462 Pat
Snowdesbury 1463, 1476 Pat
Snodgbury 1700 Marr

Upton was originally a separate vill and first appears as *Upton Stephani* in 1212 Fees 139. It is called *Upton juxta Snodebure* in 1280 (*For*), *super Snoddysbury* in 1366 (IpmR) and the two together are called *Upton Snodesbury* in 1327 (SR). The 'church-town' lies slightly above the rest of the parish and must be the *Upton*. The *Stephanus* cannot now be identified. The first element in Snodsbury is a pers. name *Snodd*, not found in independent use but clearly present in Snodshill (W), *Snoddeshelle*, in BCS 754, Snodland (K), *Snoddingland* in BCS 418, the lost Snodderswick (Db), *Snodeswic* in O.S. Facs. iii. 47, and (in a weak form) in Snowdenham (Sr), 1260 FF *Snodeham* and *Snoddanfleot* (BCS 949). This may be the same as the pers. name *Snode* found in DB and also lie behind the second name in Ceolla *Snoding* as noted by Redin (130). Hence 'Snodd's burh.' This same *Snodd* gave his name to a *Snoddeslea* mentioned in the boundaries of Crowle and this parish (BCS 428) and to a *boscus de Snodington* recorded here in 1271 (*For*).

COWSDEN [kouzən]

Colleduna c. 1150 Surv
Coulesduna c. 1190 *EveA*, c. 1220 (15th) *AOMB* 28 b
Coulesdon a. 1198 (15th) *AOMB* 61, 1242 P, 1262 *For*, 1275 SR (p), 1327 SR (p)
Collesdon 1275 *Ass*, 1500 Ipm, 1531 Lytt, 1600 QSR, 1654 Wills
Caulesdone 1280 *For*
Koulisdone 1285 *FF*
Couliston 1316 Ipm (p)

Coolsonne 1583 Wills
Coulston 1590 Wills
Colsdon 1600–1619 QSR
Coulsden 1682 Wills
Cousdown 1855 Kelly   *Cowsdown* 1892 ib.

Professors Ekwall and Zachrisson suggest that in this name we have as the first element an OE pers. name *Cūfel*, a diminutive of the well-established *Cūfa*. *fl* was early assimilated to *ll*, at least in certain of the forms. Hence 'hill of Cufel,' *v.* dun. Cf. Cowesfield and Coulston (W) with the same pers. name (PN W 64–5). There was a *Couleswelle* in Wo, not very far off, c. 1250 (*AOMB* 61).

DADSLEY BARN (6″)

Dodeslough 15th VCH iv. 209 n. 13

The second element in this name is uncertain, probably it is *sloh*, 'slough, mire.' The first would seem to be the pers. name *Dode* or Dodd recorded in this parish in 1275 (SR) and 1341 (NI).

Wick by Pershore

WICK BY PERSHORE 81 H 1

Wiche 1086 DB   *Wicha Inardi* c. 1150 Surv
(*la Wike*) 1261 Ipm
Wyke 1275 SR

v. wic. For the *Inardus* cf. Innerstone and Insoll *supra* 157 and *infra* 241. It included manors known as Wyke *Waryn* or *Warren*, the *Warin* family having been holders here already in 1275 (SR) and *Wyke Burnell* (1366 IpmR), this manor having been sold to Bishop Robert Burnell in 1281 (VCH iv. 169).

Yardley[1]

YARDLEY 72 D 6

Gyrdleah 972 (c. 1050) BCS 1282
Gerlei 1086 DB
Gardelegia c. 1086 (1190) *EveA*
Ierdele 1220 Bracton, 1275 SR, 1305 Wigorn

[1] Transferred to Halfshire in 1760.

Yerdel' c. 1237 *Bodl* 43, 44, 45
Jordele 1255 *FF*, 1259 Pat
Zerdeleye, Gerdeley 1291 Tax
Yerdeleye c. 1300 BM, 1478 Pat
Erdeley 1478 Pat
Yardeley 1541 BM

This name must be a compound of OE *gyrd*, 'yard, rod, twig' and leah. It is difficult to say in what sense *gyrd* can be used in this compound, perhaps that of 'twig, stick' is the likeliest, hence 'twig-clearing.' Cf. Yardley (So), KCD 816 *Gyrdley*, Yardley (Ess, Nth). It might however refer to some boundary-mark, cf. Stalybridge (Ch), Staveley (La) and Staveley (Db). Ekwall (PN La 29) suggests that here we have a compound of OE *stæf*, 'staff, stave,' used in the sense suggested. In *gyrdweg* (BCS 955) and *gyrdford* (BCS 778) it perhaps refers to a road or a ford marked out by stakes or something of that kind.

ACOCK'S GREEN

This must take its name from the family of Richard *Acock* who is mentioned in Fines (1652–90).

BILLESLEY FM

Billesleye 1275 *Ass*, SR (p)

'Clearing of *Bill*,' *v.* leah.

THE BIRCHES

atte Birches 1334 AD i

Self-explanatory.

FOX HOLLIES HALL

atte Holies, de Holies 1275, 1327 SR

v. holegn.

GREET

Grete, Greth 1255 *FF*, 1275 *Ass*, 1328 Ch, 1545 LP
Greet End 1552 Ct

This must be OE greot, 'gravel,' used descriptively of the place or, possibly, of the stream on which it lies, cf. R. Greet (Nt). The name seems also to be found in:

GREETHURST (lost)

Gruthurst 1221 Ass   *Grethurst* 1275 SR, 1332 SR, both (p)
Greethurst 1279 Ipm
'Gravel wood' or 'wood on the river Greet.'

HAY MILLS

in the Hay, in le Hay 1327 SR, 1340 NI
'Enclosure,' *v.* (ge)hæg.

KINETON GREEN [1]

Cinctunes broc 972 (c. 1050) BCS 1282
OE *cyning-tun*, 'king-farm' or 'royal manor.'

LEA HALL

atte Lee 1275 SR
v. leah.

SPARKBROOK (6")

This probably takes its name from the family of *Spark(e)* recorded in Yardley in 1275 and 1327 (SR). It first appears as 'a torrent called *Sparkbroke*' in a 1511 rental of Bordesley Manor (Dugdale Society, vol. iv. 41).

STECHFORD

Stichesford 1267 Ipm
Stigford 1275 *Ass*
Stifford 1275 SR
Stichford 1296, 1318 AD i, 1670 FF, c. 1830 O
Sticheford, Stycheford 1303 Wigorn, 1410 AD i, 1583 Wills

The forms are late but consistent with derivation from OE *stȳfic*, 'stump.' Possibly therefore 'ford by the stump.' There are no *u*-forms but such are commonly absent in the case of *stȳfa- stȳfic-* names, perhaps owing to the following labial, cf. Stewkley (PN Bk 72).

SWANSHURST

Swaneshurst 1221, 1255 *Ass*, 1345 *FF*, all (p)
Swanhurste 1275 SR (p)
Swanneshurste 1332 SR (p)
Swanshurst 1677 FF

[1] Partly in Warwickshire.

It is impossible to say whether the first element in this name is OE *swann*, 'swan,' or OE *swān*, 'peasant.' The *swān* alternative is the more probable. The second is hyrst.

TYSELEY [taizli]

> *Tisseleye* 1327 SR (p)   *Tiseley* c. 1830 O

The pers. name *Tyssa* is not on record in OE but it, or a strong form *Tyssi*, lies behind Tisbury which is *Tyssesburg* in the letters of St Boniface[1] and *Tyssebirig* in BCS 591. Hence 'Tyssa's clearing,' *v.* leah. The modern pronunciation is clearly artificial. A name *Tissi* from *Tīdsige* would be easier to explain and it should be added that there are no later forms in *Tusse*- for Tisbury (PN W 162), and this again points to *Tisse*. It is however difficult to get by the 8th cent. form *Tysses*-.

YARDLEY WOOD

> *atte Wode* 1275, 1327 SR

Self-explanatory.

IV. CRESSELAU HUNDRED

Cresselau 1086 DB
Kerselau c. 1150 Surv

This Hundred consisted of 12 manors assessed at 100 hides. It lay compactly to the north-east of Doddingtree Hundred. The site of the meeting-place is unknown. In the 13th century this Hundred, with the exception of Wolverley and Hartlebury, was merged in the Hundred of Halfshire in which it still remains. The name itself is a compound of OE cærse and hlaw, hence 'hill on or by which cress grows.'

Chaddesley Corbett

CHADDESLEY CORBETT [tʃædʒli] 71 H 12

> *Ceadresleahge* 816 (11th) BCS 356
> *æt Ceadresleage, Cedresleage, Ceadesleage* 816 (11th) BCS 357
> *Ceaddes Leage* 11th Heming
> *Cedeslai* 1086 DB

---

[1] Stevenson MSS.

Chedlega 1167 P
Chedeslega 1167 P
Caddislega 1189 P
Cheddesle(ga) Hy 2 (1300) Ch, 1270 Ch
Chaddesleye, Chadesley 1275 SR, 1290 Ipm, (*Corbet*) 1431 FA
Cheddesley 1577 Saxton
Chedderley 1675 Ogilby

The first element in this name would seem to be a pers. name in which we have an *r*-extension of an earlier *Ceadda* or *Ceadd*, such as is dealt with under Pixham *supra* 225. Such an extension, if it be assumed, would suggest that this method of pers. name formation was still in use after the English settlement, for the name *Ceadd(a)* must be of Celtic origin, though the palatalisation suggests that the English must have become acquainted with it at a very early date, by what chance we know not. It is difficult to say how far the post-Conquest forms of this place-name (with the exception of the contracted form from the Pipe Roll) are to be explained as due to early loss of *r* or as from an alternative form of the name in which the unextended *Ceadd* is used. For such alternative forms cf. Chadwick in Hartlebury *infra* 243. The name then means 'clearing of *Ceadder*' or 'of *Ceadd*.' See further Introd. xxiii.

The manor came into the possession of the *Corbet* family at the end of the 12th cent. (VCH iii. 38).

ASTWOOD HILL (Old 1″)

Askewode 1505 *MinAcct*

As this lies on the eastern boundary of the parish it is clear that this is 'east wood' and that the only early form is corrupt.

BARROW HILL

atte Berewe 1327 SR

v. beorg. This hill has a barrow on it, said to be a pre-historic burial mound (VCH iv. 433).

BELLINGTON FM

Belintones 1086 DB   *Belinton* 1224 *FF*, 1275 SR
Bellington 1665 FF

Probably OE *Bellingtūn,* 'Bella's farm,' *v.* ingtun. A pers. name *Bela* or *Bella* may be inferred from *bellan ford* (BCS 454) and such place-names as Bellingdon (PN Bk 224) and Belford (PN NbDu 16). The plural is used in DB as it was held 'as two manors.'

BLUNTINGTON

Bluntindon 1275 *Ass,* 1291 Ipm   *Blontindon* 1275 SR (p)

OE *Bluntingdūn,* 'Blunt's hill,' *v.* dun and ing (used with the same force as in ingtun names). For this pers. name *v.* Bluntisham (PN BedsHu 204) and cf. further Blunt's Hall (Ess), earlier *Blunteshale.*

BRADFORD HOUSE and BRIDGE (6″)

La Brodeford 1229 Ch   *Bradeford* 1275 *Ass* (p)
Bradefordebrugge 1300 Pat
Self-explanatory.

BROCKENCOTE

Brochamcote 1275 SR
Bro(a)kencote 1505 *MinAcct,* 1656 BM, 1671 FF

'Cottage by (Doverdale) brook-homestead,' *v.* broc, ham, cote, cf. Brockamin in Leigh *supra* 205.

CAKEBOLE

Kakebale, Cakebale 1270 AD vi (p), 1275 SR (p), 1656 BM
Cakeballe 1280 *For* (p)
Cokebale 1322 Cl
Cakebowe 1656 WillsP
Cakebould 1708 FF

The first element in this name and in Cakemore *infra* 293, and in a lost *Kakewelle* in Fladbury (1260 *RBB*), must be the pers. name which is found also in Cakeham or Cackham (Sx), *Cacham* 1263 *FF,* 1262 (1338) Ch, and in Cavick in Wymondham (Nf), *Cakewyc* 1332 BM, *Cakewyck* 1453 AD iii. This name is not on independent record in OE but there is evidence for Germanic cognates of such an OE name as *Caca* or *Cacca.* Förstemann (PN 57) records a pers. name *Cac(c)o* and a more doubtful *Cacho*. From this were formed place-names *Cachinga* and *Cakingeham* (ON i. 1623)[1].

The second element is probably a lost OE *beall*, 'ball,' used of a rounded hill. Such a use is recorded in the EDD in Somerset and a good illustration is the well-known Cloutsham Ball in that county. This dialectal use of *ball* and its presence in a Worcestershire place-name tend to confirm Björkman's view (*Scand. Loan-words* 229) that the word *ball* in ME was not a Scand. loan-word but an OE word of which we only happen to have record of the diminutive form *bealluc*. See further PN La 165. The whole name, if this is the right view, means 'Caca's rounded hill.' The *d* of the 18th cent. form is the common vulgarism whereby *d* develops after final *l*, as in *vild* for *vile*.

CHADDESLEY WOOD

de Bosco, atte Wode 1275, 1327 SR

Self-explanatory.

DORHALL FM

Dorewall 1505 *MinAcct*

This is probably for OE *dēorwælle*, 'spring where animals water,' *v.* deor, wielle.

DRAYTON

Dreiton 1200 Dugd. ii. 76   *Drayton* 1255 *Ass*

v. dræg, tun. This place lies on a stream where it is crossed by the road. The exact sense of *dræg* cannot be determined here.

FENNY ROUGH

Fenney in Harueington 1654 WillsP

The first part of this name must be OE fenn-eg, descriptive of an island in marshland.

---

[1] The history of Kigbeare (D) suggests another possibility for the origin of this pers. name. This has forms DB *Cacheberga*, 1242 Fees *Cakeber*, 1310 Ipm *Cadekebera*, 1256 *Ass Cadekeber*. Here it is clear we have a pers. name *Cadoc*, a diminutive of OE *Cada* and that this name might appear, as early as DB, as *Cache*. For the forms of this name we are indebted to Mr J. E. B. Gover.

HARVINGTON

Herwynton 1275 SR, 1311 Cl, 1327 SR, all (p)
Herewinton 1275 SR, 1326 Pat, 1342 *FF*
Horinton 1323 Ipm (p)
Herwyngton 1325 Pat (p)
Harwytone 1545 Wills

'Farm of *Herewynn*,' that being an OE fem. pers. name. The *v* of the modern form is irregular but we may compare Kinvaston (St), *Kynwaldestun* in the Wolverhampton foundation charter, Rivenhall (Ess), DB *Ruwenhale* and Waveney (Nf), 1275 *Wahenhe*, 1465 *Wawneye*. See also *s.n.* Evenlode *supra* 123. The history of this name is quite different from that of Harvington in Oswaldslow *supra* 134.

HILLPOOL

Hulle 1255 *Ass*, 1275 SR   *Hilpoole* 1612 Wills
Self-explanatory.

PLEREMORE

Pleybmere 1275 SR (p)   *Blebermer* 1327 SR (p)

SWANCOTE FM

Swenecote 1271 *For*
Swanecote 1280 *For*, 1324 FF
Swannecote 1505 *MinAcct*

This place, like Sannacott (D), is from OE *swāna cot(u)*, 'cottages of the peasants,' *v.* swan, cot.

TAGG BARN

Tagburnesyche, Taggeburne 1505 *MinAcct*
For this name *v.* Tagwell Lane in Droitwich *infra* 288.

TANWOOD

Twenewode 1290 Ipm (p)   *Twynewod* 1291 Ipm
Tanwood 1789 Gough

This house is between two woods and that is doubtless the origin of the name, it is '(be)tween woods.' Cf. Twyning (Gl), which is *Bituinæum* in BCS 350, a similar compound of *ēa*, 'river,' also Twembrook (Ch), 1288 *Twenebrok*.

WINTERFOLD

Wynterfold 1275 SR, 1290 Ipm (p)
Wintrefelde 1507 *MinAcct*

The name is self-explanatory. The place lies in a sheltered position.

WOODHAMCOTE (lost)

Wudhamcote 1221 *Ass* (p)   *Wodehamcote* 1275 SR (p)
Wodecote 1431 FA

Self-explanatory.

WOODHOUSE FM (6")

Wodhous 1505 *MinAcct*   *le Woodhouse* 1548 Pat

v. similar names in Upper Arley, Pensax, Grafton Flyford *supra* 33, 68, 201 and Ombersley *infra* 273.

WOODROW

Wodrewe 1505 *MinAcct*   *Woodrow* 1655 WillsP

Probably used of a row of trees, a thin wood. *v.* **raw, ræw** and cf. *hæselræwe* (BCS 1282).

YIELDINGTREE

Gyldintre 1275 SR
Gildentre 13th StSwith (p)
Yildyntre 1327 SR (p)
Yalyngtre, Yelyngtree 1505 *MinAcct*
Ildintre, Ildentre, Yldontre 1341 Pat (p), 1544, 1545 Wills

Gilda may be a pet-form for such OE names as *Ēadgīld*, *Ingild*, *Swǣfgild* and the name mean 'Gilda's tree,' but it is difficult to be sure. The forms with *ing* are so late in appearing that connexion with the word *yielding* is very unlikely.

Doverdale

DOVERDALE [dɔ·dəl] 81 A 11

on Douerdale, andlang Douerdæles 706 (12th) BCS 116
andlang Doferdæles 817 (11th) BCS 362
Lunvredele 1086 DB
Duverdale 1166 RBE
Douredela 1166 P (p)
Dovredal' 1212 Fees 140

Douerdale 1262 *For*, 1275 SR, 1294 Wigorn, 1316 Ipm, 1327
SR, all (p)
Dorydale 1451 Pat
Doverdall 1546 LP
Dardall, Dordall 1558 Wills

This village takes its name from the stream, which is called
in succession Dordale Brook, Elmley Brook and Hadley Brook.
The second element in the stream-name is OE **dæl**, the first is
explained in IPN 24. See also Dordale *infra* 275.

HILL FM
othe Hulle 1327 SR, 1340 NI
Self-explanatory.

SOUTHALL
Southale 1327 SR (p)
'South nook of land,' *v.* healh. It is in the south of the parish.

Elmley Lovett

ELMLEY LOVETT 71 J 11
Elmesetene gemære 817 (11th) BCS 361
Elmsetena gemære 980 (11th) KCD 627
Ælmeleia 1086 DB
Almelega Ricardi de Portes c. 1150 Surv
Aumeleg(a) 1210 RBE, 1212 Fees 140
Almeleye Lovet 1275 SR
Elmeleye Lovet 1327 SR
Awmeley Lovet 1428 FA

OE *elma-lēage* (dat.), 'clearing of the elm-trees,' *v.* leah. For
the *Alm-*, *Aum-* forms *v.* Zachrisson, *A. N. Influence* 147. In
the first forms we have the usual irrational addition of sæte to
the first element of a place-name, to denote its inhabitants. The
Portes family continued to hold land in Elmley till 1327 (VCH
iii. 107), and one *Richard* was holding in 1166 (RBE), but the
Lovett family inter-married with them early in the 13th cent.

ACTON
Akton 1275 SR (p)
Acton juxta Elmele Lovett 1342 FF
'Oak-farm,' *v.* ac, tun.

BALLHILL COTTAGES (6″)

This may take its name from the *Balle* family mentioned in 1327 (SR), especially as Townsend (1644) gives the old name as Ball Hall.

CALLOWS FM (6″)

This must take its name from the family of *le Calewe*, 'the bald,' recorded in 1275 and 1327 (SR).

CUTNALL GREEN [kʌtlənd]

Cuttenhall Green 1642 Townsend   *Cutnall* 1644 ib.

The forms are too late for any certainty to be possible. In a good many *Cut-* names, as in Cutcombe (So), Cutslow (O) and Cutsdean (*supra* 120) we have pers. names *Cudd(a)* or *Codd*, with later unvoicing of *d* to *t*, but such unvoicing before *n* is not very probable.

FELGATE (lost)

Felegate 1275 SR   *Felgate* 1327 SR, 1644 Townsend

There is very little to go upon. Possibly this is for *Thelegate*, 'gate made of planks' (*v.* þel), with the common confusion of initial *th* and *f*.

GOLDSMITHS FM[1]

This must take its name from the family of *Goldsmyth* recorded in 1327 (SR).

INSOLL (lost)

Inerdeshell, Ynardeshull 1275 *Ass*
Inneshale 1327 SR (p)
Insale 1340 NI (p)
Insoll 1642 Townsend

'The hill of I(s)nard,' *v.* hyll. For this pers. name and its significance in Wo *v.* Innerstone *supra* 157.

MERRINGTON (lost)

Merynton 1375 AD iv, 1388 IpmR, 1389 Pat

Possibly 'farm of *Mǣra*' (*v.* ingtun), *Mǣra* being a shortened form of one of the OE names in *Mǣr-*, found also in Meering

---

[1] On the lithographed 1″ map.

(Nt) and Kirk Merrington (Du). This estate however lay on the borders of three parishes and it is possible therefore that the name stands for OE *mǣringa-tun*, 'farm of the dwellers on the *meare* or boundary,' *v.* (ge)mære.

ROLLES ORCHARD (Old 1″)

This takes its name from the family of *Rowles* mentioned in a Will of 1568. It is called *Rowles Orchard* in 1644 (Townsend).

RYELANDS FM

Middil Rilande 1524 LP

This is clearly a plural of 'rye-land,' i.e. where such is grown (*v.* **ryge, lond**).

SAPCOTT (lost)

Sapercote(s) 1275 SR (p), 1543 LP
Sapcote 1327 SR (p)
Sapcott 1640 Townsend

No attempt can be made to solve this difficult name until similar names in other counties, e.g. Sapperton (Db, Sx, Gl), have been fully documented.

UPTON FM

Upton 1275 SR, 1345 *FF*
Self-explanatory. It stands on a hill.

WALTON FM (6″)

Walton 1255 *Ass*, 1299 (18th) *RBB*, 1323 Pat, 1327 SR
v. **wealh, tun** and cf. Walton in Clent *infra* 280.

Hartlebury

HARTLEBURY 71 J 10

Heortlabyrig 817 (17th) BCS 361, 980 (11th) KCD 627
Heortlanbyrig, Heortlaford n.d. (12th) BCS 1320, 985 (11th) KCD 653
Huerteberie 1086 DB
Hurtlebery c. 1086 (1190) *EveB*
Hertlebery, Hertlebyr c. 1150 Surv, 1255 Ch
Hurklebery 1271 *For* (p)
Heortelbury 1346 FA
Hurtlebury 1349 *Bodl* 67 (p)

The first element in this name is a pers. name *Heortla*, a diminutive of a name derived from the common word *heorot*, 'hart,' cf. OGer *Hirz* and *Hirzil* in Förstemann PN 845. Hence 'Heortla's burh.' Cf. Hartlington (Y).

ASHRIDGE (lost)

Esruge 1249 *FF*   *Asserugge* 1275 *Ass*
Self-explanatory.

CHADWICK

Cheddewic 1182 (18th) *RBB*
Chedelwyke al. *Cheddewyche* 1299 (18th) *RBB*
Chadewyke 13th (17th) Hab   *Chedewyke* 1327 SR (p)
Cherwick c. 1830 O
'Ceadda's dairy farm,' *v.* wic, with a variant form from the diminutive *Ceadela*.

CHARLTON

Cherletona 1182 (18th) *RBB*, 13th (17th) Hab
Chorlton 1327 SR (p)
v. ceorl, tun.

CROSSWAY GREEN

de Cruce, atte Croys 1275, 1327 SR (p)
Self-explanatory. This cross may well have been the 'cross of Waresle' (VCH iii. 381). For the form *croys v.* Cruise Hill *supra* 26.

GOLDNESS HO

Goldeneye 1332 SR (p)   *Goodnes, Goldnes* 1562 Wills, OrdBk
This must be a manorial name derived from a family called *Goldney, Goldness* standing for *Goldney's.*

LEAPGATE COTTAGE (6″)

(of þæm) hlypgeat 980 (11th) KCD 627
Such a gate is defined in the NED as 'a low gate in a fence, which can be leaped by deer, while keeping sheep from straying,' but, as Dr Grundy points out, its true function was to allow the deer to return to their *haga* when they had come out of it.

The normal development would be Lypiatt, as in the Gloucester-shire place of that name. The present form is a modern re-spelling.

LINCOMB

> *Lincumbe, Lyncumbe* 706 (12th) BCS 116, 1275 *Ass*, 1299 (18th) *RBB*, 1451 StSwith
> *Lyncombe, Lincombe* 1606 Wills, 1676 OrdBk
> 'Flax-valley,' *v.* lin, cumb.

THE MOUNT

> *de Monte* 1275 SR
> Self-explanatory.

NORCHARD

> *atte Norchard* 1327 SR (p)   *Oldeorchard* 1332 *FF*
> *Norchard* 1599 Wills
> *v.* Norchard in Rock *supra* 73 and orceard.

PANSINGTON FM[1]

> *Punchamton* 1221 *Ass*, 1266 Pat, Ipm
> *Poughamton* 1275 SR (p), 1299 (18th) *RBB*
> *Punchampton* 1275 *Ass*
> *Pouchampton* 1327 SR (p)

It is difficult to do anything with this name. The *u* of the second and fourth forms is presumably an error of transcription for *n*. If we take *Punch-* to be the correct form of the first part of the name, it should perhaps be associated with the first element in Ponsworthy (D), *Puneceswurði* in BCS 1323, and the first element taken to be the pers. name *Punec(a)*. *Punec(a)* is a diminutive of the pers. name found in Poynings (Sx), cf. PN in -*ing* 62. The second element is hamtun.

UPPER MOORS FM[2], LOWER MOORS FM (6″)

> *in the More* 1299 (18th) *RBB*
> Self-explanatory.

---

[1] This identification is probable though the intervening links are missing. *u* is often unrounded to *a* and final *hampton* is very commonly reduced to *ington*.
[2] Lithographed 1″ map.

PEPWELL FM (6″)

> *Pepewell* 1200, 1201 Cur, 1281 Wigorn, 1332 *FF*
> *Peopewell* 1274 AD iv, 1339 AD v
> *Pepewall* 1275 SR (p)
> *Popewell* 1331 *FF*, c. 1375 AD iv
> *Pip(e)well* 1375 AD iii, 1379 Cl
> *Peppewall* 1463 IpmR
> *Pepwell* 1649 Surv
> *Peppall, Pephall* 1591 Wills, AD v

If we compare this name with the forms of Peopleton *supra* 216 it is clear that behind this name lies the pers. name *Pypba* found in the Mercian genealogy as the name of the father of Penda. From this would come a name *Pyppa*, hence 'Pyppa's spring,' *v.* wielle.

PERRY HO

> *Pyre* 1275 SR (p)   *Perry* 1585 Wills
> *v.* pyrige.

POOLLANDS FM (6″)

> *pasture called Pull* 1451 StSwith
> Self-explanatory.

PYEHILL FM (6″)

Thus recorded c. 1600 (OrdBk). It probably takes its name from the family of *Pye* in 1275 (SR).

TINFIELD (lost)

> *Tendefeld* 1480 OrdBk   *Tynnefilde* 1557 ib.

This may possibly be 'enclosed field,' from the past part. of *tȳnan*, 'to enclose,' though we should expect ME *tinde-* or *tunde-* rather than *tende-* in this part of the country. Cf. *Tinfielde* as a field-name in Clent in 1838.

TITTON

> *Tidelintona* 1182 (18th) *RBB*
> *Tittlington* 1266 Ipm
> *Tydinton, Tyddington* 1275 SR (p), 1299 (18th) *RBB*, 1451
>   StSwith

T

Tidlintona 13th (17th) Hab
Titton al. *Tiddington* al. *Teddington* VCH iii. 380

This must be 'farm of Tidel' with the suffix ingtun. *Tīdel* is a pet-form of OE *Tīdhelm* or some other such name.

TORTON

Tortintuna 1182 (18th) *RBB*
Torchinton 1229 Ch
Torketon 1275 *Ass*
Torton 1275 *Ass*, 1480 OrdBk, 1627 QSR
Toruthone 1300 *Pat*
Thorton 1329 *FF*

This may be from *Torhtwine-tun*, 'farm of Torhtwine,' or more probably from *Torhtingtun*, 'Torhta's farm,' *Torhta* being a pet-form of one of the numerous OE names in *Torht*, *v*. ingtun.

WARESLEY

Wæresleage 817 (17th) BCS 361
Wereslæge 980 (11th) KCD 627
Wæreslege c. 1150 Surv
Waresleia, Waresle(ga) c. 1150 Surv, 1200 Cur, 1208 Fees 37,
    1221 *FF*, 1275 SR (p)
Warslei 1269 AD iv

'*Wǣr's* clearing,' *v*. leah. *Wǣr* is a shortened form of one of the numerous OE names in *Wǣr-* and is found also in Warwick (Wa) and Waresley (Hu).

WHITLINGE

æt hwitan hlince 969 (11th) BCS 1241
Whiteling, Whyteling, Whitelyngge 1221 *Ass* (p), 1309 *FF*,
    1337 Pat
Wittelinge 1221 *Ass* (p)
Wyteling 1240 WoP, 1275 *Ass*, 1316 Cl, all (p)
Wyklinge 1275 SR (p)
Whitling 1642 QSR, 1669 FF, c. 1830 O
Whitlench c. 1890 Lithog 1″

'White ridge,' *v*. hlinc, hwit. Cf. *on hwitan hlinces* (BCS 1213).

WILDEN

Wineladuna 1182 (17th) Hab
Winelduna 1182 (18th) *RBB*
Wybeldone 1275 SR (p)
Wiveldon 1299 Cl (p)
Weldon 1327 SR (p)
Wildon 1480 Deed (p), Eliz ChancP

The 1275 form makes it certain that the *n* of the earliest forms is an error of transcription for *u*. There is good ground for assuming an OE pers. name *Wīfel(a)*, a weak form of *Wīfel*, which is common in place-names and we probably have here 'Wifela's hill,' *v.* dun.

Kidderminster

KIDDERMINSTER[1] 71 G 10

Chideminstre 1086 DB
Kedeleministre 1154 RBE
Kidemenistra 1168 P
Kedemenistra 1190 P
Kyderemunstre c. 1200 BM
Kydeministre 1232 Cl
Kiddeministre 1242 Cl
Kydiminstre 1270 Cl
Kydermunstre 1275 SR, 1315 Cl
Kederminster, Kedermynstre 1419, 1435 IpmR
Kyddermynster, Kedermistre, Kethermyster 1550 Pat
Kedermister 1610 Speed
Kidderminster al. *Kederminster* 1675 Ogilby

The OE pers. names *Cyda, Cydda, Cyddi* are well established, and a derivative *Cydel(a)* lies behind Kidlington (O). If the

[1] There are four unidentified berewicks of Kidderminster, recorded in DB as *Bristitune, Fastochesfelde, Teulesberge, Sudwale*. The first is probably for OE *Beorhtingtūn*, 'Beorhta's farm,' the second contains an unrecorded pers. name *Fæstoc*. OE names in *Fast-* seem all to be of Scand. origin, but an OE name *Fæsta* may have existed and for a diminutive *Fæstoc* we may compare OGer *Fastiko* recorded in Förstemann PN 501. The third name may contain the OE pers. name *Teoful* found in the old life of St Gregory, though it is possible that here and even in that OE name itself we really have an OE *þēofela*, a diminutive of *þēof*, which has its parallel in OE *þēofeca* recorded in *þēofecan hyl* (BCS 1237) and in OGer *Thiebiko* noted by Förstemann PN 1409. *Sudwale* is probably for *Sūðwælle*, 'south spring.'

form of 1154 is genuine it suggests that Kidderminster contains the latter name and that subsequent forms with *r* are due to Anglo-Norman confusion of *l* and *r* (IPN 106). The permanent replacement of *l* by *r* would be somewhat unusual and the 1154 form is only derived from a 13th cent. copy of the lost Pipe Roll of 1 Hy 2. It is perhaps more probable that the name contains an *r*-extension of *Cydda* (cf. Chaddesley *supra* 234, and Dodderhill *infra* 281) and that the *l* form is the isolated exception. The second element is clearly OE mynster. This is probably the monastery for which Ethelbald of Mercia granted land to Cyniberht by the river Stour in 736 (BCS 154). The site is traditionally at Broadwaters (VCH iii. 458). The original name of Kidderminster before the founding of the monastery was probably *æt Sture* as in BCS 220[1]. See further Introd. xxiii.

AGGBOROUGH FM

Akberewe 1275 SR
Agberwe, Hagberewe 1307, 1316 Ipm
Ackebarewe 1323 Ipm
Agburrow 1686 FF

'Oak-hill,' *v.* ac, beorg and cf. Aggberrow in Longdon and a lost *Aggborough* in Madresfield *supra* 208, 210.

BLACKSTONE

atte Blakestone 1275 SR   *Blackstone* 1673 FF

This is a high rock, dark in colour, so called in contrast to Redstone (*supra* 35) three miles lower down the Severn. This also had a hermitage.

CALDWALL HALL (6″)

Caldewelle 1249 FF, 1255, 1275 *Ass*   *Caldewall* 1335 Ch
Caldwall 1505 IpmR   *Cawdewall* VCH iii. 170

'Cold spring,' *v.* cald, wielle.

---

[1] Of Kidderminster streets Mill Street and High Street are old and obvious. The present Blackwell Street is *Black Star* Street in 1753, *Blaxter Strete* in 1485 and *Blakestanstret* in 14th cent. (VCH iii. 161 ff.). As this road does not lead to Blackstone it is probable that the last form is corrupt and that the first part of the name is an unrecorded *blackestre*, an agent noun denoting one who dyes things black. There was a Joh. *le Blaxtere* in Kidderminster in 1281 and a Ricardus *le Blakestare* in Chaddesley in 1275 (SR).

COMBERTON FM

Cumbrintone 1275 SR   *Comberton* 1390 AD iii, 1545 LP
Commerton 1787 Cary
'Cumbra's farm,' *v.* ingtun. Cf. Cumberwood and Comberton *supra* 193.

EYMORE WOOD

Eymore 1294 Ipm, 1352 CompR
As noted by Duignan (PN Wo 60) the farm lies opposite an island in the Severn and the name doubtless means 'marshland by the island,' *v.* eg, mor.

FRANCHE

Frenesse 1086 DB
Frenysse 1249 FF
Frechene, Frenes 1275 *Ass* (p)
Freynes 1275 SR (p)
Fraynsh 1307 Ipm (p)
Fraynysche 1421 BM
Franyshe 1545 Wills
Fraunche 1587 Wills

In explaining Fring (Nf), Professor Ekwall (PN in -*ing* 77) assumes a pet-form from OE names in *Frēa*- to explain the early forms *Frainges, Freing, Frenges* of that name. Behind Franche we may have the same pers. name *Frēa*, followed in this case by *æsc*. Hence *Frēanæsc*, 'Frea's ash-tree.' The same pers. name may be found in Freeford (St), DB *Fraiforde*, 12th c. *Freiforde*.

GUILDINGS FM (6")

This probably takes its name from the *Gilding* family, founders of a charity in Dowles, just across the river (VCH iv. 316). This may be the same name as *le Guldene* found as a pers. name in Trimpley in Kidderminster in SR (1275, 1327).

HABBERLEY

Harburgelei 1086 DB
Haberlega, Haberley(e), Haburley 1183 P (p), 1275 SR (p), 1319 Ipm, 1333 FF, 1425 IpmR, 1550 Pat

This is probably the 'clearing of a woman named *Hēahburh*.' If that is the case, the first *r* in the DB form must be an error due to anticipation of the *r* later in the word. The name *Hereburh* seems to be ruled out by the early and persistent *a* and the improbable early disappearance of *r* involved in this explanation.

HEATHY MILL (6")[1]

Hethei, Hethye, Hetheye 1221 *Ass*, 1275 *FF*, 1275 SR *et passim*

'Heath-island,' *v.* hæð, eg.

HOARSTONE FM

Horstan 1240 Wigorn (p)
othehoreston, de Horeston 1275 SR, 1307 Ipm
Hoarstone 1651 FF

'Boundary-stone' (*v.* har), possibly one on the bounds of Wyre forest. This is a very common term in the West Country, cf. *Horestone* Furlong in Overbury, *Whoarston* Grove in Himbleton, from the 1649 Survey.

HOO FM (6") and HOOBROOK

de Hou, de la Ho(o) 1180 P, 1275 *Ass*, SR, 1302 Wigorn
The Whooe, Hooe 1610 Wills, 1661 FF

v. hoh.

HURCOTT

Worcote 1086 DB
Hurchcote Hy 2 LyttCh (p)
Hurecote 1227 FF
Holecote 1275 *Ass*
Horecote, Horkote 1275 SR (p), 1390 AD iii
Harcote, Harcoote 1294 Ipm (p), 1579 Wills
Harpcote 1315 Ipm (p), 1477 Pat
Hurdecote 1545 LP
Hurcott 1570 Wills
Hutchcott 1652 FF

It is clear that there has been corruption in some of the forms given here. Probably behind them all ultimately lies OE

---

[1] It is possible that the lost DB manor of *Hatete* (evidently a corrupt form) should be identified with Heathy. It included a mill.

hierde-cot(u), 'herdsmen-cottages.' The normal development of this, in this area, would be to ME *hurdecote*. The *d* would tend to be lost from the consonant group *rdc* and then confusion must have arisen with the various words beginning with *Hor-* (from har and horh) and possibly also with names like Hardwick, from OE heordewic, cf. Hurcott (So), Hurdcote and Hurdcott Ho (W) which undoubtedly have the etymology suggested for this name.

NETHERTON (Old 1″)

de la, atte Netherton 1275, 1327 SR

'Lower farm,' *v.* neoðera, tun. 'Nether' in relation to Wribbenhall. It is half a mile lower down the Severn.

NORTH WOOD

Northu' 1127 (1421) Dugd iii. 448
Northwud 1241 Cl

Self-explanatory. It is in the north of the parish.

OFFMOOR FM

Affemere 1335 Ch

The second element is mere. There is a pool close at hand. If the one form is to be relied on, the pool belonged to one *Æffa*. The modern form is corrupt.

OLDINGTON FM

Aldintone 1086 DB
Haldintone 1275 *Ass*
Eldintone 1275 SR
Oldin(g)ton 13th AD ii (p), 1390 AD iii

'Ealda's farm,' *v.* ingtun.

PARK ATTWOOD[1]

ate Wode, atte Wode 1319 Ipm, 1362 Ch

In 1362 John *atte Wode* was granted a licence to impark, the reference evidently being to this particular estate.

---

[1] The 6″ map has the curious form Parkatt Wood for the wood itself, as distinct from the house. The form is said to be used locally.

Park Hall

Parcheys 1405 Pat, IpmR

'Park enclosures,' *v.* pearroc, (ge)hæg.

Puxton

Pokeleston 1240 WoP
Pokleston 1275 SR, 1294, 1307 Ipm, all (p)
Pokelstone 1333 FF
Powkelston 1553 Wills
Buxson, Puxon 1561 Wills, 1700 FF

OE *pūcel* is a 'goblin' and this place might mean 'goblin's farm.' More probably it is that word used as a pers. name, cf. the weak form found in Pucklechurch (Gl), *Pucelancyrcan* (BCS 887).

Rhydd Covert

This place is referred to in a fine of 1327 where we have mention of certain tenements in *Ryde*. This is the same name as that explained in Rhydd Green *supra* 212.

Sutton Common and Fm

Sudtone 1086 DB   *Sutton* 1275 SR (p)

'Farm south of Kidderminster,' *v.* suð, tun.

Trimpley

Trinpelei 1086 DB
Thrympelege 1255 *Ass* (p)
Trympelege, Trimpeleye, Trympeley 1255 FF, 1275 *Ass*, SR, 1550 Pat
Trumpeleye 1255 *Ass* (p), 1281 Misc
Tryenpeleye 1275 SR
Trimpley 17th FF *passim*
Trempley 1787 Cary

This is a difficult name, but we are probably right in assuming that the first element is an OE pers. name *Trympa*. This would seem to be a form, with *i*-mutation of the stem vowel, of the pers. name *Trumpa* which must lie behind Trumpington (C). This *Trumpa* is probably a pet-form for OE *Trumbeorht*. Another derivative of this name-stem may lie behind Trimstone (D), *Trempelstan* in 1238, *Trympeston* in 1330.

WANNERTON FM

Wenuerton 1086 DB
Wenfertone 1275 SR
Wenforton 1327 SR
Wynfurtone 1369 WoCh (p)
Wannerton 1591 QSR, 1672 FF

There can be no doubt that this farm (*v.* tun) takes its name from the *Wenferð* stream, mentioned in BCS 514 in the bounds of Wolverley (*v. supra* 16).

WARSHILL TOP FM (6"), WASSELL WOOD

Warseld 1275 SR (p)
Wassall c. 1780 Nash

There is an ancient earth-work here (VCH iv. 425) and the name itself doubtless records the fact. It is the OE *weard-setl*, used of a guard-house or watch-tower, here employed to describe the earthwork on this commanding hill-top. Stevenson in the Crawford Charters (p. 72) shows that it may be possible to identify another *weard-setl* in Devon with a Beacon Hill, while the *weard-setl* which appears in so many Hampshire charters from the Clere district has been shown by Grundy to be Beacon Hill in that county (*Arch. Journ.* lxxviii. 132). A further example of this name is found in Wassel Grove and Wast Hills *infra* 293, 335. It is apparently a name of the same type as Totternhoe, discussed in PN BedsHu 139.

WRIBBENHALL

Gurberhale 1086 DB
Wrbenhala n.d. (11th) Dugd i. 607
Wrubbenhale c. 1160 (c. 1240) WoC
Wrubbehale c. 1200 (c. 1250) WoC
Wurbenli 1203 (1308) AnnMon iv. 392
Wurbenhale, Wrubenhale, Wrobbenhale 1240 WoP
Wrignall 1565 WillsP
Rignall 1581 Wills
Ripenhall 1619 QSR
Ribbenhall, Rybbenhall 1633 QSR, 1678 FF
Wrewbenhall 1666 FF

The first element in this name furnishes a difficulty, but it becomes somewhat clearer if we bring it into relation with certain other names. In the neighbouring parish of Wolverley we find in the Subsidy Rolls of 1275 and 1327 pers. names containing the place-name *Wrobbecumbe* or *Wrybbecumbe*. This place must have been named from someone bearing the same name as the founder of Wribbenhall, probably from that man himself. Similarly, Ribden in Farley (St) is *Wrybbedon* in 1327 (BM). All these names point to an OE pers. name *Wrybba*. An allied *Wrobba* is found in Robley (Ha), *wrobban lea* in BCS 625[1], and Rabley (Herts), *Wrobbele* in 1317 Cl. In the Essex place-name Wrabness, DB *Wrabenasa* we may have a pers. name *Wraba* from another grade of the same stem. Side by side with *Wrybba* a metathesised form *Wyrba* seems to have been found, which would account for early forms in *Wurb-*. In the DB form we have Anglo-Norman *g* for initial *w* and common confusion of *n* and *r*. The name has also been influenced by Ribbesford.

Upper and Lower Mitton[2]

MITTON, UPPER and LOWER 71 H 9 and 10

Myttun 841 (11th) BCS 433
Mettune 1086 DB
Ouermittun 1221 FF
Mutton(e) 1227, 1270 Ch, *(Walter)* 1275 SR, *(Nethere)* FF, 1340 Ipm, *(Ouermutton)* 1359 FF
Nether Mytton 1420 FF

v. myðetun. The farm was so called because it stands at the junction of the Stour and the Severn, cf. Mitton in Bredon *supra* 102. Lower Mitton is now merged in Stourport. The *Walter*, called *Walter dominus de Mutton* in 1275 (SR), is unknown.

BURLISH COMMON

Bourlasshe 1378 IpmR, 1379 Pat   *Bourlash* 1390 AD iii

The forms are few and late but the second element appears to be æsc. The first may be a pers. name *Burgela*, a weak form of the name *Burgel*, itself a diminutive form of *Burga*. For these pers. names *v.* Redin 45, 139. Hence 'Burgela's ash-tree.'

---

[1] Duignan (PN Wo 184) calls attention to this parallel.
[2] Upper Mitton is actually in Oswaldslow Hundred.

LICKHILL HO

> *Lekhull* 1375 Wigorn
> *Leykhull, Leykhill* 1420, 1429 *FF*
> *Lickhyll* 1558 Wills, 1659 FF

'Garlic-hill,' a compound of OE *lēac*, 'leek, garlic' and hyll.

Rushock

RUSHOCK 71 J 12

> *Russococ* 1086 DB
> *Rossoc* 1166 RBE
> *Roissoc* 1167 P (p)
> *Russoc, Russok(e)* 1200 Cur, 1212 Fees 140, 1223 Pat, 1226
>   Ipm, 1285 Wigorn, 1327 SR
> *Roshoke* 1210 RBE
> *Rossehocke* 1275 *Ass*
> *Rushok* 1292 *FF*, 1359 Ch
> *Rushuc* 1296 Ipm
> *Russchucke* 1300 *Pat*
> *Rysshok* 1435 IpmR

This is probably a compound of OE **hrysc** and hoc. The parish lies in a sharp bend of Elmley Brook. Hence, 'hook of land grown over with rushes.' Rushock in Kington (He) seems to have a similar origin. *v.* Addenda *supra, s.n.* Rushwick.

Stone

STONE 71 G 11

> *Stanes* 1086 DB, 1212 Fees 140, 1275, 1327 SR
> *Stone* 1346 FA

It is impossible to say just what these *stones* or rocks were.

DUNCLENT FM

> *Dunclent* 1086 DB, 1212 Fees 140, 1275 1327 SR
> *Dounclent* 1316 *FF*, 1346 FA
> *Dunklet* 1527 Wills
> *Dunklyn, Dunklin* 1577 Saxton, 1675 Ogilby

Dunclent lies a good five or six miles south-east of the Clent Hills proper, but as the ground slopes continuously down the whole way, it is impossible to avoid the conclusion that the term Clent may have been applied to a fairly large district and that *Down*-clent was the name given to the village which lay at the foot of it. If that is the case we have a very early example of the use of that element in place-name compounds. *Down* Ampney (Gl) was so called in contrast to *Up* Ampney or Ampney Crucis. It is on slightly lower ground, but here the *Down* is probably used to describe a place which is lower down a stream, viz. Ampney Brook. The earliest reference for *Doun*-in this name that has been noted is 1284 (FA).

SHENSTONE

> *Senestone* 1221 *Ass*
> *Schenestone* 1275 *Ass*, SR (p)
> *Scefneston* 1275 *Ass* ·
> *Shenston* 1327 SR (p), (*in Kidderminster*) 1410 IpmR
> *Sheynstone* 1654 FF

The absence of any *stan*-forms, and the presence of the form *Scefneston*, seems to make derivation from OE sciene, stan impossible. There is the possibility of an OE pers. name *Scēaf* (if it is not of purely mythological origin, *v.* Redin 22) and a weak form *Sceua* (ib. 78). An *-en* derivative of this name (cf. Pensham *supra* 221) would give rise to an OE *Scēafnes-tūn* and this may be the source of the name.

Wolverley

WOLVERLEY 71 F 10

> *Wulfferdinleh* 866 (18th) BCS 513
> *Wlfwardilea, Wlfordilea* 866 (11th) BCS 514
> *Wulfweardiglea* 11th (11th) KCD 766
> *Ulwardelei, Ulwardelea* 1086 DB, c. 1140 (c. 1240) *WoC*
> *Wlfwardile* 11th Heming
> *Wluardele(ge)* 1227 *FF*, 1240 WoP
> *Wolffardeleye* 1275 SR
> *Wolwardeleye* 1291 Tax
> *Wolvardelegh, -ley* 1292, 1321 Pat, 1411 IpmR
> *Wolfordleye* 1327 SR
> *Wolverley* 1535 VE

In BCS 513 *Wul(f)ferd* makes an exchange of land at Wolverley with Burgred of Mercia and there can be little doubt that

Wolverley was actually named from this very *Wulferd*, the full form of whose name was *Wulfweard*. The place was called in full *Wulfweardingléah*. For the force of the connecting -*ing*, *v*. EPN. It is a good example of the use of -*ing* to denote simply 'having to do with' or 'possessed by.'

AUSTCLIFF

> *Astenes Clive* 1240 WoP
> *Alstanesclive, Alstone Clive* 1275 SR (p), 1411 IpmR
> *Ausclif, Austcliffe* 1589 Wills, 1649 Surv
> *Alsclife* 1614 WillsP
> *Horse Cliff* c. 1830 O

'Cliff of *Ealhstān* or of *Ælfstān*,' *v*. clif. The 'cliff' is above the Stour, cf. Austerley (Y), Austerson (Ch).

AXBOROUGH FM

> *Heasecan beorh* 866 (11th) BCS 514, 964 (11th) BCS 1134
> *Hatchbury Hill* c. 1830 O

No OE name *Heaseca* is on record, but such diminutive formation from the adj. *h(e)aso*, 'grey,' is quite possible and has its parallel in a series of names *Has(u)o, Hasig, Hesiko, Hasilo* given by Förstemann (PN 787) as from this same stem. Hence 'Heaseca's hill,' *v*. beorg.

BLAKESHALL

> *Blakesole* c. 1190 (c. 1250) *WoC* (bis), 1327 SR
> *Blakesal* 1275 (p)
> *Blakesall, Blackshall* 1575 Wills, 1649 Surv
> *Blacksoll* 1625 WillsP

'Black miry pool,' *v*. blæc, sol.

CAUNSALL

> *Conneshale* 1240 WoP, 1327 SR (p)
> *Con(n)sall* 1558 Wills, 1649 Surv
> *Counsall* 1614 WillsP
> *Cornsall* c. 1830 O

There can be no doubt that there was an OGer name-stem *Kan-*, found in various place-names such as Cannings (W) (*Caningamersc* ASC), and in the Flemish Caneghem, earlier

Caningahem (Mansion, *Oud-Gentsche Naamkunde* 27). See further Förstemann, ON i. 1641–2. It may actually occur independently in OE *Cana, Cane* (Redin 88, 133) which are of doubtful origin. *Can(n)* would be the strong form of this name and in the West Country we should expect *Conn*. The name is therefore 'Can(n)'s healh.'

COOKLEY

> *Culnan clif* 964 (11th) BCS 1134
> *Culleclive, Culla clife* 11th Heming, 1166 (c. 1240) *WoC*, 1240 WoP
> *Colecliff* 1275 SR
> *Cookley* 1608 QSR, 1649 Surv
> *Cookecliffe* 1649 Surv

The first element looks like a pers. name *Cūlna*. Such a name is at least possible. On the basis of the pers. name *Cūla*, which may be assumed from Cooling (K), *Culingas* BCS 778, Culham (O), *Culanham* BCS 759, and *Cullanbyrig* BCS 61, a name in -*n*- may well have been formed in the same way as the *Tilne*, *Wilne* and *Lifne* noted by Redin (160–1). Hence 'Culna's clif.' The cliff is above the Stour. See further Introd. xxiii.

DEBDALE FM (6")

> *Diepedale, Depedale* 1187 P (p), 1240 WoP, 1327 SR (p)
> *Debdale* 1649 Surv

'Deep dale,' *v.* deop, dæl.

DRAKELOW

> *Brakelowe* (sic) 1240 WoP
> *Drakelow, Dracloe* 1582 Wills, 1649 Surv

'Dragon-hill' or 'barrow,' *v.* draca, hlaw and cf. Drakelow (Db), *Dracanhlawen* in BCS 772.

HOBRO FM

> *High Holborough* 1601 QSR   *Holbro* c. 1830 O

'Hollow hill,' *v.* holh, beorg.

HORSELEY HILLS FM

> *Horsle(ge), Horsley* c. 1160 (c. 1240) *WoC*, 1189 P (p), 1240 WoP, 1255 Ass, 1275 SR (p), 1308 Ipm (p)
> *Horselegh, Horseley* 1223, 1321 Pat, c. 1830 O

'Horses' clearing,' *v.* hors, leah. It is clear that this lay just by the *horsabroc*, 'horses' brook' of the bounds of Wolverley and Cookley (BCS 513, 1134). There was also a *Horsestana* close at hand (*WoC* 5b). Cf. Horsebrook *supra* 12.

KINGSFORD

    Cenungaford 964 (11th) BCS 1134
    Keningeford 1189–96 (c. 1250) *WoC*, 1275 SR, 1306 FF
    Kiningeford c. 1200 (c. 1250) *WoC*
    Keingford 1240 WoP
    Kenigford 1255 *Ass*
    Kemingford 1316 Ipm
    Kyngesford, Kingsford 1346 FA, 1427 SR, 1649 FF

'Ford of the people of *C(o)ēn* or *C(o)ēna*,' *v.* ingas. At a later stage *e* was raised to *i* before *ng*, the process being helped by folk-etymological association with *king*.

LEA CASTLE

    le Le, le Lee 1292 Ipm, 1369 Pat
    The Lee, Lea Hall 1649 Surv, c. 1830 O

v. leah. This must come from the oblique case form *lea*.

THE LOWE (6″)

    la Lawe 1221 FF, 1240 WoP, 1255 *Ass* (p)
    de (la) Lowe, atte Lowe 1255 *Ass*, 1275 SR, 1327 *FF*
    The Lowe 1649 Surv

v. hlaw.

SOLCUM FM (6″)

    Socombe n.d. VCH iii. 568   *Solcan* 1649 Surv

There is very little material to go on. The farm lies at the head of a little valley, with a spring in it, which may have given rise to a sol or miry place. Hence 'miry-valley,' *v.* cumb.

UPTON HOUSE (lost), now SIONHILL HOUSE

    Uptun 1240 WoP   *Upton* 1275 SR (p), 1649 Surv

Self-explanatory, the house lying on high ground above the Stour valley.

WOODHAMCOTE (lost)

Wodehancot 1240 WoP   *Woddamcote* 1591 Wills

Self-explanatory. Cf. Brockencote *supra* 236.

V. FISHBOROUGH HUNDRED

Fissesberga 1086 DB

This hundred consisted of 11 manors, assessed at 65 hides. It was a compact area, except that Ombersley lay separate and in contact with five other hundreds, while Oldberrow, stated in DB to be 12 acres of land, was far away to the north and almost surrounded by Warwickshire. Some time soon after the Norman Conquest this hundred, with the addition of Abbots Morton, Atch Lench, Sheriff's Lench, (part of) Church Lench, and the Wo part of Bevington (Wa) from Esch Hundred, formed the new hundred of Blackenhurst *supra* 17. The name must be derived from the pers. name *Fisc*, found as a name in DB but not on record in OE.

Aldington

ALDINGTON 82 H 4

Aldintona 709 (c. 1200) BCS 125, c. 1086 (1190) *EveA*, 1086 DB, 1291 Tax

Aldington 1227, 1270 Ch

Aunton or *Aldington* 16th VCH ii. 355

'*Ealda's* farm,' *v.* ingtun.

Badsey

BADSEY 82 H 4

Baddeseia 709 (c. 1200) BCS 125

Baddesege 714 (16th) BCS 130

Badsetenagemære c. 850 (c. 1200) BCS 482

Baddesig c. 860 (c. 1200) KCD 289 (iii. 396)

Badesei 1086 DB, c. 1086 (1190) *EveA*

Baddesham 1251 Ch

Baddesheye 1275 SR

Baddeseye 1291 Tax

Badsey 1535 VE

This would seem to contain a strong name *Bæddi* corresponding to the pers. name *Bad(d)a* which is well established. It is presumably a pet-form of an OE name in *Beadu-*, cf. Badshaw Lane (Ha), *beaddescagan* in BCS 622. The village stands at the confluence of three streams, hence 'Bæddi's well-watered land,' *v. eg.* The same man must have given his name to *Bædeswellan* (BCS 1282) which lies on the bounds of Broadway where they coincide with those of Badsey.

SHRAWNELL (lost)

    Schrewenhulle c. 1330 ChronEve
    Shrawnell 1535 VE, 1544 LP, 1571 D

In a Devonshire Charter (BCS 723) we have a place called *scræwanleg*. There and in the Wo place-name we have compounds of leah and hyll respectively, formed either with the animal name *screawa*, '*shrew*-mouse,' or with a pers. name derived from it.

Bretforton

BRETFORTON 82 H 5

    Bretfertona 709 (c. 1200) BCS 125
    Brotfortun 716 (16th) BCS 130
    Bradferdtuna c. 860 (c. 1200) KCD 289 (iii. 396)
    Bratfortune 1086 DB
    Brotfortona c. 1086 (1190) *EveA*
    Bretfortone 13th ChronEve
    Bratforton 1235 FF (p), 14th ChronEve
    Bradforton 1249 FF (p) 1346 FA
    Bretferton 1250 FF
    Brefferton 1251 Ch
    Bretforton 1275 SR
    Bretfordton 1286 Wigorn (p)
    Bretfordon 1365 FF
    Brodforton 1546 Marr

The first two forms are of no authority and count for little in the solution of this difficult name. We may compare its forms with those of Harvington in Oswaldslow Hundred *supra* 134, where we saw how medial *-ford-* might be weakened to *-ferd-* and *-verd-*. If the second element is *ford*, the first may possibly

U

be **brad,** 'broad,' with later unvoicing of *d* to *t* before *f*. The development of the *Bret*-forms would be however quite irregular and could only be explained as due to some confusion, e.g. with Bretford (Wa).

LARKBOROUGH

Lauerkeboerge, Lauergeboerge 709 (12th) BCS 125

'Lark-hill,' *v.* lawerce, beorg. Middendorf quotes similar compounds *laweorcdun* (BCS 870), *laurocan beorg* (ib. 1005), *lafercan beorh* (ib. 1237, 1299). The last two examples are from Evenlode and Cutsdean in this county.

Evesham

EVESHAM[1] [iˑvʃem], [iˑviʃəm], [eisəm], [iˑʃəm], [iˑsəm], olim [iˑzəm] 82 H 3

(1) *Ethom* 706 (14th) BCS 117, 710 (14th) BCS 127, 716 (14th) BCS 134

   Homme 709 (c. 1200) BCS 125

(2) *Cronuchomme* 706 (14th) BCS 116, 708 (14th) ib. 120, 716 (14th) ib. 138

   Cronochomme 706 (14th) BCS 511

   Cronuchamme c. 860 (c. 1200) BCS 511

(3) *Eveshomme* 709 (c. 1200) BCS 124

   Eouesham 714 (16th) BCS 130, 1016 (c. 1200) KCD 723

   Eoueshamme, Eofeshamme 1017–23 Earle 235

   Eoueshom 1033–8 Earle 238

---

[1] Of Evesham streets, Bridge Street goes back to *Bruggestrete* (13th), Oat Street to *le Odestret* (14th) which is probably for *Wodestrete*, and Cowl Street to *Col(e)strete* (13th). The last two were perhaps so called because wood and coal were sold there. High Street is the *Magnus* or *Altus vicus* of the 13th and 14th cents. There was also a *Bruttestret* or *Brutaynstret* which appears in 1546 (LP) as *Britten* Street and in 1794 as *Briton* Street, which seems to be 'Britons' Street.' The 13th and 14th cent. *Runhuile, Ruynhulle* appears in 1546 (LP) as *Ryvell*, an error of transcription for *Rynell*, as *Runhill Lane* in a deed of 1584 and Rynal Street at the present day (*ex inf.* Mr E. A. Barnard, F.S.A.). Is this 'ruin-hill,' a term of reproach (cf. *Ruinestrete,* a 13th cent. street-name in Droitwich)? Such a term of reproach is certainly found in *Rotton Rewe* in 1546 (LP), 'rats' row,' cf. Ratton Row in PN NbDu 162. (The forms for the Evesham street-names are all from the *Chronicle of Evesham* except where otherwise stated.)

Heofeshamm 1037 C (12th) ASC
Eofeshamm 1045 D, 1054 C (12th) ASC
Euesham 1077 E (12th) ASC
Evesham 1229–52 Ch, 1232 Cl
Evesholm vulg. *Esam* 1675 Ogilby
(4) *æt Ecguines hamme* c. 874 (c. 1200) BCS 482

The place must have been originally named from the great hamm or bend in the river here, the prefixed *Et-* being a late spelling for OE *æt*. It seems at times to have been distinguished from other such *hamms* by the distinctive addition of *Cronuc-*, from OE *cornoc, cranoc*, 'crane,' or (possibly) 'heron,' from the presence of one or other of these birds. An alternative method of distinguishing it was to associate it with the name of one *Ēof*, an OE name only found elsewhere in the Kentish forms *Iab, Iof*, and this was the name which was destined to survive. This *Eof* is, in a 16th cent. copy of a charter of Bishop Ecgwine's, said to have been a shepherd to whom the Virgin Mary revealed herself at this spot, but as the form of his name there given is *Eoves*, clearly a back-formation from *Eovesham* itself, one should not attach too much weight to the story, especially as the vision is ascribed to Ecgwine himself and not to *Eof* in another charter (BCS 125). Finally, the place seems to have been occasionally named after Bishop Ecgwine himself, the founder of the monastery established there.

MERSTOW GREEN (6″)

In the *Chronicle of Evesham* we have a series of references from the 13th cent. to 'terra in *Merstowe*' and in 1546 (LP) to a messuage in *le Merstowe*. Merstow Green lies just to the north of the wall built by Abbot Chyryton early in the 14th cent., which divides off the Abbey and its grounds from the town of Evesham. Probably the whole site of the Abbey and its grounds was once known as *mǣre stow*, 'famous place,' stow being used in its specialised sense of land dedicated to some religious purpose. The green adjoining it preserves the name.

Church Honeybourne

CHURCH HONEYBOURNE [hʌnibʌn] 82 H 6

Huniburna 709 (c. 1200) BCS 125, c. 1086 (1190) *EveA*
Huniburne 1086 DB, 1251 Ch
Hunigburne 1221 *Ass*
Honiburne 1275 SR, 1291 Tax
Churchoniborne 1535 VE

For this name *v*. Honeybrook *supra* 11. *Church* in distinction from Cow Honeybourne (Gl). This last was also known as *Chappell Honniborne* (1623 Marr), being a chapelry of Church Honeybourne.

PODEN

Poddenho (also *Podemore, Podenhomme*)[1] 709 (c. 1200) BCS
    125, 1251 Ch
Podeho c. 1190 *EveA*, 1256 Pat
Poddeho 1275 SR (p)
Podone c. 1306 ChronEve
Podenho 1327 SR (p), 1340 NI (p)
Powden 1535 VE, 1545 LP

'Podda's *hoh*,' with later loss of suffix, cf. Podmore (St). It is easy enough to find a **mor** and a **hamm** here but there is no hoh except to the north-east of the site of the present farm.

Norton-and-Lenchwick

NORTON-AND-LENCHWICK 82 G 3

NORTON

Nortun 709 (c. 1200) BCS 125, 1086 DB

'North farm,' probably so called from its relation to Lenchwick itself.

LENCHWICK

Lenchwic 709 (c. 1200) BCS 125
Lencuueke 714 (16th) BCS 130

---

[1] Mr C. S. Seyler has identified these with a brook still called locally *Puddenham* or *Puddimore* and fields called *Puddenham* in the neighbouring parishes of Saintsbury and Willersey (Gl). A further reference to the stream is probably to be found in *Wudanhammesbroc* (BCS 482) in the bounds of Willersey, with the common mistake of *w* for *p*.

Lenchewic 1086 DB
Lenchwic, Lenchwyk(e) c. 1086 (1190) *EveA*, 1238 *FF*,
1262 *For*

'The **wic** or dairy farm by *Lench*'; for this name *v.* Lench
supra 148.

CHADBURY

Ceadweallan byrig c. 860 (c. 1200) KCD 289 (iii. 396)
castellum de Chadelburi 13th ChronEve
Chedelesburie 13th ChronEve
Chadelesburne 1275 *Ass*
'*Ceadwealla's* stronghold,' *v.* burh.

TWYFORD

Twiford, Tuiford 709 (16th) BCS 125, 714 (16th) ib. 130

v. **twi, ford.** Two tracks lead down from the Alcester-
Evesham road to the Avon and the present Offenham Ferry.
North of the ferry we have Deadman's Ait, once clearly an
island. At present a backwater is all that remains of the branch
of the Avon which must once have run on its west side. Probably the northern track originally crossed first this branch, then
the ait and then the Avon itself and so to Offenham, giving a
'double' ford. The analysis of the materials for the early history
of Evesham suggests that Twyford was the original name of all
the land within the great bend of the Avon on which the
monastery and town of Evesham afterwards arose.

North, Middle and South Littleton

LITTLETON 82 G 4

Litletona 709 (c. 1200) BCS 125
Lytletun et alia Litletun 714 (16th) BCS 130
þry litlen tunes c. 860 (c. 1200) KCD 289 (iii. 395)
Liteltune 1086 DB, c. 1086 (1190) *EveA*
Lutleton 1227 *FF*
Lytlinton 1249 *FF*
Sutlitinton, Northlitleton, Middleton 1251 Ch
Lutlinton 1275 SR, 1327 SR
Luttilton 1332 SR
Lytleton, Lettleton 1535 VE

'Little farm,' *v.* lytel, tun. The *three* farms go back to very early times.

PICKERSOM (local)[1]

> *Picereshomme* 709 (c. 1200) BCS 125
> *Picereshamme* c. 860 (c. 1200) KCD 289 (iii. 396)
> *Pickersum Hill* 1649 Surv

Cf. Pixham in Powick *supra* 225 which is identical in origin.

SHEENHILL FM

> *Shynehill* 1657 FF   *Shynnell* 1662 FF   *Shin Hill* 1820 G

It is certain that this hill is the same as the *scenedun* of BCS 125, in the bounds of the Evesham manors. It is mentioned just after *Buggildstret*, and Buckle Street is a quarter of a mile east of Sheen Hill. This identification makes it clear that we must take the first element as OE sciene, so that the name means 'bright hill.'

Offenham

OFFENHAM [ʌfənəm] 82 G 4

> *Offeham* (also *Offepol*) 709 (c. 1200) BCS 125
> *Vffaham* 714 (16th) BCS 130
> *Uffenham* c. 860 (c. 1200) KCD 289 (iii. 395), 1392 Pat
> *Afanhamme*[2] 1058 BM
> *Offenham* 1086 DB, 1535 VE
> *Offam* 1251 Ch
> *Hoffenham* 1275 SR, 1340 NI
> *Uffenam, Uffnam, Uphnam* 1584 Marr, 1590 Wills, 1677 Marr

'The hamm of *Uffa*.' It lies in a bend of the Avon. Here, as in Uffmoor in Hasbury *infra* 295, it is clear that there was early confusion between the pers. names *Offa* and *Uffa*, a confusion commented on by Redin (102–3). Here the more common form *Offa* ultimately prevailed. For another *Uff*-form, cf. *uffanlege* in Himbleton (BCS 542) and *Uffanhealas* in Ombersley (BCS 116).

---

[1] This identification is due to the kindness of Mr C. A. Seyler.
[2] This form is probably due to association with the Avon, on which it lies.

FAULK MILL (6")

Fokemulne 13th ChronEve

This may possibly be for *folke-mulne*, 'people's mill,' or from *Folcan-myln* with the pers. name *Folca* found in *Folcanstan* = Folkestone (K). For the phonetic development cf. Faulkland (So), earlier *Folclond* (1316 FA).

Oldberrow[1]

OLDBERROW 82 A 6

Ulenbeorge 709 (c. 1200) BCS 124
Ulbeorge 714 (16th) BCS 130
Oleberge 1086 DB
Ulleberga 1190 P
Ulleberwe 13th ChronEve, 1307 Wigorn
Huleberge 1252 Ch
Hullesbarewe 1265 Misc
Hulleberwe 1275 SR
Ulleburwe, Houleburewe 1280 *For*
Oulebererwe 1305 Wigorn
Ullebererwe 1311, 1369 Pat
Olbarwe 1321 AD ii
Olberewe 1327 SR
Ollebarewe 1340 NI
Ulbarewe 1346 FA
Wolbarowe 1535 VE, 1542 LP
Owlbarrow 1545 Wills
Owburrow 1622 WillsP

The first element is doubtless the same as that found in *ulanwyllan* in the same charter as *Ulenbeorge* and in the neighbouring Ullenhall (Wa)[2]. The triple occurrence of this first element in the names of three not very distant objects is in favour of a pers. name rather than the bird-name *ūle*, 'owl,' but we have no definite evidence for a pers. name *Ūla* in OE though there is a possibility of a parallel in OGer, cf. Förstemann PN 1476. The later forms show hesitation between *Ull-*

---

[1] Recently transferred to Warwickshire.
[2] DB *Holenhale*, 1242, 1268 Ipm *Ulnhale*, 1251 Fees *Hulenhale*, 13th AD ii *Ullenhale*, 1316 FA *Olenhale*, 1302 AD iv *Olenhale* (from forms kindly supplied by Major Laffan).

with trisyllabic shortening and retention of the long vowel
under the influence of *owl* itself. The second element is beorg,
hence 'owl-hill' or '*Ula's* hill.'

WHORE NAP (Old 1″)

This lies on the bounds of Warwickshire and Worcestershire
and we clearly have a case of OE har as in Warstock in King's
Norton *infra* 357.

Ombersley

OMBERSLEY 81 B 10

> *Ambreslege, Ombreswelle* 706 (12th) BCS 116
> *Ombersetena gemære* 817 (11th) BCS 361, 980 (11th) KCD
>   627
> *Ambresleie, Ambresley, Ambreslege* 714 (16th) BCS 130, 1166
>   RBE, 1182 P, 1200 Cur, 1283 Wigorn, 1327 SR, 1359 Ch
> *Hambreslega* c. 1086 (1190) *EveA*
> *Ombresleye* c. 1300 *Bodl* 57 a (p)
> *Aumbresleg, Aumbresley* 1229–51 Ch, 1280 ib. (p)
> *Ambersley* 1675 Ogilby

The history of this very difficult name would seem to go
along with that of Amesbury (W), c. 1000 *Ambresbyrig* (Saints),
Amberesburg (BCS 494), Ambersham (Sx), *Aembresham,*
Embresham (BCS 1114), *Ambresham* 1166 P, 1284 Winton
Ambrosden (O), DB *Ambresdene* and an *Ambresmedwe* in the
Feckenham district (*AOMB* 61) c. 1200. The suggestion which
has been made that these names should be taken as representing
OE names formed from the pers. name *Éanbeorht,* cannot be
entertained in the case of Amesbury and Ombersley, and is very
doubtful for Ambersham and Ambrosden, and that for two
reasons. In the first place it is impossible to believe that the
t could have disappeared so completely, and in the second we
should have expected numerous forms in *Emb-*. None are
however to be found, except for Ambersham. Rather we must
associate it as does Alexander (PN O 39) with the base *Ambr-*
recorded in the archaic Vandal pers. name *Ambri* and in the
fairly common diminutives *Ambrichus, Ambricho* given by
Förstemann (PN 98). The former would appear in OE as
Ambre and in the West Country as *Ombre*. See further
Introd. xx. Hence 'Ambre's clearing,' *v.* leah. A spring (*v.*

wielle) was named after the same man, while in the third form we have a reference to the boundary of the people of Ombersley, the suffix being added to the first element in the name as in Broadwas *supra* 103.

ACTON

Acton 1175 P (p), 1275 SR (p), *et passim*
'Oak-farm,' *v.* ac, tun.

BARNHALL FM

Bernewell 1264, 1327 SR (p)
'*Beorna's* spring,' *v.* **wielle**.

BORELEY

Barlege c. 1190 *EveA*   *Borleye* 1275 *Ass*, SR (p)
Boreley 1527, 1570 Wills
This is a compound of OE **bar** and **leah**, 'boar clearing.'

BOURNES DINGLE (6″)

This clearly takes its name from the family of Sir John *Bourne* who held Ombersley in the 16th cent. (VCH iii. 463).

BROOKHAMPTON [brukən]

Brokhamton, Brochamton 1215–22 (c. 1250) *WoC*, 1275 *Ass*, SR (p)
Brockington 1655 WillsP
'The hamtun by the brook,' cf. Brookhampton in Astley *supra* 33.

CHATLEY

Chatley, Chatteley 1539, 1545 Wills
'*Ceatta's* clearing,' *v.* leah.

COMHAMPTON [kəmən]

Cumbehampton 1275 *Ass*   *Comphampton* 1275 *FF* (p)
Comanton 1567 Wills
'The hamtun by the cumb or valley.'

THE CROSS (6″)

de Cruce, atte Croys 1275, 1327 SR
Self-explanatory. For the form *croys v.* Cruise Hill *supra* 26.

Dean's Wood (6″)

In a fine of 1275 and in the Assize Roll of the same year we have a family taking their name from *la Dene*. Either the wood takes its name from this *dene* itself, when the *s* is pseudo-manorial, or it is named from that family. The wood lies at the south end of a small valley.

Dunhampton [dʌnən]

Dunhampton 1222 *FF*, 1275 *Ass*
Dunhamton 1275, 1327 SR (p)
Dudhampton 1582 Wills

'The hamtun by the hill.'

Gardner's Grove (6″)

This probably takes its name from the family of *Gardener* mentioned in 1604 (Wills).

Hadley

Haddeley(e) 13th ChronEve, 1327 (18th) Nash
Hadley 1581 Wills, 1656 FF

The twice-repeated double *d* makes it probable that the name is '*Headda's* clearing,' rather than 'heath-clearing,' *v.* leah, hæð.

Harford Hill

Hertford 1275 SR (p)   *Herford* 1327 SR·(p)
Harpford 1570 Wills

'Stag-ford,' *v.* heorot.

Hawford

Hageford 1182 (18th) *RBB*
Haweford 1262 *For* (p), 1304 Ipm
Hauford 1275, 1327, 1332 SR, all (p)
Hawford 1352 (18th) Nash
Hausforde 1358 AD ii (p)
Havard 1638 QSR
Halford 1649 Surv

'Ford by the hedge' or 'ford by the enclosure,' *v.* haga.

Lenchford Ferry

Linchford 1612 VCH iii. 463

'Ford by the ridge,' *v.* hlinc.

LINEHOLT [linjəl]

Lynholt, Linholt 1358, 1379 Pat, 1612 VCH iii. 463
Lyneholt 1596 WillsP
Linnal 1820 G

'Limetree-wood,' v. lind, holt.

MAYHOUSE FM

Maiothous 1330 FF   Mayhouse 1540 Wills, 1654 WillsP
Mayeux 1580 Wills, 1820 G

The identification of the first form is probable if not certain. Mayhouse is on the Droitwich border of Ombersley parish and Maiothous is a messuage in Droitwich. The forms do not admit of any certain etymology.

NORTHAMPTON

Northamtun c. 1190 EveA
Norhamton 1223 Pat (p)
Northam(p)ton 1275 Ass (p), 1327 SR (p), 1579 Wills

'The north hamtun,' in contrast to Suddington infra.

OSMONDS (6″)

As suggested by Duignan (PN Wo 122), this doubtless takes its name from the family of Philip Osmund and Richard Osmond (1275, 1327 SR) found in this vill.

POWERS

Powereswere 1450 IpmR

There are six Poers and two Powers in the 1275 Subsidy Roll. They are not definitely associated with Ombersley or Holt on the opposite side of the river, but William le Poer had land in Ombersley in 1203 (ChronEve).

SUDDINGTON

Suthinton' 1257 AD i (p)
Over Sudyngton, Sodynton 1351 FF, Pat
Over and Nether Suddington 1547 Pat
Sinton Close 1613 QSR

v. Sodington supra 60. This lies in the south of the parish, in contrast to Northampton supra. The form Sinton actually survives in Sinton Fm (6″) hard by[1]. For this form cf. Leigh Sinton *supra* 207. In the Evesham Cartulary (c. 1200) there is a form *Sudurton* which points to an alternative *sūðera tun*, 'southern farm.'

SYTCHAMPTON [sitʃən]

Sychampton 1575–89 Wills

'The hamtun by the sic or watercourse.'

TAPENHALL FM (6″)

Toppehale 1275 SR (p)   *Tapenhale* 1327 SR (p)
Tapenhill 1612 VCH iii. 463   *Tapenhall* 1655 WillsP

If the first form is correct, the first element is the weak form *Toppa*, otherwise unknown, but evidently connected with the pers. name *Topp*, found in Topsham (D), *Toppesham* BCS 721, Toppesfield, Toppinghoe (Ess), with later unrounding of *o* to *a*. It is however likely that it is the same name as Tapenhall in Claines *supra* 114, a mile away.

TYTCHNEY (6″)

la Twichene 1275 SR (p)
Twychene, Twichene 1308 Wigorn (p), 1371, 1375 AD iv, 1389 Pat (p)

This is OE *twicen(e)*, 'place where two roads meet,' found also in Touchen End (Berks), *la Twychene* in IPM 1351, 1360 and in *twycene* in Pershore (BCS 1282) and *Twichene* in Pensax (1240 WoP) and very commonly in Devon. There is a road-crossing just north of Tytchney.

UPHAMPTON [upətən], [ʌpən]

Uphampton 1275 *Ass*
Huphamton 1275 SR (p)
Ophampton, Uponton 1337 WoCh, 1570 Wills

'The hamtun on high ground.'

WINNALL

Wilenhale c. 1190 *EveA*
Wylnehale 1275 SR (p)

---

[1] For a similar pair of forms cf. Phepson *supra* 137.

Wylenhale, Whilenhale 1327 SR (p)
Wynnalds 1649 Surv

This is probably 'Willa's healh.' The final form shows the common excrescent *d* of *vild* for *vile*.

WOOD HOUSE (6")

la Wodehuse 1275 SR (p)

'House by the wood,' *v.* Woodhouse in Pensax *supra* 68.

YOUNGS FM (6")

This probably takes its name from the family of *Yonge* or *Young* mentioned in Wills of 1614 and 1630.

Wickhamford

WICKHAMFORD 82 J 4

Wicwona 709 (c. 1200) BCS 125
Wigorne 714 (16th) BCS 130
Wycweoniga gemære c. 860 (c. 1200) KCD 289
Wiquene 1086 DB
Wichwana c. 1086 (1190) *EveA*
Wikkewan 1251 Ch
Wike Waneford 1255 *Ass*, 1275 SR
Wikewone, Wikewane, Wykewane 1327, 1332 SR, 1397 Pat
Wykeword 1346 FA
Wyk(e)wansford 1389 Pat, 1545 LP
Wikewanford 1471 IpmR
Wycanford 1550 Pat
Wikenford 1577 Saxton
Wic(k)hamford 1593 Wills, 17th FF
Wicconford 1634 QSR
Wickwanford 1657 FF

This name must be taken together with Childs Wickham (Gl), *Childeswicwon* in BCS 117, which lies on the same small stream, now called Badsey Brook. For Childs Wickham we have another form in BCS 1282, viz. *Uuiguuennan* (dat.). Little can be done with this name. Professor Ekwall calls attention to the apt parallel *Wigewen broke* (KCD 706) in Bradford-on-Avon (W). The diversity of the early forms clearly points to a Celtic original which the English settlers had difficulty in handling.

HACKNEY (local)[1]

(*H*)*echeneige* 709 (c. 1200) BCS 125

'Well-watered land of *Hæcca*,' *v.* eg. This name is not on actual record, but cf. *Hacca, Hæcci.*

PRESS-MEADOW (local)[1]

Prestesmede 709 (c. 1200) BCS 125
Prestemede 1233 (13th) ChronEve

'Priest's mead,' *v.* mæd, surviving to this day in a field-name.

VI. CLENT HUNDRED

Clent 1086 DB

Clent Hundred consisted of 21 manors assessed at 97 hides. It lay to the east of Cresseau Hundred. It was compact, except that the north and south portions were divided by a small projection of Came Hundred. The meeting-place was presumably somewhere near Clent. All the manors of Clent were later merged in the Hundred of Halfshire.

Belbroughton

BELBROUGHTON 71 G 13

This includes the two settlements called in OE *Beolne* and *Broctun.* The first survives in:

BELL HALL, HEATH, END and MILL

Beolne 817 (11th) BCS 360, 11th Heming, 1300 *Pat*
Bellem 1086 DB
Belna, Belne c. 1150 Surv, 1181 P, 1212 Fees 140, (*Bruyn*) 1255 *Ass*, 1292 Ipm
Bellene 1275 *Ass*
Bellenbrun 1280 *For*
Bolne 1346 FA
Bryncebellum 1556 AD vi

For the identification of these field-names we are indebted to Mr C. A. Seyler.

BROUGHTON appears as

Broctun 817 (11th) BCS 360, 11th Heming
Brocton 1086 DB, 1292 Ipm

They are merged into Belbroughton which appears as

Bellebrocton 1292 Wigorn (p)
Belnebrocton 1298, 1313 Wigorn (p), 1323 Ipm (p)
Belvebrotton, Belnebrotton 1323 Cl, 1362 Pat
Bellibroughton, Bellebroughton 1368 Pat, 1431 FA

Broughton is clearly 'farm by the brook.' That brook, before it reaches the present village of Belbroughton, has passed through the various places called *Bell* which are enumerated above, and *Belne* is the old name for the brook, cf. *Pat* 1300 (Mctcs of Feckenham Forest), *aqua q. v. Beolne*. The *Bruyn* family came in in the 13th cent. and from them the manor was often spoken of as *Brians Bell* (VCH iii. 16).

BRANTHILL FM (6″)

Branthyles 1556 AD vi

'Burnt-hills' (*v*. brende). This interpretation is made probable by its being near to a *Brandgoste*, i.e. 'burnt gorse,' in the reference cited above.

BROOM HILL

Bromhull 1275, 1327 SR (p)   *Bromhill* 1531 Wills
Self-explanatory.

DORDALE

Doverdale 1275 SR (p)

This is the name of a farm and district in Belbroughton, but they lie on a stream which, if one follows its course southwards, becomes that stream which is for a time called Elmley Brook and afterwards forms the western boundary of Doverdale (*v. supra* 239).

FAIRFIELD

Forfeld(e) 817 (11th) BCS 360, 11th Heming, 1275 *Ass*
Forfeud 1255 For, 1262 *Ass*
Forefeld 1271 For, 1275 *Ass*, 1279, 1292, 1316 Ipm
Fortfeld 1280 *Ass*

Forfeild 1474 IpmR
Forfield 1616 QSR
Forefield 1820 G

This place lies on the northern edge of Feckenham Forest. The feld is the open country outside that forest-land. We may adopt Duignan's suggestion (PN Wo 60) that the prefix is OE *fore*, 'in front,' and then interpret the whole name as descriptive of land lying just in front of the forest-land. Cf. OE *fore-burg, -duru, -scyttels, -tīege, -weall, -weard* for similar compounds. The Forhill *infra* 333 provides a further parallel and other examples of the same type of compound are Fordon in the East Riding, Forwood in Henley-in-Arden (Wa) and Fore Wood in Crowhurst (Sx), Farwood (D) in Colyton (DB *Forohoda*, 1198 FF *Forewode*) all thrusting themselves prominently forward. The form *Fortfeld* suggests confusion with the prefix *forð-*. Such confusion has its parallel in the double forms *forð-tīege* and *fore-tīege* in OE. For *forð* cf. Furtho (Nth) and Forty Green *supra* 202.

FENN FM (6″)

de la Fenne, atte Fenne 1275, 1327 SR

GORSE FM

de la Gorste 1275 SR
v. gorst. Both these names are self-explanatory.

HARTLE

Herthul(le) c. 1260 *Bodl* 36, 1275 SR, 1291 Ipm, 1312 *FF*, 1327 SR, 1334 LyttCh, all (p)
Herthill 1318 Ipm (p)
'Hart-hill,' *v.* heorot, hyll.

HAYES FM (6″)

usque hesam sub domum Adam de la Haye 1255 *FF*
v. hese. The reference is to woodland country near a forest 'hay' (*v.* (ge)hæg) belonging to one *Adam*.

HILL FM (6″)

de la Hulle 1275 SR

HURST FM

la Hurste 1275 SR

Both these names are self-explanatory.

INSETTON

Insington c. 1830 O

The form is too late to do anything with. Possibly we should compare 'a house called le *Insetun*hous' in Solihull (Wa) in AD i. 1349.

MADLEY HEATH

Maydeneleye 1300 *Pat*
Madeley 1553, 1605 Wills
Madley 1587 Wills
Maidley c. 1830 O

'Maidens' clearing,' *v.* leah. For this type of name *v.* Medbury (PN BedsHu 71).

MOOR HALL

de la More 1275 SR   *More Hall* 1347 Pat
Morehalbellum 1556 AD vi   *Morehall Bell* 1656 BM

Self-explanatory, except that the *Bell(um)* refers to its being part of *Beolne*. It was often called Moorhall Bell (VCH iii. 16).

PEPPER WOOD

Pup(p)erode 1230 P, c. 1255 *For*, 1276 RH, 1314 Pat
Pepperod(e) 1251 Ch, 1463 IpmR
Purperode c. 1255 *For*, 1276 RH, 1314 Pat
Pipperod 1262 *For*, 1275 *Ass*
Popperod 1271 *For*
Pypperode 1494 IpmR
Pyperode Wood c. 1830 O

It is clear that in this name we have the same pers. name *Pypba* or *Pyppa* which is found in Pepwell and Peopleton *supra* 216, 245 and Pedmore *infra* 305. The suffix is rod and the whole name means 'Pypba's clearing.' This is all part of an old forest-area.

x

WILDMOOR (6")

> *Wildmore* 1270 Inq aqd
> *de la Wildemore, atte Wildemore* 1275, 1327 SR

Self-explanatory.

Broom

BROOM[1] 71 F 12

> *Brome* 1169 P   *Broome* 1343 LyttCh

Self-explanatory.

REDHALL FM

> *Le Redewall* 1373 LyttCh

'Red-spring,' *v.* read, wielle, cf. Redhall Fm in Ridgeacre *infra* 300.

Churchill

CHURCHILL 71 F 12

> *Cercehalle* 1086 DB
> *Chirhulle* c. 1250 Dugd v. 83
> *Chyrchull* 1275 SR
> *Churchulle* 1292 Ipm, 1298 Wigorn

In the Worcester episcopal Registers (1307) it is distinguished from Churchill in Oswaldslow as *Chirchehull* in the forest of *Kynefar* or Kinver. It is also known as Churchill near Kidderminster and as Churchill in Halfshire. For the etymology *v.* Churchill *supra* 106.

ISMERE HOUSE

> *Husmeræ* 736 BCS 154
> *Provincia Usmerorum* c. 760 (11th) BCS 220
> (*in*) *Usmerum* 781 (11th) BCS 241
> *Usmere* 964 (11th) BCS 1134

In the first reference we have the name of a *provincia*, in the third the name is presumably in the dat. pl. after the preposition *in*. In the second we have a latinized gen. pl. of *Usmere*. The lake or rather chain of lakes from which this district took its name is that which runs from the present Broadwaters in Kidderminster to Churchill (*v.* mere). The first element is

---

[1] In Staffs. from early 13th cent. till 1844.

difficult. Professor Ekwall (*Anglia Beiblatt* xxxvi. 279) and Professor Zachrisson (*English PN and River-names* 15), take the first element here to be the common river-name *Use* with early loss of *e* from the compound *Use-mere*. They note a further compound of this river-name and mere in the *usan-mere* of BCS 123[1]. Ismere House must take its name from the province rather than from the 'meres' themselves for it lies more than a mile to the north-east of them.

Clent[2]

Clent 71 F 13

Clent 11th Hcming, 1086 DB, 1186 P, 1258 Pat

This name is difficult. There is a ME *clint*, 'hard flinty rock,' a Scandinavian loan-word which has its origin in Dan, Sw *klint*, but this cannot be the source of *clent* in England, with its persistent *e* and further, as a Worcestershire place-name of the 11th cent., and almost certainly of far earlier date, it can hardly be Scandinavian at all. In the North Frisian dialects we have in place-names the forms *klant*, *klent* and *klunt* (Schmidt-Petersen, *Die Orts- und Flurnamen Nordfrieslands* 40). The first two go back to a Germanic *klent* which is the source of Danish *klint* and which, had it been found in OE, would have given *klint*. The third form goes back to a Germanic *klant* which, in the forms *klant*, *klatt* (all with the same sense) is found in modern Norwegian (Torp, *Nynorsk Etym. Ordbog s.v.*), and suggest that *klant* was a common Germanic form showing a different grade of the same stem. There may have been an *i*-noun formed from this grade in OE, giving a lost OE *clent*, 'rock,' a suitable name for a hill. The word *clent* in this sense is found once in a ME text in the phrase 'a *clent* hille.' The NED (*s.v.*) suggests that this is allied to *clint*, if not the same word. The text is a northern one so that it may be that we have an isolated bad spelling for the Scandinavian word but it does not seem very probable[3].

---

[1] Not 125, as in Zachrisson's text. It should be added that *Hellerelege* is not near Worcester but near King's Norton as shown by the identifications *s.n.* Lindsworth and Chyndhouse *infra* 355, 352.

[2] In Staffordshire from early 13th cent. till 1844.

[3] For certain points in this article we are indebted to Professor W. E. Collinson.

CALCOTT HILL

Caldecote 1327 SR (p)   *Kalcotthyll* 1609 Wills

'Cold cottage(s),' *v.* cald, cot.

NIMMINGS PLANTATION (6")

This is probably the same as 'land in Churchill called *Nemmynges*,' 1429 LyttCh. In any case it is an example of OE *niming*, used of land taken into cultivation or enclosed. *v.* PN in *-ing* 25. Cf. Nimmings Fm *infra* 346.

OLDNALL FM (6")

Hodenhull 1237 Ipm

Duignan (PN Wo 120) gives a series of forms, *Aldenhulle, Oldenhull*, etc., which we have been unable to track down, which suggest that this may be '*Ealda's* hill,' *v.* hyll. Their identification is however uncertain.

THICKNALL FM

Thyckennaile 1304 Ct (p)   *Thicknoll* 1592 Wills

The history of this name is not certain. It might be from OE *atte thickenhale*, i.e. 'at the thick nook or corner,' but the sense is not clear. There is a name *Thikenolre* found in the 1327 Subsidy Roll in this vill which looks as if it might be from the same place. If it is, the use of the epithet is clearer, for it looks like a derivative of OE *alor*, 'alder,' cf. Orleton *supra* 67.

WALTON HILL, HO, and POOL

Walton 1275 SR (p), 1545 Wills

v. wealh, tun and cf. Walton in Elmley Lovett *supra* 242.

Crutch

CRUTCH 81 A 12

Cruchia Hy 2 (1285) Ch
Cruch 1178 (c. 1240) WoC
Crouch(e) 1538 LP, 1701 FF, 1820 G
Croyche juxta Wyche Eliz ChancP
Crowche 1653 FF

The place doubtless takes its name from Crutch Hill in which we have the same British word for a hill noted under Crookbarrow *supra* 178. See further IPN 25.

Dodderhill

DODDERHILL 81 B 12

Dudrenhull 1096–1180 (c. 1250) *WoC* (quater)
Duderhull 1175 (c. 1250) *WoC*, (18th) Thomas, c. 1150 (18th)
  Hearne's *Heming* 536
Doderhull 13th Wigorn *passim*
Dodderhull, Doderhyll 1535 VE

This points clearly to a pers. name *Dudra*, an *r*-derivative of OE *Duda*. For such *r*-derivatives cf. Doddershall (PN Bk 110) and Pixham *supra* 225.

ASTWOOD

Estw(o)d(e) c. 1086 (1190) *EveB*, 1212 Fees 140, 1212 RBE
Astwude juxta Wychebaud 1270 Ipm
Astwode Roberti 1242 Fees 960   *Wylliesastwode* 1271 *FF*
Astwode 1287 Ipm, 1300 *Pat*

Self-explanatory. It is in the east of the parish, near Wychbold. *William* Savage held land in Astwood in 1258 (Ipm). Astwood *Roberti* was another manor in this vill.

BROOKHOUSE FM (6″)

atte Broke 1275, 1327 SR
Self-explanatory.

COLLEY PIT (6″)

atte Colle 1275 SR   *Colleyhulle* 14th VCH iii. 59
The pit is in a slight valley running up into a low hill. There is no stream now but there may have been one and its name may have been *Colle* (*v.* Cole, R. *supra* 10). The pit probably refers to a large pond.

FORD FM

atte Forde 1275, 1327 SR   *Fourde* 1398 *Pat*
The Forde 1576, 1585 Wills   *The Furde* 1602 WillsP
Self-explanatory.

HELPRIDGE FM

Helperic 1086 DB
Helpriche 1558 Wills   *Helpridge* 1576 Wills
Elbridge c. 1830 O

The identification of this hitherto lost brine-pit of Droitwich is made clear by the fact that Helpridge is two miles from Droitwich and that a quarter of a mile to the south-west of it lies Brinepits Fm, probably the very brine-pit, with its seventeen salt-pans, of which Domesday speaks. The brook which runs past Brinepits Fm is called Salty Brook. There are a good many early stream-names in *-ic* but this seems only to be added to elements of Celtic origin. Professor Ekwall therefore suggests that, like a good many other stream-, mill-names and the like, it is humorous in origin and that is a playful application of the OE pers. name *Helperic*, lit. 'helpful,' to a particularly rich brine-pit. In the same way he would take the stream-name *Til(l)nōþ* (BCS 217, 299) to be the OE pers. name of that form, meaning 'excellent, useful one,' perhaps from its power of driving mills.

HENBROOK

Hensbroc 770 (11th) BCS 204   *Hennebroc* 1201 (c. 1240) *WoC*
Henbrook 1559 Wills

Sievers (*Angelsächsische Grammatik*, 289, n. 3) explains this name as containing the word *hens*, a noun with an *s*-suffix which would be the English cognate of ON *hæns*, a collective plural denoting poultry. Hence 'hens' (i.e. probably moorhens') brook.'

HILL FM (6")

atte Hulle 1275, 1327 SR
Self-explanatory.

HOBDEN (6")

Obeden 1375 Wigorn (p)
Abdon 1558 Wills
Obden 1613 Wills, 1649 Surv, 1892 Kelly
Hobon 1772 T, 1789 Gough

There is a pers. name *Oba* which is well established, but there is no doubt that, at least in the majority of cases, it stands for OE *Ofa* rather than for *Obba*, which we must assume to explain the present name. *Obba* is found once (in one text) for a man who is otherwise called *Ova* (Redin 102). It may possibly be a hypocoristic form of that name, with gemination of medial *f*. On the other hand it may be that there was a name *Obba* of an entirely different origin. *Obba* would be a regular hypocoristic form for such a pers. name as OE *Ordbeorht*. Hence 'Obba's valley,' *v.* denu.

HUNTINGTRAP FM[1]

Huntingthrop 1271 For
Huntindrop(e) 1300 Pat, 1485 (18th) Nash
Hountingthrope 1327 SR
Hundingtrope 1398 Pat
Huntingthorp 1550 Pat

This contains as its first element the pers. name *Hunta* linked to the second element þorp by the element *ing* as in the *ingtun*-names. Hence 'Hunta's village.' Cf. Huntingtree *infra* 295.

IMPNEY

Ymeneia, Imenea, Imeneye, Ymeneye 1176 P, 1210 RBE, 1212 Fees 140, 1271 For
Impney 1658 FF

'Imma's low-lying well-watered ground,' *v.* eg. For· this name cf. Immingham (L) and *ymman holigne* in the bounds of Old Swinford (BCS 1023).

KINGSHILL FM[2]

Kingeslaunde 1271 For
Kyngeslonde, Kingeslonde 1275 SR (p), 1287, 1308 Ipm, 1300 Pat, 1327 SR (p), 1377 Cl, 1389, 1408 IpmR
Kingsland Hill 1789 Gough

As we are in woodland country, the suffix is probably ME launde rather than land.

---

[1] Now in Hanbury.
[2] As late as the directory of 1923 the place is called Kingsland Hill Farm. The shortened form is a good example from modern times of the tendency, noted by Ritter, to drop the middle element of three in a triple-compound name.

KNOTTENHILL[1] (lost)

> *Knoteshull, Cnoteshull, Cnotteshull* 1240 Cl, 1267 Ch
> *Knothull* 1255 *For*
> *Knottenhull(e)* 1276 RH, 1291 Tax, 1386 Pat

'Cnott(a)'s hill,' *v.* hyll. For this pers. name *v.* Knotting (PN BedsHu 15).

LEATHER BRIDGE

> *Letherenebruge* 1229 Ch
> la *Lethernebrugge* 1300 (18th) *Pat*
> *Leathorne Bridge, Leatham Bridge* 1635 QSR

It is impossible to avoid the conclusion that the bridge must have acquired its distinctive name from some use of leather in some part of the original structure.

PRIDZOR WOOD (6″)

> *Prudesouere* 1270 FF (p)   *Purdesore* 1456 VCH iii. 79

There is a Cornish name *Prud*, but this must probably be ruled out of the question. There is also an English pers. name *Prūda* which survived until the 13th cent. A strong form of this would explain the present name. For the suffix ofer, cf. Hadzor *infra* 291.

RASHWOOD

> *Eshide* 1221 *Ass*
> *Aschide* 1227 FF
> *Esside, Essyda* c. 1300, 1303 AD v, vi
> *Raschehede prope Wyche* 1535 VE
> *Rasshid* 1550 Pat
> *Rash(e)wood* 1581, 1615 Wills, 17th Hab

This name must be a compound of OE æsc and hid and describe an estate of one hide on which ash-trees grew in plenty. The initial *r* developed from such forms as ME *at ther asshide* becoming *at the rasshide*. Cf. Ryknild Street *supra* 2.

---

[1] This estate of Bordesley Abbey was in an *Astwood*. An entry in the Assize Roll of 1275 suggests that it was in Astwood *Robert* (281 *supra*) and thus in Dodderhill.

SAGEBURY FM

Savagebure, Savagebury 1275 SR (p), 1350 Ch, 1406 *FF*
Savegebury al. *Astwood Savage* 1366 VCH iii. 63, n. 78
Savegesbury 1431 FA
Sagebury, Sageburie 13th WoCh (p), 1550 Pat, 1561 Wills
Sedgebury c. 1830 O

This is the manor (*v.* burh) of the *Savage* family who held it
in the 13th cent. (VCH iii. 63). Cf. Astwood *supra* 281.

WYCHBOLD

Uuicbold, Wicbold 692 (11th) BCS 77, 831 BCS 400
Wicelbold 1086 DB
Wichebald 1160 P
Wychebaut 1283 FF
Wichebaud 1275, 1308 Ipm
Wychingbald 1275 *Ass*
Whichebaud 1276 RH

This is clearly a compound of **wic** and **bold** just as Witton
infra 289 is a compound of **wic** and **tun**. The whole name means
'buildings by the **wic**,' referring possibly to Droitwich itself.

Droitwich

DROITWICH[1] 81 B 12

Wiccium emptorium 716 (14th) BCS 134
(*in*) *Wico emptorio salis quem nos Saltwich vocamus* 717 (12th)
   BCS 138
Saltwic 888 (13th) BCS 557
(*æt þære*) *sealtwic* 1017 KCD 1313
Wich 1086 DB
Drihtwych, Dryghtwych 1347, 1356 Pat, 1466 IpmR
Drytwyche 1353 *FF*, 1397 Pat
Dertwych 1396, 1426 Pat, 1469 IpmR, 1485 Ipm, 1486 Pat
Drythewiche 1446 Pat
Dirtewych, Dyrtwyche 1460 Pat, 1485–97 Ipm *passim*, 1480,
   1491 StratGild

[1] Of lost Droitwich streets we may note *Ruinestret, Ruyenestret* (13th,
1343 AD ii, iii) which may have the same first element as *Ruynhulle* in
Evesham *supra* 262, n. 1, *le Barrestret* (1335, AD i) taking its name from some
barre or gate. The *Rafunestrete* of 1229 (Ch) appears as *Runestrete* in the *WoC*
copy of the same document and shows that the Charter Roll form is bad.

Dertwich vel *Droitwich* 1466 IpmR
Droittewich 1473 IpmR
Drethwyche 1503 Ipm
Droytwiche, Droytwych 1515–40, 1547 LP
Draytewiche 1533–42 LP
Dartewyche 1536 LP
Dortewych 1538 LP
Durtewiche 1540 LP
Droitwich vulg. *Durtwich* 1675 Ogilby[1]

The use here of OE wic is fully discussed in EPN *s.v.* It is simply descriptive of a settlement. That the word *wic* itself has no such sense as 'brine-pit' is shown further by the fact that *sealt* could be prefixed to it. Such a compound would be pointless if the word *wic* itself implied the presence of salt. There can be little doubt that the first element in the present form of the name is the ordinary word *dirt* (*v*. NED for the various ME forms of it). The place is low-lying and would doubtless be muddy and 'dirty[2].' For such a name there is a curious Cheshire parallel. There is a Fullwich (Ch) near Malpas, earlier *Ful(l)euuic* (*Chartulary of Chester Abbey*, ed. Tait, 18, 55) which doubtless means 'foul or dirty wic.' It was low-lying and there were salt-pits there. This place was apparently known alternatively as *Dirtwich* or at any rate there was a place of that name quite near it, for the Egertons, who had land in Over and Nether Fulwich, also had lands in *Droytwich* al. *Durtwich* in the manor of Malpas. Leland (*Itinerary*, ed. Toulmin Smith iv. 7; v. 6) speaks of this *Dertwich* or *Dyrtwich* as lying in a low bottom. Later corruptions of the name are doubtless due to attempts to disguise the unpleasant associations of the name. The only difficulty in this explanation is the presence of the forms *Dryghtwych*, but these are probably simply bad spellings. One might take them to be for OE *dryhten*, ME *dryght(en)* 'lord,' but that word is extremely archaic except in application to the

---

[1] To the Rev. Dr Whitley we are indebted for a full list of 15th and 16th cent. forms of the name as it appears in the Borough records from the time that it first appears with a prefix: *Durt-* (1495), *Droyt-, Droit-* (1495 onwards, *passim*), *Dyrth-* (1496), *Drowthwheche* (1498), *Dert-* (1508), *Dryt-* (1528) with occasional *Wiche, Wyche, Wheche.*

[2] 'Durt-wich some terme it, of the salt pits and the wettish ground' (Camden, *Britannia*, tr. Holland, 574).

deity himself, and it is inconceivable that it should have given rise to a place-name in the 14th cent.

In addition to the main wic of Droitwich there were also

UPWICH (lost)

Upwic 962 (11th) BCS 1087   *Upewic* 1086 DB
Uppewich 1275 *Ass*   *Upwich* 17th FF

MIDDLEWICH (lost)

Middelwic 972 (18th) BCS 1284, 972 (c. 1050) BCS 1282
Midelwic 1086 DB   *Middewich* 1275 *Ass*
Middelwich Hy 7 (17th) Hab

NETHERWICH (6")

neodemestan wic (acc.) 972 (c. 1050) BCS 1282
Neoþomæst wic 972 (18th) BCS 1284
Netherwich Hy 7 (17th) Hab

These *wyches* or buildings at the different brine-pits were probably so distinguished from their position in relation to the Salwarpe. Netherwich was certainly the lowest down the river, *neoðomæst* being the old superlative form of neoðor.

BRIAR MILL (6")

molendinum voc. Brerhulle n.d. Dudg vi. 1004
Bryerhylle 1535 VE

'Briar-(hill)-mill.' *v.* **brær, hyll,** with omission of the middle element in the triple-compound.

FALSAM PITS

Falsham field 1456 VCH iii. 79   *Falfordes pit* 1456 ib.
Falsone pit 18th Nash

There is very little to go upon, but the first element may be a pers. name *Fæle* which is perhaps also found in *Fælesgræfe* (BCS 1282) in this county, and allied to OE *fæle*, 'pleasant.' The second element may be either **ham** or **hamm.**

GILTON BROOK (6")

Grytenbrook 1456 VCH iii. 79
Giltonbrook 17th (18th) Nash

The first element is probably a lost OE adj. *grŷten*, a derivative of greot or grot, meaning 'sandy, pebbly.'

GOSFORD (lost)

Goseford' 1276 RH

One of the numerous geese-haunted fords (*v.* gos, ford). It was the ford where now a bridge at the end of Queen Street (once Gosford Street) carries the Bromsgrove road over the Salwarpe.

LOLLAYCROSS (lost)[1]

This cross is mentioned in the VCH (iii. 80) and would seem to have been identical with 'The Cross,' the old name given to the point where the Alcester-Kidderminster road crosses that from Selly Oak to Worcester. Two hundred yards south-south-east on the Holloway is a field called *Lullo's* which must be the *Loulleleye, Lulleleye* of AD iii (1333 and 1343) and have given rise to the name Lollay Cross. The name means 'Lulla's clearing,' *v.* leah.

PRIMSLAND

Prymmes Lane 1456 VCH iii. 79
Primsland Lane 17th (18th) Nash

This doubtless contains the pers. name *Prime* found occasionally in Wo in 1273 and 1327 (SR). There is a very doubtful OE name *Prim*. *v.* Redin 34.

TAGWELL LANE (6″)

Tagwall spring 1456 VCH iii. 79
Taggewell 17th (18th) Nash

There can be little doubt that here and in Tagg Barn in Chaddesley Corbett *supra* 238, also in *Taggemere* in Bishampton (Nash), we have the word *tag* used in the west and south-west for a sheep, apparently a variation of the more usual *tegg*. Hitherto the form *tag* has only been known from modern dialect, but the forms here given show that *tagge* was already in use in the 13th cent. and suggests that the two forms *teg* and *tag* go back to an OE *tacga*, *teg* being a common dialectal development of *a* to *e*. Cf. Zachrisson in *Englische Studien* lix. 353. For the name we may compare Sw *tacka*, 'ewe, sheep.'

---

[1] For the topography of Lollay Cross we are indebted to the kindness of Dr Whitley.

WITTON

Wittona 716 (14th) BCS 134, (*juxta Wyche*) 1378 IpmR
Wictun 817 (17th) BCS 361
Wittun 972 (18th) BCS 1284
Witone in Wich 1086 DB

It is clear that here, as in Wyton (Hu), Market Weighton (Y), we have a compound of OE **wic** and **tun**, meaning 'enclosure by the wic,' cf. Wychbold *supra* 285. Professor Tait calls attention to the parallel of Witton by Northwich (Ch). It contains the parish church of Northwich, just as Droitwich is (or was) mainly in the parishes of St Andrew and St Peter de Witton. In both cases it looks as if the *wic* was the industrial centre and the *wictun* the dwelling-place.

Dudley

DUDLEY 71 C 14

Dudelei 1086 DB, 1199 Cur
Dodelega 1190 P (p)
Duddelaege, Duddelege, Duddeleye c. 1140 Chron. of John of
    Worc, 1229 Ch, 1264 Ipm, 1275 SR
Doddele(ye) 1289 Wigorn, 1327 SR

'*Dudda's* clearing,' *v.* leah. The forms of this name have often been confused with those of Diglis in St Peters-without-Worcester *supra* 162.

FREEBODIES (Old 1")

A name of the manorial type, deriving from the family of *Frebodi* found in Dudley in 1275 and 1327 (SR).

HOLLYHALL

atte Holie 1327 SR
Self-explanatory.

NETHERTON

Nederton 1487 Ipm   *Netherton* 1573 Wills

This is on relatively high ground, but it must have been given its name in contrast to a lost *Ouertone* (*Ass* 1275) which was still higher.

RUSSELL'S HALL (6")

This must take its name from the family of *Russel* recorded in Dudley in the Subsidy Rolls of 1275 and 1327, and it is spoken of as *Russelleshalle* in 1315 (Ipm).

WRENS NEST HILL[1]

> *de la Wrosne* 1273 Ipm, 1275 SR, *Ass*, 1278 *FF* (p)
> *Wrosne* 1278 *FF*
> *Wrosene* 1291 Tax
> *ate Wrosne* 1293 Ipm
> *atte Wrosome* 1395 Ipm

This is a prominent isolated hill and it is probable that Skeat is right in identifying the name with the OE word *wrāsn*, 'chain, fetter,' but used also as a gloss for the Latin *nodus*, so that it may appropriately refer to what may be described as a hill-knot, cf. Bowland Knotts (Y), Blawith Knott (La).

Elmbridge

ELMBRIDGE 81 A 12

> *Elmerige* 1086 DB
> *Elingbrige* 1211 RBE
> *Elmrugge* 1212 Fees 960
> *Aumbrug'* 1212 Fees 140
> *Aumerugg'* c. 1280 Ipm
> *Ellebrug'* 1235 Fees 526
> *Elm(e)brug(g)e* 1270 Ch (p), 1275 SR, 1308 Ipm, 1431 FA, 1492 Ipm
> *Almeringge* (sic) 1287 Ipm
> *Elmerugge* 1308 Ipm, 1337 Ch, 1346, 1428 FA
> *Elinbrugge* 1378 IpmR, (*alias dict' Elinrugge*) 1397 IpmR

As Elmbridge is very definitely on a ridge, and there is no bridge near, we must interpret this name as OE *elma-hrycg*, 'ridge of the elm-trees,' with early intrusive *b*, *v.* elm, hrycg. Cf. Keybridge *infra* 305. For *Alm-*, *Aum-* *v.* Elmley Lovett *supra* 240.

---

[1] In Staffordshire.

ADDIS FM

This must take its name from the *Adys* family, recorded in 1685 (FF).

BROAD COMMON and ALLEY

These are probably referred to in the *Brodefeld* of 1327 (SR), *le Brode* of 1418 (*FF*) and *Brode* (Hab). The name is self-explanatory.

CASHES FM

Casseyesplace, Casseyes Land 1447 Pat, (*juxta Wyche*) 1478 IpmR

Cassies 1545 LP   *Cashies* 1892 Kelly

The family of Cassey of Droitwich (*Cassi* 1240 WoP, *Cassy* 1275, 1327 SR) must have had interests in Elmbridge and given their name to this farm.

PURSHULL [pəˑsəl]

Pershulle 1210 RBE, 1275 SR

Purshull' 1242 Fees 960, 1286 Ipm, 1335 Ch, 1346, 1431 FA, 1439 IpmR

Pursill, Pursell, Pursall 1549 Pat, 1558, 1579 Wills

It is difficult to make any suggestion in explanation of these forms as they stand, but Habington (i. 462) gives a form *Purteshull* which, if it is correct, makes a suggestion possible. There is some evidence for an OE pers. name *Purta*, cf. *Purtanig* (W) in BCS 1093, Purfleet (Ess), earlier *Pourteflete*, a lost Portpool (Mx)[1], 1203 *Purtepol*. If this name existed, a strong form *Pyrti*, with mutation of the stem vowel, would explain the forms of Purshull. Hence (possibly) 'Pyrti's hill,' *v.* hyll.

Hadzor

HADZOR 81 B 13

Headdesofre 11th Heming

Hadesore 1086 DB

Haddesour 1212 Fees 140, 1218 *FF*

Had(d)esouere c. 1215 *Bodl* 1, 1235 Fees 527, 1300 *Pat*, 1428 FA

[1] Surviving in Portpool Lane in Holborn.

Hadeshoure 1249 *FF*
Eddes(h)ore 1271, 1280 *For*
Addesoure 1275 *Ass*, 1282 Wigorn
Haddesor 1327 SR, 1366, 1486 Pat
Hadser, Hadsore 1533 LP, 1535 VE
'*Headdi's* bank,' *v.* ofer.

Hagley

HAGLEY 71 F 13

Hageleia 1086 DB
Hagelega 1168 P (p)
Haggele(ge), Haggeleg, Haggeley 1212, 1235 Fees 527, 1255
   Pat (p), 1275 SR, 1323 Ipm, 1327 SR, 1340 NI, 1346 FA
Aggelegh 1221 *Ass*
Haygheleghe 1349 *FF*
Hageley, Hagley 1462, 1485 Pat
'*Hæcga's* clearing,' *v.* leah. This name is found once inde-
pendently in OE and is also found in *hacggen hamm* (BCS 432).

HARBOROUGH HILL

Herdeberewe John LyttCh, 1275 SR (p)
Hardeberewe 1367 LyttCh
Harborow 1500 AD i
Harborough 1787 Cary, 1820 G
Harberrow c. 1830 O, 1892 Kelly
'Herdsman-hill,' cf. Harborough (Wa), DB *Herdeberge*[1].

HOLLIER'S FM (6")

This must take its name from the family of Elizabeth *Hollier*,
an 18th cent. benefactor of Hagley (VCH iii. 135).

WASSEL GROVE

Warselde 1275 SR (p)
Warsfelde 1327 SR (p)
Wartelde 1340 NI (p)
Wassell 1558 Wills, 1662 FF
This has the same history as Warshill, Wassell in Kidder-

---

[1] Duignan (PN Wa 66) is in error in identifying this with *Hereburgebyrig*
(KCD 710). Probably it is Harbury (Wa).

minster *supra* 253 and Wast Hills *infra* 335. The grove stands
high.

WYCHBURY HILL

There is a conspicuous hill here. The burh is doubtless the
very strong camp which crowns it (VCH iv. 424). The first
element can hardly be the *wice* or 'wych-elm' in this situation,
and it is just possible that here we have another trace of the
Hwicce. Cf. Wichenford *supra* 179.

Halesowen

HALESOWEN[1] 72 D 1

Hala 1086 DB
Hales Regis 12th VCH iii. 136
Hales 1227 Cl, (*Owayn*) 1272 Ct, 1276 LyttCh
Halesowing 1690 Marr

'Nooks' of land, *v.* healh. *Owen* from *Owen*, a Welsh prince
who married a sister of Henry II (VCH iii. 142) and in distinction from Hailes Abbey (Gl). *Regis* because for a time the
manor was forfeited to the crown (ib.)[2].

The parish includes:

Cakemore

CAKEMORE (6″) v. NW

Cackemore, Cakkemore 1270 Ct, 1303 Pat
Cakmore 1500 (18th) Nash
Cackemor 1535 Wills

'Cacca's marshy land,' *v.* mor. For this pers. name *v.*
Cakebole *supra* 236. The present form suggests a spelling
pronunciation.

COCKSHOT

Cockeshete Grove 1448 LyttCh
v. Cockshoot in Wichenford *supra* 180.

---

[1] Almost the whole of the parish was transferred from Worcestershire to
Shropshire early in the 12th cent. and it remained in that county till 1832–44.
[2] There are streets called Cornbow and Rumbow in Halesowen. The
former is *Cornbowe* in 1297 Ct, 1371 LyttCh, for the latter no early forms have
been noted. Both cross streams and the second element is probably *bow*
denoting a bridge (cf. Bow Brook *supra* 10) but the origin of the first part of
each name is obscure.

Y

Cradley

CRADLEY 71 D 13 [kreidli]
> *Cradelei* 1086 DB
> *Crandelega* (sic) 1179 P
> *Cradelega* 1180–88 P *passim*
> *Cradele(ye)* 1272 Ct, 1275 *Ass*, SR, 1310 *Bodl* 50 (p), 1327 SR, 1340 NI, 1485 Pat

This is a very difficult name and we cannot be sure of the position of the original nucleus of Cradley. It probably lay however by the Stour, with high ground north and south of it and Professor Zachrisson suggests that this leah may have been so called because it lay in a *cradol* or 'cradle' of land.

COLMAN HILL (Old 1")
> The pers. name *Colemon* is frequent in Court Rolls (1271–1295) and the hill is called Colemans Hill in 1820 (G).

LYDE GREEN (6")
> *de la Lyde, atte Lythe* 1278, 1282 Ct

This is from OE hlið. The place lies on a slope and we may compare The Lyde (PN Bk 169).

NETHEREND
> *Netherend* 1275 SR, 1304 Ct, both (p)

Self-explanatory. There is an *Overend* for which no early forms have been noted.

Hasbury

HASBURY [heizbəri] 72 E 1
> *Haselburi* 1270 Ct
> *Hasulbury* 1500 (18th) Nash
> *Halesburg(h)* 1535 VE, 1538 LP
> *Halesbury* 1544 FF

'Hazel-burh,' i.e. marked by the presence of such. The forms in *Hales-* are probably due to the influence of Halesowen itself, though it should be noted that *halse* is found as a dialectal form of *hazel*, cf. Hazelbury (W).

HAYLEY GREEN[1]

haia apud Hayleya 1274 Ct

The *Hay-* is the same as the *haia* and the whole name denotes a leah marked by a (ge)hæg, 'a clearing with an enclosure.'

HIGHFIELDS PARK (6″)

le Hyefeld, le Heghefeld, le Hyghefeld 1346, 1372, 1383 LyttCh

'High open country,' *v.* heah, feld.

HUNTINGTREE (6″)

Huntintre, Huntingtre 1278 Ct, 1347 LyttCh
Hundyntre 1306 Ct

This is probably from OE *Huntingtrēo*, 'Hunta's tree' (cf. Huntingdon in PN BedsHu 261) and Huntingtrap *supra* 283.

LYDIATE LANE (local)

Nonemones Lydyate 1280, 1293 Ct, E 1 LyttCh
a la Lidgate 1275 SR
Nomons Lideyate 1435 Ct

For this name *v.* hlidgeat. Its lack of any certain owner is interesting.

UFFMOOR FM (6″)

Hoffemor c. 1255 Bodl 7 (p)
Huffemor c. 1260 Bodl 36 (p)
Offemor 1272 Ct
Uffemor(e) 1292 Ct, 1327 SR (p)
Offemore Grange 1415 LyttCh
Houghmoor c. 1830 O
Huffmore 1855 Kelly

'*Offa's* marshland,' *v.* mor. For the *Uff-* forms, cf. Offenham *infra* 266. In this case we must take the *h* to be inorganic. If it is original, then we have to do with a lost OE pers. name *Huffa*, a regular hypocoristic form for *Hūnfrið*.

---

[1] This should be in Lutley.

Hawne

HAWNE BANK and FM (6") iv. NE

Hamletus de Halen 1294 Ct
Halon 1500 (18th) Nash
Hawne 1581 Wills
Hallen al. *Hawne* 1770 Ct

This is from OE *hēalum*, the dat. pl. of the word healh, of which we have the nominative in Halesowen itself. The name is identical with Halam (Nt), *Healum* in BCS 1348.

Hill

HILL (6") v. SW

Hulle 1271 Ct   *Hyll* 1560 Wills
Self-explanatory.

COOMBESWOOD and THE COOMBES (6")

Close of Cumbes Hy 3 LyttCh
boscus de Combes 1271 Ct

'Valleys,' v. cumb.

GORSTY HILL

Gorstes 1270 Ct (p)

These probably refer to the same place and take their name from the presence of gorst or gorse.

HELL GRANGE (lost)

de la Helle, de Helle c. 1260 Ipm, 1278 Ct
Hellgrange 1535 VE, 1538 LP

We have no evidence from OE charters for an element *hel(l)*, apart from the dubious *ecgerdeshel* of BCS 1230. The form *dudemæres hele* (BCS 1170) quoted by Middendorff (*s.n. hele*) is found in a charter in which *ēa* has already become *ē* and the name therefore probably comes from OE *hēale* (v. healh). The probability is therefore, as suggested by Professor Ekwall, that this is the common word *hell*, used as a term of contempt or the like.

MUCKLOW HILL

de Michelowe 1278 Ct

'Great hill,' *v.* micel, hlaw, aptly descriptive of the steep hill down which the Birmingham road descends into Halesowen.

Hunnington

HUNNINGTON FM (6″) ix. NE

Honinton 1270, 1280 Ct   *Honyton* 1500 (18th) Nash

'*Hūna's* farm,' *v.* ingtun, cf. Honington and Hunningham (Wa).

THE BREACH (Old 1″)

le Breche 1282, 1294 Ct

This is from bræc or brec and denotes land broken up by the plough. Cf. PN Bk 55, 60, 61 and Breach and Brache in PN BedsHu 81, 157.

THE GRANGE (6″)

This is probably the *Homgrang'* of 1291 Tax. The first element may be 'home' (*v.* ham), the name being descriptive of the grange of Halesowen Abbey which lay at its doors. If so, it is a much earlier example of *home* in this sense than any hitherto noted.

HOLLIES FM

de Holies, le Holies 1270, 1278 Ct

Self-explanatory.

REDHILL FM

le Redehull 1383 LyttCh

Self-explanatory.

Illey

ILLEY 72 E 1

Hillely John LyttCh
Hilleleye Hy 3 LyttCh (p)
Illeg 1255 *Ass* (p)
Illeleya 1271 Ct

There is an OE name *Hilla* on record (Redin 117) which may be a pet-form for some name in *Hild-* and, if the *h* is genuine, this place-name must be interpreted as '*Hilla's* clearing' (*v.* leah). Otherwise we must take the first element to be an OE name *Illa*. The existence of such a name is doubtful, the correct form being more probably *Ylla*. If that were found here we should expect some later forms with *u*. Cf. PN Bk 125.

Lapal

LAPAL[1] [læpəl] 72 E 2

Lappole 1227 Ch
Laphole 1272 Ct
Lappol, La Pole 1274–1307 Ct
Lappoll Hill 1591 Wills

From Lapworth (W), *Hlappawurð* in BCS 356 and from Lapley (St), DB *Lepelie*, we are probably right in assuming an OE pers. name *Hlæppa* or *Hlappa* and the whole name may be interpreted as *Hlæppan-hol*, 'Hlappa's hollow.' The place lies in a hollow. *v.* hol(h).

CARTER'S LANE (6″)

This probably takes its name from the family-name *Carter* recorded in 1304–6 (Ct).

HOWLEYGRANGE FM (6″)

Oueleya 1270 Ct
Oweleye 1271 Ct
Owley Grange 1415 LyttCh, 1500 (18th) Nash

This is possibly 'owl-clearing,' *v.* ule, leah, but the forms are difficult and inconclusive, cf. Oldberrow *supra* 267.

WEBB'S GREEN (6″)

Le Webbegreen 1407 Ch   *Le Quybbe* 1431 LyttCh

Lutley

LUTLEY 71 E 14

Ludele(ya) 1169 P, 1255 *Ass*
Ledeleye 1275 SR

---

[1] This place has been confused with *La Pulle*, i.e. Pull Court *supra* 105.

Lod(e)leye 1275 *Ass*
Lotteleye, Lutteleye 1291 Ipm
Lutleye 1327 *FF*
Lutteleye 1346 AD vi
Ludley 1500 (18th) Nash, 1535 VE

This points to a pers. name *Hlūda* or *Hlȳda*, a derivative of *hlūd*, 'loud.' For the possibility of such a pers. name stem cf. *Hludesbeorh* (BCS 741), *v.* leah.

Oldbury and Langley

LANGLEY 72 C 1

Longeleye 1270 Ct (p)   *Lang(e)ley* 1271 Ct
Longley 1500 (18th) Nash
'Long-clearing,' *v.* lang, leah.

OLDBURY [1]

Aldeberia 1174 P   *Oldebure* 1270 Ct
'*Ealda's* stronghold' or 'old stronghold,' *v.* burh.

BIRCHFIELDS LANE (6″)

Birchyfield 1646 Deed
'Open land grown over with birches,' *v.* feld.

BLAKELEY HALL (6″)

Blakeleye 1270 Ct (p), 1291 Tax, 1301 Ct, 1322 Cl, 1329 Pat,
    1415 LyttCh
Blakely 1500 (18th) Nash
Blackley c. 1830 O
OE (*æt þæm*) *blacan lēage*, i.e. 'at the black clearing,' *v.* blæc.

TITFORD

Tottefordfeld 1299 Ct   *Tetford Brugge* 1521 Deed
The first element is probably the pers. name *Tēotta* discussed under Teddington *supra* 168.

WALLOXHALL (lost)

Wallokeshall 1270, 1275 Ct   *Wollockeshale* 1275 *Ass* (p)

---

[1] In the maps in VE (vol. iii) and VCH ii. 90 this Oldbury (in Salop, c. 1200–c. 1840, and then in Brimstree Hundred), is confused with Oldbury in Morville (Sa), which is in Stottesdon Hundred and this confusion has been widespread (*Birmingham Arch. Soc. Trans.* 1919, p. 76).

Walloks 1301 Ct
Walaxhale 1500 (18th) Nash
Walloxhall 1627 WillsP

'*Wēaloc's* nook of land,' *v.* healh.

Ridgeacre

RIDGEACRE FM 72 E 2

Rugacre, Rugaker 1271, 1294 Ct, 1571 Wills
Rughaker 1272 Ct
Rugeacre 1500 (18th) Nash

'Ploughed land on the ridge,' *v.* hrycg, æcer.

REDHALL FM

Radewill 1272 Ct
Radewelle 1275 SR, 1291 Tax, 1293 Ct, 1415 LyttCh
Radwall 1500 (18th) Nash
Rednall Field 1646 Deed
Reddall c. 1830 O

'Red spring,' *v.* read, wielle, cf. Redhall in Broom *supra* 278.

Romsley

ROMSLEY 72 F 1

Romesle(ye) 1270 Ct, 1291 Tax, 1293 Ct
Rummesleye 1355 Pat
Romisley 1500 (18th) Nash
Rameley 1538 LP
Ramsselie 1604 WillsP

It is possible that the first element in this name may be OE *hramsa*, 'wild garlic,' *rams* or *ramson* (dial.). This would appear in West Country dialect as *roms*, hence 'wild garlic clearing.' If this is the history, the form *Rummesleye*, if not an error of transcription for *Rammesleye* must be a bad spelling, with *u* for *o* due to the frequent spelling of *u* as *o* in other words. Cf. *ramesleigh* (BCS 438), in a late copy *hrameslea* (BCS 801).

Another possibility is that it is OE ramm, as in Ramsden *supra* 188.

DALES WOOD (6")

boscus de Dales 1270 Ct

This must be from the plural of OE dæl, 'valley.'

GREAT FARLEY WOOD

Farnle 1271 Ct

Farleya 1274, 1301 Ct

Farlee 1291 Tax

Fareley 1605 Wills

'Fern clearing,' *v.* fearn, leah and cf. *Farley* in Mathon *supra* 66.

KENELMSTOWE (6")

Kelmestowe 1277, 1304 Ct, 1473 Pat

de Sci Kenelmi 1293, 1295 Ct

Kelmstowe 1327 SR (p)

St Kellums 1577 Saxton

Kelmstowe was a settlement which grew up round the church built on the traditional site of the murder of the boy-king St Kenelm. The stow-suffix is an interesting example of the use of that word to denote a place with religious associations. The last spelling represents a fairly common dialectal pronunciation of *lm*, cf. EDG § 234.

ROMSLEY HILL

de monte de Romesle 1293 Ct

Self-explanatory.

SHUT MILL (6")

Schute Lane 1295, 1306 Ct

le Schute brok 1307 Ct

Shote, Shet Mill 1500 (18th) Nash

Presumably we have here an early example of the use of the word *shoot* to denote a rush of water. The lane must have led down to it. The earliest example of this sense (*s.v. shoot*, sb[1]) in the NED is dated 1613.

WESLEY'S FM (6")

Wesley 1270 Ct (p)

Westleye 1272 Ct

Wasteleye 1500 (18th) Nash

'West clearing,' *v.* leah. The *s* is probably pseudo-manorial. The place is in the extreme west of the parish.

Warley Salop

WARLEY SALOP 72 D 2

> *Werueslea* 1185, 1186 P (p)
> *Weruesley* 1212 Fees 140
> *Worveleg, Worveleye* 1235–6 Fees 527, 1275 SR, 1340 NI
> *Whernelege* (sic) 1255 *Ass*
> *Weruele(ye)* 1255 *Ass*, 1270 Ct, 1292 Cl, 1316 *FF*, 1327 SR, 1336 *FF*
> *Worneleigh, Wernelegh* 1291 Ipm
> *Worley* 1500 (18th) Nash, 1521 Deeds
> *Wareley* 1763 Bowen

There can be little doubt that *Werv-* or *Worv-* is the correct form rather than *Wern-*. The clearing (*v.* leah) probably took its name from a lost stream-name, cf. Worsley *supra* 74. For Salop *v. infra* 303.

CASTLE LANE (6")

The *Castle* is clearly that named in the 'placea vocata *le Castel*' in 1306 (Ct) but we do not know anything else about it.

KNOTTSALL LODGE (6")

> *Cnotteshala* 1294 Ct

'*Cnott's* nook of land,' *v.* healh. For this pers. name cf. Knotting (PN BedsHu 15) and *Knottenhill supra* 284.

LIGHTWOODS PARK[1]

> *Lythewood* 1297 Ct

'Light wood,' *v.* liht, wudu and cf. Lightwood in Cotheridge *supra* 117.

Warley Wigorn

WARLEY WIGORN (c. 1830 O)

The grant of the manor of Halesowen to Earl Roger (before 1086) did not include certain estates in the parish of Hales, viz. Cradley, Warley Wigorn and Lutley. These manors therefore

---

[1] Partly in Smethwick.

remained in Wo when the rest of the parish was transferred to Shropshire c. 1109 and became known as Warley Salop. Warley Wigorn consists of some sixteen isolated patches, most of them surrounded (before 1832) by Shropshire. Many of them were less than five acres in extent.

BRAND HALL

la Brende Halle 1309 LyttCh *Brandehalle* 1320 *FF*

'The burnt hall' (*v.* brende), referring to some incident in the past history of the place or, if *halle*, as so often, be for earlier *hale*, it might be the 'burned or cleared nook of land.'

BRISTNALL HALL

Brusenhull 1299 Salt Soc. vii. 54 (p)
Brussenhulle 13th (Duignan PN Wo 27)

'The burst hill,' referring to some breach or landslide, the first element being ME *bursten, brusten*, the old past part. of *burst*. Cf. *to borsenan beorge*, a similar compound found in BCS 743.

PERRY HILL

atte Piries 1306 Ct
'Pear-tree,' *v.* pirige.

Hampton Lovett

HAMPTON LOVETT 81 A 12

Hamtona juxta Wiccium emptorium 714 (14th) BCS 134
Hātun 817 (11th) BCS 360
Heamtun 11th Heming
Hamtune 1086 DB
Hamton 1200 Cur, (*Louet*) 1315 *FF*
Hampton' 1242 Fees 961

This must be OE hamtun. It is not on a hamm and names compounded with that element appear later as *Homtun*, cf. Hampton Lucy (Wa). The *Lovet* family had a holding here from the beginning of the 13th cent. (VCH iii. 154).

BOYCOTT FM (6")

Boicote c. 1189 Dugd vi. 1004, 1322 BM
Boykote, Boycote 1275 *Ass*, 1318 *FF*

Names in *Boy-* offer a good deal of difficulty. Boycott (PN Bk 48) has the same narrow range of forms as this place-name and so has Boycott (Sa). Boyton End (Sf) is DB *Boituna*, Boyton (W) is DB *Boientone*, and Boyland (Nf) is DB *Boieland*. There is also an unidentified *Boiwic* (Herts) in BCS 245. Stevenson (*Crawford Charters* 130) notes also the name *Boga*, *Boia* found from the 10th cent. onwards and the names *Boga*, *Boia*, *Boge(a)*, *Boie*, *Boiga* found as the names of moneyers from Alfred to Edward the Confessor. The occurrence of the name in such frequency among moneyers would tend to confirm Forssner's suggestion (*s.n.*) that the name is of continental origin, having its parallel in OS and East Gothic *Boio*, but its widespread use in English place-names suggests the possibility that it was also native in English. The question further arises in that case as to what its history may be. Stevenson quotes the name Edwig *Boga* (BCS 1244), where it is clearly used as a second and probably as a nickname, and the compound *Maneboia* (BCS 1130, p. 371), which one would incline to take as a compound of *mann* and *boia*[1]. Is it possible that here we have the original form of the word *boy* which first appears in English c. 1300 (NED *s.v.*)? Such a suggestion throws no light on the ultimate etymology of that difficult word, but if *boia* or *boga* was a significant word in OE it would be a little easier to understand its threefold occurrence with cot, twofold with tun and single with wic and, so far as has been noted, with no other second element.

FIBDEN FM

> *Fibbedone* 1241 FF
> *Fybedune* 1275 SR (p)
> *Febedon* 1349 Pat
> *Ffybdon* 1576 Wills

No certainty is possible about this name. If there was an OE pers. name *Feolu-beorht*, and such a compound is quite likely, *Febba* or *Fibba* is a possible pet-form from it. Hence, possibly, 'Febba's dun.'

---

[1] Note also Roger *Boye* in SR 1275.

FICKENAPPLETREE (lost)

> *Thiccan apel treo* 11th Heming
> *Tichenapletreu* 1086 DB
> *Tikenapeltre, Tinkenapeltre* 1200 Cur
> *Thik(e)nap(p)eltre* 1249 *FF* (p), 1275 SR (p), 1321 Cl, 1393 *FF*
> *Ykenapeltre* 1275 *Ass*
> *Fikelnapletre, Fecknapletre* 1346 FA, 1542 Deed
> *Thirkenappeltre* al. *Fikenappeltre* 1439 IpmR
> *Faukenapeltre, Fiknantre* 1546 LP, 1550 Pat

The meaning is obvious but the corruptions of form are interesting. Cf. Thicknall *supra* 280.

HORTON FMS

> *Hortun* 972 (c. 1050) BCS 1282, 1086 DB

'Muddy farm,' *v.* horh, tun. The estate lies on low ground.

KEYBRIDGE FM [keibridʒ] (6″)

> *Cauerigge* 1275 *Ass*
> *Caverugge* 1275 SR (p)
> *Caberugge* 1502 WoCh
> *Caveridge, Caverige* 1535 VE
> *Caverudge* 1539 LP
> *Kabridge* 1591 Wills

This is a difficult name. There is the possibility of an OE pers. name *Cāfa* of which we have derivatives in the *Cæfca* of the Crawford Charters (p. 61) and the *Cæfel* of a coin. OE *Cāfanhrycg* may have become *Căveridge* with trisyllabic shortening. It is clear that at a later stage the history of the word has been obscured by some folk-etymologising process. Hence 'Cafa's ridge.' *v.* hrycg.

UPPER HALL FM

> *Overhall* 1431 FA, 1623 FF   *Upperhall* 1542 Deed

Self-explanatory.

Pedmore

PEDMORE 71 E 13

> *Pevemore* 1086 DB
> *Pubemora* 1176 P
> *Pebb(e)more* 1291 Ipm, 1346 FA

Pebemore 1212 Fees 140
Pedmore c. 1270 LyttCh, 1431 FA
Pedmer 1275 SR
Pebmore 1291 Ipm, 1323 Cl, IpmR, 1327 SR
Pobmore 1323 Ipm
Pedemore 1406 Pat
Pobbemore 1428 FA

The first element in this name is probably the pers. name *Pypba* found in Peopleton, Pepwell and Pepper Wood *supra* 216, 245, 277. In addition to the assimilation to *Pyppa* there may have been another to *Pybba* which would account for the forms found here. For the interchange between *b* and *d* we may compare the history of Bedgrove (PN Bk 166), earlier *Bebgrove*. The process seems to be a species of dissimilation.

FOXCOTE

Foxcotun (dat.) c. 950 (c. 1400) BCS 1023
Foxcote 1273, 1293 Ipm (p), 1338 *FF*
'Fox-infested cottages,' or 'fox-earths,' *v.* fox, cot.

Salwarpe

SALWARPE [sɔlwʌp] olim [sæləp] 81 C 12

Salewerpæn (acc.) 706 (12th) BCS 116
Saluuerpe 717 (11th) BCS 137, 770 BCS 203
Saluuarpe 767 (12th) BCS 202
Salouuearpan (dat.), *Salouuarpe* 817 (11th) BCS 360
Salowearpe, Saleworp, Saloworpan (acc.), *Salewearpan* (acc.)
 n.d. (17th) BCS 361
Salouuarpan, Salwarpan, Saloworpe, Salewarpe n.d. (11th)
 BCS 362
Sealeweorpan (acc.) 982 (c. 1050) BCS 1282
Salewarpe 1086 DB, 1438 IpmR
Saleuuarpa Wm 1 (1313) Ch
Salop(e) 1275 *Ass*, 1307 Ipm, both (p)
Salwarp 1327 SR
Sallopia in Wigorn 1590 Wills

Most of the early references are to the stream on which Salwarpe stands and it is clear that the place takes its name from the stream.

The river Salwarpe runs in a sinuous course with a very slight fall. Habington (ii. 296) says that it runs 'close by the brynckes of thease saltpyttes....If, as sometymes happenethe, the fresh water with exceedynge fluddes overfloweth the baulkes and for a season drowneth the salt-wells, etc.' This suggests that the river Salwarpe might have been so called because it deposits *warp* or 'alluvial sediment, silt.' This word *warp* is only recorded from the 17th cent. (NED), but it may well have existed earlier. The NED on the basis of the Yorkshire place-name Ruswarpe and the common use of the word *warp* in this sense in Lincs and Yorks suggests that it is from ON *varp* in an unrecorded sense. The Worcestershire place-name and (to a less degree) the occurrence of *warp* in Northamptonshire dialect suggest that the word may have been native English also, or even alone. The idea which lies behind the word is that of something which is 'thrown' (cf. OE *weorpan*, 'to throw'). This element is found elsewhere in the Germanic dialects, but there it has the sense of something which is thrown up and heaped so as to form a dam or dyke. This is seen in the history of Antwerp (Förstemann, *Die Deutsche Ortsnamen* 45) which is a compound of this element and *and-*, *ant-*, 'against,' and in such names as *Warp*, *Neuwarp*. The usual term in OE for such a dam or bank is *gewyrp*, an *i*-formation from a different grade of the same stem (cf. Middendorff *s.v.*). The first element, as suggested by Middendorff *s.v.*, may be OE *salu, sealu,* 'dark-coloured, sallow,' and the element be descriptive of the colour of the alluvium.

CHAUSON

Celvestune 1086 DB
Chalveston c. 1150 Surv, 1275, 1327 SR (p)
Selvestona 1240 WoP
Chelvestone 1324 FF
Schalveton 1330 Dugd i. 614 (p)
Chanston (sic) 1581 Wills
Chalson, Chauson 1656 BM, 1665 VCH ii. 208

'*Cealf's* farm.' For this pers. name cf. Chawston (PN BedsHu 65). It is just possible that we have the significant cealf, 'calf,' here, but it is not very likely.

COPCUT

> *Coppecot(e)* c. 1255 *For*, 1277 RH, 1316 Ipm
> *Coppicote* 1291 CompR, Wigorn
> *Capcote, Copcote* 1560 Wills, c. 1830 O

Copcut lies on the top of a hill, almost at its highest point, so probably this name means 'cot or cottage(s) on the copp or top of the hill.' The form *Coppi-* and persistent *Coppe-* suggest however that we may have to do with a pers. name *Coppa*, cf. Copford (Ess), KCD 699 *Coppanford* and Copley (So), BCS 300 *Coppanleighe*[1] and Copson (K), *Coppanstan* in BCS 367, *coppaneg* (KCD 612) in Wolverton.

HIGLEY BARN (6″)

> *Huggelegha, Huggeleye, Huggele* 1232 Bracton (p), 1316 Ipm, 1327 SR (p), 1340 NI
> *Hygley* 1558 Wills

'*Hycga's* clearing,' *v.* leah. For this pers. name *v.* PN Bk 182.

HILL END

> *atte Hulle* 1275 SR, 1316 Ipm   *Hill End* 1550 Pat
> Self-explanatory.

LADYWOOD

> *Leuediwode* 1316 Ipm   *Ladywood* 1558 Wills
> Self-explanatory.

MIDDLETON FM (6″)

> *Mideltone* 1275 *Ass*

Self-explanatory. It lies half-way between the Church Town and the southern boundary of the parish.

OAKLEY

> *Akelege, Acele* 1255 *Ass*
> *Ockle(y)* 1275 SR (p), c. 1300 *Pat*, 1623 WillsP
> *Okley, Ocley(e)* 1275 SR, 1316 Ipm, 1327 SR, all (p)
> *Ocle* 1535 VE

Self-explanatory. The modern form is due to the influence of the independent word.

---

[1] An identification due to Mr C. A. Seyler.

PULLEY (6")

Wulle lea (sic)[1] 817 (11th) BCS 362
Pullege, Pulley(e) 1255, 1275 *Ass* (p), 1298 Wigorn (p), c. 1300
  (18th) Nash, 1560 Wills
Polleye 1275 SR (p)

This is probably OE *pull-leage* (dat.), 'clearing by the pool,'
v. pull, leah.

Old Swinford

OLD SWINFORD 71 E 12

Swinford c. 950 (c. 1400) BCS 1023, 1210 RBE
Suineford 1086 DB
Swyneford, Swineford 1235 Fees 527, 1275 SR, 1291 Tax
Old Swynford 1291 Ipm
Oldeswyneford, Woldswynford 1327 SR, 1438 Pat

'Pig or boar ford,' *v*. swin, ford. 'Old' in contrast to King-
swinford (St) which sometimes appears as New Swinford.
wold is a dialectal pronunciation of *old*.

AMBLECOTE[2]

Elmelecote 1086 DB
Amelecote 1255 *Ass*, 1316 FA
Amecote 1284 FA
Hamelcote 1317 AD iv
Amulcote 1333 SR
Amelcote 1338 AD iv
Hamblecote 1540 FF
Amblecote 1622 WillsP

The DB form is almost certainly corrupt, the first *l* being an
error. Assuming that to be the case, we may suggest that the
first element is a pers. name *Æmela*, a weak form of the pers.
name *Æmele* found once in a signature to a charter of King
Offa (BCS 208). The name therefore means 'Æmela's cottages.'

BEDCOTE MILL (6")

Betecote 1221 *Ass* (p)
Beccote 1255 *Ass*

---

[1] Heming has what must be the correct reading, viz. *pulle lea*.
[2] In Staffordshire though in Old Swinford Parish.

z

Bettecote 1275 SR (p), 1290 *FF*, 1317 AD iv, 1371 *FF*,
  1365 LyttCh
Bedcote 1461 IpmR
Bedcott 1540 FF
Bedcoate, Bedcutt, Bedcott 1621, 1655 FF

There is evidence for an OE fem. name *Bettu*. This, or OE
Beta, Bettica, which are probably allied to it, would account for
the first element in this name. *v.* cot.

CARELESS GREEN

This probably contains the family name of John *Carles* of
Lye in Old Swinford (Wills 1558).

THE HAYES

haya de vetere Swinforde 1312 (18th) Nash
v. (ge)hæg.

HUNGARY HILL (6″)

Though there are no old forms, there can be no doubt that
this is one of the numerous *Hunger* or *Hungry* Hills, so called
from the poorness of the soil, cf. *Hungerhulle* (13th *AOMB* 61)
in Pershore. This one is on the coal measures in contrast to the
comparative richness of the keuper sandstone of most of the
parish. There is no foundation for the legend that the hill is
so called from the glass factory started there by Hungarians.
The Henzies or Hensells who founded that industry came from
Lorraine.

LYE, commonly called 'The Lye'

de Lega, atte Leye, the Lye 1275, 1327 SR, 1550 Wills
Ley 1625 WillsP
'The clearing,' *v.* leah, cf. Leigh *supra* 204 pronounced as *Lye*.

OLDNALL FM (6″)

Holdenhale 1275 SR (p)   *Oldenhale* 1277 Ct (p)
Oldenhall 1789 Gough
'*Ealda's* nook,' *v.* healh.

PIRCOTE GRANGE (lost)

Piricote, Pyricote 1270 Ct (*Hales*) (p), c. 1295 Wigorn
Pirecock 1270 Ct
Pyr(e)cote 1291 Tax, 1535 VE
'Cottage by the pear-tree,' *v.* pyrige, cot.

PLATT (lost)

de la Platte 1241 *FF*, 1242 P

This is the word *plat*, 'piece of ground,' for which Ekwall (PN La 31) adduces an example c. 1230, *Adames-plat*. Here we have further examples of its early use. It is only recorded in the NED from the 16th cent. on.

STAMBERMILL

Stanburn(e) 1271 Ct (*Hales*) (p), 1275, 1327 SR (p)
Stambourn Mill 17th (18th) Nash
'Stony stream,' *v.* stan, burna.

STOURBRIDGE [stə˙bridʒ]

Sturbrug, Sturesbrige 1255 *Ass* (p)
Self-explanatory.

WOLLASTON

Wullaston 1241 *FF*
Wollaueston 1275 *Ass*
Wolaston 1305 Wigorn, 1365 LyttCh, 1591 Wills
Wolarston 1327 SR (p)
Woolweston 1708 FF
'*Wulflāf's* farm,' *v.* tun, cf. Woollashill *supra* 196.

WOLLESCOTE

Wlfrescote, Wollscot, Woolescote 1275 SR (p), 1552, 1587 Wills
'Wulfhere's cottage,' *v.* cot.

Upton Warren

UPTON WARREN 81 A 13

Upton(a) 716 (14th) BCS 134, 1212 Fees 140
Uptune 1086 DB

Opton 1255 *Ass,* (*Warini*) 1290 Wigorn
Shirreue Upton 1300 *Pat*
Shirreues Upton juxta Bremesgrave 1319 *FF*

As the village lies on low ground it is probably called *Up* from its position up the Salwarpe in relation to Droitwich, and not from its height above the surrounding country. William fitz *Warin* was here already in 1254 (Pat). The Beauchamps, the hereditary sheriffs of Worcestershire, were the overlords till the 15th cent.

BADGE COURT

Bachecote 1221, 1275 *Ass,* 1327 SR (p), 1383 Cl (p)
Bachecott 1547 Pat   *Batch Court* c. 1830 O

'Cottage(s) by the stream,' *v.* bæc, cot.

COOKSEY GREEN

Cocheseie 1086 DB
Choceseia c. 1086 (1190) *EveA*
Kokese(*ye*), *Cokeseya* 1200 Cur, 1212 Fees 140, 1255 *FF,*
    1269 Wigorn
Parua Cokesheye 1262 *For*
Cokeseye 1316 Ipm, 1327 SR
Cukeseye 1327 *FF*
Cokesay 1550 Pat
Cooksey 1616 Wills

Despite the long run of spellings with *o,* the modern form and comparative evidence suggest a pers. name *Cucc,* found also in Cooksland (St) DB *Cuchesland,* 1140 P *Cokeslonia,* Cuxham (O), KCD 691 *Cuceshamm,* and in a weak form in Cookley (Sf), DB *Cokelei,* 1251–1300 Ch *Cuckele, Kukeleia,* Cookbury (D), 1242 Fees *Cukebyr,* Cookworthy (D), 1238 *Ass Kokewrthy* and in the unidentified *Cucanhealas* of BCS 936. A diminutive of it is found in *Cucolanstan* (BCS 548) for Cuxton (K). The place lies high and it is difficult to see that it is an eg or island even in the widest use of that term. The suffix is therefore probably (*h*)*eye* from OE (ge)hæg and denotes 'woodland enclosure.'

Cutpursey Coppice (6″)

Cutbaldesheye 1271, 1293 *For*, 1300 *Pat*
Cobbaldesheye 1271 *For*
Cudballeshey 1300 Ch
Cotebaldeshey 1335 Ch
Cudbaldesheye 1349 *FF*
Cadbaldeshey 1411 IpmR
Cuttpurse Coppice 1650 Surv
'*Cūðbeald's* enclosure,' *v.* (ge)hæg.

Durrance Fm

Durrance 1573 Wills   *Durrans* 1787 Cary
The name *Duran*, presumably the same name as *Durrant*, is found in Hartlebury not so very far away in 1275 (SR). It is possible therefore that this may be a name of the manorial type derived from this family.

Poislands (6″)

Pyes Deane 1650 Surv   *Piezlands* c. 1830 O
This is probably from the family name *Pye* rather than from the bird. Walter *le Pye* and Thomas *Pye* are on record in 1275 (SR) in Bromsgrove and Hartlebury respectively.

Westwood Park

Westwood 81 B 11

æt Westwuda 972 (18th) BCS 1284, 1172 P
The name is self-explanatory. The 'wood' was to the west of Droitwich.

Clethale (lost)

Clethehale 1168 (18th) Nash
Clethale 1178 (c. 1240) *WoC*, 1542 LP
Clithale, Clethale 1275 SR
Clethall 1539 LP
Professors Ekwall and Zachrisson suggest that here we have an OE *clǣte*, a side-form with *i*-mutation of OE *clāte*, found as ME *clet, clete*, 'burdock.' It has survived as dial. *cleat*, 'colts-foot.'

VII. ESCH HUNDRED

Esch 1086 DB
Naisshe 1086 DB (Herefordshire)
Æsc, Leisse c. 1150 Surv

This Hundred, with fifteen manors, assessed at 95 hides, lay in the middle east of the county. The major part of it was a continuous area, but two islands of other Hundreds (viz. Stock-and-Bradley and Dormston) thrust themselves into it. The remainder consisted of the isolated manors of Cleeve Prior and Crowle. The meeting-place of the Hundred is unknown, but, as suggested in VCH iv. 1, it may well have been at the manor of *Haisse*, recorded in the document (c. 1190) which we have called *Evesham A*.

Of the fifteen manors of Esch, three were transferred to Halfshire, viz. Feckenham, Kington, and Church Lench. Cleeve Prior, Crowle, Hanbury and Inkberrow went to Oswaldslow, while Abbots Morton, Sheriffs Lench and Atch Lench went to Blackenhurst Hundred.

Cleeve Prior

CLEEVE PRIOR 82 F 5

Clyve, Clive 11th Heming, 1086 DB, (*Prioris*) 1240 *WoC*
Priours Cleve 1535 VE

v. clif. It stands on a conspicuous ridge and was held by the Prior of Worcester. *Prior's* in contrast to *Bishop's* Cleeve (Gl), which was held by the Bishop of Worcester.

MARLCLIFF HILL

Marnan Clive, Mearnan clyfe c. 872 (11th) BCS 537
Marle Clyve 1280 *For*
Marclive 1340 FF, 1772 T
Marke Cleeve 1649 Surv

Duignan (PN Wo 109), on the strength of Nash's statement that 'here are quarries of very good stone...some of it bears a very fine polish, like Derbyshire marble' (i. 236), thinks that the first element must be the gen. sg. *marman* of OE *marma*, 'marble.' This is much open to question on more than one ground. First, it involves believing that the form found in the charter is already corrupt; second, it is difficult to believe that the term *marble* could ever have been applied to the hard bands in the lias of Cleeve Prior, for that is what the stone here is; and thirdly, it involves an awkward compound, 'cliff of marble,' rather than 'marble-cliff' which would be the normal type[1].

The parallel of Marnham (Nt), DB *Marneham*, makes it almost certain however that we have to do with a pers. name. For the possibility of such a pers. name we may note the place-name *Marningum* recorded by Förstemann (ON ii. 214), which seems to be an *ing*-derivative of a similar Germanic pers. name.

An OE pers. name *Mearna, Marna* could be associated with the *marn*- grade of the verb *murnan*, 'mourn.'

Crowle

CROWLE 81 D 13

> *Croglea* (dat.) 836 BCS 416
> *Crohlea* 840 (11th) BCS 428, 1086 DB

Cf. also *crohwællan* in the bounds of Crowle (BCS 428) and a reference to the bounds of Crowle in the *crohhæma gemære* of BCS 1108.

> *Croelai* 1086 DB
> *Croela Gualteri, Croela Odonis* c. 1086 (1190) *EveA*
> *Croule(ga), Crouleia* c. 1150 Surv, 1201 Cur, 1208 Fees 36, 1241 *FF*
> *Croeley* 1182 (18th) *RBB*
> *Crawlega* 1182 (18th) *RBB*
> *Craulega* 1185 P
> *Craule* 1201 Cur, 1224 ClR
> *Crolea* 1212 Fees 140
> *Croule* 1232 Ch, 1240 WoP, 1300 Ch, 1308 Ipm, (*Haket*) 1359 *FF*, 1540–4 LP
> *Crauleia* 1241 *FF*
> *Crouley* 1286 Ipm
> *Croullee* 1299 (18th) *RBB*
> *Croulee* 1425 Ipm
> *Croll* 1481 IpmR

---

[1] It is difficult to say what is the relation of the difficult and unidentified form *marana clive* in KCD 714. It was in Oxfordshire.

Crowele R 3 *Bodl* 81
Crule 1513 *Bodl* 107
Crowley 1535 VE, 1540 LP

This name cannot be considered apart from certain other English place-names. Crowhurst (Sx) appears as *Crochyrst*, *Croghyrst* (BCS 208, 834), Croydon (Sr) as *Crogdene*, *Crogdæne* in BCS 529, 1132, Crookham (Berks) as *Crohhamm* in BCS 802, none of them in original charters but all in respectable texts. In addition to these we have from post-Conquest documents Croughton (Ch), DB *Crostona*, St Werburgh Cartulary *Croctona*, *Croghtona*, *Crostona*, *Crochtona*, *Crouhton*, Crafton (Bk), DB *Croustone*, Croom in Sledmere (Y), DB *Crogun*, Joh *Crohum* (BM). The only OE words which can be associated with these are (*a*) OE *croh*, 'saffron' (with an adjectival derivative *croged*, *croced*, 'the colour of saffron'), (*b*) OE *crōg*, *crōh*, 'vessel, pitcher, crock,' (*c*) a rare *crohha* found in the OE vocabularies as a gloss for *luteum*, 'mud,' and possibly connected with the dialectal *crock*, 'smut, dirt,' (*d*) a similarly rare *crōh*, 'tendril.' It is very difficult to say how far any of these may be connected with some of the names in question. With regard to the saffron-*croh* we do not know how far it may have been cultivated in early times. *Saffron* as a flavouring belongs probably to post-Crusade times, when the autumn crocus was imported from the east, but saffron was a very common dye among the Romans and it may be that they actually cultivated it when in Britain and that afterwards it went out of fashion. The vessel-*croh* could only have been used in place-names from some fancied resemblance of the ground, and such is always hard to establish. In some ways the last two terms are the most likely, but we know very little about the words and for the present these names must remain an unsolved problem.

Odonis from Odo, a sub-tenant of Roger de Laci in DB, *Gualteri*, probably from *Walter* Hacket's holding in the late 12th cent. (VCH iii. 331), *Haket* from the same holding.

COMMANDRY FM [kɔmaˑndəri]

Le Commaunders 1535 VE

Lands in Crowle were confirmed to the Hospital of St

Wulfstan in 1232 (Ch), and ultimately took their name from the Master of the Hospital, known as its *commander* (VCH ii. 175 n. 1). For these terms *v.* NED *commander* and *commandery*.

FROXMERE COURT

> *Froxmere* 1240 WoP, 1275 SR, (*Droitwich*) 1327 SR, 1431 FA, all (p)
> *Johannes Froxmer del Wych* 1398 Pat

This is a manorial name rather than a pure place-name. The Froxmeres were a family belonging to Droitwich (*le Wych*). Wherever they may have come from originally, it is clear that their name is from a place-name *Forsca-mere*, 'frogs' pool,' *v.* forsc.

STANLEY WOOD (6")

> *Standesley Hill* 1649 Surv

Feckenham

FECKENHAM [feknəm] 82 C 2

> *Feccanhom* 804 (11th) BCS 313
> *Feccanham* c. 960 (11th) BCS 1006
> *Fec(c)heham* 1086 DB, Hy 2 (1266) Ch, R 1 (1326) Ch
> *Feckeham, Fekkeham* c. 1086 (1190) *EveA*, Matilda (1266) Ch, 1233, 1244 Cl
> *Fekeham* Matilda (1266) Ch, 1233 Cl, 1275 SR
> *Feccaham* Hy 2 (1313) Ch
> *Fekkam* R 1 (1266) Ch
> *Fecham* 1232 Ch, Cl
> *Fe(c)kenham* 1233 Cl, Ch, 1312 Ch
> *Fayknam* 1524 Middleton
> *Feckingham* 1675 Ogilby
> *Fecnom* 1699 Marr

In DB we have pers. names *Fech* and *Feche* which seem to be the same as the pers. name which must lie behind *fecceswudu* (KCD 752). Here we seem to have a pers. name in a weak form corresponding to this. The *cc* would normally be palatalised in this name and some of the later spellings suggest this but, as often, we get a *k*-pronunciation developing before *n*. The *hamm* is probably that spoken of under Ham Green *infra* 319, just half a mile to the north of the church.

ASTWOOD COURT, etc.

> *Estwode de Strech* 1221 *FF*
> *Estwude* 1244 Cl
> *Astwode* 1259 Ipm, (*Strecches*) 1319 Pat, (*Musarde*) 1427 StratGild
> *Stretcheast(e)wood* 1497 AD i

The wood lies on the east side of the parish. In 1243 (FineR) the wood is spoken of as formerly the property of Richard *Strecche*. The *Musard* family held another manor in Astwood, coming in before the end of the 14th cent.

BEANHALL FMS (6″)

> *Beansetum* (dat. pl.) 836 BCS 416
> *Benhala, -hale* 1175 P (p), 1262 *For*, 1364 Pat
> *Bonhale* 1262 *For*
> *Benhall* 1430 AD ii
> *Benehall* 1471 IpmR
> *Benhull* 1592 QSR
> *Beanall* 1701 FF

'Nook of land where beans grow,' *v.* bean, healh. In the first example we have sæte, 'inhabitants,' suffixed in the usual irrational fashion to the first element in the compound name. Cf. Broadwas *supra* 103.

BECKNOR (lost)

> *Bokenouera* 1216 (1408) *EcclVar* (p)
> *Beckenore* 1300 *Pat*
> *Beckenoure, Beckenovere* 1387 IpmR, 1392 Middleton
> 'Becca's bank,' *v.* ofer.

BERROW HILL

> *la bergh* 1221 *Ass*   *atte Berewe* 1275, 1327 SR
> *Berrow* 1655 WillsP
> *v.* beorg.

CALLOW HILL

> *Kalewan hulle* 1221 *Ass*   *Callow Hill* 1613 QSR

v. calu, hyll. 'Bare hill,' cf. *Kalouhille* (1275 SR) in Broadwas, *calwan hyll* in Oddingley (BCS 1108) and *calawan hylle* in Bredicote (KCD 683).

CRABBS CROSS

No early forms have been found, but the pers. name *Crabbe* is common in Bromsgrove and perhaps we have the same name here.

CRUMP FIELD

This is probably named from the family of Peter *Crumpe* who was living in this vill in 1275 (SR).

FORD MILL (6″)

atte Forde 1275 SR

Self-explanatory.

HAM GREEN

Hamm(e) 1240 Ch (p), 1271 Ipm, 1280 *For*
Homme 1275 SR (p), 1364, 1376 Pat
Home 1275 SR (p), 1603 SR, 1617 QSR
Hom 1656 WillsP

v. hamm. It is situated in the bend of a stream.

HUNT END

The pers. name *le Hunte, Hounte* is found in 1275, 1327 SR and this probably lies behind *Hunt* End, first mentioned in 1637 (QSR).

IPPLESBOROUGH HILL (1841 Tithe Award)

Ipples berhge c. 960 (11th) BCS 1006
Ipplesbergh, Ipplesberewe 14th AlmBk

A pers. name *Ip(p)(a)* is found in *Ipanlea* (KCD 1281), *Ippanbeorge* (BCS 917), *Ippesford* in Yardley (1316 Ipm). Here we have a diminutive *Ippel(a)* found also in Ipplepen (D), *Iplanpenne* (BCS 952). Iping (Sx) may contain the same pers. name (PN in -*ing* 59).

KING'S PARK (Old 1″)

This is what in 1306 (Cl) is spoken of as 'the King's hay called *le Park.*'

THE LECHE (lost)

(*andlang*) *lecc* c. 960 (11th) BCS 1006   *Leche* c. 1300 AlmBk

This is the word lache, leche found in ME and surviving as

the dialectal *latch, letch* or *leach*. This form is interesting as giving the OE nom. and acc. sg. form for this word, not hitherto noticed. It is clearly the same word for a stream as *lecke*, noted by Jellinghaus, *Die Westfälischen Ortsnamen* 128.

LUKE'S COPPICE (6″)

Lukesfeld, Lukeslone 1399 AD iii
Lukes 1467 AD iii

The coppice, field and lane probably all took their name from the same man *Luke*.

NORGROVE COURT

Northgrove 1378 IpmR, 1471 Pat *Norgrove* 1548 Wills
Self-explanatory. It lies in the extreme north of the parish.

SHURNOCK

sciran ac, sciren ac c. 960 (11th) BCS 1006
Schirnach, Scyrnach, Shirnak 1175 P, 1240 WoP, 1237 *FF*,
 1292 Pat, 1327 SR, 1396 IpmR
Sirnac 1197 *FF*, 1200 Cur
Chirnache 1240 WoP
Shyrnacke 1524 More

'(At the) bright oak,' *v.* scir, ac, probably so called from some distinctive feature of its foliage.

SILLINS

Sulyen 1262 For
Le Sulyon 1464 Pat

The identification is not certain and the forms are scanty, but this may be OE *sulh*, dat. *sylh*, 'plough,' and later 'plough-land' in the dat. pl. In the NED *s.v. sullow* we have a quotation from Layamon, *twenti sulhene* (or *solȝene*) *lond*. There is a *Sullyon Hylle* in the demesne-land of Bordesley (VE) and a dike called *le Sulyon* near to Bridley Moor in Tardebigge which must refer to the same land. This would be some three miles from Sillins, but as there is a continuous rise in ground, which may be the '*hill*,' it is possible that all three names should be linked together.

TOOKEYS FM

We have a pers. name *Tok(e)y* here in a 13th cent. WoCh and in 1327 (SR). The farm is called Tookes Farm in 1619 (VCH iii. 119, n. 20) and Tuckers on the old 1″ map. It is clearly named from the family. *Tookey* itself is probably of Scandinavian origin, from ON *Tóki*.

WALKWOOD

> *Wercwude* 1230 P
> *Werkewode* 1240 WoP, Ch (p), 1451 Pat
> *la Werkwode, le Werkwode, le Wercwode* 1255 *FF*, 1262 Ipm, 1271 *For*
> *Worcwode* 1280 *For*
> *Warkewood* 1519 Ct, 1597, 1656 Wills
> *Warkwood* 1789 Gough, c. 1830 O

There is ample evidence for OE names *Weorc, Weorce* and probably *Weorca, v.* PN NbDu 207. Hence 'Weorca's wood.'

WHEATING HILL

> *Wytenhull* 14th AlmBk
> *Wheating Close, Sweeten Hill* 1841 Tithe Award

This is probably OE *hwītan hylle* (dat.), 'white hill.'

Hanbury

HANBURY 82 B 1

> *Heanburh* c. 765 (11th) BCS 220
> *Heanbyr(i)g, Heanbirige* 831 BCS 416
> *Norð Heanbyrig* 11th BCS 1320
> *Hambyrie, Hambir'* 1086 DB, 1208 Fees 38
> *Hamburga, Hambyry* c. 1086 (1190) *EveA & B*
> *Hembiri juxta Wych* 1190 (1335) Ch
> *Hamberi* 1201 Cur
> *Hambury* 1275, 1327 SR
> *Hembure* 1291 Tax
> *Hanbury juxta Wych* 1379 Pat
> *Handbury* 1686 Marr

'(At the) high burh.' 'North,' 'By Droitwich,' in distinction from Henbury (Gl) which is the same name (*Heanburg* BCS 75).

The latter is commonly distinguished as *in salso marisco*. Both were Bishop's manors.

BIERT (now WARDS FM)

Berte 1299 (18th) *RBB* (p)
Beart Hy 8 VCH iii. 374
The Pert 1820 G
Biert 1895 O

Professor Ekwall suggests that this may be the old name of the Dean Brook, which was perhaps once distinguished as *beorhte*, 'bright.'

BRICKLEY (Old 1″)

Blickelege 1255, 1275 *Ass*, 1299 (18th) *RBB*
Blikelege, Blykeleye 1271 Ipm, *For*, 1275, 1332 SR, all (p), (*juxta Hambury*) 1355 *FF*
Blukeleye 1327 SR (p)
Blyckley 1634 QSR
Blickley 1671 FF

The pers. name *Blike* is found in Wo in 1275 (SR). It is doubtless to be associated with the pers. name *Bliccel* or *Blicla* which lies behind Blickling (Nf), cf. Ekwall, PN in *-ing* 76. Hence 'Blic(a)'s clearing,' *v.* leah. For such a pers. name there is definite evidence in the *terra Blic* in Felstead (Ess) in a 12th cent. cartulary[1].

BROUGHTON GREEN and TEMPLE BROUGHTON FM (6″)

Broghton 1255 *For*   *Brocton Templar* 1271 *For*
Temple Broughton 1705 FF

'Brook-farm' (*v.* broc, tun) in the possession of the Templars (VCH iii. 377), cf. Domus Templi Jerusolymulitani in Broctone (*RBB*).

DITCHFORD BANK

Dichesford, Dychford 1255 *For*, 1327, 1332 SR, all (p)

The farm stands on a bank some 40 ft. above Seeley Brook. The dic is probably the brook itself.

[1] *ex inf.* Dr O. K. Schram.

GOOSEHILL GREEN
Goshull(e) 1255 *For* (p), 1276 RH, 1299 (18th) *RBB*
Gosehill 1485 (18th) Nash, 1592 Wills
Goosehill 1633 QSR
Self-explanatory. Cf. *gosa beorg* (BCS 956).

HOLLOW COURT, HOLLOWFIELDS FM
Holewei, Haloede 1086 DB
Holoweie c. 1086 (1190) *EveA*
Holeweia, Holeway 1136 (1266) Ch, 1230 Ch, 1233 Pat,
    1255 *For*, (*juxta Feckenham*) 1376 IpmR
Holew' Hy 2 (1266) Ch
Holwey 1550 Pat
Hollowey 1576 Wills
Holy Fields 18th Nash
'Hollow road' (*v.* hol, **weg**), the name presumably of the
road, now represented by a series of footpaths and tracks, which
runs straight north from Hollow Court past the various Hollow-
fields farms on to the Saltway. Its course lies low. It is just
possible that it is the *holanwege* of BCS 1006.

MERE GREEN, MERE HALL
de la Mere 1271 *For*
atte Mere 1275, 1327 SR
Meare Green 1599 QSR
v. mere.

THE MOORLANDS (6")
Cf. *Morcroft* 1299 (18th) *RBB*
Self-explanatory.

MOORWAYS END (6")
Moreweye 1299 (18th) *RBB* (p)
Morewisend 1545 LP   *Murrwayes end* 1652 Comp
Moorwaisend 1655 FF
'End of the way across the **mor** or marshy place.'

PARKHALL FM
Parc(k)hall(e) 1344 (17th) Hab, 1364 AD ii, 1376 Pat

This was the estate attached to the hereditary office of 'parker' of Feckenham Forest (VCH iii. 376).

PUCK HILL (6″)

This hill (1649 Surv) may take its name from the Jordan *Pouk'* who is found in Hanbury in 1275 (SR). His name must by origin have been a nickname from OE *pūca*, 'goblin.'

WEBBHOUSE FM

Wybbes 1408 *EcclVar*, 1580 VCH iii. 378
Webbhouse 1660 ib.

The family of *Webb* is found in this vill in 1275 (SR) and the name is of the manorial type.

WESTFIELD FM

Westefeld 1323 AD vi

Self-explanatory. It lies in the extreme west of the parish.

Inkberrow

INKBERROW 82 D 2

Intanbeorgas 789 (11th) BCS 256
Intanbe(o)rgum (dat. pl.) 803 (11th) BCS 308
Intebeorgan 803 (c. 1000) Middleton
Incsetena gemære 963 (11th) BCS 1110
æt Intanbeorgan 977 (11th) KCD 613
Intebyrgan (dat. pl.) c. 1012 KCD 898
Inteberge, Inteberga 1086 DB, c. 1086 (1190) *EveA & B*
Hinteberge 1187 P
Inteberg(h) 1230 Ch, 1233 Cl, 1261 Ipm, (*Parua*) 1262 *For*,
  1315 BM
Major Intelberghe 1275 *Ass*
Inkbarewe 1275 SR
Inteberwe 1327 SR
Jyntebarowe 1336 Pat
Inteburgh 1400 IpmR
Ynkbarow, Inckbarrow 1535 VE, 16th Wills
Inkebarry 1577 Saxton

The pers. name *Inta* is found in OE and has its OGer cognate in *Inzo* (Förstemann PN 956), cf. Intwood (Nf). There are several hills here (*v.* beorg) and it is clear that the name was originally 'Inta's hills.' Confusion between *t* and *k* is very common, cf. Collett's Green in Powick *supra* 225.

BOUTS

Boltes 1271 *For*, 1357 Pat
Bulces 1275 SR (p)
Bultus 1383 Ct, 1439 StratGild
Boulters 1559 Wills
Boults 1654, 1662 FF

Jellinghaus (*Die Westfälischen ON* 32) notes an element *bolte* or *bult* denoting a small rounded hill. This is the MLG *bulte*, ModLG *bulte*, Dutch *bult*, Swiss *bulzi*, all used with much the same sense of something rounded, a heap, a small hill. From Low German it was loaned into the various Scandinavian dialects and appears as Dan *bylt*, Swed *bylte*, Norw *bulten*, Shetland *bolt*. The word clearly belongs to the West Germanic dialects and must have had two forms of the stem, *bulti* and *bulta*. The latter must have given rise to a lost OE *bult* in which, contrary to the usual rule, *u* was preserved owing to the initial *b* and possibly also because of the following *l*, cf. Wright, *OE Grammar* § 108 for other similar words. For the full history of its cognates *v.* Falk og Torp, *Etymologisk Ordbog*, *s.v.* bylte and Torp, *Nynorsk Etym. Ordbog*, *s.v. bulten*. Small hills suit the site of Bouts and Lower Bouts, for there are two or three small isolated hills in the neighbourhood. *v.* Bilford *supra* 111 for a possible example of the mutated *bylte*[1].

CLADSWELL

Cloddesheale c. 1012 KCD 898
Glodeshale Marescalli 1167–8 P
Clodeshala, -*hale* 1180 P, 1253 Pat, 1255 *Ass*, FF, 1327 SR (p), 1357 Pat
Cloddeshale 1182 P, 1494 Ipm
Clotsall 1535 VE
Clodeshaw al. *Clodsall* 1542 LP
Cladsole 1650 FF

---

[1] For certain details we are indebted to the kindness of Professor W. E. Collinson.

AA

The word *clod* first appears independently as *clodde* in the 14th cent. (NED *s.v.*), but, as the editors remark, it must have existed in OE, to judge by such a compound as *clod-hangra* (BCS 963). That word *clodd* must have been used as a pers. name, probably of the nickname type, and have given rise to this place-name, 'Clodd's nook' (*v.* healh). The existence of such a pers. name in Worcestershire is made the more probable by the place-names *cloddeslæhge* and *cloddeswællan* found in the bounds of Tardebigge as given by Heming (362). The first of these names survives as *Cloddesley Felde* in 1535 (VE). These places are some nine miles away from Cladswell. *Marescalli* from the family of *Marshal* (VCH iii. 421).

Cook Hill

Cochilla, Chokhille 1155, 1185 P
Kochull, Cochull, Cokhull 1227 Pat, 1241 Cl, 1261 Ipm,
    1275 *Ass*, 1316 Ipm, 1326, 1357 Pat, 1494 Ipm
Cochelle c. 1270 Gerv
Cokehill 1450 Pat
Cockhull 1451 Pat
Cokkyll 1527 Wills
Cokehill 1542 LP

This probably simply means 'cock-hill,' a very common type of place-name, *v.* cocc, hyll, cf. PN BedsHu 38. The modern form is deceptive.

Edgiock

Eghoc 1221 Ass
Hegehok 1255 *For*
Eggenok 1296 Ipm
Eggeok, Eggeoc 1307 Ipm, 1383 Cl, both (p)
Eghok 1327 SR (p)
Edgiocke 1553 Wills
Egiocke al. *Edgehogge* 1661 FF
Edge Oak 1892 Kelly

'Ecga's oak' (*v.* ac) or, more probably, 'Ecga's hook or corner of land' (*v.* hoc and cf. Rushock *supra* 255). If the suffix were *ac* we should on the whole have expected (*h*)*ac* in 1221.

GANNOW FM and WOOD (6″)

Gannowe 1407 IpmR *Ganowe* 1550 (17th) Hab

For this name *v.* Gannow Green *infra* 341.

HOCKLEY HILL (lost)

Hauecle 1255 For (p) *Hauekele* 1275 SR (p)
Hockley Hill 1817 Map[1]

'Hawks' clearing,' because frequented by them, *v.* heafoc, leah.

HOLBERROW GREEN

Holbarewe 1275 FF
Holeburwe 1280 FF
Holeboregh 1306 Ipm
Holebargh 1307 Cl
Hulleberewe 1327 SR
Holbarwe 1331 AD iii
Holberwe 1357 Pat
Holborough 1628 QSR

There does not seem to be any particular topographical reason why this hill should be called 'hollow' (*v.* holh) and the forms, especially that in *Hulle-* are against such a suggestion. Rather we must take the first element to be OE *hulu*, 'hovel,' and take the whole name to mean 'hovel-hill,' that is, hill with hovels on or by it. For the use of such an element *v.* Hulcott (PN Bk 152). The *o* forms are at first common spellings of *u* as *o*; later they led to actual confusion with the more common first element *Hol-* from holh.

HOOKEY'S FM

Hochie 1255 For (p)
Okheye 1271 For (p)
Ocheye 1275 Ass
Hokeye 1275 Ass
Okeye 1275 SR (p)
Hockeye 1320 Pat (p)
Okhei 1327 SR (p)

---

[1] Parish and other maps accompanying list of names in possession of the O.S. department and kindly communicated by Mr O. G. S. Crawford.

This is probably a compound of hoc and (ge)hæg, 'enclosure on the hook of land.' The farm lies on a little projecting hill. The modern form is pseudo-manorial.

KNIGHTON

> *Cnittetone, Knitteton* 1241 Cl, 1271 *For*
> *Knythindon* 1275 *Ass*
> *Knytynton* 1357 Pat
> *Cnyton, Kniton* 1383 Ct, 1715 *Map*[1]

'Farm of the *cnihts*,' *v.* cniht, tun and cf. Knighton *supra* 52.

LITTLE INKBERROW

> *Lytelincbarroo* 1398 Pat

Self-explanatory.

MEARSE FM

> *de la Merche* 1275 SR
> *ate Merse, de la Mers* 1301 Ipm, 1303 *FF*
> *atte March* 1316 Ipm
> *Mea(r)se Field* 1817 *Map*

This is probably the OFr *marche* rather than OE mearc, as the latter should have come out as *mark* (*v.* march in NED). The place lies near the bounds of Feckenham Forest and the name therefore means 'farm on the *march* or boundary.' For confusion of final *ch* and *s*, *v.* IPN 102[2]. Similarly, though we have no early forms, Mearse Fm, Lane and Coppice in Belbroughton are on the bounds of Fairfield or of Feckenham Forest, and Mearse House in Chaddesley Corbett is probably on the bounds of the old manor of Bellington.

MORTON UNDERHILL

> *Holberwe Morton* 1275 *FF*
> *Morton apud Salterestret* 1275 *Ass*
> *Morthone Underhull* 1280 *For*
> *Morton juxta Indeberg* 1289 Wigorn
> *Comynes Morton* 14th VCH iii. 423

---

[1] See note 327 *supra*.
[2] Some of the entries may belong to the *mersce* of BCS 120 which is on the bounds of Inkberrow and Abbots Morton, some two miles south of Mearse Fm.

This 'marsh-farm' (*v.* **mor, tun**) is distinguished from other Mortons in the county as by Holberrow, by Salters Street (*v. supra* 7), under the hills of Inkberrow, and by Inkberrow itself. Held by the *Comyn* family in the 14th cent. (VCH, *loc. cit.*).

GREAT and LITTLE NOBURY

Neubyri, Neubire 1255, 1275 *Ass*, 1276 RH
Nubure, Nubery 1280 *For*, 1439 StratGild
Neubery 1355 Ipm
Newbury 1383 Ct, 1715 *Map*
Newherye juxta Intebarowe 1415 IpmR
Nobere, Nobury 1558 Wills, 1817 *Map*
'The new burh,' cf. Nobold (Sa) = Newbold.

STOCK GREEN and WOOD

la Stolke (sic) 1271 *For*   *de Stoke* 1275 SR
atte Stocke 1327 SR   *Stoke* 1364 Pat
Stoke Green 1558 Wills
v. stocc.

THORNE

þordune, þornhæmadic 963 (11th) BCS 1110
Thorndona 1208 Fees 37
Thorndune, -duna c. 1235 Wulst, 1271 *For*
Thorndon 1275 *Ass*, 1428 FA, 1494 Ipm
Thorne 1431 FA, 1535 VE
'Thorn-tree hill' (*v.* þorn, dun) with later loss of the second element. The second form shows the suffixing of hæme to the first element noted under Doddenham *supra* 46. It has been noted (*Word-Lore* i. 172) that these *Thorne* names are specially common on or near parish boundaries. The explanation of this is of course that suggested by a correspondent in the same paper (i. 216), viz. that thorntrees or bushes were very commonly used as boundary marks.

Kington

KINGTON [kaintən] 82 D 2

Cyngtun 972 (c. 1050) BCS 1282
Chintune 1086 DB
Kinton(a), *Kynton* c. 1086 (1190) *EveA*, 1246 *FF*, 1327 SR
Kyngton 1235 Fees 527, 1275 SR, 1315 Ipm, 1327 Pat
Chincton 1266 Pat
Kyneton, *Kineton* 1290 Wigorn, 1577 Saxton, 1730 Marr

This may be from OE *cyne-tun*, 'royal farm' or 'manor,' with later alteration under the influence of the common word 'king,' cf. OE *cynedom* now represented by *kingdom*, or the name may actually have been *cyningtun* in OE, though a compound of this type does not seem very probable. For similar hesitation elsewhere cf. Kineton (Wa), *Cyngtun* in BCS 1234. Note also Kinton (Sa), earlier *Kinton* and *Kyngton* (PN Sa 134) and Kinton (He), DB *Chingtune*.

Church Lench

CHURCH LENCH 82 F 3

æt Lench 860–5 (c. 1200) BCS 511
Chirichlench, *Ciricleinc* 1054, 1070 (13th) ChronEve
Lenche Roculf 1230 *FF*   *Lench Rokulf* 1346, 1428 FA

ATCH LENCH

Achelenz 1086 DB
Hecheslenz c. 1086 (1190) *EveA*
Eche Lenz, *Eacesleinc*, *Echeslenc* 13th ChronEve
Aches Lenche 1262 *For*, 1275 *Ass*, 1291 Pat, 1300 *Pat*
Lench Sacriste 1275 SR
Ashelenche 1291 Tax
Eccheslenz 13th AD ii
Acch(e)lench 1495 Pat, 1535 VE
Atchelenche 1574 Wills
Archlench 1618 Wills

SHERIFFS LENCH

Lench Alnod 716 (14th) BCS 134
Lenz Bernardi c. 1086 (1190) *EveA*

Lench Alnoth juxta Chadelbure 14th *Harl* 3763
Schyruelench 1271 *For*   *Shirreve Lench* 1275 SR
Shrewlinche 1560 VCH iii. 47
Lench Shrives 1610 Speed
Shrevese Lench 1619 Marr

v. Abbots Lench *supra* 148. *Church*, presumably from the possession of a church before the other Lenches had one. *Roculf* from its lord in the days of Hy 3 (VCH iii. 46). *Atch* Lench from its possession by some unknown *Æcci*. In the case of Sheriffs Lench the holders *Alnod* (OE *Ælfnōð*) and *Bernard* are unknown. Odo, Bishop of Bayeux, gave it to Urse the *Sheriff* (VCH iii. 46). For *Shrewlinche* cf. Shrewton (W) with the same first element.

Abbots Morton

ABBOTS MORTON 82 E 3
Mortun 708 (c. 1200) BCS 120, 714 (16th) BCS 130, 1086 DB, c. 1086 (1190) *EveA*
Abbotes Morton 1418 Pat   *Morton Abbat* 1428 FA
Stonie Morton 1610 QSR
Stony Moreton 1787 Cary
'Marsh farm,' *v.* mor, tun. It was held by the Abbot of Evesham till the time of the Dissolution and the prefix distinguished it from Morton Underhill, three miles away.

BEVINGTON WASTE[1]
Biuintona c. 1086 (1190) *EveA*, 1316 FA
Biuington 1262 *For*
Beuynton 1332 SR
This would seem to contain a pers. name *Bifa* allied to the OGer names *Bibo*, *Biba* (Förstemann PN 299–300), of which we have a geminated form in the OE pers. name *Bibba* only found in the place-name *bibban hlincg* (BCS 758). Hence 'Bifa's farm,' *v.* ingtun.

MORTON WOOD FM
boscus de Morton Abbatis 1271 *For*
Self-explanatory.

---

[1] Partly in Warwickshire.

REDWAY (Old 1")

Cf. *reade sloh* in the bounds of Abbots Morton (BCS 120), the adjective in both cases referring to the colour of the soil.

VIII. CAME HUNDRED

Came 1086 DB
Kamel c. 1150 Surv

This was a compact Hundred containing 14 manors and assessed at 82¾ hides. It occupied the north-east of the county. Nothing is known of the origin of the name or of the meeting-place of the Hundred. When the Hundred of Halfshire was formed, three of the Came manors, viz. Alvechurch, Stoke Prior and Osmerley (lost) went to Oswaldslow, the rest to Halfshire. For the loss of final *l* we may compare DB *Ripam* (acc.) for Ribble, R. earlier *Rippel*.

Alvechurch

ALVECHURCH[1] [ɔ·ltʃə·tʃ] 72 H 3

Alviethe Cyrice, Aluieuecerche, Ælfiðe cyrce 11th Heming
Ælfgyðe cyrcan n.d. (c. 1200) BCS 1320
Alvievecherche 1086 DB
Aluithechirche c. 1086 (1190) *EveB*, 1212 ClR, 1240 (c. 1240) *WoC*
Alvichech' 1208 Fees 38
Alvinechurche 1244 *FF*
Alvechirche 1275 SR
Alvenechurch 1285 Pat
Alninechirch 1291 Tax
Alvynechirche 1292 Pat
Aumthechirche 13th AD i
Alderyche 1521 LP
Allchurch 16th Wills, 1675 Ogilby

'The church of *Ælfgýð*,' with early confusion with another OE woman's name, viz. *Ælfgiefu*, ME *Alvive*. For *Ælfgýð* cf.

---

[1] In the bounds of West Hill (BCS 455) we have a *crawan hyll*. This must be the same as *Croweshull* in the 1299 Survey of Hopwood (*RBB*).

Elueþelond in Leigh (c. 1270). Forms which should have *u* or *v* have often been transcribed by editors as containing *n*. For this interesting example of an 'owned' church in the possession of a woman, cf. Mawer, *Place-names and History* 26. For similar reduction of the same OE name cf. Alveley (Sa), pronounced [ɑ·vli], and Aveley (Ess). It has developed differently in Allacott in Shebbear (D), *Alvethecote* in 1426.

ALCOTT FM (6″)

Alecote 1275 SR (p)   *Alcote* 1299 (18th) *RBB*
Alcoteȝelde 1408 *EcclVar*   *Awcot* 1587 AD iii
Alcott yeild 1650 Comp

'Aella's cottages,' *v.* cot. For *-ȝelde v.* Burcot in Bromsgrove *infra* 339.

ARROWFIELD TOP

Harewemede c. 1300 *EcclVar*   *Harrowfield* c. 1830 O

This must contain as its first element the old heathen word hearg and the 'mead' or 'field' have been a place of heathen worship. It is only five or six miles from another heathen site at Weoley (*infra* 350). The modern form is doubtless due to association with the neighbouring river Arrow.

BITTELL FM

This is probably named from the family of *Bytilde* (1275 Subsidy Roll), *Bettilde, Butilde* 1299 *RBB*.

BROCKHILL LANE and DINGLE (6″)

atte Brochole 1275 SR, 1299 (18th) *RBB*
'Badger-hole,' *v.* brocc-hol.

FORHILL [fɔrəl]

Forhulle 1299 (18th) *RBB*   *The Forrell* 1623 WillsP

This is probably for OE *fore-hyll*, 'hill-in-front.' It stands out prominently at the head of the Arrow valley. For other similar names cf. Fairfield *supra* 275 and cf. *Forhull* in Ripple (1408 *EcclVar*).

HOPWOOD

Hopwudeswic, Hopwuda (dat.) 849 (11th) BCS 455
Hopwuda (dat.) 934 (11th) BCS 701

Hopwod 1208 Fees 38, 1273 Ipm, 1275 Wigorn
Hoppewode 1255 *Ass*
Hupwode (ter), *Hupwodezelde* 1299 (18th) *RBB*
Hopewodezelde 1408 *EcclVar*
Hopewode 1591 Wills

'Wood in the valley,' *v.* hop, wudu. The first form denotes the wic or dairy farm belonging to Hopwood, and it is an interesting example of the genitival type of compound. For *zelde v.* Burcot in Bromsgrove *infra* 338 and cf. *Pentonzelde infra* and *Alcotezelde supra* 333.

LEA END[1]

de la Lee 1271 *For*   de la Leye (bis) 1275 SR
in the Lee (bis) ib.
atte Leye 1299 (18th) *RBB*   le Ley 1550 Pat
v. leah.

OSMERLEY (lost)

Osmeresle(ia) 1138 BM, 1156 (1266) Ch, 13th AD ii
Osmerley 1227, 1244 *FF*, (*Over and Nether*) 1535 VE
'*Ōsmǽr's* clearing,' *v.* leah.

PINTON (lost)[2]

Pynitone, Pinyton 1244 *FF*, 1317, 1340 Pat
Pynintone 1299 (18th) *RBB*
Peenton c. 1300 *EcclVar*
Pentonzelde 1408 *EcclVar*

'Pinna's farm,' *v.* ingtun. The pers. name *Pinna* is not on record before the Conquest but occurs in the *Inquisitio Eliensis* as the name of a juror in Radfield Hundred (C); in two MSS it is written *Pinna* and in one *Pinnæ*. The strong form *Pin* occurs in the Gloucester DB as the name of a pre-Conquest holder of Hackpen and the name must be found in Pinden (K), *Pinindene* in BCS 1322 and Pennicott (D), *Pynnecote* in 1274. *Pinca* is a diminutive of it and so is *Pinnel*, found in *Pinnelesfeld* (BCS 282). For *-zelde v.* Burcot in Bromsgrove *infra* 338.

---

[1] It is very difficult to keep this name separate from Lea Green in King's Norton *infra* 354.
[2] The site must have been near Pinfields Wood in Bromsgrove, *v. infra* 343.

RADFORD FM

> *Radeford* 1182 (18th) *RBB* (p)
> 'Red ford' (*v.* read, ford), from the colour of the soil.

ROWNEY GREEN

> *Ruenheye, Rowenheye* 1244 *FF*, 1275 SR, both (p)
> *la Rowenheye* 1276 AD ii
> *Rowney* 1669 FF

OE (*æt þæm*) *rūgan gehæge*, '(at the) rough enclosure,' *v.* ruh, gehæg, a very common name.

SANDHILLS FM (6″)

> *Sanden* 1262, 1271 *For*, 1295 Wigorn, 1340 Pat
> *Newesondene, Oldsondene, Sandene* 1299 (18th) *RBB*
> *Saandene* 1319 Pat
> *Sandal* 1820 G

Originally sand-denu, 'sand-valley,' *dale* would seem, as often, to have been substituted for *dene* and then, in the unstressed position, to have undergone further corruption.

SWAN'S HILL

> *Swanneshull* 1546 AD iii

This name probably means what it says. Cf. Swanshurst *supra* 233.

TONGE (lost)

> *Tonge* 1086 DB, c. 1086 (1190) *EveA* & *B*, 1521, 1531 LP
> *la Tange* 14th (18th) Nash

This is doubtless OE *tang*, 'tongs,' used in a transferred sense of some place at a junction of streams, as explained by Ekwall (PN La 18). It is unlucky that we have no knowledge of the site of the place in question.

WAST HILLS [waˑstəl] (West Hill 6″)

> *æt Wærsetfelda* 780 BCS 234
> *Wearsetfeld* 780 (endorsement) BCS 234
> *Weorsethyll* 849 (11th) BCS 455
> *Werstfeld, Wærsethyll* 934 (11th) BCS 701
> *Warestel* c. 1086 (1190) *EveB*

Wasthill 1221 *Ass* (p)
Wasthull 1275 SR, 1289 Wigorn, 1305 Abbr, 1357 Pat, all (p)
Warstelle 1521, 1531 LP
High Wastells 1546 AD iii
Wasie Hills, Wastill c. 1830 O

Professor Ekwall and Mr Bruce Dickins agree in suggesting that the first element here is the OE *weardsetl*, already noted in Wassel Grove in Hagley *supra* 292 and Warshill Top and Wassell Wood in Kidderminster *supra* 253. Such an interpretation would suit the site. *Wærsetfeld* was the subject of a grant by Offa and it is clear from the topography of the charters that it was an estate in the neighbourhood of *Wærsethyll*.

WEATHEROAK HILL

la Wederake 1221 *Ass* (p)
Wederoke 1299 (18th) *RBB*
Wederokes Hull 1299 (18th) *RBB*, 1439 StratGild
Wederhoke 1327 SR (p)
atte Woderok 1340 NI
Wetherock Hill 1603 SR

It is impossible to attain any certainty with regard to this name. The first element may be OE *weder* and the name may have been given to some particular oak on this summit point which, for some reason or other, could be used for weather-prophecy. It may be OE *weðer*, 'sheep,' and the oak have been so called from some association with sheep, because they took shelter under it. Finally, it should be borne in mind that there is evidence for a pers. name *Weder(a)* as in Wetheringsett (Sf) (*v.* PN Sf 85), Weathergrove (So), *Wederangraf* in BCS 730, 931. In that case it means 'Wedera's oak.'

Bromsgrove

BROMSGROVE 72 J 1

Bremesgraf 803 (11th) BCS 308, 803 (c. 1000) Middleton 206
Bremergrafan (dat.) 803 (c. 1000) Middleton 206
Bremesgrefan (dat.) 803 (11th) BCS 308, 804 (11th) BCS 313
Bremesgrave 1086 DB, c. 1086 (1190) *EveA*, 1174 P, 1176
    P (p), 1180, 1181 P, 1232 Ch, c. 1235 *Bodl* 42 b, 1242 P
    1267 Ch, 1271 Ipm (p), c. 1285 *Bodl* 42 a, 1387 ib. 76

Brimesgrav 1161–76 P (except four instances), 1182, 1185 P
Brumesgrava 1162, 1173 (ChancR *Brimesgraua*), 1186, 1187,
    1190 P, 1235 Pat
Bromesgrava 1167 P, 1232 Ch
Brunesgrave 1171, 1172 P, 1317 Ch
Brimmegrave 1200 Cur
Brimmesgrave, *Brummesgrave* 1216 Cl, 1317 Ch
Bremmisgrave 1259 Pat
Bremmesgrave 1261 Pat
Brymesgrove 1373 Pat, 1424 IpmR
Bromesgrove al. *Brommesgrove* 1441 Pat

From the pers. name *Breme* in DB, from this name and from
the unidentified *Bremesburh* (ASC s.a. 909 D) Redin (11) and
Ritter (115 and n. 1) are doubtless right in assuming an OE pers.
name *Brēme* from the adj. *brēme*, 'famous.' The second element
shows common confusion of the forms **graf(a)** and **græfa**, hence
'Breme's grove or thicket.' This should normally have developed
to *Bremsgrove* or *Brimsgrove*, but the rarity of the first element,
ready folk-association with *broom* (*v.* **brom**), and the near
neighbourhood of two other places, viz. Birmingham and
Bromwich, with similar sounding first elements, played havoc
with its development.

Professor Zachrisson suggests that the development may, in
part at least, be due to a definite phonological development,
thus *brim* > *brym* > *brum*. Cf. ModEng *rosin* for *resin*.

ALFREDS WELL
    Offads Well c. 1830 O
    It is probable that, as suggested by Duignan (PN Wo 119),
this well derives its name from the family of *Orford* found in
Bromsgrove from the 16th cent., who are said to have lived by
this spring in the early 19th cent.

ASHBOROUGH (6″)
    Asseberga 1086 DB, 1221 *Ass* (p)
    Esberuwe, *Esberowe* c. 1200 NQB, c. 1210 ib. (p)
    Assebarewe 1262 For
    Esseberowe 1275 SR (p)
    Ashberwe 1327 SR (p)
    'Ash-tree hill,' *v.* **æsc, beorg.**

BARNSLEYHALL FM (6")

> *Barndesley* 1255 Pat
> *Barndele(ye)* 1259 Ipm (p), 1275 *FF*, SR
> *Barndley* c. 1300 (18th) Nash
> *Brandeleie* 1347 Pat (p)
> *Barnsley* 1564 Wills

'The leah of *Beornmōd* or of *Beornnōð*,' for the former cf. Barnsley (PN Gl 15).

BARNT GREEN

> *Barnte* 1290 *FF*
> *Brante* (pasture of) 1317 Pat
> *Barne Green* 1468 StratGild
> *Brantyrene* (sic) 1535 VE
> *Barn(e) Green* 1591, 1612 Wills, 1789 Gough

Close at hand is *Brantesford* (1244 *FF*).
This is probably OE *bærnet* and denotes a place cleared by burning, some forms showing metathesis. Such a name in this old woodland area is very probable.

BONE HILL (Old 1")

> *Bolenhull* 1262 *For*
> *Bolhull* 1275 SR (p)
> *Bollenhull* 1280 *For*, 1473 IpmR
> *Bonehill* 1685 FF
> *Bunnill* 1780 Nash

'Bolla's hill,' *v.* hyll. For the pers. name *v.* Bolnhurst and Bolnoe or Bone End (PN BedsHu 13, 28). Cf. Bonehill (PN St 20).

BUNGAY LAKE FM

> *Bongey Lane* 1504 Ct (NQB)

The pers. name *Bungy* occurs in the Subsidy Rolls of 1275 and 1327 in Chaddesley Corbett hard by. Presumably the name ultimately derives from Bungay (Sf).

BURCOT

> *Bericote* 1086 DB
> *Biricote* 1221, 1275 *Ass*, 1380 LibPens

Buricote 1255 *FF*, 1275 *Ass*
Byrcote 1275 SR, 1504 Ct (NQB)
Bercote c. 1300 (18th) Nash
Burcott Yeld 1595 Wills
Bircoate 1653 FF

This must be a compound of OE **byrig** (gen. sg.) and **cot**
just as Bierton (PN Bk 147) seems to be a compound of *byrh*
(gen. sg.) and *tun*. This place would be related to the royal
manor of Bromsgrove in the same way that Bierton was to
Aylesbury (Bk). *Elde, Yelde* or *Yield* is the name given to the
areas into which certain parishes, notably Bromsgrove, Alvechurch and King's Norton, were divided for purposes of
taxation. It must be associated with OE *gieldan*, 'to pay,'
gield, 'payment.'

BURNFORD (lost)

Burneford[1] 1240 WoP, 1244 *FF*, 1380 LibPens, 1653 FF
Burnford 1275 *Ass* (p), (*Elde*) 1427 Ct (NQB)

Presumably 'ford across the stream,' though a pers. name
Byrna is possible (PN Bk 216). For *Elde v.* Burcot *supra.*

CATSHILL

Catteshulle 1221 *Ass*, 1262 Ipm (p), 1275 SR (p)
Chateshull c. 1245 Wulst (p), 1255 *FF*
Cadeshull 1300 *Pat*
Catshill Elde 1427 Ct (NQB)

'*Catt's* hill' or '(wild) cat's hill,' *v.* hyll. This name seems to
be a duplicate of Catshill in Godalming (Sr), which appears as
Chatishille (c. 1151) in BM. For the pers. name *v.* Catworth
(PN BedsHu 237). For *Elde v.* Burcot *supra.*

CHADWICH FM

Celdvic 1086 DB
Chaldeswic c. 1086 (1190) *EveA*
Chadelwic 1196 FF, 1232 Ch
Chadeleswyz c. 1235 *Bodl* 42 b
Chadeswych 1240 WoP, 1421 *FF*, 1445 AD vi
Chadeleswich, -wych c. 1245 *Bodl* 26, 27, 30, 1289, 1349 *FF*

[1] Possibly also the *Broneford* of 1182 (P).

Chedereswike 1255 FF

Chadleswich, -wych c. 1255 *Bodl* 6, 7, c. 1280 ib. 37, c. 1295 ib. 47, 48

Chaddelewyz c. 1260 *Bodl* 35

Chaddewych 1380 LibPens

Chaddelwyche 1387 *Bodl* 76

Chaddeswych 1485 (18th) Nash

'The wic or dairy-farm of *Ceadel(a)*.' For this pers. name and for its strong and weak forms *v*. Chalfont (PN Bk 218–9).

CHARFORD

Cherleford 1231 Pat, 1275 SR (p), 1300 *Pat*

Cherlesford 1231 Pat

Charvard, Charford 1654–5 WillsP

OE *ceorla-ford*, 'ford of the *ceorls*,' *v*. ceorl.

COMBLE (lost)[1]

Comble 1086 DB   *Comeley* 1300 (18th) Nash, 1380 LibPens

This may be a compound of **cumb** and **leah**, but as the site is lost we cannot be sure. There is another reference to the *combe* in *kumbewalle* in Chadwich (*Bodl* 76) and to *Comble* in *Comeleford*, a pers. name in Cofton in 1275 (SR).

CROWFIELDS FM (6″)

Crowefeld 1275 SR (p)   *Croufelde* 1327 SR (p)

Self-explanatory.

DODFORD

Doddeford 1232 Cl, c. 1235 *Bodl* 92 b, 1240 WoP, 1275, 1327 SR

'Dodda's ford.'

DYERS (lost), but on the site stands the Golden Lion Inn.

Dyeres place 1403 Pat, 1425 IpmR   *Dyers* 1537 FF

Diers 1664 FF

This is probably named from the family of Robert *le Deyar* and John *le Dyere* mentioned in 1275 and 1327 (SR).

---

[1] Identified with Cobley in Tardebigge in VCH i. 285, but it can hardly be there. Nash (i. 151) gives it as one of the fifteen vills of Bromsgrove on the authority of 'a leger book of Worcester Priory.'

EACHWAY

Etchy 1795 VCH iii   *Etchey* c. 1830 O

The forms are too late for any certainty. The place stands high in old forest-land, so the suffix is probably *hey* (*v.* gehæg). It is next to Whetty Fm (*v. infra* 345), another *hey*.

FOCKBURY HO

Fockebure, -bury, Fokkebury c. 1200 NQB, 1275 SR, both (p), 1380 LibPens
Fokebire 1275 *Ass* (p)
Fukkebury 1327 Cl
Fokebury 1490 Ct (NQB), 1550 Pat
Foxbury 1562 Wills
Fockbury 1609 QSR

This points to a pers. name *Focca*, a pet-form of an OE name in *Folc-*. Hence, 'Focca's burh.'

GANNOW GREEN and GANNOW FM (6")

Gannou 1330 Ch
Gannowe 1408 IpmR, 1462 Pat, 1535 VE
le Gannowe 1421 *FF*, 1445 AD vi
Ganho 1580 WillsP
Gannow 1659 FF

The history of this name must be taken along with that of Gannow in Inkberrow *supra* 327, Gannah (He) in Holme Lacy, *Gannou, Gannowe* in 1336, 1343 Ipm, Gannow (La), *Ganhow* in 1526 (PN La 83) and croft voc. *Gannowestockynge*, pratum voc. *Gannoweslonde* in Haseley (Wa) in 1505 (*MinAccts*). It is clear that in all these names the second element is OE hoh, and Professors Ekwall and Zachrisson agree in suggesting that the first is OE *gamen*, 'game, play,' with the somewhat unusual assimilation of *mn* to *nn* at an early date. If that is the case, these *hohs* must have been places where games of some kind were held. We have one other such compound of *gamen* in Wo in *gamenhulle infra* 394, cf. also Ganfield Hundred (Berks), DB *Gamenesfelle*. Förstemann (ON i. 994) gives examples of such compounds in German names.

BB

GORSE HILL

> *Gorsthal(e)* 1275, 1327 SR (p)

'Gorse-grown nook,' *v.* gorst, healh.

THE HEATH (6″)

> *de la Heithe, atte Hethe* 1275 *Ass*, SR, 1327 SR

HOLY WELL (1″), HOLYWELL LANE and FM (6″)

> *Helliwell* 1232 Ch   *Haliwellefeld*, c. 1235 *Bodl* 42 b

Both these are self-explanatory. There is a chalybeate spring here.

HORNS HALL (6″)

> *de la Hurne* 1275 *Ass*, SR

'Corner, nook,' *v.* **hyrne.** It lies in the extreme south-east corner of the parish.

HUNDRED HO (6″)

Robert del *Hundred* is mentioned in 1275 in the Subsidy Roll for King's Norton and may have derived his name from here. Possibly the hundred courts for Halfshire were sometimes held here (cf. Duignan PN Wo 89). Cf. Hundred House in Great Witley *supra* 23.

LICKEY

> *la Lecheye, la Lekheye, la Lechay, Lekhaye* 1255 *FF*, 1271
> *For*, 1299 Ct (Hales), 1314 Pat, 1315 Orig, 1394, 1408
> IpmR
> *Lykheye, Lykehay* 1271, 1280 *For*, 1427 Ct
> *la Leckhaye* 'which is the King's Hay' 1337 Ipm
> *Lyckhay, Lickhay* 1473–5 BM, 1675 NQB
> *The Leckhay* 1781 BiblWo 70
> *Leekhay* 1792 NQB

All that can be said with certainty with respect to this name is that it was the name of a forest-enclosure (*v.* (ge)hæg). The first element might be **leac,** but there are two serious objections to it, viz. that one would not expect such an element in a forest-name and that it hardly explains the *Lyk-* forms.

LINTHURST

Lynlehurst (sic) 1504 Ct   *Linthurst* Jas 1 NQB
The Linthouse 1783 NQB

This is probably from *lindhurst* (*v.* lind, hyrst). The first form is clearly corrupt. Cf. Lynhurst (K), BCS 1295 *lindhyrst*.

PINFIELDS WOOD (6″)

Pyntonfyldes 1547 Pat

This must have taken its name from the lost *Pinton* in Alvechurch. Pinfields Wood is on the boundary of Cofton, but at one time that was part of Alvechurch.

SHEPLEY FMS

Sepeley c. 1200 NQB (p)
Schipley c. 1270 NQB
S(c)hepeley(e) 1300 Pat, 1342 LyttCh, 1380 LibPens
Shepley Elde 1427 Ct, 1550 Pat

'Sheep-clearing,' *v.* sceap, leah. For *Elde v.* Burcot *supra* 338.

SHURVENHILL (lost)

Suruehel 1086 DB
Suruenhulle 1255 *Ass* (p)
Schoruenhulle 1275 SR (p)

This place has been commonly identified with Sarehole in Yardley. The new form from the Assize Roll confirms the accuracy of the DB form and makes it extremely unlikely that Sarehole can represent it from the phonological point of view. Further, the entry concerns Bromsgrove and King's Norton and makes Yardley still more unlikely. Finally, the old identification breaks into the topographical order of the berewicks noted *infra* 356 n. The first element is probably an OE name *Scurfa*. For the possibility of this as an English in distinction from a Danish name *Scurfa* (which is well established), see Sheraton in PN NbDu 176. The name *Sceorf* (which must be allied to it) is found in Shareshill (St), DB *Servesel*.

After the above was written, there came to light in *WoC* 61 b the field-name *Scurfhemeburne* in Stoke Prior. The first part is clearly one of those irrational formations in *hæme* noted under Doddenham *supra* 46, and the 'Scurf-dwellers' from whom the burn was named clearly belonged to *Shurvenhill*. This confirms in interesting fashion the geographical arrangement of the DB berewicks of Bromsgrove. It is placed in DB between Fockbury and Woodcote, and these lie near the Stoke Prior boundary of Bromsgrove.

SIDEMOOR

> *Sidmore* 17th NQB, 1728 ib.

Probably 'broad marsh,' *v*. sid, mor.

SPADESBOURNE BROOK (6″)

> *Padston* 1275 SR
> *Padeston* 1380 LibPens, 1457 LyttCh, 1490 Ct
> *Padston Elde* 1427 Ct
> *Padestone* or *Spadesbourne* 18th Nash

The brook takes its name from a lost vill *Padston* or at least from the same man who left his name to a tun and to the neighbouring burna. The pers. name *Padda* is well established. Here we have a strong form of it. Hence 'Padd's farm and stream.' The initial *sp* for *p* seems to be a purely modern corruption. For *Elde v*. Burcot, *supra* 338.

STAPLE HILL and FM

> *le Stapul* 1485 (18th) Nash

The hill must have been distinguished by some pillar or post, cf. Stapenhill *supra* 100.

TIMBERHANGER

> *Timbrehangre* 1086 DB, 1227 Bracton
> *Timberhongle, Timberhongel, Tymbyrhongell* 1255 *FF*, 1271
>   *For*, 1331 *FF*, 1335 Ch, 1446, 1480 IpmR, 1665 FF
> *Tymberhungre* 1380 LibPens
> *Tyberhaygull* 1490 Ct
> *Tiberhunger* 1537 LP
> *Tymberhunger* 1550 LP

'Wooded slope from which timber is taken,' *v*. timber, hangra. Under AN influence the name was at one time beginning to develop on the lines of such names as Rishangles (Sf) and Barnacle (Wa), noted in EPN *s.v.* hangra.

WHETTY FM

le Wetheye 1387 *Bodl* 76

'The wet forest-enclosure,' *v.* (ge)hæg.

WHITFORD HALL[1]

Wythenford c. 1245 Wulst (p)
Witeford, Wyteford 1255 *FF*, 1267 Ipm, 1340 NI, all (p)

Either '*Hwīta's* ford' or 'white ford.'

WILLINGWICK (lost)[2]

Willingewic 1086 DB
Welingewiche 1086 DB   *Welingewic* 1196 *FF*
Walingewica c. 1086 (1190) *EveA*
Wyllingwy(c)ke 1316 LyttCh, 1319 *FF*, 1445 AD vi
Wylyngwyke 1380 LibPens
Wyllynswych 1431 FA

This is probably from OE *Willinga-wīc*, 'dairy-farm of Willa's people,' *v.* wic. The second, third and fourth forms offer difficulties however. The *e* can only be explained as due to common AN lowering of *i* to *e*, the *a* is probably due to confusion of the resultant *Wel-* with Anglian *wælle*, ME *walle* for *welle*.

WOODCOTE GREEN

Wdecote 1086 DB
Odenecote c. 1086 (1190) *EveA*
Wudecote 1218 FineR (p)
Wodecote 1275 *Ass*, SR (p), 1316 Ipm, *FF*, 1431 FA (p)
Woodcote 1485 (18th) Nash

Probably 'cottages by the wood,' though the form from the Evesham Book suggests an alternative, 'wooden cottages.'

YARNOLD LANE and FM

This may be identical with the *Ernehull* from the 1485 Rental of Dodford given by Nash. If so, it may mean 'eagle-

---

[1] *v.* Wythwood *infra* 358 for the rejection of the identification with DB *Witeurde.*
[2] It lay contiguous to Chadwich.

hill,' *v.* **earn, hyll.** The later phonological development is what one might expect. The lane leads up a hill rising 560 ft.

Cofton Hackett

COFTON HACKETT 72 G 2

> *æt Coftune* 780 BCS 234, 848 (11th) BCS 455, c. 930 (11th) BCS 701
> *Costune* 1086 DB, c. 1086 (1190) *EveA & B*
> *Costona* 1208 Fees 36, 1212 ib. 140, 1242 P, 1271 Ipm
> *Kofthon, Coftone* 1280 *For,* 1295 Ct
> *Corfton Hakett* 1431 FA
> *Korfen Hackett* 1650 *Surv*

Middendorf (28) and Duignan (PN Wo 39) agree in suggesting that the first element here is OE *cofa*, used in one or other of the varied senses that the modern English *cove* has, viz. pit, cavern, cave, shed, shelter. Professors Ekwall and Zachrisson point out that in a compound of this kind, if of early formation, the absence of any sign of the suffix -*a* is not surprising, cf. OE *gum-drēam* from *guma* and *han-crēd* from *hana*. The compound must denote a tun marked by a *cofa*. Wm. *Haket* held Cofton in 1166 (RBE).

COFTON RICHARDS FM

> *Cofton Walteri* 1309 *FF* *Corfton Richart* 1431 FA

This estate was held by one *Richard* as early as 1166 (RBE) and by a *Walter* in 1256 (Pat).

GROVELY HO

> *Grofleye* 1275 SR (p) in Frankley *Groveley* 1535 VE
> 'Grove-clearing,' *v.* **graf, leah.**

NIMMINGS FM (6″)

No forms have been noted, but the name is presumably identical with Nimmings in Clent *supra* 280.

Frankley

FRANKLEY 72 F 4

> *Franchelie* 1086 DB
> *Frangelee* 1197 FF

Frankele(ge) 1166 RBE, 1212 Fees 140, 1278 Ct (NQB)
Fraunkele(ye) 1274 Cl, 1315 *FF*, 1323 Cl, 1340 NI
Frankelowe 13th AD ii (p)

'*Franca's* clearing,' *v.* leah. The pers. name *Franca* is on record in early OE and survived in use into the 12th cent. In place-names it forms the first element of Frankton (Wa), English Frankton (Sa), Frankaborough in Broadwood Widger (D), and Frankhill in Creacombe (D). It also occurs in *Francan cumb*, an unidentified site on the boundary of Crediton (*Crawford Charters* 57).

FRANKLEY HILL

super montem, othe hulle 1275, 1327 SR

Self-explanatory.

FROGMILL FM

Froggemulle 1373 LyttCh

Self-explanatory, cf. Frogmill in Inkberrow.

KETTLES WOOD

From the pers. name *Ketel* frequent in the Court Rolls from 1271 to 1307 and found in the Subsidy Rolls for 1275 and 1327. This pers. name is of Scand. origin.

OLDENHILL (lost)

Holdenhull John LyttCh
Aldehulla Hy 3 LyttCh
·Oldenhull Hy 3 LyttCh
Oldehulle 1327 SR

All these are from pers. names, but they are probably local and not manorial, and the name denotes '*Ealda's* hill.'

Grafton Manor

GRAFTON MANOR 71 J 13

Grastone 1086 DB
Grafton(e) 1086 (c. 1190) *EveA*, 1212 Fees 140, 1275 SR, (*juxta Bremesgrave*) 1367 IpmR

'Grove-farm,' *v.* graf, tun.

WARRIDGE LODGE

Worug(g)e 1276 RH, 1293 *FF*, 1300 Pat

The hill here is of irregular outline, and the name is probably a compound of OE **woh** and **hrycg**, hence 'crooked ridge.'

Northfield[1]

NORTHFIELD 72 F 3

Nordfeld 1086 DB
Northfeld c. 1086 (1190) *EveA*
Nortfeld al. *Norfeld* 1338 Ipm
Norfeld 1577 Saxton

'Open land (*v.* feld) lying to the north of King's Norton,' which is itself to the north of an early settlement at or near Bromsgrove.

BARTLEY GREEN

Berchelai 1086 DB   *Bartley* 1657 FF

OE *beorca-lēage* (dat.), 'birchtrees' clearing' (*v.* leah, beorc), with common confusion of *k* and *t* sounds. Cf. Burtle (So), Bartley (Ha), Bartlow (C), all containing the same first element.

BROADHIDLEY HALL

Hiddeley, Hyddeley 1270 Ct (Hales), 1292 Misc, 1311, 1317 LyttCh
Hedeley 1440 LyttCh

'*Hidda's* clearing,' *v.* leah. Cf. Hidcote (Gl).

BROMWICH WOOD (6")

Bromwiche 1275 SR (p)   *Bromwychestude* 1350 LyttCh
Bromwycheslond 1410–1431 LyttCh

'Broom-grown dairy-farm,' *v.* brom, wic.

GENNERS FM

This farm is called *Jenners* in 1603 (SR) and probably takes its name from the family of *Gynour* (i.e. the engineer) mentioned in the Subsidy Rolls of 1275 and 1327. Cf. Duignan PN Wo 67.

---

[1] Incorporated in Birmingham in 1911.

HAY GREEN

in the Haye 1275 SR

v. (ge)hæg.

LEY HILL

atte Leye 1275 SR

v. leah.

MIDDLETON HALL FM (Old 1")

Middeltune c. 1200 VCH iii. 197

Middelton 1275 SR (p), 1292 Cl, Ipm

'Middle farm,' probably so called as lying between King's Norton and Northfield.

MOOR STREET

de la More 1275 *Ass*   *above the More* 1275 SR

v. mor.

RADDLEBARN (local)

Rattlebarn 1789 Gough, c. 1830 O

This is generally stated to be so called because rams were *raddled* here, but no certainty is possible.

SELLY OAK

Escelie 1086 DB

Selle(gh), *Selley(e)* 1221 *Ass* (p), 1242 Fees 468 (p), 1254 Pat, 1255 *Ass* (p), 1292, 1323 Ipm, 1323 Cl, 1327 SR, 1403, 1416 FF

This looks at first like a compound of sele and leah, which might mean 'clearing with a hall or building on it,' but there are two disturbing factors about the name. The first is the *sc* in DB, which looks as if the initial sound of the name had originally been OE *sc* rather than *s*. The second is that in the Curia Regis Rolls for 1204 (Salt Soc. ed.) we have one Gervase de *Selvele*, alternatively called Gervase de *Selleg*, bringing an action against one Bernard de *Frankele*. Frankley and Selly are very near, and there is no Shelley from earlier *Shelf-* or *Shelveley* nearer than Ess, Sx or Sf. It is difficult to avoid the conclusion therefore that here we have really an OE *scylflēage*, 'clearing on the scylf or shelf of land.' As the ground is much broken here that seems to be a possible suggestion from the topographical point of view. In quite modern times the word Oak was suffixed to the name of the manor. Tradition has it that the place took its additional name from a prominent oak-tree within the village.

TINKER'S FM

This probably takes its name from the family called *le Tynekare*, *le Tinker* in 1275 and 1327 (SR).

WEOLEY CASTLE

> *Welegh*, *Weleye* 1264 Pat, 1275 SR, 1276 RH, 1292 Misc, 1300 Wigorn
> *Woley* 1273 Ipm
> *Wleye* 1323 Ipm
> *Wheleye* 1327 SR
> *Weolegh'*, *Weoleye* 1370 AD iv, 1386 *FF*, 1420 Ipm

It is clear that this is the same as Willey (Sr), *Weoleage* in BCS 627, and an unidentified *weoleage* in Ha (KCD 712), and that in these names, as in Weedon (Bk, Nth) (cf. PN Bk 85), we have reference to a clearing where heathen worship of some kind was once carried on, the first element being the OE *wīg*, *wēoh*, 'idol,' probably also 'temple,' *v.* leah. Cf. Arrowfield Top *supra* 333.

WOODCOCK HILL

This may take its name from the family of *Wodecoc* or *Wodecoke* recorded here in 1275 and 1327 (SR), rather than directly from the bird.

King's Norton[1]

KING'S NORTON 72 F 3

> *Nortune* 1086 DB
> *Northone Regis* 1286 Wigorn　　*Kynges Norton* 1288 ib.

'North farm,' probably in relation to an early settlement at or near Bromsgrove. The manor was held by the king in DB.

---

[1] Incorporated in Birmingham in 1911, with the exception of the ecclesiastical district of Wythall.

BALSALL HEATH[1] (6", 1905 ed.) [bɔ·səl]

> *Bordeshale* 1275, 1327 SR (p), al. *Bordisley* 1322 Ipm
> *Bordishalle Hethe* 1541 *Deed*
> *Bordsall heth* 1546 *Deed*
> *Bawsoll Hethe* 1552 Bordesley Tax Roll (Dugd. Soc. iv)
> *Bossall heath* 1577 *Deed*
> *Bordeshall Heth* 1619 *Will*
> *Boswell Heath* 1650 *Surv*

This healh must have been the property of one *Bord* (cf. Bordesley *infra* 365) who gave his name to the other and neighbouring Bordesley in Aston (Wa).

BLACKGRAVE FM

> *la Blackgreue, Blackgreve* 1237 Bracton, 1252 FineR, 1362 Cl
> *la Blakegreve, le Blackgreve by Kyngesnorton* 1252 Ch, 1348 Ipm
> *la Blakgrave* 1275 Wigorn

'Black thicket,' *v.* **græfe.**

BOURNBROOK

> *Burnebrock* c. 1250 NQB (p)
> *Byrnebroc* 1275 SR (p)
> *Barnebrok, Barnbrook(s) End* 1511 AD v (p), 1574, 1592 Wills, 1789 Worc. Canal Map

This must be a compound of OE *Beorna* and broc (cf. Ritter 134). The modern form has clearly been influenced by association with **burna**, 'stream,' especially as it also forms a 'bourne' or boundary.

BRANDWOOD END

> *Brander End* 1587 Wills

The 16th cent. form may be only a colloquialism for the form which we now have in full. If so, the name means 'burnt wood,' *v.* **brende.**

---

[1] Once part of Moseley, now included in Birmingham. For the references to the Deeds (one in his own possession and the other two in the Library of the Birmingham Corporation) we are indebted to Mr W. B. Bickley. He suggests that while the Heath was in Wo, Balsall itself may have been in Wa and a part of Bordesley.

BROAD MEADOW

Brademedwe 1237 LibPens, 1275 SR, 1240 WoP, all (p)
Brademedewe 1311 Pat (p)

Self-explanatory. Here as in Broadwas and Broadway *supra* 103, 191, *Broad*- has taken the place of regular *Brad*-.

CHYNDHOUSE (lost)[1]

on ciondan, of ceondan c. 705 (12th) BCS 123
on ciondan, of ciondan 972 (c. 1050) BCS 1282
Chende 1255 *Ass*, 1275 SR, both (p)
Cheende 1339 *FF* (p)
Chwyndes 1425 Pat
Chyndehouse 1542 AD vi

From the bounds from which the first forms come it may be inferred that *ciondan* is a stream-name. The bounds of BCS 123 show that it was close to Lindsworth Fm (*infra* 355).

COLMERS FM

Colemore 1255 *For* (p)
Collemor 1275 SR, *Ass* (p)
Colmore 1327 SR (p)
Culnore 1594 Ct (NQB)
Colmers 1648 Comp

As all the forms except the last two are from pers. names it may be that the name is a manorial one and that final *s* is the correct ending. If the name is topographical it may be that the marsh (*v.* mor) took its name from a lost river Cole (*v.* Cole *supra* 10) now called the Rea. Or it may take its name from a pers. name *Cola*.

COTTERIDGE

Cotteruge 1317 Pat (p)
Coderugge 1327 SR (p)

This may be manorial, the person who gave his name to the place having come from Cotheridge in this county, *v. supra* 116. Otherwise it should be interpreted as '*Cotta's* ridge' (*v.* hrycg). It stands on a well-marked ridge.

[1] As there was 'a close called *Chendelond*' in Solihull in 1368 (AD ii), it may be inferred that the *Chind* was near where the bounds of Yardley, King's Norton and Solihull meet.

FARMONS (lost)

Fermonnes tenement 1464 Pat

This probably takes its name from the family of *Farmon* mentioned in 1327 (SR), cf. Farman's Court in Rock *supra* 71.

GRIMES HILL (6″)

Grimeshull 1185 P (p), 1221 *Ass*

GRIMPITS FM (6″)

Grimmesput 1275 *Ass*
Grimesput, Grymesput 1275 SR, *Ass*, all (p)

'Hill' and 'pit' of *Grim*. For this pers. name *v*. Grimley *supra* 126. In this case the Scand. is possible.

HAWKESLEY HALL

Hauckeslowe 1275 SR, LyttCh, 1327 SR, 1329 *FF*, all (p)
Hakeslowe 1515 LP
Hawk(e)slow(e) 1590 Wills, 1603 SR
Hawksley 1608, 1645 D

'Hawk's hill' or 'hill of a man named *Heafoc*.' Both are possible. Cf. *hafoceshlæw* (KCD 775).

HAZELWELL

Haselwell 1325 Pat (p), 1335 *FF*, 1508 Pat
Hazelwell 1705 FF
Self-explanatory.

HEADLEY HEATH

Hæðleage 849 (11th) BCS 455
Hedlege, Hedlye c. 1250 NQB, 1275, 1327 SR, all (p)
Headley Heath 1581 Wills, 1711 FF

'Heath-clearing,' *v*. hæð, leah.

HIGHTER'S HEATH

Haylers (sic) *Heth* 1549 Pat   *Hayters Heath* 1650 *Surv*

The forms are very late. Possibly they derive from the pers. name *Hayter* which Weekley (*Surnames* 81) takes to be from the Devonshire Hay Tor.

HOLLYMOOR

Hollemere 1371 Pat

'Hollow mere,' *v.* holh, mere.

HOLLY WOOD

del Holies, atte Holyes c. 1250 NQB, 1360 Wigorn

Self-explanatory.

HOUNDSFIELD FM (6″)

Hundesfeld 1086 DB, 1156 (1266) Ch (p)
Hondysfeld 1499 AD i
Houndefeld 1535 VE
Hownesfeld 1550 Pat

'Hound's open land,' though it might also contain a pers. name, cf. Mawer in *Mod. Lang. Rev.* xiv. 241–2.

INKFORD (6″)

Ennekesford 1255 *Ass*
Inkeford 1424 VCH iii. 184, n. 92
Enkeford 1545 Wills
Inckford 1586 Wills, 1603 QSR

It would seem almost certain that behind this name, as behind Ennick Ford *supra* 222, lies a lost stream-name. *v.* Inkford Brook *supra* 12.

KINGS HEATH, KINGSUCH (lost), KINGSWOOD

The earliest forms noted for these are *Kyngesheth* (1511 AD v), *King's Heath* (1650 *Surv*), *Kyngissyche, Kingsuch, Kingsitch* (c. 1270 AD i, 1544 LP, 1686 FF), *Kingswood* (1650 *Surv*). They are further survivals from the royal ownership of the manor. For the second name *v.* sic.

LEA GREEN FM (6″)

Lea 1086 DB, 1180 P (p)
de Lee, de la Lee c. 1200 NQB, 1275 SR
de la Leye 1300 *Pat*   *atte Leye* 1327 SR
atte Lye 1318 Ipm
Lee Eld, Lee Yeald 1490 Ct (NQB), 1562 Wills
Lea Green, Lay Green 1820 G, c. 1830 O

v. leah. See further Lea End in Alvechurch *supra* 334. For *Eld* and *Yeald v.* Burcot in Bromsgrove *supra* 338.

Lifford

de la Ford c. 1250 NQB, 1275 *Ass*, SR

This is the ford by which Ryknild Street crosses the Rea. It is apparently a case of the French definite article coalescing with the following English significant word, cf. Lawell House in Chudleigh (D), 1329 ExonReg. *mansum suum de la Walle.*

Lindon Hall (Old 1″)

de la Linde 1275 SR   *Lynde* 1559 Wills

'(At the) lime-tree,' *v.* lind. The modern form of the name is probably due to the alternative alien name *linden* for that tree.

Lindsworth Fm (6″)

Lindwyrðe c. 705 (12th) BCS 123
Lindeorde[1] 1086 DB
Lindewo' c. 1250 NQB (p)
Lyndewrthe c. 1275 AD ii (p)
Lyndeworth 1275 SR
Lindworth 1855 Kelly

'Enclosure by the lime-trees,' *v.* lind, worð and cf. Lindon Hall *supra.*

Monyhull

Monhull 1237 LibPens, 1275 *Ass*, SR, c. 1275 AD ii, 1293
    CompR, all (p)
Monehills 1535 VE, 1544 LP
Mon(e)yhull 1547 Pat, 1685 FF
Monyhall 1650 FF

This is probably from OE *Mannan-hyll*, 'Manna's hill,' *v.* hyll, with West Country *o* for *a*. It is clear that in modern times there has been confusion with the common word *money* by some process of folk-etymology. The suggestion in EPN

---

[1] Identified in VCH i with Linthurst, but the forms of the names do not agree. Further, all the identified berewicks of Bromsgrove occur in DB in a geographical sequence, and if *Lindeorde* = Lindsworth it is in its right position. Further, in BCS 123, it stands next to *ciondan* (cf. Chyndhouse *supra* 352), and that would seem to have been close to Lindsworth Fm.

(*s.v.* monig) that the first element is *many* must be withdrawn. The hill is a single isolated one.

MOOR GREEN

> *de Mora, super Moram* c. 1250 NQB, 1275 SR
> Self-explanatory.

MOSELEY

> *Museleie* 1086 DB
> *Moselege, Moseley* 1221, 1262 *Ass* (p), 1494, 1511 AD iv, 1549 Pat
> *Mousley* 1577 Saxton

This lies on high ground with gravel, so apart from phonological difficulties, OE mos is unlikely. Professors Ekwall and Zachrisson suggest OE *mūs(a)-lēage*, 'field-mouse or field-mice clearing' (*v.* leah). A pers. name *Mūsa* is also possible, cf. Robertus filius *Muse* in an Assize Roll of 1219. See further Mansion, *Oudgentsche Namenkunde* (88), on a Flemish name *Muse* or *Musa*. The name may have been influenced in its development by the more common type found in Moseley *supra* 128.

MOUNDSLEY HALL

> *Mundesley* 13th AD ii   *Moundsley Elde* 1427 Ct (NQB)
> *Mounesley* 1490 Ct (NQB)

Probably '*Mund's* clearing,' *v.* leah. Cf. *mundesdene* in the bounds of Yardley (BCS 1282) about two miles away. For *Elde v.* Burcot in Bromsgrove *supra* 338. There were five *yields* in King's Norton parish.

REDNAL

> *æt Wreodanhale* 780 BCS 234, 849 (11th) BCS 455, 934 (11th) BCS 701
> *Weredeshale* 1086 DB
> *Wrodenhale* 1187 P, 1342 LyttCh
> *Wredenhale* 1275 SR, 1289 *FF*, both (p)
> *Wrednall* 1427 Ct (NQB), 1589–93 Wills
> *Rednall* 1594 Wills

Professors Ekwall and Zachrisson agree in suggesting that

we have here as the first element the gen. sg. of an OE *wride*, *wreode*, a variant of OE *gewrid*, 'thicket,' from the weak grade of *wriðan*, 'to twist.' For the *o*-forms cf. Hurtlehill *supra* 73. Hence 'nook of the thicket,' *v*. healh.

RUBERY

Robery Hills 1650 *Surv*

This is an old name for part of the Lickey Hills, and it doubtless means 'rough hills,' *v*. ruh, beorg, cf. Rowberry (He) and *ruanberg* in Sedgeberrow (BCS 223).

STIRCHLEY STREET [stretli]

Stretley Streete 1658 Deed

This is on the line of Ryknild Street (*v. supra* 2). For the name cf. Streetly (St) nr. Sutton Coldfield on the same road. The form *Stirchley* is due to metathesis, found also in Sturton (Nb, Nt, L, Y) and Stirton (Y).

TESSALL FM

Thessale 1086 DB
Tessala 1186 P (p)
Tesselega 1188 P, 1424 IpmR
Teshale c. 1270 AD i
Thesale 1276 LyttCh (p)

WALKER'S HEATH

le Walkerishethe 1314 AD i   *Walkers Heath* 1650 *Surv*

There was a John fil. Ric. le *Walkere de Kyngesnorton* in 1340 (*FF*, Wa).

WARSTOCK

Le Horestok 1331 Misc   *Hoorestock* 1675 WillsP

Hoore is from OE har and is descriptive of a boundary stocc or post. The place lies where King's Norton, Solihull and Yardley meet. The development of initial *w* is dialectal, cf. Old Swinford *supra* 309, *warstone* as a field-name in Clent (Terrier 1838) = hoarstone, and *Whoarstone* in Himbleton (1649 Surv).

WEST HEATH

West Hethe c. 1270 NQB, 1299 (18th) *RBB*
Self-explanatory.

WYCHALL FM[1]

la Wythalle[2] (sic) 1253 Pat
de la Withalle 1275 SR
de la Wychalle, Wichalle c. 1275 AD i, ii
Whichehalle 1300 Wigorn (p)
Wichall acre in Norton Regis 1322 Inq aqd
la Wychall acre 1322 Cl

From the persistent double *l* this name would seem to be a compound of wic and heall, hence 'hall by or of the dairy-farm.'

WYTHALL

Wyhtehalle 1283 Wigorn
Witho Chapel 1577 Saxton
Withall, Withall Heath 1650 *Surv*, 1672 D
Withorn Chapel 1763 Bowen

In addition to the above forms we should perhaps include the unidentified *Warthuil*, a DB berewick of Bromsgrove. As Wythall was a chapelry of Bromsgrove (cf. Round in VCH i. 285), and as the geographical distribution of the definitely identifiable berewicks of Bromsgrove suggests that it is not so far from Lindsworth on the one side and Wythwood and Houndsfield on the other, it may well be that the two places are identical. If so, it is very difficult to suggest an etymology at all. The forms, apart from DB, are scanty, late and not entirely consistent with one another, and it may be that DB, apparently so corrupt, is nearer the true form, whatever that may have been. It should be added that the topography makes it unlikely that the DB suffix *-huil* is for *-hull*.

WYTHWOOD COTTAGE[3] (6″)

Witeurde 1086 DB
Withwurthe 1221 *Ass* (p)

[1] This is often confused with Wythall *infra*. Duignan (PN Wo 184) erroneously puts Wychall in Northfield and makes *de la Withalle* of SR (1275) serve both places.

[2] That this is Wychall rather than Wythall *infra* is clear from the fact that the person in question can be traced as Ricardus de *Wichalle* in several other documents.

[3] On the geographical principle mentioned above *sub* Lindsworth, while Whitford is out of the question, Wythwood would suit quite well. It was evidently at one time the name for a considerable area.

Withewrthe 1237 Bracton
Wytheworth, Wycheworth 1283 Cl, 1285 Pat, both (p)
Withworth Heath 1587 AD iii
Withworth 1661 FF
Withwood Heath and *Green* 1820 G

It is difficult to make any other suggestion than that the first element in this name must be OE wiðig, and the second worð, hence 'enclosure by the withies.' Cf. Lindsworth *supra* 355. For late confusion of *worth* and *wood*, cf. PN NbDu 268.

Stoke Prior

STOKE PRIOR[1] 81 A 14
  Stoke 770 (11th) BCS 204
  Stoche 1086 DB
  Stokes c. 1086 (1190) *EveB*, 1221 *Ass*
  Stok Prioris 1275 SR

  v. stoc. Held by the Prior of Worcester whereas Stoke Bishop (Gl) was an episcopal manor.

ASTON FIELDS
  Eastun 767 (17th) BCS 202
  Estone, Estona 1086 DB, c. 1086 (1190) *EveB*, (*in Stokes*)
    1221 *Ass*, 1227 *FF*
  Astone End 1391 LibPens
  Aston Fields 1649 Surv

  'East farm,' in relation to Bromsgrove.

BADDINGTON MILL (Old 1")
  Bedindone, -dona 1086 DB, c. 1086 (1190) *EveB*, 1521, 1531
    LP
  Badington 1255 *Ass*
  Baddington Mill 1649 Surv

  '*Bǣda's* hill,' *v.* dun. The two elements are linked by the use of *ing* as in the ingtun-names.

BRIDENBRIDGE (lost)
  (*in*) *bridenan brygge* 770 (11th) BCS 204
  bridenebricge 11th Heming (362)

---

[1] In the metes of Stoke Prior (BCS 204) we have a *werdun broc* and a *teouelege, teofelege*. The former appears as *Wardebroke* in *Pat* 1300 and SR (1327), the latter as *Thavelege* in 1240 (WoP).

This contains the OE *breden*, *briden* or *bryden*, an adj. de-noting 'made of planks,' from OE *bred*, 'plank,' and brycg, so that the whole name means 'plank-bridge.' A further example of this name is found in the Halesowen Court Rolls, in the form *Bredenbruge*, *la Brydenebrug* s.a. 1306 and 1307. It is possible that a last trace of this name is to be found in the *Breedon* Brook of the 1649 Survey of Stoke.

BROOMHOUSE FM (6″)

de Brome, *ate Brome* 1240 WoP, 1275, 1327 SR, 1340 NI
Broomhouse 1649 Surv
Self-explanatory.

CASPIDGE FM

cærsa bæt 770 (11th) BCS 204
Casbridge 1649 Surv, 1820 G
Caspidge c. 1830 O

It is clear that *bæt* is a bad form for bæc and that the first element is OE cærse, hence 'cress stream.'

FINSTALL

Vinstal-stude 1295 Wigorn
le Vynestallstede 1368 (18th) Nash

The first is an entry in connexion with the lease of a salt-pit. The term *vinstal* or *finstal* is explained by an entry in the Charter Rolls (1328) in which Peter de Stodleye grants to the canons of Witton in Droitwich two *salinæ*, i.e. brine-pits, and a *finstallus*, i.e. a place for heaping firewood, from OE *fīn*, 'heap of wood,' and steall.

GAMBOLDS, UPPER and LOWER (6″)

This is a name of the manorial type, *Gamel* being found as a pers. name in this vill in 1240 (WoP).

GRIMLEY HALL

de Grimley 1275 SR

This may be the name of a migrant from Grimley elsewhere in the county. *v. supra* 126.

HILL FM

de Monte, othe Hull 1275, 1327 SR

Self-explanatory.

KINCHFORDS (lost)

This lost name is recorded by Nash (ii. 38) and represents the *Kingesford* of the metes of Feckenham Forest (*Pat* 1300). It is an interesting development for which no parallel has so far been noted.

THE OAKALLS (6″)

This is probably to be identified with the *Okholt* found in pers. names in 1240 (WoP) and 1275 (SR), cf. Oakhall in Grimley *supra* 128.

ST GODWALDS

sancto Godewalde 1275 *Ass*

This was a chapelry of Stoke Prior. St Gudwald of Brittany (7th cent.) has four dedications to him in English churches.

SALOP BRIDGE (lost)

This name is found in the 1649 Survey and is interesting as preserving the old pronunciation of the name of the river Salwarpe *supra* 306.

SHARPWAY GATE

sceap weg (sic), *scearp weg* 770 (11th) BCS 204

Sharpway Gate 1649 Surv

The 'Gate' must have been on the Feckenham-Wychbold road at a point where there is a steepish descent.

WHITFORD BRIDGE

Whyteford 1408 *EcclVar* (p)

The identification is probable, though not certain. The ford was so called in contrast to a *Blakeford* which appears in the metes of Stoke Prior (*Pat* 1300), and this is probably the same as the pers. name *Blackforde* found in Tardebigge in 1327 (SR).

Tardebigge[1]

TARDEBIGGE 72 J 2 dim[taˑbik]

Tærdebicgan (dat.) 974 (11th) BCS 1317
Terdebiggan 11th Heming (bis)
Tyrdebicgan 11th Heming
Terdebigan 11th (17th) Hickes no. 45
Terdeberie 1086 DB
Terde(s)bigga R 1 (1266) Ch
Terdebigga 1138 BM, 1169–92 P (*passim*), 1275, 1327 SR
Terdebig 1230 Cl
Therdebigge 1258 FF
Tertebigge 1275 *Ass*
Terbygge 1486, 1499 Pat
Tardbick 1675 Ogilby
Tarbeck 1680 FF
Tarbick, Tarbeck, Tarbigg, Torbick, Turbick 17th QSR

It is impossible to make any headway with this name. The early forms suggest possible association with the pers. name *Tyrdda* found in Tredington *supra* 172. As *æ* becomes *a* in ME in this county it is possible that the first form *Tærd-* is for *Terd-*. If it were not we should have expected ME *Tard-*. The suffix with its *cg* looks more like English than Celtic, but no suggestion can be made as to its meaning.

Tardebigge includes (*A*) Tutnall-and-Cobley.

BLACKWELL FM (6")

Blakewell Hy 3, LyttCh
Self-explanatory.

BROCKHILL FM

Brokhyll 15th VCH   *Brockehull* 1535 VE
Probably 'badger-hill,' *v.* brocc, hyll.

COBLEY HILL

Cobesleie 12th Dugd v. 409
Cobbele(ye) 1271 *For* (p), 1299 (18th) *RBB*
Cobley Hill 1535 VE

---

[1] In Staffs. from c. 1100 to 1266 and then in Warw. till 1844.

This contains a pers. name *Cobb(a)* occurring as *Cobbe* in the 12th cent. and also contained in Cobley (Ha), *Cobbanlea* BCS 974, and probably also in Cobham (K), *Cobbahamm* BCS 741.

HEWELL GRANGE

Hewell(e) 1275 *Ass*, 1276 RH, 1291 Tax

'High stream,' *v.* heah, wielle.

SHORTWOOD FM, GREAT

Surthewode 1249 AD ii   *Sortewode* 13th AD ii
Schortewodde 1535 VE

Self-explanatory.

THE SIDNALS (6″)

Sidenhale c. 1245 *Bodl*, 1265 Wulst, 1275 *Ass*

OE *sidan hēale*, 'broad corner of land,' *v.* sid, healh. The *s* is pseudo-manorial.

TUTNALL

Tothehal 1086 DB
Tottenhull 1262 *For*, 1380 LibPens
Totenhull 1275 *Ass*, SR (p), 1473 Ct, 1535 VE
Totynhyll 1542 LP
Toutnell 1675 Ogilby

'Hill of Tot(t)a,' *v.* hyll. The DB form is probably corrupt.

TYNSALL (lost)[1]

Tuneslega 1086 DB
T(h)eneshale Matilda, Hy 2, R 1 (1266) Ch
Tunneshal(l) 1230 Ch, 1276 RH
Tuneshale 1230 Cl, 13th AD ii, 1244 *FF*, 1276 RH
Tunsale 1327 SR (p)
Tynsall Filde 1535 VE

The identity of the above places is not quite certain, but the variant forms of the suffix have their parallel in those of Bordesley *infra* 365. There is an OE pers. name *Tun(n)a*. A strong

---

[1] In DB in Bromsgrove. The site of the place is approximately fixed by its being demesne land of Bordesley Abbey in the manor of Hewell (VE iii. 271).

form of this, with later development of *u* to *i*, as noted *supra* 163, will explain all the forms except the second. This may be an error for *Toneshale*. If it is not, then we must take the pers. name to have been *Tynni* rather than *Tunni*.

(*B*) Webb Heath

FOXLYDIATE

Foxhuntleyates c. 1300 *Pat*   *Foxenlydeyate* 1464 Pat
Foxlydiate 1591, 1594 Wills   *Fox Liddet* 1675 Ogilby

'Swing-gate used by the fox-hunt or hunters,' *v.* hlidgeat and cf. Lydiate Lane in Hasbury *supra* 295. In the metes of Feckenham Forest (1300 *Pat*) we have mention of *Foxhuntwey* voc. *le Ruggeway*, *v. supra* 4.

HOLYOAKE'S FM

le Haliok 1255 *Ass*   *Holiok* (p) 1275 SR[1]

Self-explanatory. Cf. Holyoakes (Lei). Pseudo-manorial.

RAGLIS (Old 1")

This is probably manorial in origin. The surname *de Raggeleye* is found in the Subsidy Roll of 1275, the family doubtless coming from Ragley (Wa).

SHELTWOOD FM

Sylkwode 1256 *FF*
Siltwode c. 1260 AD ii
Schiltewode, Shyltewode 1275 *Ass*, 1276 RH, 1388 IpmR, 1468 StratGild
Schildwode 1275 *Ass*
Schiltwode, Shiltwode 1279 RH, 1314 Ipm (p), 1374 Pat
Saltwod 1291 Tax

From the point of view of form the first element might well be explained as OE *scielet*, a word assumed in the NED (*s.v. shillet*) to explain dialectal *shillet, shilt*, 'sort of rock, clay-slate.' The application of the name to the site is not obvious.

(*C*) Redditch

REDDITCH 82 A 3

de Rubeo Fossato c. 1200 Madox, *Formulare* no. 623
la Rededich, le Rededych 1247 FF, 1300 *Pat*, 1348 Pat

---

[1] In Bromsgrove.

Reddich, Reddyche 1394 Pat, 1441 StratGild, 1535 VE
The Rediche, le Redyche 1446 AD ii, 1464 Pat
The Redde Dych 1536 Wills
Readdich prope Terbig 1558 Wills

'Red ditch' (*v.* read, dic), from the colour of the soil. Cf. Reddish (La).

BATCHLEY (6″)

Bacheley 1464 Pat

'Valley-clearing,' *v.* bæc, leah.

BORDESLEY

Bordeslega 1138 (1266) Ch
Bordesley, Borsly 1535 VE, LP
Bursley 1577 Saxton
Boresley 1650 *Surv*

Other forms are without interest. It denotes the clearing of land (*v.* leah) owned by one *Bord*, cf. Bozen Green (Herts), DB *Bordesdene* and Balsall Heath *supra* 351. The name *Borda* is found in DB. It probably has a parallel in OGer *Borto*, *Porto, Porzo* (Förstemann PN 328–9), cf. Bordesley in Aston (Wa).

BRIDLEY MOOR (6″)

Bridleymore 1464 Pat

The first element may be ME *bridde*, 'bird,' but the forms are too late for certainty. *v.* leah.

EASEMORE FM (6″)

Eyesmore 1535 VE

This may be a late compound of ME *eye* and *more*, 'marshy place of the well-watered land' (*v.* eg), referring to land by the Arrow.

HEADLESS CROSS

Hedley 1275 SR, 1294 Ipm, 1327 SR, all (p)
Smethehedley 1300 *Pat*
Hedley Cross 1464 Pat
Hedles Crosse 1549 Pat
Headleys Cross 1789 *Canal Map*, 1820 G

'Heath-clearing,' *v.* hæð, leah. From Hedley developed Hedley's Cross, and this was later corrupted as above, cf. Duignan PN Wo 80. *Smethe* = 'smooth, level.'

(*D*) BENTLEY PAUNCEFOTE 82 A 2

   Beneslei 1086 DB
   Benetlega, -lege 1185 P, 1197 *FF*, (*Pancevot*) 1212 Fees 140
   Bunetleg 1280 *For*
   Benetley in Fekenham forest 1281 Ch
   Benteley in Tardebigg 1499 Pat
   Stretch Bentley 1578 Wills

   v. beonet, leah and cf. Bentley in Holt *supra* 141. Richard *Panzeuot* held land here in 1185 and the *Streche* family was holding an estate in Bentley in 1275 (SR).

JEFFERIES' FM

   Named from the *Jeffreys* family who held the manor of Bentley Pauncefote in the 16th cent. (VCH iii. 226).

THE THRIFT

   atte Frithe 1275 SR

   'The wood,' *v.* fyrhþe. Cf. Marston Thrift and Salem Thrift (PN BedsHu 80, 30) and Thrift Wood in Crowle (*Thrid* c. 1830 O).

THE ELEMENTS, APART FROM PERSONAL NAMES, FOUND IN WORCESTERSHIRE PLACE-NAMES

This list confines itself for the most part to elements used in the second part of place-names or in uncompounded place-names. Under each element the examples are arranged in three categories, (*a*) those in which the first element is a significant word and not a pers. name, (*b*) those in which the first element is a pers. name, (*c*) those in which the character of the first element is uncertain. Where no statement is made it may be assumed that the examples belong to type (*a*). Elements which are not dealt with in the *Chief Elements used in English Place-names* are distinguished by an (n) after them.

ac (a) Aggberrow (2), Aggborough (2), High Oak, Holy-oake's Fm, Noak, Noken, Rock, Shurnock, (b) Edgiock (?), (c) Weatheroak.

æcer Linacres, Ridgeacre.

æppeltun Napleton.

æsc (a) Nash (3), Rashwood, *Esch*, (b) Burlish, Botany (?), (c) Franche (?).

alor Clifton Arles, Orleton, Thicknall (?).

ancor (n) Ankerdine.

anstig Ayngstree.

bæc (a) *Batch*, Badge Court, Brookpatch, Caspidge, *Foxbatch*, Hawkbatch.

bærnet The Barnets, Barnt Green.

*beall (b) Cakebole.

bearu (b) Bagburrow, Sedgeberrow.

bedd Ashbed, Hollybed, Ribbesford.

beonet Bentley (2).

beorc Bartley.

beorg Aggberrow (2), Aggborough (2), Ashborough, Barham, Barrow Hill, Berrow (3), The Burf, Burhill, Crookbarrow, *Fishborough*, Harborough, Hobro, Holberrow, *Ildeberg*, Lark-borough, Limberrow, Rubery, Wadborough, (b) Allesborough, Axborough, Inkberrow, Ipplesborough, (c) Gadbury, Old-berrow.

beretun *Barton*.

bern Barneshall, Barn Hill (?).

ME *berse (n) *Berse*.

OE bicere (n) Bickley (?).

bierce Six examples of this element.

binnan *Binholme*.

blæc Blaythorn.

boc Baughton, Buckridge.

bocen *Bucknell*.

ME boie (n) Boycott (?).

bold Newbold, Wychbold, Boughton.

bræc The Breach.

breden (n) *Bridenbridge*.

brende Brand Hall, Brandwood, Branthill.

broc (a) Five uncompounded, Claybrook, Gilton Brook, Henbrook, Stanbrook, (b) Bournbrook. See also river-names.

brochol Brockhill.

brom Broom.

bromig Bromley.

brycg *Bridenbridge*, Hawbridge, Leather Bridge, *Maybridge*, Stourbridge.

*bult (n) Bouts.

bur *Bower*, Bowercourt.

burh (a) Barley, Burcot, Bury, Buryend, Buryfield, Hanbury, Hasbury, Libbery, Nobury, Oldbury, Overbury, Tenbury, Woodbury, (b) Banbury, Chadbury, Eastbury, Elbury, Fladbury, Fockbury, Hartlebury, Snodsbury, and (manorial) Sagebury, (c) Buckbury, Comer, Oldbury, Spilsbury, Wychbury.

burhtun Burton.

burna (a) Atterburn, Barbourne, Bourne Bank, Honeybourne, Stambermill, (b) Isbourne, (c) Washbourne.

ME bursten, brusten (n) Bristnall.

*bylte (n) Bilford.

cærse Caspidge, *Cresselau*, Kerswell.

ME calenge (n) Callans Wood.

calu Callow Hill (2).

ceafor Cheveridge (?).

ceaster Worcester.

ceorl Charford, Charlton.

cirice (b) Alvechurch.

*clæte, OE (n) *Clethale*, Clethill.

*clent, OE (n) Clent, Dunclent.

clif (a) Cleeve (2), Clevelode, (b) Austcliff, Cookley, Marlcliff.

cluse (n) Clows.

cnafa Knavenhill, *Knaveslade*.

cniht Knighton (2), Knightwick.

cnoll Knowle.

cocc Cook Hill.

cofa Cofton.

corn Cornbrook, Cornwood.

cot (a) Brockencote, Burcot, Calcott, Colkett's Fm, Draycott
(2), Foxcote, Gorcott, Hurcott, *Pircote*, Swancote, Walcote,
Woodcote, *Woodhamcote*, Woodmancote, (b) Alcott, Amblecote, Armscott, Bedcote, Bredicot, Darlingscott, Wollescote,
(c) Boycott, Copcut, Goldicote, *Sapcott*, Westmancote, Woodhamcote.

cradol (n) Cradley (?).

cran Cromer.

crawe Craycombe.

croft (a) *Calvecroft*, Deptcroft, (b) Caddecroft, Pitchcroft.

cros Cross (2), Cruise Hill.

crumb (n) Croome.

crundel Crundall, Crundelend.

cumb (a) Comble, Comhampton, Coombe, The Coombes,
Craycombe, Lincomb, Merecombe, Norcombe, Solcum,
(b) Iccomb.

dæl Dales Wood, Debdale, Doverdale.

deað (n) Deaseland.

denu (a) Dean Brook, Ramsden, Saldon, Sandhills, Timberdine,
(b) Hobden.

dic Ditchford (2), Redditch.

dræg Draycott (2), Drayton.

dun (a) Bredon, Longdon (3), Ramsden (3), Ridon, Thorndon,
Thorne, Waddon, (b) Baddington, Bluntington, Cowsden,
Fibden, Stildon, Warndon, Wilden, (c) Carton.

ea Rea (2).

eg (a) Bevere, Fenny, Forty (2), Heathy, Rye, (b) Cainey, Hackney, Impney, Kempsey, (c) Sapey.

elm Two uncompounded examples.

ende Brockamin, Buryend, Indhouse, Moorend, Nash End, Netherend, Northend, Southend.

fæsten Holdfast.

fald Deerfold, Winterfold.

feld (a) Arrowfield, Buryfield, Crowfields, Fairfield, Field Fm (2), Fieldhouse, Fieldy, Gadfield, Hatfield, Highfields, North-field, Pinfields, Westfield, (b) Easerfield, Eldersfield, Madres-field, Woodsfield, (c) Houndsfield, *Tinfield*.

fen (a) Fen Fm, (b) Edvin, Pinvin.

fin Finstall.

folc Faulk Mill (?).

ford (a) Blackford, Bradford (2), Charford, Defford, Ditchford (2), Ford Fm, Ford Mill, *Gosford*, Harford, Hawford, *Hol-ford*, *Kinchfords*, Larford, Lenchford, Lifford, *Perryford*, Radford (2), Ribbesford, Rochford, Sandford, Shatterford, Stakenford, Stanford, Stratford, Swinford, Twyford, Whit-ford, Wichenford, Wickhamford, (b) *Balsford*, Bastonford, Besford, Daylesford, Dodford, Guarlford, Inkford, Kings-ford, Paxford, Payford, Pudford, *Symondford*, Tilesford, Titford, (c) Bilford, Bransford, *Burnford*, Nafford.

fore (n) Fairfield, Forhill.

forð (n) *Forty Green*.

fyrhð Frith Fm, The Thrift.

gamen (n) Gannow (2).

geat *Felgate*, Meneatt, Oldyates Fm (?), Thornsgate, Wood-gates.

gild *Ildeberg*.

glædene (n) Gleden Brook.

gorst Gorse Fm, Gorsty Hill.

græfe (a) Blackgrave, (b) Bromsgrove.

graf(a) Grove (2), Norgrove (2), Thorngrove.

grene Three uncompounded examples.

greot Greet.

gryten (n) Gilton Brook.

gyrd (n) Yardley.

(ge)hæg (a) Churches, Cliffey, Hay Green, Hayes (2), Hay

Mills, *Hay Oak*, Hayswood, Hookey's, Lickey (?), Menith-wood, Oxhey, Rowney, Whetty, (b) Cooksey (?), Cutpursey, (c) Eachway.

hæsel Hasbury, Hazel Fm.

hæð Heath (9), Headless Cross, Headley.

hætt (n) Hathitch, Hathouse.

haga Hallow, Hawbridge, Hawford.

ham (a) *Barham*, Horsham, Newnham, (b) Doddenham, Falsam (?), Kinsham, Strensham.

hamm (a) Ankerdine, *Asham*, *Binholme*, Brockamin, Eastham, The Fullhams, Ham (4), *Kingesham*, (b) Birlingham, Evesham, Falsam (?), Feckenham, Mildenham, Offenham, Pensham, Pickersom, Pixham.

hamstede Dunhampstead.

hamtun (a) Brookhampton (2), Comhampton, Dunhampton, Glasshampton, Hampton Lovett, Northampton, Oakhampton, *Sevenhampton*, Sytchampton, Uphampton, Woodhampton, (b) Pansington, (c) Bishampton, Yarhampton.

hangra Timberhanger.

har Warstock, Whore Nap.

heafoc Halfridge, *Hockley*, Ockeridge.

heafod Swinesherd.

healh (a) Beanhall, Broomhall, *Clethale*, *Coldnalls*, Fernhalls, Gorse Hill, Hales, *Hall*, Hawne, *Northal*, Oxnall, Rednall, Ryall, The Sidnals, Southall, Stonehall, Thicknall (?), Wychall, (b) *Baldenhall*, Balsall, Battenhall, Bastenhall, Baynhall, Caunsall, Cladswell, Knottsall, Oldnall, Tapenhall (2), *Tynsall*, Uckinghall, *Walloxhall*, *Wennal*, Winnall, Wribbenhall, Yessel, (c) Tessall.

heall (a) Brand Hall, Hall Fm, Oldhall, Parkhall, Upper Hall, Wood Hall (3), Wychall, (c) Wythall (?).

hearg Arrowfield.

hege Hallow.

hens (n) Henbrook.

heordewic Three examples.

hese Hayes Fm.

hid Hyde (3), *Quinzehides*, Rashwood.

hielde Clethill.

hierde Harborough, Hurcott, Hursley.

higna Henwick.

hlaw (a) *Cresselau*, Drakelow, The Lowe (2), Low Hill, Mucklow, (c) Hawkesley, Kidley's Fm, Oswaldslow.

*hlenc (n) Lench, Lenchwick.

hleo Libbery.

hlidgeat Foxlydiate, Lydiate Lane.

hlinc Lenchford, Link, Sandlin, Whitlinge.

hliǒ Lyde Green.

hlose Lowesmoor.

hlype Clerkenleap, Hindlip.

hlypgeat Leapgate.

hoc (a) Hook (2), Rushock (?), (b) Edgiock.

hoh (a) Gannow (2), Hoo Fm, (b) Kersoe, Poden.

holegn Hollies (2), Hollin, Holling, Hollybed, Hollyhall, Holly Wood.

holh (b) Lapal.

holt Holt, Birchall, Oakhall (2), Lineholt, Sherrard's Green (?).

hop (a) Hope, Hopehouse, Hopwood, (b) Easinghope.

hramse (n) Romsley (?).

hrycg (a) *Ashridge*, Buckridge, Coldridge, Elmbridge, Halfridge, Lindridge, Ockeridge, Rodge, Rugg's Place, Sherridge (?), Warridge, (b) Cotheridge, Cotteridge (?), (c) Cheveridge, Keybridge, Tiltridge.

hryding Priory Redding, Reddings.

hulu (n) Holberrow.

hus Five examples of Woodhouse.

hyll (a) Branthill, Bristnall, Brockhill (3), Broom Hill, Burhill, Callow Hill (2), Churchill (2), Cook Hill, Fernhill, Forhill, Goosehill, Gorst Hill, Hartle, Hill (21), Hull, Lickhill, North Hill, Penn Hill, Queenhill, Redhill (2), Stapenhill, Swan's Hill, Tickenhill, Underhill, Wheating Hill, Witnells End (?), Yarnold (?), (b) Bone Hill, *Bucknell*, Cherkenhill, Doddenhill, Dodderhill, Greenhill, Grimes Hill, Howsell, *Insoll*, *Knottenhill*, Monyhull, Mucknell, *Oldenhill*, Oldnall, Purshull, *Shurvenhill*, Trotshill, Tutnal (2), Windhill, Woollashill, (c) Catshill, Hockerills, Howsell, Ravenshill, Sarn Hill, *Shrawnell*, Tutshill, Winthill.

hymel Himbleton.

hyrne Horns Hall.

hyrst (a) Bullockhurst, *Greethurst*, Hurst (3), Linthurst, Swanshurst, (b) Shakenhurst.

iggoð Aits, Neight.

ingtun (a) Eastington, Heightington, Northington, Norton, Sindon's Mill, Sinton (2), Sintons End, Sodington, Suddington, (b) Abberton, Aldington, Alton, Bellington, Berrington, Bevington, Bockleton, Chevington, Comberton (2), Eckington, Huddington, Hunnington, Oldington, Peopleton, *Pinton*, Quinton (?), Talton, Teddington, Tibberton, Tidmington, Titton, Torton, Tredington, Whittington, Wolverton, Woodston, (c) *Merrington*.

kidde, ME (n) Kidley's Fm (?)

lacu *Timberlake*.

(ge)lad (a) Clevelode, Saxon's Lode, (b) Evenlode.

læfer Larford.

land (a) Deaseland, Newland(s) (3), No Man's Land, Ryelands, (b) Kitlands.

launde Kingsland.

leah (a) Areley, Arley, Astley, Barley, Bartley, Batchley, Bentley (2), Beoley, Birchley, Blakeley, Boreley, Bradley, Bromley, Bushley, Castle Green, *Comble*, Cowleigh, Cradley (?), Crowle, Elmley (2), Farley (2), Grovely, Hanley (2), Hawkley, Hayley, Headless Cross, Headley (2), *Hockley*, Horseley, Hursley, Hurtlehill, Langley, Lea (3), Leigh, Ley(s) (2), Lye, Madley, Moseley, Oakley, Pulley, Redmarley (2), Selly, Shepley, Shrawley, *Southley*, Spetchley, Stirchley, Weoley, Wesley's Fm, Witley, Worsley, Yardley, (b) Abberley, Barnsley, Billesley, Blockley, Bordesley, Broadhidley, Chaddesley, Chaceley, Chatley, Cobley, Cudley, Diglis, Dudley, Dunley, Frankley, Garmsley, Grimley, Habberley, Hagley, Harpley, Higley, Illey, Kinnersley, *Lollay*, Lulsley, Lutley, Moundsley, Oddingley, Ombersley, *Osmerley*, Peachley, Seckley, Seeley, Tiddesley, Trimpley, Tyseley, Waresley, Warley, Wolverley, (c) Bickley, Bordley, Gatley, *Harley*, Howley, Martley, Moseley, Playley, Prickley, Romsley, Shelsley, Suckley, Syntley, Wordley.

*lecc, OE *The Leche*.

lind Limberrow, Lindon (2), Lindsworth, Lineholt, Linthurst.

mæd Three examples of *meadow*.

mægden Madley, *Maybridge*.

mæne (n) Meneatt, Menithwood.

(ge)mære Marbrook, Marl Brook, Mary Brook, Mere Brook, Merry Brook.

maðð(u)m (n) Mathon (?).

mearð Martley (?).

mere (a) Blakemore, Cromer, Hollymoor, Ismere, Langmorehill, Lowesmoor, Mere Green, Redmarley (2), Throckmorton, (b) Offmoor.

mersc Four examples.

micel Mucklow.

mor (a) Ashmoor, Blackmore, Eymore, Moor (12), Sidemoor, Smithmoor, Wildmoor, (b) Cakemore, Easemore, Hipsmoor, Pedmore, Rumblesmore, Uffmoor, (c) Colmers (?), Clattsmore.

mos Moseley.

mot *Emmots*, *Portsmouth*.

motte, ME (n) Moat Court.

myln (a) *Cutmill*, Frogmill, (c) Pye Mill.

mynster (b) Kidderminster.

myðe Maythorn, Mitton (2), *Mythe*.

næss Claines.

neat Nafford (?).

nest (n) Crowneast, Culverness.

niming, ME (n) Nimmings (2).

niwe Naunton (2), Nobury.

ofer (a) Haselor, *Over*, (b) *Becknor*, Hadzor, *Mapnors* (?), Pridzor.

ora Pershore.

orceard Norchard (2).

oter Atterburne.

oðer (n) Otherton.

pal (n) Pole Elm.

pearroc King's Park.

*persc, OE (n) Pershore.

pirige Five examples of Perry, *Pircote*, Pirton.

plæsc Splash Bridge.

platte, ME (n) *Platt*.

pol Pool (2).

port Portfields, *Portsmouth*, Port Street, Portway.

preost Press-meadow.
pull Pull Court, Pulley, Pool Brook, Poolfields, Poollands.
pytt (a) *Pithouse*, (b) Grimpits.
ræcce (n) Rochford.
ramm Ramsden (?), Romsley (?).
ribbe (n) Ribbesford.
rippel (n) Ripple
rod Pepper Wood.
(ge)ryd, ME ridde Rhydd Court, Rhydd Green
sænget (n) Syntley (?).
*salegn (n) Sallings
*scelde (n) Shclsley (?).
sceolh Shoulton.
scielet (n) Sheltwood.
sciene Sherridge (?).
*sciete (n) Cockshoot, Cockshot.
scitere (n) Shatterford.
scræf (n) Shrawley.
scræwa (n) Shrawnell (?)
scylf Selly (?), Shell.
sealh Saldon, Sale Green, Salford.
secrestein, ME (n) Saxon's Lode (?).
sic Sytchampton, Hathitch, *Kingsuch*.
slæd *Knaveslade*.
sloh·(n) (b) Dadsley.
snæd Snead.
sol Blakeshall, Solcum.
spæc (n) Spetchley.
stakyng, ME (n) Stakenford.
stan Blackstone, Hextons (?), Hoarstone, Redstone, Southstone,
  Stone, *Whitstones*.
stapol Stapenhill (?), Staple Hill.
steall Finstall.
steort Sturt.
stoc Severn Stoke, Stoke Bliss, Stoke Prior, *Wiburgestoke*.
stocc Stock (3), Warstock.
stocking Benstoken, Mogstocking.
stol (n) Stoulton.
stow Kenelmstowe, Merstow.

stræt Greenstreet, Port Street, Stirchley, Stratford.

sulh Sillins (?), Southstone.

sundor (n) Cinders Wood.

sundorland *Sunderland*.

swan Swancote, Swanshurst (?).

swann Swanshurst (?).

*tæcga (n) Tagg Barn, Tagwell.

tang *Tonge*.

teld (n) Tiltridge (?).

þicce *Fickenappletree*, Thicknall.

þorn (a) Blaythorn, (b) Cropthorne.

þorp (a) Upthorpe, (*b*) Huntingtrap.

*þrocc (n) Throckmorton.

ticcen Tickenhill.

trenche, ME (n) Trench Lane.

treo (a) *Fickenappletree*, (b) Doddingtree, Hagtree, Huntingtree, Hussingtree, *Wimburntree*, Yieldingtree.

tun (a) Acton (3), Alderminster, Aston (4), Baughton, Bough-
ton, Bretforton, Broughton (4), Charlton (2), Clifton (2),
Clopton, Cofton, Drayton, Grafton (3), Hampton, Harving-
ton, Hillhampton, Himbleton, Horton, *Hylton*, Kineton,
Kington, Knighton (2), Littleton, Middleton (2), Martin,
Minton, Mitton (2), Moreton's, Morton (4), Naunton (3),
Netherton (4), Norton (4), Noverton, Nurton's Fm, Orleton,
Otherton, Oughton (?), Pirton, Shipston, Shoulton, Staunton,
Stockton, Stoulton, Sutton (2), Throckmorton, Town,
Upton (6), Walton (2), Wannerton, Weston, Witton, Wooton's
Fm, (b) Alstone, Bayton, Bricklehampton, Chauson, Cuts-
dean, Dormston, Eardiston, Harvington, Howsen, Inner-
stone, Offerton, *Padstone*, Pitmaston, Structon's Heath,
Wollaston, Woodston, (c) Conderton, Phepson, Puxton,
Shenstone (?), Woodmanton. *v.* ingtun, beretun, burhtun.

twicene (n) Tytchney.

(bi)twihn (n) Tanwood.

wæsc Shipston.

weald Cotswolds, Upton Wold.

wealh Walcote, Walton (2).

weardsetl Warshill, Wassell, Wassel Grove, Wast Hills

*wearpe (n) Salwarpe.

weg Broadway, Hayway, Meadows, Moorways, Portway, Ridge Way, Sharpway.

wete (n) Whetty.

wic (a) Bromwich, Droitwich, Henwick, Knightwick, Lench-wick, *Middlewich*, Netherwich, Northwick (2), Rushwick, *Upwich*, Wick (4), Witton, Wychall, Wychbold, (b) Alfrick, Chadwich, Chadwick, *Colewick*, Conningswick, *Goldenwick*, Kenswick, Powick, *Willingwick*, Winricks.

wielle, Angl. **wælle** (a) Blackwell (2), Caldewell, Caldwall, Dorhall, Hazelwell, Hewell, Holywell (2), *Horwell*, Kerswell, Littals, Oxhall, Redhall (2), Salford, Tagwell, Woodhall, (b) Barnhall, Baywell, Luckalls Fm, Pepwell, Perdiswell, Sneachill, Trotshill, (c) Barn Hill.

wielm, Angl. **wælm** Walmspout.

wig (n) Weoley.

wiht (n) Witley.

wildor (n) *v.* Marshend.

wind (n) Winthill (?).

wiðig Wythwood.

woh Warridge.

worð (a) Lindsworth, Wythwood, (*b*) Bengeworth, Cumber-wood.

worðign (b) Bedwardine, Tolladine.

wrasn (n) Wrens Nest.

*wride, **wreode** (n) Rednall.

wudu (a) Astwood (4), *Bastwood*, Cornwood, Hayswood, Hop-wood, King's Wood, Kyrewood, Ladywood, Lightwood (2), Monk Wood, North Wood, Oldwood, Sheltwood, Shortwood, Tanwood, Westwood (2), Yardley Wood, (b) Walkwood.

NOTES ON THE DISTRIBUTION OF THESE ELEMENTS

A few notes upon the distribution of certain place-name elements may be given, but in the present state of our comparative knowledge of the material for other counties, the remarks can to a large extent only be tentative.

bæc = stream-valley. This suffix is about equally common in

Wo, He, Sa. It is also found occasionally in Ch, Db, Lei, Gl, L, Nf, Sf, Nth. The bæc in So and W is *bæc*, 'hill,' and not this word *bæc*.

bold. The Wo evidence confirms the statement in EPN 7 that this element is characteristic of the Central and West Midlands and we may note the evidence *s.n.* Boughton *supra* 90 for a compound *bold-tun*, a parallel form to the NCy *boðltun* or Bolton. *v.* also Introd. xix, n.

broc, burna. In this county, as in Beds, Bk, Hu, it may be noted that, as a result of intensive study of the place-names of the county, the number of *brooks* increased considerably, while the number of *burns* remained practically stationary, pointing to the application of *brook* to something definitely smaller than what is known as a *burn*.

cot(e). This suffix is relatively about as frequent here as it is in Sa, St, Gl, but rather more frequent than in Db and Lei. It is much less frequent than in Wa, O, Bk, Berks and slightly less frequent than in Beds, Nth and W.

cumb. Intensive study here as elsewhere tends to increase considerably the number of *coombes* and to prove its widespread use in minor names.

(ge)hæg. There are relatively a large number of place-names with this element, as was to be expected in a county which includes much forest-land. They are names of very small places.

ham in this county, as in St, Sa, He, Gl, Wa, O, Db, Lei, Nth, is relatively a very rare suffix, and it may be that some of those given under this element should be taken as examples of **hamm** and still further diminish the proportion. **hamm** is fairly common, but the places are often very small.

hamtun. There are 14 clear examples of this element in Wo. The counties which come nearest to it in the frequency of its use are O, Gl, W, Do. Eleven of these are in the adjoining parishes of Astley and Ombersley, one in the adjoining parish of Hartlebury, while Hampton Lovett is one parish away and only one is in a different part of the county, suggesting a curious local fashion in the use of this suffix. *Sevenhampton* was also in the parish of Astley and Hillhampton adjoins it. Here the suffix is *hæma-tun* (*v.* hæme) rather than hamtun.

hoh here, as in Sa, St, Gl is rare.

hyll is far commoner than either beorg or (still more) hlaw.

ing(as) and ingaham. No examples have been noted in this county, but there is one *ingahamm*.

ingtun. The first group, with a significant first element—*north, south, east, height*—are confined to the north-west of the county, to the parishes of Mamble, Rock, Grimley, Ombersley, Suckley, Acton Beauchamp and Leigh, with the exception of Eastington in Longdon-on-Severn. Of those compounded with pers. names, Chevington, Eckington, Abberton, Aldington, Bevington, Comberton, Tidmington, Peopleton, Wolverton group themselves around Pershore, within a radius of five or six miles, while Huddington, Tibberton and Whittington lie a few miles to the north-west of this group. After that we have a gap and then there is a group consisting of Bellington, Comberton, Oldington, Titton, Torton and *Merrington* in the adjacent parishes of Hartlebury, Kidderminster and Chaddesley Corbett with Hunnington to the north-east. The only ones west of the Severn are in the north-west—Alton in Rock, Berrington in Tenbury, Woodston in Lindridge and Bockleton. In the extreme south-east, in the detached parts of Worcestershire, we have Talton, Tredington and Tidmington. *Pinton* in Alvechurch lay by itself in the north-east of the county.

leah is very common in this well-wooded area, only a little less common than in St.

þorp is very rare, as it is in St and Wa. It seems to be unknown in Sa and Ch. It is much more common in Gl and O.

tun. If we include the ingtun and hamtun names, this is the commonest of all Wo elements. It is worthy of note that there are 84 examples with a significant first element as against 17 with a pers. name as the first element. When a pers. name was compounded ingtun was clearly preferred to simple tun.

weardsetl. The triple use of this element, not surviving elsewhere, is an interesting local peculiarity.

wic. The form *wich* is fairly common, especially in the salt-district, and the proportion of names in *wic* compounded with a pers. name is larger than usual.

worð is very rare, as it is in Sa, St, He, O and only a little less rare than it is in Ch, Wa. In Gl and W it is a good deal more common. None were added as the result of intensive study.

worðign is very rare, as it is in Ch and Gl. The proportion in He and Sa is a good deal higher. It has not been noted in St.

PERSONAL-NAMES COMPOUNDED IN WORCESTERSHIRE PLACE-NAMES

Names not found in independent use are marked with a single asterisk if their existence can be inferred from evidence other than that of the particular place-name in question. Such names may be regarded as hardly less certain than those which have no asterisk. Those for which no such evidence can be found are marked with a double star.

Æbba	Abbots Lench (?)
Æcci	Atch Lench
Æffa	Offmoor
Ælfgȳð (f)	Alvechurch
Ælfsige	Alstone
Ælfstān	Austcliff (?)
Ælla	Alcott
Ælli	Allesborough
Æmela	Amblecote
Ætti	Atchen Hill
*Ambre	Ombersley
Bacga	Bagburrow
Bǣda	Baddington
Bǣga	Baynhall, Baywell
*Bænincg	Banbury
*Bæsta	Bastenhall
Bata	Battenhall
Bēage (f)	Bayton
*Beald	*Balsford*
Bealda	*Baldenhall*
Becca	*Becknor*
Bēda	Bedwardine
*Bela	Bellington
Be(o)nna	Bengeworth

Beorhthelm	Bricklehampton
Beorhtstān	Bastonford (?)
Beorna	Bournbrook, Barn Hill (?),
Beornmōd	Barnsley (?) [Barnhall
Beornnōð	Barnsley (?)
Beornstān	Bastonford (?)
Bera	Berrington
Betti	Besford
Bettu (f)	Bedcote
Bica	Bickley (?)
*Bifa	Bevington
Bill	Billesley
Bisa	Bishampton (?)
*Blica	Brickley
*Blocca	Blockley
Blunt	Bluntington
*Boccel	Bockleton
Boia	Boycote (?)
Bolla	Bone Hill
Bord	Bordesley, Balsall Heath
Bōta	Botany
Brāda	Bredicot
Brēme	Bromsgrove
Bucca	Buckbury
*Burgela	Burlish
Burghild (f)	Buckle Street
*Byrle	Birlingham
*Byrna	Burnford
**Cac(c)a	Cakebole, Cakemore
Cada	Caddecroft
*Cāfa	Keybridge
*Cann	Caunsall
*Cæntwaru	Conderton (?)
*Catt	Catshill
*Catta	Gatley
Cāua	Cainey
Ceadd, *Ceadder	Chaddesley
Ceadd, *Ceadela	Chadwick

*Ceadela	Chadwich
Ceadwealla	Chadbury
*Ceafor	Cheveridge (?)
*Cealf	Chauson (?)
Ceatta	Chatley
**Ceatwe	Chaceley
*Cēca	Kenswick
*Celm, Cylm	Kinsham
*Cemmi	Kempsey (?)
Cēna	Kingsford
*Cifa	Chevington
*Clodd	Cladswell
**Clott	Clattsmore
*Cnott	Knottsall
*Cnotta	*Knottenhill*
Cobba	Cobley
*Codd	Cotswolds, Cutsdean
*Codda	Cotheridge
Cola	*Colewick*, Conningswick
*Coppa	Copcut
**Criddi	Kersoe
*Croppa	Cropthorne
*Cucc	Cooksey
Cūda	Cudley
*Cūfel	Cowsden
**Cūlna	Cookley
Cumbra	Comberton (2), Cumberwood
Cūðbeald	Cutpursey
*Cwēna	Quinton
*Cydela	Kidderminster (?)
**Cydera	Kidderminster (?)
Cyneheard	Kinnersley
*Dægel	Daylesford
*Dēorling	Darlingscott
Dēormōd	Dormston
Dodda	Dodford, Doddenham, Doddenhill
Dudda	Diglis, Doddingtree, Dudley

*Dudra	Dodderhill
Dunna, Dūna	Dunley
Ēadbeorht	Abberton
Ēadmund	Armscott
Ealda	Aldington, Oldbury (?)
	Oldenhill, Oldington, Old-
	nall (2)
Ealdbeald	Abberley
Ealdhere	Eldersfield (?)
Ealhrǣd	Alfrick
Ealhstān	Austcliff (?)
Ealhðrȳð (f)	Offerton
Ēanwulf	Alton
Eardwulf	Eardiston, Yessel
**Ēar	Eastbury
*Earna	Areley (?), Arley (?)
Ecci, Ecca	Eckington
Ecga	Edgiock
*Ela	Elbury
Eof	Evesham
Eofa	Evelench
*Eofla	Evenlode (?)
Eowla	Evenlode (?)
Ēsi	Easinghope, Isbourne
**Ēswald	Easerfield (?)
*Fǣle	Falsam
**Febba, Fibba	Fibdon
*Fecca	Feckenham
*Fisc	*Fishborough*
*Flǣde (f)	Fladbury
*Focca	Fockbury
Franca	Frankley
*Frēa	Franche
*Gǣrla	Guarlford (?)
Gārmund	Garmsley (?)
*Geagga	Hagtree

Geddi, *Gedda	Edvin
Gerlo (OGer)	Guarlford (?)
*Gilda	Yieldingtree (?)
*Golda	Goldicote
Goldgiefu (f)	*Goldenwick*
*Grīma	Grimley, Greenhill
Grímr (ON)	Grimes Hill, Grimpits
Gunnbiǫrn (ON)	Gumborn
*Hæbba	Abbots Lench (?)
*Hæcca	Hackney
Hæcga	Hagley
Headdi	Hadzor
*Heafoc	Hawkesley (?)
Hēahburh (f)	Habberley
**Hearpa	Harpley (?)
*Heaseca	Axborough
*Heortla	Hartlebury
Herewynn (f)	Harvington
Hidda	Broadhidley
Hilla	Illey (?)
*Hlæppa	Lapal
*Hlūda, Hlȳda	Lutley
Hræfn	Ravenshill
Hūd(a)	Huddington
**Huffa	Uffmoor (?)
Hugo (OGer)	Howsell
Hugelin (OGer)	Howsen (?)
Hūna	Hunnington
*Hund	Houndsfield
Hunta	Huntingtrap, Huntingtree
Hūsa	Hussingtree
Huwæl (OWelsh)	Howsen (?)
Hwīta	Whittington, Whitford (?)
*Hycga	Higley
**Hyppi	Hipsmoor (?)
*Icca	Iccomb
*Illa	Illey (?)

Imma	Impney
Inta	Inkberrow
*Ippel	*Ipplesborough*
Isnard (OGer)	Innerstone, Insoll
*Luc(c)a	Luckalls Fm
Lull(a)	*Lollay*, Lulsley
Mǣðhere	Madresfield
Manna	Monyhull
**Mappa	*Mapnors* (?)
*Mearna	Marlcliff
Mucca	Mucknell
Mund	Moundsley
*Mūsa	Moseley (?)
*Mylda	Mildenham
*Nata	Nafford (?)
Obba	Obden (?)
*Odda	Oddingley
Ōsmǣr	*Osmerley*
Ōsweald	*Oswaldslow*
Padd(i)	Spadesbourne
*Pæcc	Paxford
Pǣga	Payford
*Pecci	Peachley
*Ped(e)n	Pensham
Penda	Pinvin
*Peohtmann	Pitmaston
**Perdi	Perdiswell (?)
*Pīcer	Pickersom, Pixham
*Pinna	*Pinton*
*Plega	Playley (?)
Poda	Poden
*Pohha	Powick
Prūd(a)	Pridzor
*Pūcel	Puxton (?)

Puda	Pudford
*Puneca	Pansington
Pybba, Pypba	Pedmore, Pepper Wood,
*Pyppel, *Pybbel	Peopleton [Pepwell
*Pyrt(a)	Purshull (?)
Rūmweald	Rumblesmore
*Scæcca	Shakenhurst
**Scēafen	Shenstone (?)
*Scrēawa	Shrawnell (?)
*Scurfa	*Shurvenhill*
Scyld	Shelsley (?)
Secg	Seckley, Sedgeberrow
Siga	Seeley (?)
Sigemǣr	*Symondford*
*Snǣti	Sneachill
*Snodd	Snodsbury
**Spēol	Spilsbury
*Stilla	Stildon
*Strenge	Strensham
*Succa	Suckley
*Tǣse	Tessall
*Tǣtel	Talton
*Tapa	Tapenhall (2)
*Teolta	Tiltridge
*Tēotta	Teddington, Titford
Tīdbeorht	Tibberton
Tiddi	Tiddesley
*Tīdel	Titton
Tīdhelm	Tidmington
*Þȳfel	Tilesford (?)
Tóli (ON)	Tolladine (?)
*Tolla	Tolladine (?)
*Toppa	Tapenhall (?)
*Torhta	Torton
Tota, Totta	Tutnall
**Treda	Tredington (?)

*Tropinel (OFr)	Trapnell Brook
*Trott	Trotshill
*Trympa	Trimpley
*Tunni, *Tynni	*Tynsall*
Tyrdda	Tredington (?)
*Tyssi	Tyseley
*Ucca	Uckinghall
Uffa	Offenham, Uffmoor (?)
*Ūla	Oldberrow (?)
*Wǣr	Waresley
*Wǣrma	Warndon
*Wassa	Washbourne
Wēaloc	*Walloxhall*
*Wedera	Weatheroak (?)
*Weorca	Walkwood
*Weorð	Woodsfield, Wordley (?)
*Wifela	Wilden
Wīga	Windhill
Wīgburh (f)	*Wiburgestoke*
Wihtlāf	*Wihtlafestun*
Willa	*Willingwick*
Winta	Winthill (?)
*Wrybba	Wribbenhall
Wuduman	Woodmanton (?)
*Wudusige	Woodston
Wulfhere	Wollescote, Wolverton
Wulflāf	Wollaston, Woollashill
Wulfweard	Wolverley
*Wylla	Winnall
Wynburh (f)	*Wimburntree*
*Wynwaru (f)	Winricks

FEUDAL NAMES

Acton Beauchamp, Areley Kings, White Ladies Aston, Bentley Pauncefote, Broughton Hackett, Drake's Broughton, Temple Broughton, Chaddesley Corbett, Cleeve Prior, Cofton

Hackett and Cofton Richard(s), Croome D'Abitot, Earls Croome, Edvin Loach, Elmley Lovett, Halesowen, Hampton Lovett, Hanley Child (?), Hanley William, Temple Laughern, Brace's Leigh, Abbots or Ab Lench, Atch Lench, Rous Lench, Sheriffs Lench, Abbots Morton, Birtsmorton, Naunton Beauchamp, King's Norton, Park Attwood, Redmarley D'Abitot, Stoke Prior, Shelsley Beauchamp, Shelsley Walsh, Stoke Bliss, Upton Warren, Wick Episcopi.

MANORIAL NAMES

(i) *bury*-names: Sagebury.

(ii) *Possessive*-forms: Abbinton's Fm, Arundle's Fm, Bannall's Fm, Barnards Green, Barrett's Fm, The Blanquettes, Callows Fm, Cashes Fm, Chambers Ct, Durrance Fm, Earl's Ct, Farman's Ct, Gambolds, Goldness Fm, Goldsmiths Fm, Grimer's Fm, Gunnice, Holdings Fm, Larkins, Osmonds, Pickard's Fm, Powers, Raglis, Russell's Hall, Spellis Fm, Stretches, Terrills Fm, Tomkins, Tookeys Fm, Willett's Fm.

(iii) Forms without the possessive *s*: Beauchamp Ct, Froxmere Ct, Gumborn Fm, Hopton Ct.

(iv) Doubtful. Kidley's Fm, Oldyates Fm, Sevington Fm, Witnells End, Woolstan's Fm.

(v) Pseudo-manorial: *Coldnalls*, Colkett's Fm, Fernhalls Fm, Hill's Fm, Luckalls Fm, Moreton's Fm, Norgrovesend, Nurton's Fm, Rugg's Place, Sindon's Mill, Sintons End, Structon's Heath, Wesley's Fm, Wooton's Fm.

FIELD AND OTHER MINOR NAMES

In collecting material for the interpretation of the place-names (i.e. those found on the O.S. maps) a good deal of material has been gathered in the form of field and other minor names, especially those of boundary marks. It is impossible to deal with these exhaustively, first because they are too numerous, and secondly because many of them are without much interest, consisting largely of forms which are common in all field-names; further, it is but rarely that one has a succession of forms in an individual name such as is usually necessary if any satisfactory interpretation is to be attempted.

An analysis of these elements, with illustrations of their use, follows. Those elements that have been already fully illustrated in the major place-names are for the most part left unnoticed.

ærs, ears (n), *Oxan ers* (10th BCS, 1282), 'ox's arse.' This element is still fairly common in field-names, used generally of a rounded hill.

apulder, *Apperley* (1240), *bradan apoldre* (10th).

ME barbecane (n), loc. dict. *la Barbecane* (c. 1240) in Pershore (*AOMB* 61) carries this word further back than the NED.

ME berse (n). In Feckenham Forest we have *Bersa* (1230 P, 1262 *For*) and *la Berse* (1270 Ipm). These must be from an unrecorded ME *berse*. Ducange has a LL *bersa* for which he quotes from a charter of Hy 3 the phrase *intra bersas forestae*. He defines *bersa* as 'crates vimineae seu sepes ex palis contextis, quibus silvæ vel parci undique incinguntur, ut nullis cervis... ad egressum pateat aditus.' This must be the same as MLG *bersa*, *birsa*, 'pleached hedge' (Förstemann ON i. 431).

brycg. We may note *eorðbrycg* (10th, BCS 1023), *Eorthen-brugge* (14th), referring to bridges of earth or turves, *Troubrugge* (13th) to one of wood (*v.* treo), *Crukedebrugge* (13th), and *Standefast Brigge* (15th), presumably so narrow that there were frequent blocks in the traffic.

byht, *byht* (9th, BCS 542), *le Buyghte* (1419).

byrgen (n), 'burial place,' *Ealhmundes byrigenne* (11th, Heming 362).

bytme (n), 'bottom,' *le Byttemfeld*, *Betemefeld* (1456).

camp, *pullescamp* (8th, BCS 219).

ME clere, 'glade.' Evidence for this word was given *s.n.* Clearfields (PN Bk 119). It is found again in Hanley Castle in the 16th cent. as the name of a wood, viz. *Cleres*.

croft is common. We may note *Horsacroft* (10th, BCS 1139), *Grascroft* (13th), *Ruscroft* (1240), i.e. rush-croft, *Heth-*, *Whet-*, *Pery-croft* (1472), with heath, wheat and pear-tree, *Bencroft* (1182), with beans, *Salecroft* (1275), with willows (*v.* sealh), *Nettelcroft* (1408), *Bollucus Croft* (1373), i.e. bullock's, *Sparwe-croft* (c. 1250), *Menecroft* (Hy 3) with the element *mene* noticed under Menithwood *supra* 58.

EE

dingle (n), *la Dingle* (1275 SR) and *la Dyngle* (1299 *RBB*) add two more examples of this very rare word denoting a hollow or valley, *v.* NED *s.v.*

dor, *heandore* (10th, BCS 1282), *heador* (11th, Heming 362).

dræg. A new compound of this word has been noted in a 'saltpan called in English *Draiburne*' (c. 1150) in *WoC* 21. This may help ultimately to throw light on this difficult element (cf. EPN *s.v.*).

edisc, *Wynburhedisc* (10th, BCS 1282), *bradan edisc* (9th, BCS 349).

efn (n), 'level,' is found in *Euneberghe* (1304) and *efna lea* (Heming 356).

ME fallinge (n). In 1349 (LyttCh) we have *le Vallyng* which seems to be the Midland equivalent of *The Felling* as noted in PN NbDu 84. It is possible that we have an earlier form of this in the word *fælinge* in BCS 455. It denotes a place where trees have been felled.

flint (n), 'flint, rock,' *Flinthulle* (c. 1200).

ME grepe (n), meaning 'trench, ditch,' is found in *le Greep de la Dene* in AD vi (1334).

haga, *kyningeshaga* (9th, BCS 462), *le Hawe* (1299), *wulfhaga* (BCS 1282).

hamstede. There is one example in *hamstude* (1301) in Halesowen.

hangra. We have one example of the very common compound of this element and clæg in *Clehungere* (1299).

hemm (n). In the Halesowen Court Rolls we have in the 13th cent. pers. names *de Hem*, *de la Heme*, *in le Hem*, *ythehem*, which point to the use of the word *hem* to denote edge or border of a piece of country, cf. the *holte hemmes* in the quotation from the *Morte Arthur* in NED *s.v.*

hielde. Two examples have been noted in the form *le Helde* (13th, 1408). Note also *Kekeshelde* (c. 1220).

hryding is common in field-names.

ingaham. Though there are no examples of this element in Wo place-names that have survived, we may note among field-

names *Hunulingham* or *Humelingeham* (WoP, *WoC*) in the
13th cent. in Broadwas, *Badmingham* or *Bodmingeham*, *Dering-
ham* (WoP) from the same time and *Bedelingeham* in *RBB* (1299).

læs, *Somerleswe* (1316), *Oxonleese* (15th), *Oxlese* (1408),
Calverneleasowe (16th).

land is very common. The first element may denote the state
of cultivation as in *mæðland*, 'land for mowing' (BCS 362),
earðland (ib.) or *erthelond* (13th), 'ploughing-land,' the crop
that grows on it as in *Poeselond* (1326), *wadlond* (BCS 356),
'woad-land.' Reference is made to the animals on it in *henne-
lond* (1408), *culand* (1299). There is one case of the difficult
banlond (1326) discussed under Bandland (PN Bk 23).

ME leyne (n). In 1327 (Pat) we have a field-name *la Leyne*
in Dudley which seems to be another example of the obscure
word noted under *lain, leyne* in the NED, denoting a 'layer,'
but not hitherto recorded of a layer of soil until the 16th cent.

myln. *Frogmulle* and *Froggemulle* are found in Worcester and
in Frankley in 1408 and 1373, *Stewemulne* (13th), 'mill by the
stew-pond' in St Johns. We have a *Pukemulle*, 'goblin-mill'
(1255), in Dodderhill and a *Lyther mill* (14th), 'bad mill,' in
Cotheridge.

ofesc (n). In BCS 462 we have *be þære alra ofesce* (repeated
in BCS 1139). Middendorff (*s.n.*) takes this to be the same as
ME *ouese, ouise*, Somerset Dial. *ovvis* from a variant of OE *efes*,
'edge,' 'eaves,' so that the whole phrase means 'along the edge
of the alders.' The correct form would be *ofes* rather than *ofesc*.
v. NED *s.v.* eaves.

pearroc, as used of a small enclosure, is found in *le Parrock*
(1381), *Malkinsparrok* (1455), *Stoniepirruch* (sic) (c. 1300).

ME pewite (n). *Pewytelowe* in Cleeve Prior from a 13th cent.
document quoted in VCH iii. 309 carries the history of the
bird-name *pewit* some 200 or 300 years earlier than the forms
in the NED.

pytt. Among the compounds of this word we may note
þyrspyt (BCS 537), 'giant-pit,' *Poukeput* (1408), 'goblin-pit,'
horpytt (BCS 1243), 'dirty pit,' *lampytt* (Heming 246), 'loam-
pit,' *marleput* (14th), 'marl-pit.'

ME queche (n). In the Halesowen Ct Rolls (1307) we have *la queche*, 'thicket,' carrying back this word 150 years earlier than the earliest form in the NED.

sceaga is curiously rare in this county. We may note *Alresawe*, 'aldershaw,' in Yardley (1240), *Gorssawe* (p), 'dirty wood,' in King's Norton (1275), *Grenesawe* in Fladbury (1299).

seað does not seem to have survived in any Wo place-name, but we may note the compounds found in OE charters from this county, viz. *lamseað, sandseað*, referring to pits from which loam and sand were taken, *wulfseað*, 'pit in which wolves were snared,' *ducanseað*, 'duck-pit,' i.e. where they swam, and *mor-seað*, 'marshy pit' (BCS 183, 542, 1282, KCD 683).

sidling (n), 'sideways, oblique, inclined to one side,' found in *sidlingweg* (BCS 957) has also been noted in *Sidlinghull* near Pershore (13th, *AOMB* 61).

sihtra (n), 'water-course,' is found in BCS 233 and 361. In the former it is synonymous with sic. The word does not seem to be found later in Wo. Middendorff (116) quotes the interesting parallel of East Frisian *sichter*, used of a small channel of water.

sol. Twice we have this element compounded with heorot (BCS 204, 455), referring to a wallowing-place for stags. We also have a *Blakesole* in Halesowen (1272).

ME sperte (n). In Hadzor in 1249 (*FF*) we have *Spert*, in Worcester in 1334 (*Bodl* 71), *la Sperte*, in Bromsgrove in 1280 (*For*) *Spretemede* (sic) and *Spertmeadow* in Bredicot (1649). These, like Spurt St (PN Bk 158), carry back *spirt*, meaning 'jet of water,' for here it clearly denotes a spring, some 500 years earlier than the earliest recorded use of the word in the NED.

strod is found in *secglages strod* (BCS 1282) in the bounds of Powick.

stycc (n), 'piece of land,' in *cattes stycc* (BCS 356) in Hallow.

styfecung (n). In BCS 542, 1208 we have *styfecing, styfecinc*. This must be for earlier *styfecung* the noun denoting action which is derived from OE *styfecian*, 'to clear of stumps,' and so denote a clearing in a wood (*v.* styfic).

ME tininge (n). In the 1649 Survey we have *tining* (*v.* NED) in field-names in Bredicot and in Broadwas. It denotes a hedged enclosure.

weg. Of compounds with *way* we may note in BCS 1282 *bradan wænweg*, 'broad-waggonway,' *Muleweye* (Hy 3), probably 'millway' (ME *mulne*), *scomeleswey* (13th), 'road to the shambles,' *Sakereswei* (c. 1200), 'robber's way,' from OE *scēacere*, *gerdweg* (BCS 1242), for which *v.* Yardley *supra* 231, *Twyseleweg* (1275), 'forked road,' *Wynterwey* (14th), *Dryuyngwey* (c. 1300) and *syllweg* (BCS 219), 'road made of baulks of timber' (OE *syll*). Cf. *sylbeam* (BCS 1282).

wic. There is a lost *Elliswyche*, *Eleswych* in the SR of 1275, mentioned in connexion with one John *Elys*, which suggests that the suffix *wic* was still a living element in the 13th cent.

wielle (Anglian *wælle*). We have reference to the soil by the spring or stream in *clægwyllan* (BCS 1282), *Sondwalle* (1275), to the animals which frequent it in *wolfwelle* (1299), *derewalle* (13th), *bulan wyllan* (BCS 1282), to the plants growing by or in it in *reodwellan* (BCS 183) or *le Redewall* (1373), *bromwall* (13th), to its hidden character in *Dernwell* (1240, 13th) (*v.* dierne) beside other more common and obvious compounds. *Sponwælle* (BCS 356) with the first element spon, 'chip, shaving,' is more difficult.

worðign. In the form *weorðing* it is found in BCS 455 in the phrase *inwiððan weorðing* in Cofton Hackett. As *Worthin* it is found in Lindridge in the 13th cent. It is found as part of pers. names in *de Worthine*, *atte Worthyne* (1276 SR). Compounds of it are found in *Bolewardyn* (i.e. bull-enclosure), 13th cent. and *Wodeworthin*, part of a pers. name in 1275. The word must have been in living use in the 13th cent. for in *WoC* (39 b) we have *worþinum Edredi* and *unum worþinum quod Adam f. Esberni tenet*. We may note also the series of *Wrthins* and half *Wrthins* in Droitwich (WoP 95 b). It clearly denoted little if anything more than a small close. *Worthing* is a 16th cent. field-name in Elmley Castle. worð is never thus used.

Among miscellaneous names we may note (i) a group descriptive of trees of various kinds. We have clumps of three and five oaks in *þreom ac* and *fifacan* (BCS 219, 356), a 'famous' oak in *mæranac* (BCS 1282), a tall oak in *þa langan æc* (BCS 1282), a rough oak in *rugan ac* (BCS 1088), a black oak in *blæcan æc* (BCS 1282), a boundary oak in *mærac* (BCS 204), an ivy-covered oak in *ifihtan ac* (BCS 204), a down-bent oak in *niðerbogenan ac* (KCD 765), a *crokede ac* (13th). We have also a *cyrstel mæl ac*, 'oak with a cross on it or by a cross' (BCS 204), cf. cristel mæl. We have a great and a crooked lime-tree in *greata lindan* (Heming), *wowlinde* (1262), a *greatan æspan* (BCS 219) or aspen-tree, a *bradan apoldre* and a *mærapeldran* denoting a broad and a 'boundary' apple-tree and a *hwitan biricean* (BCS 1264), a white birch-tree. (ii) References to vineyards in Gt Hampton, Pershore and Leigh in *Wynyearde* (1535), *Wynyarde* (1547), *Wynyȝard* (1338), and to a winter-pear tree in *Winter-pirye* (1182). (iii) References to places for games and sports in *Gomenhulle*, *Gamenhulle* (1299, 1408), *Pleistude* (1310), *le Pley plas* (1421).

Threferthendeles (AD iii) in a deed of 1312 carries back the word *farthingdeal*, 'fourth part of an acre' some 200 years earlier than the first quotation in the NED. *Calvestayles* (16th), *Goodwyvesfurlong* (1587), *Dewgore* (1408), *Clerkenbath* (1456), *Smocacre* (1240) are worth recording.

In OE charters we have *þeofa dene* (BCS 356), 'thieves' valley.'

Three references to heathen burial places have been noted, a *hæðenbeorgas*, 'heathen barrows,' in Bengeworth (KCD 1299) and *hæðenan byrig(g)else*, 'heathen burial place,' in Shipston (Heming 347), in Hallow (BCS 356).

PERSONAL-NAMES IN FIELD AND OTHER MINOR NAMES

Ægel	*Ægleslonan* (10th)
Ælfgār	*Algaresbrok* (1326)
Ælflǣd (f)	*Ælflæde brycge* (11th)
Ælfrīc	*Ælfrices gemære* (10th), *Alurichesdoun* (1299)
Ælfstān	*Ælfstanesbrycg* (9th)
Æþelflǣd (f)	*Æþelflæde stige* (10th)

Æþelhere	*Athelrescroft* (1316)
Æþelmund	*Æþelmundes gemære* (10th)
Æþelnōð	*Æþelnoðescroft* (9th)
Æþelsige	*Ethelsii clausum* (10th)
Æþelstān	*Æþelstanes graf* (10th)
Æþelweard	*Alwardeshull* (1311)
*Amma	*Ammanbroc* (10th)
Asbjörn (ON)	*Osebarneshulle* (1276), *Osbarnbuttes* (13th)
Babba	*Bahban fælinge* (9th), *Babbanbeorg* (10th)
*Babbel	*Babelesbeorgan* (10th)
Bacga	*Bacga slæd* (9th), *Baggeford* (1275)
Badda	*Baddanæsc* (11th)
Bealdrīc	*Baldrices gemære* (10th), *Baldricheswelle* (14th)
*Bearda	*Beardyncg ford* (10th)
Becca	*Beccan leahe* (10th)
*Bēdel	*Bedlynghamm* (1408)
Beonna	*Beonnan þorn* (9th)
Beorhtðrȳð (f)	*Bertrithestockyng* (1240)
Beornweald	*Beornwoldes sætan* (10th)
Beornwynn (f)	*Beornwynne dene* (10th)
*Bill(a)	*Bilincgbroc* (10th)
Brāda	*Bradingleage* (9th)
Brūnstān	*Brunstanespurye* (1229)
**Brutta	*Bruttangeat* (10th)
Budda	*Buddinc wican* (9th), *Buddanbroc* (10th)
*Butt(a)	*Buttingc graf* (8th)
*Byliga	*Byligan fenn* (10th)
*Byrna	*Byrnan scylf* (10th)
*Byrnhelm	*Byrnhelmes gemære* (9th)
*Carda	*Cardanstigele* (10th)
Cēnbeorht	*Coenberhtes græfe* (9th)
Cēola	*Ceolanheafdon* (10th)
Cēolfrið	*Ceolferðes mor* (9th)
*Cēolm	*Ceolmes gemære* (10th)
Cēolðrȳð (f)	*Ceoldryðe bece* (8th)
*Cetta	*Cettantreo* (8th)

Colling	*Collingeshull* (1299)
*Cott	*Cottesberwe* (1323)
Crēoda	*Creodan ac* (9th)
*Cugga	*Cuggan hyll* (10th)
Cunda	*Cundincg æceras* (10th)
Cūðrǣd	*Cuðredes treo* (9th)
*Cybbel	*Cyblesweorðig* (9th)
*Cȳli	*Cylesdene* (9th)
*Cylla	*Kyllanhrige* (8th)
**Cymede	*Cymedeshealh* (8th)
*Cymma	*Cymman leahe* (10th)
Cynehild (f)	*Cyneldeweorðe* (10th)
Cyneðegn	*Cyneðegnes gemære* (10th)
Cyneweard	*Kynewardesfeld* (13th)

*Dægheard	*Dagardingweg* (10th)
*Daga	*Daganoran* (11th)
Deneheard	*Dæneheardes hegeræwe* (9th)
Deneweald	*Denewaldincg homm* (10th)
Dēora	*Deringham* (1240)
Dēorhelm	*Deorelmesdic* (10th)
*Dyddi	*Dydincotan* (9th) '

*Eabba	*Eabbincg wylle* (9th)
Ēadhere	*Ederesbroc* (8th)
Ēadrēd	*Eadredesselde* (11th), *Eadredesfeld* (9th)
Ēadrīc	*Edrices ford* (9th)
Ēadweald	*Eadwoldincgleahe* (10th)
Ēadwine	*Edwyneshull* (1293)
Ēadwulf	*Eadulfi clausum* (11th)
Ealhheard	*Alcherdesford* (8th)
Ealhmund	*Ealhmundes byrigenne* (11th)
*Ealubeard	*Alebeardes ac* (10th)
*Eamba	*Eambanerne* (9th)
Earnweald	*Ernaldescroft* (1299)
Earnwīg	*Ernwislond* (1276)
Ecgbeorht	*Egcbyrhttige croft* (9th)
Eomǣr	*Eomeres medwa* (10th)

*Feolumǣr	*Fealamæres broc* (8th)
Frēawine	*Frewinispit* (1272)
*Fulgod	*Fulgodes mædland* (9th)

*Geofa	*Geofandene* (8th)
*Gīsla	*Gislan forda* (10th)
Glædwine	*Gladwynes parrock* (1304)
Gōdgiefu (f)	*Godivuwega* (c. 1220)
Gōding	*Godincges gemære* (9th)
*Grant(a)	*Grantesforlong* (13th)
Grawulf (OGer)	*Graulfeswik* (13th)
Grimbald (OGer)	*Grimbaldesmede* (13th)
Gūðmund	*Gouchmonesgrene* (12th)

*Hǣring	*Heringeshame* (1232)
Haraldr (ON)	*Haraldesfeld, Haroldeswelle* (1319)
Hēahstān	*Hehstanes pytt* (9th)
Heaðoburh (f)	*Heaðeburhe weorðyg* (10th)
Hemming	*Hemmingesik* (1232)
Hengest	*Hengesteshealh* (10th)
*Heoden	*Heodenes sceagan* (9th)
Herefrið	*Hereferðes maduan* (10th)
Hereweald	*Herewaldesmor* (1276)
Hereweard	*Herewardeslond* (1329)
Hoccà	*Hoccanstig* (10th)
*Hōd	*Hodes ac* (10th)
Hrólfr (ON)	*Rolvesfeld* (1324)
Hūnweald	*Hunwaldeleye* (13th)

Lamberd (OGer)	*Lamberdi campum* (10th)
Lēofcild	*Lofchildescroft* (c. 1220)
Lēofmann	*Leommanningweg* (10th)
Lēofric	*Leofrici finis* (10th), *Levericheshull* (1299)

*Meregeat	*Meriteslond* (1244)
Mūl	*Muleshlæw* (9th)

*Nægl	*Nælesbroc* (9th)

Oba	*Obantreow* (10th)
Ordgiefu (f)	*Ordivecroft* (1275)
*Ordrǣd	*Oredeshamm* (10th)
Ōsrīc	*Osricespull* (9th)
*Ōswynn (f)	*Oswynna bæc* (8th)

Pacga	*Paggeford* (1280)
*P(e)atta	*Pattelake* (1410)
*Pecg	*Pecgesford* (10th)
*Pedda	*Pedenhale* (13th)
Penda	*Pendiford* (1240)
Peohthūn	*Pehtunes triowan* (10th)
Pippa	*Pippanleah* (10th)
Porta	*Portan mære* (10th)
*Pott	*Potintun* (11th)

*Regenhere (OGer) *Reinnersstocking* (13th)

*Sǣbrond	*Sebrondescroft* (12th)
*Scobba	*Scobbestan* (10th)
Scotta	*Scottan pæð* (10th)
*Scytta	*Scyttanfen* (10th)
Sigemund	*Simondesacre* (12th)
Sigeðrȳð	*Siðryðe wellan* (8th)
Sigeweard	*Sewardeshull* (14th)
Sīðweald	*Sethwaldesfeld* (13th)
Snell (OE, ON)	*Snelleslie* (1294)
**Steorfa	*Steorfanhalh* (10th), *Stervenhale* (1299)
Strēon(a)	*Streonenhealh* (10th), *Streonesheal* (11th)
Sveinn (ON)	*Sweynesfeld* (1319)

*Tad(d)a	*Taddelone* (13th)
*Tæccel	*Teclesmor* (10th)
*Tēobba	*Tebbeleye* (13th)
*Teoloweald	*Teolowaldingcoto* (9th)
Þēodgiefu (f)	*Thudgiuecroft* (1275)
*Þēofeca	*þeofecan hyl* (10th)
Þórketill (ON)	*Thorkellesfeld* (c. 1300)
Þórsteinn (ON)	*Thurstanecroft* (1299)

Þórúlfr (ON)	*Thurulfi viam* (10th)
Tilðegn	*Tilðegnes triowan* (10th)
*Titta	*Tittandun* (10th), *Tittenhalh* (10th)
Tucca	*Tuckenhale* (1297)
Tudda	*Tuddanham* (9th)
*Tuddel	*Tuddeles þorn* (9th)
*Turtla	*Turtlincgford* (10th)
*Tȳda	*Tydanlegh* (10th)
Uffa	*Uffanheales* (8th), *Uffanleage* (9th)
Wǣrburh (f)	*Wærburgerod* (9th)
Wǣrlāf	*Wærlafesdun* (10th)
Wǣrmund	*Wermundesern* (9th), *Wermundingford* (10th)
Waubert (OGer)	*Wauberdescroft* (1255)
Wealhhere	*Wallersrudyng* (13th)
Wicga	*Wyggeleye* (1182)
Wīgbeald	*Wyboldeshale* (c. 1250)
Wīgferð	*Wiferðes mæduan* (10th)
*Wīggār	*Wigarescroft* (1255)
Wīgstān	*Wistanesbricge* (11th)
Wilheard	*Wylheardestrie* (9th)
**Wīma	*Wimyncg wyllan* (11th)
Wine	*Wyneswyrðe* (8th), *Winesbrycg* (10th)
*Wiðergēat	*Widerieteswei* (c. 1205)
Wulfgār	*Wulfgares gemære* (11th)
Wulfgiefu (f)	*Wlfgiuegrave* (c. 1200)
Wulfrīc	*Wulfrices gemære* (11th)
Wulfsige	*Wulfsigescroft* (10th), *Wulsiefurlong* (1314)
Wynburh (f)	*Wynburhedisc* (10th)
Wynsige	*Wynsiesmede* (1314)
Witel	*Wytlesleage* (10th)

INDEX

OF PLACE-NAMES IN WORCESTERSHIRE
INCLUDING THOSE ONCE IN WORCESTERSHIRE
BUT NOW IN OTHER COUNTIES

The primary reference to a place is marked by the use of clarendon type.

Abberley, 23
Abberton, 184
Abbinton's Fm, 179
Abbots Lench, v. Lench, Abbots
Abbots Morton, v. Morton, Abbots
Acock's Green, 232
Acton (Elmley Lovett), 240
Acton (Ombersley), 269
Acton Beauchamp (He), 25, 43
Acton Green (He), 26
Addis Fm, 291
Aggberrow Wood, 208, 210
Aggborough, 210, 248
Aggborough Fm (Kidderminster), 248
Alcott Fm, 333
Alderminster, 184
Aldington, 260
Alfreds Well, 337
Alfrick, 28, 140
Allesborough Hill, 217
Alstone (Gl), 88
Alton Lodge, 70
Alvechurch, 332
Amblecote (St), 309
Ambrose Fm, 89
Ankerdine Hill, 46
Apple Cross, 56
Areley Kings, 29, 30
Arley, Upper, 29, 30
Armscott, 172
Arrow, R., 9, 333
Arrowfield Top, 333
Arundle's Fm, 180
Asham Common, 188
Ashborough, 337
Ashmoor Common, 145
Ashridge, 243
Astley, 33
Aston Court (Knighton-on-Teme), 53
Aston Fields (Stoke Prior), 359
Aston Magna (Blockley), 98
Aston, White Ladies, 88
Astwood (Claines), 110
Astwood (Dodderhill), 281

Astwood Court (Feckenham), 318
Astwood Hill (Chaddesley Corbett), 235
Atchen Hill, 90
Atch Lench, v. Lench, Atch
Atterburn Brook, 110
Austcliff, 257
Avon, R., 9
Axborough Fm, 257
Ayngstree Fm, 43

Baddington Mill, 359
Badge Court, 312
Badsey, 260
Bagburrow Wood (He), 66
Baldenhall, 210
Ballhill Cottages, 241
Ball Mill, 141
Balsall Heath, 351, 365
Balsford Hall, 187
Banbury Stone, xxi, 196
Bannall's Fm, 56
Barbourne, 110
Barham, 169
Barley House, 141
Barnards Green, 211
Barneshall Fm, 162
Barnets, The, 37, 83
Barnhall Fm, 269
Barn Hill Coppice, 185
Barnsleyhall Fm, 338
Barnt Green, 338
Barrett's Fm, 70
Barrow Hill, 235
Bartley Green, 348
Barton, 205
Bastenhall, xxiii, 82
Bastonford, 224
Bastwood, 48, 77, 141
Batch, 67
Batchley, 365
Battenhall Fms, 162
Baughton, 119
Baughton Hill, 119
Baynhall, 145
Bayton, 38, 145

Baywell Wood, 121, 145
Beanhall Fms, 318
Beauchamp Court, 224
Becknor, 318
Bedcote Mill, 309
Bedwardine, 89
Beehive Coppice, 79
Belbroughton, 9, 274
Bell End, Hall, Heath and Mill, 274
Bell, R., 9
Bellington Fm, 235
Bengeworth, 95, 144
Benstoken Coppice, 205
Bentley Fm (Holt), 141, 366
Bentley Pauncefote, 366
Beoley, 186
Berr Ends, 156
Berrington Green, 83
Berrow (Oswaldslow Hund.), 96
Berrow Hill (Feckenham), 318
Berrow Hill and Green (Martley), 63
Besford, 187
Bevere Island, 111
Bevington Waste, 331
Bewdley, 40, 186
Bickley, 53
Biert, 322
Bilford, 111
Billesley Fm, 232
Binholme, 217
Birchall Green, 127
Birchend Fm (Bedwardine), 90
Birchend Fm (Wichenford), 180
Birchen Grove, 90
Birches, Little (Bockleton), 41
Birches, The (Yardley), 232
Birch Fm (Severn Stoke), 227
Birch Fm (Shelsley Beauchamp), 77
Birchfields Lane (Oldbury), 299
Birchley Fm, 41
Birlingham, 188
Birtsmorton, 213
Bishampton, 97
Bittell Fm, 333
Blackenhurst Hundred, 17
Blackford Mill, 156
Blackgrave Fm, 351
Blackmore Park, 202
Blackpit Lane, 136
Blackstone, 248
Blackwell (Tredington), 172
Blackwell Fm (Tardebigge), 362
Blakeley Hall (Oldbury), 299
Blakemore Fm, 70

Blakeshall, 257
Blanquettes, The, 111
Blaythorn Fm, 218
Blockley, 98
Bluntington, 236
Bockleton, 41
Body Brook, 9
Bone Hill, 338
Bordesley, 365
Boreley, 269
Bossil Wood, 142
Bosworth's Fm, 224
Botany Bay 151
Boughton Park, 90
Bournbrook (K. Norton), 351
Bourne Bank, Fm and Brook (Defford), 194
Bournes Dingle, 269
Bouts, xxiv, 111, 325
Bow Brook, 10, 135, 143, 167, 293
Bower, 30, 70
Bowercourt Fm, 70
Boycott Fm, 303
Brace's Leigh, *v.* Leigh, Brace's
Bradford (Eldersfield), 197
Bradford Ho and Bridge (Chaddesley), 236
Bradley (Stock and), 166
Brand Hall, 303
Brandwood End, 351
Bran Mill, 98
Bransford, 189
Branthill Fm, 275
Breach, The, 297
Bredicot, 101
Bredon, 101
Bredon's Hardwick, *v.* Hardwick, Bredon's
Bredons Norton, *v.* Norton, Bredons
Bretforton, 261
Briar Mill, 287
Bricklehampton, 190, 195
Brickley, 322
Bridenbridge, 359
Bridley Moor, 365
Bristnall Hall, 303
Broad Common and Alley (Elmbridge), 291
Broad Green (Broadwas), 104
Broad Heath (Hanley Child), 51
Broadheath, Upper and Lower (Bedwardine), 90
Broadhidley Hall, 348
Broad Meadow, 352

Broadwas, 103, 352
Broadway, 191, 352
Brockamin, 205, 237
Brockencote, 236, 260
Brockhill (Shelsley Beauchamp), 77
Brockhill Fm (Beoley), 187
Brockhill Fm (Tardebigge), 187, 362
Brockhill Lane and Dingle (Alvechurch), 333
Bromley Fm, 30
Bromwich Wood, 348
Bromsgrove, xxii, 336
Brookend (Abberley), 24
Brook End (Kempsey), 145
Brook Fm (Bransford), 190
Brook Fm (Rock), 70
Brook Fm (Tenbury), 84
Brookhampton (Astley), 33
Brookhampton (Ombersley), 269
Brookhouse Fm, 281
Brookpatch Fm, 28
Broom, 278
Broomhall Fms, 145
Broom Hill (Belbroughton), 275
Broomhouse Fm, 360
Broughton, Drake's, 218
Broughton Fm, Temple, 322
Broughton Green (Hanbury), 322
Broughton Hackett, 192
Buckbury, 208
Buckle Street, 2
Bucknell Wood, 187
Buckridge, 71
Bullockhurst Fm, 71
Bungay Lake Fm, 338
Burcot, 338
Burf, The, 33
Burhill, 191
Burlish Common, 254
Burnford, 339
Burton Court, 75
Bury Court and Mill (Redmarley), 156
Buryendbush Fm, 180
Buryend Town, 180
Buryfield, 174
Bushley, 104
Busk Coppice, 79
Buttfield, 43

Caddecroft Fm, 218
Cainey, 53
Cakebole, xxiv, 236, 293
Cakemore, 293

Calcott Hill, 280
Caldewell (Pershore), 218
Caldwall Hall, 248
Callans Wood, 218
Callow End, 224
Callow Hill (Eastham), 48
Callow Hill (Feckenham), 48, 318
Callows Fm, 241
Calvecroft, 221
Came Hundred, 332
Careless Green, 310
Carpenter's Fm, 157
Carrant Brook, 10
Carter's Lane, 298
Carton Fm, 38
Cashes Fm, 291
Caspidge Fm, 360
Castle Green (Leigh), 205
Castle Lane (Warley Salop), 302
Catshill, 339
Caunsall, 257
Cellers Grove, 104
Chaceley, xx, 192
Chaceley Stock, 193
Chadbury, 265
Chaddesley Corbett, xxiii, 193, 234, 248
Chaddesley Wood, 237
Chadwich Fm (Bromsgrove), 339
Chadwick (Hartlebury), 235, 243
Chambers Court, 208
Charford, 340
Charlton (Oswaldslow Hund.), 105
Charlton (Hartlebury), 243
Chase End, 96, 214
Chatley, 269
Chauson, 307
Cherkenhill Fm, 205
Cherry Orchard, 162
Cheveridge Fm, 51
Chevington Fm, xxi, 219
Chind, R., 10
Churches Fm, 157
Churchill (Clent Hund.), 278
Churchill (Oswaldslow Hund.), 106, 278
Churchill Wood, 109
Church Lench, *v.* Lench, Church
Chyndhouse, 10, 352
Cinders Wood and Mill, 84, 175
Cladswell, 152, 325
Claines, 110
Clattsmore, 152
Claybrook Barn, 71
Cleeve House (Pendock), 154

Cleeve Prior, 154, 314
Clent, xxiv, 279
Clent Hundred, 274
Clerkenleap, 145
Clethale, 313
Clethill, 54
Clevelode, 224
Cliffey Wood and Fm, 202
Clifton (Severn Stoke), 224, 227
Clifton Arles, 228
Clifton-on-Teme, 43
Clopton, 91
Clows Top, 39
Cobhouse Fm, 180
Cobley Hill, 340, 362
Cockshoot Fm (Wichenford), 180, 293
Cockshot (Cakemore), 293
Cofton Hackett, 346
Cofton Richards Fm, 346
Cold Grove and Place, 82
Cold Hill, 46
Coldnalls, 319
Coldridge Wood, 30
Cole, R., 10
Coles Green, 82, 206
Colewick, 91, 225
Colkett's Fm, 181
Collett's Green, 225, 325
Colley Pit, 281
Colman Hill, 294
Colmers Fm, 352
Comberton, Great and Little, 193
Comberton Aits, 194
Comberton Fm (Kidderminster), 249
Comble, 340
Comer Gardens, 91
Comhampton, 269
Commandry Fm, 316
Conderton, xix, 115
Conningswick Fm, 71
Cook Hill, 326
Cookley, xxiii, 258
Cooksey Green, 312
Cooks House, 79
Coombe Fm (Alderminster), 185
Coombeswood, The Coombes (Hill in Halesowen), 296
Copcut, 308
Coppins Court, 194
Corn Brook, 10, 54
Cornwood, 10, 54
Corse Lawn, 197, 227
Cotheridge, 116, 121

Cotswolds, The, 1, 121
Cotteridge, 352
Cowleigh Park, 206
Cowsden, 230
Crabbs Cross, 319
Cradley, 294
Craycombe Hill, 126
Cresselau Hundred, 234
Cromer Fm, 198
Cromer Green, 154
Crookbarrow Hill, 108, 178
Croome d'Abitot, 119
Croome Perry Wood, 223
Croome, Earls, 118
Croome, Hill, 118
Cropthorne, 119
Cross, The (Ombersley), 269
Crossway Green, 243
Crowfields Fm, 340
Crowle, 175, 205, 315
Crowneast Court, 39, 91
Cruise Hill (He), 26, 243, 269
Crump Field, 319
Crundall Coppice, 58
Crundelend Fms, 24
Crutch, 280
Cudley Court, 160
Culverness Ho, 39
Cumberwood (Gl), 193
Cutmill, 91
Cutnall Green, 241
Cutpursey Coppice, 313
Cutsdean, 120, 241

Dadsley Barn, 231
Dales Wood, 301
Darlingscott, 173
Dauncies, 177
Daws Hill, 225
Daylesford, 121
Dean Brook, 136
Dean's Wood, 270
Deaseland Fm, 71
Debdale Fm, 258
Deerfold Wood, 219
Defford, 194
Deptcroft, 54
Diglis Locks, 162, 289
Dines Green, 92
Ditchford (Blockley), 3, 98
Ditchford Bank (Hanbury), 322
Doddenham, 23, 46
Doddenhill Fms, 58
Dodderhill, xxiii, 281
Doddingtree Hundred, 23, 46, 58, 86

Dodford, 340
Doleham Bridge, 79
Dordale, 275
Dorhall Fm, 237
Dormston, 195
Dorn, 99
Doverdale, 239
Dowles, 47
Dowles Brook, 10
Drakelow, 258
Drake's Broughton, v. Broughton, Drake's
Draycott (Blockley), 99, 145
Draycott (Kempsey), 145
Drayton (Chaddesley), 237
Drinkers-end, 198
Drinkwater's Fm, 208
Droitwich, 285
Droitwich street-names, 285 n.
Dudley, 289
Dunclent Fm, 255
Dunhampstead, 136
Dunhampton, 270
Dunley, 29
Durrance Fm, 313
Dyers, 340

Eachway, 341
Eardiston, 58
Earl's Common, 136
Earl's Court, 92
Earls Croome, v. Croome, Earls
Easemore Fm, 365
Easerfield Coppice, 56
Easinghope Fm, 47
Eastbury Manor, xxi, 129
Eastham 48
Eastington Hall, 209
Eckington, 47, 195
Edgiock, 326
Edvin Loach (He), 49
Elbury Hill, 111
Eldersfield, 197
Elmbridge, 290
Elmley Castle, 122
Elmley Lovett, 122, 240
Elms, The (Hallow), 131
Elms, The (St Johns), 92
Emmots, 153
Ennick, R., 11
Ennick Ford, 222
Erse, R., 11, 179
Ersfield Fm, 179
Esch Hundred, 314
Evelench Fm, 170

Evenlode, 123, 238
Evenlode, R., 11, 123
Evesham, 123, 171, 262
Evesham street-names, 262 n.
Eymore Wood, 249

Fairfield, 275
Falsam Pits, 287
Farley (He), 66
Farley Wood, Great, 301
Farman's Court, 71
Farmons, 353
Faulk Mill, 267
Feckenham, 317
Felgate, 241
Fenn Fm, 276
Fenny Rough, 237
Fepsinton, 137
Fernhalls Fm, 71
Fernhill Heath, 111
Fibden Fm, 304
Fickenappletree, 305
Field Fm (Abberley), 24
Field Fm (Knighton-on-Teme), 54
Fieldhouse Fm, 72
Fieldy Fm, 131
Finstall, 360
Fishborough Hundred, 18, 260
Fladbury, xxi, 126
Flint's Dingle, 57
Flyford Flavell, 199
Fockbury Ho, 341
Foleys Wood, 153
Ford Fm (Dodderhill), 281
Ford Mill (Feckenham), 319
Foredraught Lane, 136
Forhill, 203, 276, 333
Forty Green (Hanley Castle), 202, 276
Forty Green (Redmarley), 202, 276
Fosse Way, 3, 99
Four Shire Stone, 124
Foxbatch, 104
Foxcote, 306
Fox Hollies Hall, 232
Foxlydiate, 364
Franche, 249
Frankley, 346
Frankley Hill, 347
Freebodies, 289
Frith Fm, 84
Frogmill Fm, 347
Froxmere Court, 317
Fullhams, The, 51
Furnace Fm, 79

Gadbury Bank, 198
Gadfield Elm, 198
Gambolds, Upper and Lower, 360
Gannow Fm and Wood (Inkberrow), 327, 341
Gannow Green and Fm (Bromsgrove), 327, 341
Gardner's Grove, 270
Garmsley and Garmsley Camp, 80
Gatley, 43, 185
Genners Fm, 348
Gettes Ashbed, 42
Gilbert's End, 204
Gilton Brook, 287
Gladder Brook, 11
Glasshampton, 34
Glazen Bridge, 34
Gleden Brook, 11
Glynch Brook, 11
Goldenwick, 92, 95, 124
Goldicote Ho, 185
Goldness Ho, 243
Goldsmiths Fm, 241
Good's Green, 30
Goosehill Green, 323
Gorcott Hill, 187
Gorse Fm (Belbroughton), 276
Gorse Hill (Bromsgrove), 342
Gorst Hill (Rock), 72
Gorsty Hill (Hill in Halesowen) 296
Gosford, 288
Grafton (Bockleton), 42
Grafton Flyford, 200
Grafton Manor (Came Hund.), 347
Grange, The (Hunnington), 297
Greenhill Fm, 131
Greenstreet Fm, 3, 131
Greet, 232
Greethurst, 233
Grimer's Fm, 157
Grimes Hill, 353
Grimley (Oswaldslow Hund.), 126, 131, 353, 360
Grimley Brook, 11, 141
Grimley Hall (Stoke Prior), 360
Grimpits Fm, 353
Grove Hill, 82
Grovely Ho, 346
Guarlford, 211
Guildings Fm, 249
Gumborn Fm, 127
Gunnice, 209
Gurnox, 43, 47

Habberley, 249

Hackney, 274
Hadley (Ombersley), 270
Hadzor, 291
Hagley, 292
Hagtree Fm (He), 26
Halesowen, 293
Halesowen street-names, 293 n.
Halfridge Fm (He), 26, 142
Halfshire, 17
Hall Court (Bredons Norton), 152
Hall Fm (Bransford), 190
Hall Fm, Upper (Hampton Lovett), 305
Hallow, 129
Hallow Heath, 132
Hamcastle Fm, 43
Ham Fm (Clifton), 44
Ham Green (Feckenham), 317, 319
Ham Green (Mathon) (He), 66
Hampton, Great and Little, 133, 157
Hampton Lovett, 303
Hanbury, 321
Hanley Castle, 201
Hanley Child, 50, 53
Hanley William, 51
Harborough Hill, 292
Hardwick, Bredon's, 101
Hardwick Green (Eldersfield), 198
Hardwick's Spring, 93
Harford Hill, 270
Harley, 219
Harman's Hill, 137
Harpley, 75
Hartle, 276
Hartlebury, 242
Harvington (Chaddesley), 237
Harvington (Oswaldslow Hund.), 134, 238
Harvington Hill (Oswaldslow Hund.) 134
Hasbury, 294
Haselor Ho, 106
Hatfield, 151
Hathitch Fm, 76
Hathouse Fm, 76
Hawbridge, 167
Hawford, 167, 270
Hawkbatch, 31
Hawker's Fm, 193
Hawkesley Hall, 353
Hawkley Fm, 67
Hawne Bank and Fm, 296
Hayes, The (Old Swinford), 310
Hayes Fm (Belbroughton), 276
Hayes Fm (Tenbury), 85

Hay Green (Northfield), 349
Hayley Green, 295
Hay Mills, 233
Hay Oak, 24
Hayswood Fm, 210
Hayway Fm, 191
Hazel Fm, 72
Hazelwell, 353
Headless Cross, 365
Headley Heath, 353
Heath, The (Bromsgrove), 342
Heath End Fm (Evenlode), 126
Heath Fm (Pensax), 67
Heathy Mill, 250
Heightington, 72
Hell Grange, 296
Helpridge Fm, 282
Henbrook, 282
Henwick, 132
Heriots Fm, 211
Hermitage Fm, 219
Hethelpit Cross and Gate, 227
Hewell Grange, 363
Hextons Fm, 31
Highfields Park, 295
High Oak Coppice, 68
Highter's Heath, 353
Higley Barn, 308
Hill (Halesowen), 296
Hill, The (Severn Stoke), 228
Hill and Moor, 135
Hill Copse (Stanford-on-Teme), 79
Hill Court (Grafton Flyford), 201
Hill Croome, v. Croome, Hill
Hillend (Chaceley), 193
Hillend Court (Castle Morton), 214
Hill End (Salwarpe), 308
Hill Fm (Belbroughton), 276
Hill Fm (Bockleton), 42
Hill Fm (Dodderhill), 282
Hill Fm (Doverdale), 240
Hill Fm (Eldersfield), 198
Hill Fm (Hallow), 132
Hill Fm (Rock), 72
Hill Fm (Stoke Prior), 361
Hillhampton, 52
Hillhouse (Upper Arley), 31
Hill Ho (Longdon), 209
Hillpool, 238
Hill's Fm (Hanley Castle), 204
Hilltop Fm, 85
Hillwood Fm, 49
Himble Brook, 10, 135
Himbleton, 135

Hindlip, 139
Hipsmoor Fm, 63
Hoarstone Fm (Kidderminster), 250
Hobden, 282
Hobro Fm, 258
Hockerills Fm, 49
Hockham's Fm, 63
Hockley Hill, 327
Holberrow Green (Inkberrow), 327
Holdfast Hall, 140
Holdings Fm, 146
Holford, 157
Hollands Mill, 44
Hollier's Fm, 292
Hollies Fm (Hunnington), 297
Hollin Fms (Rock), 72
Holling Fms (Martley), 42, 63
Holling's Hill (He), 66
Hollow Court, 323
Hollowfields Fm, 323
Hollybed Common, 68, 214
Holly Green, 158
Hollyhall, 289
Hollymoor, 354
Holly Wood (King's Norton), 354
Holt, 141
Holy Claines Fm, 111
Holyoake's Fm, 364
Holy Well, Holywell Lane and Fm (Bromsgrove), 342
Holywell (Hanley Child), 51
Honeybourne, Church, 264
Honeybrook, 12
Hoo Fm, Hoobrook, 250
Hook Barn (Ribbesford), 69
Hook Fm (Welland), 177
Hookey's Fm, 327
Hope Fm (Edvin Loach) (He), 50
Hopehouse Fm, 63
Hopton Court, 206
Hopwood, 333
Hornhill Wood, 137
Horns Hall, 342
Horsage Fm, 181
Horsebrook, 12
Horseley Hills Fm, 258
Horsham, 64
Horton Fms (Hampton Lovett), 305
Horwell, 228
Houndsfield Fm, 354
Howleygrange Fm, 298
Howsell, Upper and Lower, 206
Howsen, 117

Huddington, 142
Hull Fm, 57
Hundred Ho (Bromsgrove), 342
Hundred Ho (Great Witley), 23
Hungary Hill, 310
Hunnington, 297
Hunt End, 319
Huntingtrap Fm, 283
Huntingtree, 295
Hurcott, 250
Hursley Fm, 57
Hurst Fm (Belbroughton), 277
Hurst Fm (Holt), 142
Hurst Fm (Pershore), 220
Hurtlehill Fm, 73
Hyde Fm (Pershore), 220
Hyde Fm (Stoke Bliss), 81
Hyde Fm, South (He), 66
Hylton, 132

Iccomb, Church, 143
Icknield Street, 2
Ildeberg, 124
Illey, 297
Impney, 283
Indhouse Coppice, 44
Inkberrow, xxiii, 324
Inkberrow, Little, 328
Inkford (King's Norton), 354
Inkford Brook, 12, 354
Innerstone, 157, 192, 231, 241
Insetton, 277
Insoll, 231, 241
Ipplesborough Hill, 319
Isbourne, R., 12
Ismere House, 278

Jefferies' Fm, 366

Kempsey, 144
Kenelmstowe, 301
Kenswick, 147
Kersoe, 122
Kerswell Green, 146
Ketches Fm, 184
Kettles Wood, 347
Keybridge Fm, 290, 305
Keyses Fm, 214
Kidderminster, xxiii, 247
Kidderminster street-names, 248 *n.*
Kidley's Fm (He), 26
Kinchfords, 361
Kinefolka, 18
Kineton Green, 233
Kingesham, 93

Kings End (Powick), 225
Kingsford, 259
King's Green (Redmarley), 157
King's Green (Wichenford), 181
Kings Heath (King's Norton), 354
Kingshill Fm, 283
King's Norton, *v.* Norton, King's
King's Park (Feckenham), 319
Kingsuch, 354
King's Wood (Himbleton), 137
Kingswood (King's Norton), 354
Kington, 330
Kinnersley, 228
Kinsham, 102
Kitlands Coppice, 31
Knacker's Hole, 49
Knavenhill, 186
Knighton (Inkberrow), 328
Knighton-on-Teme, 52, 148, 328
Knightwick, 147
Knottenhill, 284, 302
Knottsall Lodge, 302
Knowle Hill (Bengeworth), 96
Kyre, Little, 56
Kyre Brook, 12
Kyre Magna, 55
Kyrewood, 85

Ladywood, 308
Langley (Halesowen), 299
Lapal, 298
Larford, 34
Larkborough, 262
Larkins, 64
Laughern, 93
Laughern, Temple, 94
Laughern Brook, 12
Lea Castle (Wolverley), 259
Leadon, R., 13
Lea End (Alvechurch), 334
Lea Green Fm (King's Norton), 334, 354
Lea Hall (Yardley), 233
Leapgate Cottage, 139, 243
Leather Bridge, 284
Leche, The, 319
Leigh, 204, 310
Leigh, Brace's, 190
Leigh Sinton, *v.* Sinton, Leigh
Lench, Abbots, 148
Lench, Atch, 330
Lench, Church, 330
Lench, Rous, 149
Lench, Sheriffs, 148, 265, 330
Lenchford Ferry, 270

Lenchwick (and Norton), 264
Leopard Grange, 161
Ley Fm (Strensham), 229
Ley Hill (Northfield), 349
Leys, The (He), 66
Libbery, 201
Lickey, 342
Lickhill Ho, 255
Lifford, 355
Lightwood (Cotheridge), 117, 302
Lightwoods Park (Warley Salop), 302
Limberrow Cottages, 215
Linacres Fm, 111
Lincomb, 244
Lindon, 57, 73
Lindon Hall (King's Norton), 355
Lindridge, 57
Lindsworth Fm, 279, 355, 359
Lineholt, 271
Link Common, 207
Linthurst, 343, 355
Littals, 44
Little Brook, 13
Little Kyre, v. Kyre, Little
Littleton, North, Middle and South 265
Lollaycross, 288
Longdon (Pershore Hund.), 173, 208
Longdon Fm (Tredington), 173, 208
Longdon Heath (Upton-on-Severn), 174
Longdon Hill (Bengeworth), 96
Longdon Marsh (Pershore Hund.), 209
Longmorehill Fm, 34
Lovells, The, 177
Lowe, The (Wolverley), 58, 259
Lowe Fm, The (Lindridge), 58
Lowesmoor, 112
Low Hill, 89
Luckalls Fm, 28
Luke's Coppice, 320
Lulsley, 59
Lutley, 298
Lyde Green, 294
Lydiate Lane, 295, 364
Lye (Old Swinford), 310

Madley Heath, 277
Madresfield, 209
Mail St, 44
Mallender's Cottage, 181

Malvern, Great, 210
Malvern, Little, 150
Malvern Link, 207
Mamble, 60
Mapnors, 148
Marbrook, 13
Marl Brook, 13
Marlcliff Hill, 314
Marsh Court (Eldersfield), 198
Marshend (Longdon in Pershore Hund.), 209
Marshes, The (Churchill in Oswaldslow Hund.), 109
Martin Hussingtree, 213
Martley, 62
Mary Brook, 13
Mathon (He), 65
Maybridge Closes, 143
Mayhouse Fm, 271
Maythorn, 55
Meadows Mill, 58
Mearse Fm, 328
Meneatt Fm, 77
Menithwood, 58, 205
Mere Brook, 13
Merecomb, 153
Mere Green and Hall, 323
Merriman's Hill, 112
Merrington, 241
Merry Brook, 13
Merstow Green, 263
Middleton Fm (Salwarpe), 308
Middleton Fm (Northfield), 349
Middlewich, 287
Mildenham Mill, 112
Miller's Court, 214
Minton, 49
Mitton (Bredon), 102
Mitton, Upper and Lower, 254
Moat Court, 212
Mogstocking, 229
Monk Wood, 127
Monyhull, 355
Moor End (Tibberton), 171
Moorend Cross (Mathon) (He), 66
Moorend Fm (Mamble), 60
Moor Fm, 59
Moor Green (King's Norton), 356
Moor Hall (Belbroughton), 277
Moorfields Fm (Clifton), 45
Moorlands, The (Hanbury), 323
Moors, The (Birlingham), 188
Moors Fm, Upper (Hartlebury), 244
Moor St (Northfield), 349

Moorways End, 323
Moreton's Fm, 102
Morton, Abbots, 331
Morton, Castle, 214
Morton Underhill, 328, 331
Morton Wood Fm (Abbots Morton) 331
Moseley (Grimley), 128
Moseley (King's Norton), 356
Moundsley Hall, 356
Mount, The (Hartlebury), 244
Mucklow Hill, 297
Mucknell Fm, 167
Munn's Green, 47
Murrell's End, 157
Mutlows, 178
Mythe, 220

Nafford, 188
Napleton, 146
Nash, The (Kempsey), 25, 146
Nash End (Upper Arley), 31
Nash End (Eldersfield), 199
Naunton (Ripple), 158
Naunton (Severn Stoke), 158, 228
Naunton Beauchamp, 158, 215, 228
Naunton, Sheriffs, 215
Neight Hill, 137
Netherend (Cradley), 294
Netherton (Dudley), 289
Netherton (Kidderminster), 251
Netherton (Oswaldslow Hund.), 150
Netherton Fm (Abberley), 24
Netherwich, 287
Newbold-on-Stour, 173
Newland (Pershore Hund.), 215
Newlands (Pershore), 220
Newlands.Fm (Norton-juxta-Kempsey), 151
Newnham, 55
Nimmings Fm (Cofton), 346
Nimmings Plantation (Clent), 280
Noak, The, 64
Nobury, Great and Little, 329
Noken Fm, 128
No Man's Land, 191
Norchard (Hartlebury), 244
Norchard Fms (Rock), 73, 244
Norcombe Wood, 99
Norgrove Court, 320
Norgrovesend Fm, 40
Northal, 228
Northampton, 271
Northend Fm, 204

Northfield, 348
North Hill, 212
Northingtown Fm, 128
Northwick (Claines), 113
Northwick Park (Blockley), 99
North Wood (Kidderminster), 251
Norton-and-Lenchwick, 264
Norton Fm (Suckley), 82
Norton-juxta-Kempsey, 151
Norton, Bredons, 151
Norton, King's, 350
Noverton (Stanford-on-Teme), 79
Noxons Fm, 104
Nunnery Wood, 161
Nurton's Fm, 25, 31, 73, 79

Oakalls, The, 361
Oakhall Green, 127, 128, 361
Oakhampton, 35
Oakley (Salwarpe), 308
Ockeridge Wood, 142
Oddingley, 152
Offenham, 266
Offerton Fm, 139
Offmoor Fm, 251
Oldberrow (Wa), 267
Oldbury (Halesowen), 299
Oldbury Fm (St Johns), 94
Oldenhill (Frankley), 347
Oldhall Fm (Rock), 73
Oldington Fm, 251
Oldnall Fm (Clent), 280
Oldnall Fm (Old Swinford), 310
Old Swinford, *v.* Swinford, Old
Oldwood Common, 85
Oldyates Fm, 25
Ombersley, xx, 268
Orleton, 67, 228, 280
Osmerley, 334
Osmonds, 271
Oswaldslow Hundred, 87
Otherton Fm, 117
Oughton Wells, 28
Over, 113
Overbury, 96, 153
Oxhall, 55, 76
Oxhey Fm, 105
Oxnall Fm, 55

Padstone, 344
Palmers Gate, 85
Pansington Fm, 244
Park Attwood, 251
Park Hall (Kidderminster), 252
Parkhall Fm (Hanbury), 323

Parret, R., 13
Partridge Fm, 132
Paxford, 100
Payford Bridge, 157
Peachley, 133
Peasebrook Fm, 192
Pedmore, xxii, 305
Pendock, 154
Pendock Moor, 154
Penn Hall, 68
Pensax, 67
Pensham, xxiii, 221, 256
Peopleton, xxii, 135, 216, 306
Pepper Wood, xxii, 277
Pepwell Fm, xxii, 245, 277, 306
Perdiswell Hall, 113
Perry Fm (Stoke Bliss), 81
Perry Hill (Warley Wigorn), 303
Perry Ho (Hartlebury), 245
Perry Wood (St Martins), 161
Perryford, 120
Pershore, 217
Pershore Hundred, 183
Pershore street-names, 217 *n.*
Pewtrice Fm, 215
Phepson, xviii, 137
Pickard's Fm, 32
Pickersleigh, 226
Pickersom, xxii, 266
Piddle, North, 222
Piddle, Wyre, 155
Piddle Brook, 14
Pigeon Lane, 153
Pinfields Wood, 334, 343
Pin's Green, 216
Pinton, 334
Pinvin, xxii, xxiii, 223
Pircote Grange, 311
Pirton, 223
Pitchcroft, 113
Pithouse, 148
Pitmaston Ho, 94
Pittensarys Fm, 94
Pixham, xxii, xxiii, 225, 235, 266, 281
Platt, 311
Playley Green, 158
Pleremore, 238
Poden, 264
Poislands, 313
Pole Elm, 226
Pool Brook (Gt Malvern), 212
Pool Cottage (Stoke Bliss), 81
Pool House (Astley), 35
Poolfields, 182
Poollands Fm, 245

Portefields Fm, 114
Portershill Fm, Porter's Mill, 114
Portsmouth, 217
Port Street, 3, 96
Portway Fm, 3
Powers, 271
Powick, 223
Press-meadow, 274.
Prickley Green, 64
Pridzor Wood, 284
Primsland, 288
Priors Court, 154
Priory Redding, *v.* Redding, Priory
Puck Hill, 324
Pudford Fm, 65
Pull Court, 105
Pulley, 309
Pursers Fm, 226
Purshull, 291
Puxton, 252
Pyehill Fm, 245
Pye Mill, 100

Queenhill, 155
Quinton, 42
Quinzehides, 87

Raddlebarn, 349
Radford (Rous Lench), 150
Radford Fm (Alvechurch), 335
Raglis, 364
Ramsden, 188
Rashwood, 284
Ravenshill Fm, 171
Rea, R. (Birmingham), 14
Rea, R. (Knighton-on-Teme), 14
Redding, Priory, 82
Reddings, The, 141
Redditch, 364
Redhall Fm (Broom), 278
Redhall Fm (Ridgeacre), 300
Red Hill (St Peters), 163
Redhill Fm (Hunnington), 297
Redmarley (Gt Witley), 86
Redmarley d'Abitot, 156
Rednal, 356
Redstone Rock, 35, 248
Redway, 332
Rhydd Covert (Kidderminster), 252
Rhydd Green (Gt Malvern), 212
Ribbesford, 68
Ridgeacre, 300
Ridge Way, 4
Ridon Ho, 106
Ripple, 158

Robert's End, 204
Rochford, 69
Rock, 69
Rock Moor, 73
Rodge Hill, 65
Rolles Orchard, 242
Romsley, 300
Romsley Hill, 301
Ronkswood, 161
Rous Lench, *v.* Lench, Rous
Rowney Green, 335
Rubery, 357
Rugg's Place, 182
Rumblesmore, 153
Rushock, 255, 326
Rushwick, 94
Russell's Hall, 290
Ryall, 158
Rye Fm and Street, 97
Ryelands Fm 242
Ryknild Street, 2, 284

Sagebury Fm, 285
St Clair's Barn, 25, 37
St Godwalds, 361
Saldon Wood, 138
Sale Green, 143
Saleway, 138
Salford Court, 45
Sallings Common, 42
Salop Bridge, 361
Saltways, 4, 14
Salwarpe, 306
Salwarpe, R., 14
Sandford, 229
Sandhills Fm, 335
Sandlin Fm, 207
Sankyn's Green, 79
Sapcott, 242
Sapey, Lower, 75
Sarn Hill Wood, 105
Saw Brook, 14
Saxon's Lode, 159
Seckley Wood, 32, 100
Sedgeberrow, 164
Seeley Brook, 14
Selly Oak, 349
Sevenhampton, 35
Severn, R., 14
Severn End, 204
Severn Stoke, *v.* Stoke, Severn
Sevington Fm, 27
Shakenhurst, 40, 126
Sharpway Gate, 361
Shatterford, 32

Sheenhill Fm, 266
Shell, 138
Shelsley Beauchamp, 76
Shelsley Kings, 77
Shelsley Walsh, 78, 125
Sheltwood Fm, 364
Shenstone, 256
Shepley Fms, 343
Sheriffs Lench, *v.* Lench, Sheriffs
Sheriffs Naunton, v. Naunton, Sheriffs
Shernal Green, 139
Sherrard's Green, 212
Sherridge Ho, 207
Shipston-on-Stour, 164
Shire Ditch, 212
Shortwood Fm, Great, 363
Shoulton, 133
Shrawley, 78
Shrawnell, 261
Shurnock, 320
Shurvenhill, 343
Shut Mill, 301
Sidemoor, 344
Sidnals, The, 363
Sillins, 320
Sindon's Mill, 82
Sinton (Grimley), 61, 83, 128
Sinton Fm (Ombersley), 83, 272
Sinton, Leigh, 207, 272
Sinton End, 207
Sintons End (Acton Beauchamp) (He), 27, 83
Smite Hill and Fm, 15, 140
Smite, R., 15, 140
Smithmoor Common, 118
Sneachill, 166
Snead Fm and Common, 74
Snig's End, 227
Snodsbury, Upton, 230
Sodington Hall, 60, 82, 83, 128, 207, 209
Solcum Fm, 259
Southall, 240
Southend Fm (Upton-on-Severn), 174
South Hyde Fm, *v.* Hyde Fm, South
Southley, 159
Southstone Rock, 79
Southwood, 77
Spadesbourne Brook, 344
Sparkbrook, 233
Sparrow Fields Fm, 161
Spellis Fm, 114
Spetchley, 165

Spilsbury Hill, 61
Splash Bridge, 85
Stakenbridge, 150
Stakenford Bridge, 150
Stambermill, 311
Stanbrook, 226
Stanford-on-Teme, 79
Stanley Wood (Crowle), 317
Stapenhill Fm, 100, 344
Staple Hill and Fm, 344
Staunton, 226
Stechford, 233
Stildon Manor, 74
Stirchley Street, 357
Stock-and-Bradley, 166
Stock Green and Wood (Inkberrow), 329
Stockton-on-Teme, 80
Stoke Bliss, 80
Stoke Prior, 359
Stoke, Severn, 227
Stone, 255
Stonebow, 167
Stonehall, 146
Stony Cross, 55
Stoulton, 166
Stour, R., 15
Stourbridge, 311
Stratford, 160
Strensham, xx, 229
Stretches, 51
Structon's Heath, 52
Sturt Coppice, 208
Suckley, 81
Suddington, 271
Sunderland, 175
Sutton (Tenbury), 85
Sutton Common and Fm (Kidderminster), 252
Swancote Fm, 238
Swan's Hill, 335
Swanshurst, 233
Swinesherd, 87–8, 161, 167
Swinford, Old, 309
Symondford Brook, 116
Syntley Fm, 36
Sytchampton, 272

Tagg Barn, 238
Tagwell Lane, 288
Talton Fm, 173
Tanwood, 238
Tapenhall Fm (Claines), 114, 272
Tapenhall Fm (Ombersley), 272
Tardebigge, 362

Teddington, 168, 299
Teme, R., 15
Temple Broughton Fm, v. Broughton, Temple
Temple Dingle, 79
Temple Laughern, v. Laughern, Temple
Tenbury, 83
Terrills Fm, 85
Tessall Fm, 357
Thicknall Fm, 280
Thorndon Fm, 220
Thorne, 329
Thorngrove, 128
Thornsgate, 40
Thrift, The, 366
Throckmorton, 169
Tibberton, 170
Tickenhill, 41
Tiddesley Wood, 222
Tidmington, 171
Tilesford Fm, 170
Tiltridge Fm, 174
Timberdine Fm, 163
Timberhanger, 344
Timberlake, 40
Tinfield, 245
Tinker's Fm, 350
Tirle Brook, 15
Tirle Mill, 15
Tirle Way, 15
Titford, 299
Titton, 245
Tolladine Fms, 114
Tomkins, 25
Tonge, 335
Tookeys Fm, 321
Torton, 246
Town House (He), 66
Trapnell Brook, 16
Tredington, 172, 362
Trench Lane and Wood, 143
Trimpley, 252
Trotshill, 175
Trundalls Wood, 69
Tutnall (Claines), 115
Tutnall (Tardebigge), 362, 363
Tuts Hill, 199
Twyford, 265
Tynsall, 363
Tyseley, 234
Tytchney, 272

Uckinghall, 160
Uffmoor Fm, 295

Underhill Fm, 97
Uphampton, 272
Upper Arley, v. Arley, Upper
Upper Hall Fm, v. Hall, Upper
Upper Moors Fm, v. Moors Fm, Upper
Upthorpe Fm, 186
Upton Fm (Elmley Lovett), 242
Upton Ho (Wolverley), 259
Upton-on-Severn, 174
Upton Snodsbury, 230
Upton Warren, 311
Upton Wold Fm, 101
Upwich, 287

Valentia Wood, 32

Wadborough, 220
Waddon Hill, 165
Walcot, 221
Walker's Heath, 357
Walkwood, 321
Wall House, 86
Walloxhall, 299
Walmspout Coppice (He), 67
Walton Fm (Elmley Lovett), 242, 280
Walton Hill, Ho and Pool (Clent), 280
Wannerton Fm, 253
Waresley, 246
Warley Salop, 302
Warley Wigorn, 302
Warndon, 175
Warridge Lodge, 348
Warshill Top Fm, 253
Warstock, 268, 357
Washbourne, Little (Gl), 79, 176
Wassel Grove (Hagley), 292
Wassell Wood (Kidderminster), 253, 292, 336
Wast Hills, 335
Waste Hill Wood, 79
Weatheroak Hill, 336
Webbhouse Fm, 324
Webb's Green, 298
Welland, 177
Wenferth, R., 16
Weoley Castle, 186, 350
Wesley's Fm, 301
Westfield Fm (Hanbury), 324
West Heath (King's Norton), 357
West Hills, v. Wast Hills
Westmancote, 103
West Meadow, 192

Weston Fm (Bockleton), 42
Westwood (in Clent Hundred), 313
Westwood Fm (Mamble), 61
Wheating Hill, 321
Whetty Fm, 345
White Ladies Aston, v. Aston, White Ladies
Whitford Bridge (Stoke Prior), 361
Whitford Hall (Bromsgrove), 345 358
Whitlinge, 246
Whitstones, 110, 115
Whitsun Brook, xix, 16
Whittington, 178
Whore Nap, 268
Wiburgestoke, 134
Wichenford, 179, 293
Wick by Pershore, 231
Wick Episcopi, 95
Wick, Lower and Upper, 95
Wickhamford, 273
Wilden, 247
Wildmoor (Belbroughton), 278
Willett's Fm, 74
Willingwick, 345
Wimburntree Hundred, 23, 87
Windhill Fm, 62
Windrush, R., 17
Winnall, 272
Winricks Wood, 62
Winterfold, 238
Winthill (He), 27
Witley, Great, 86
Witley, Little, 183
Witnells End, 33
Witton, 285, 289
Wollaston, 311
Wollescote, 311
Wolverley, 256
Wolverton, Upper and Lower, 168
Woodbury Hill, 86
Woodcock Hill, 350
Woodcote Green, 345
Woodend Fm, 182
Woodgates Green, 55
Wood Hall (Norton-juxta-Kempsey), 133, 151
Woodhall Fm (Hallow), 133
Woodhall Fms (Kempsey), 147
Woodhall Fm (Wichenford), 182
Woodhamcote (Chaddesley), 239
Woodhamcote (Wolverley), 260
Woodhampton Ho, 37
Woodhouse End Fm (Grafton Flyford), 201, 239

Wood House (Ombersley), 273
Woodhouse (Pensax), 68, 201, 239, 273
Woodhouse Fm (Upper Arley), 33, 201, 239
Woodhouse Fm (Chaddesley), 239
Woodmancote, 195
Woodmanton Fm, 45
Woodrow (Chaddesley), 239
Woodsfield, 226
Woodston Manor, 59
Woollashill, Woollas Hall, 196
Woolstan's Fm, 52
Wooton's Fm (Acton Beauchamp) (He), 27
Worcester, 1, 19
Worcester street-names, 21
Worcestershire, 1
Worcestershire Hundreds, 17
Wordley Fm, 37, 226
Worsley Fm, 37, 74, 302

Wrens Nest Hill (St), 290
Wribbenhall, 253
Wyats Copse, 182
Wychall Fm, 358
Wychbold, 285
Wychbury Hill, 293
Wyndbrook, 17, 177
Wyre Forest, 1, 20
Wyre Piddle, v. Piddle, Wyre
Wythall, 358
Wythwood Cottage, 358

Yardley, 231
Yardley Wood, 234
Yarhampton, 37
Yarnold Lane and Fm, 345
Yarringtons, 29
Yessel Fm, 106
Yieldingtree, 239
Youngs Fm (Ombersley), 273

INDEX

OF PLACE-NAMES IN COUNTIES OTHER THAN WORCESTERSHIRE

[References to place-names in Bk, Beds, Hu are not included as these have been fully dealt with in the volumes already issued upon the names of those counties.]

Abdon Burf (Sa), 33
Ab Kettleby (Lei), 149
Addlethorpe (L, Y), 58
Alciston (Sx), 88
Aldermaston (Berks), 185
Allacott (D), 333
Alston (So), 88
Alveley (Sa), 333
Alveston (Wa), 70, 168
Ambersham (Sx), 268
Ambrosden (O), 268
Amesbury (W), 268
Ampney, Down (Gl), 256
Ardley (O), 58
Arrow, R., (He), 9
Ashbrook (Gl), 145
Atcham (Sa), 90
Austerley (Y), 257
Austerson (Ch), 257
Aveley (Ess), 333

Badshaw Lane (Ha), 261
Baltington (Do), 187
Banwell (So), 56
Barnacle (Wa), 345
Barnetts Wood (Ha), 83
Barnettwood (Sr), 83
Barnet Wood (He), 83
Barnsley (Gl), 338
Barston (Wa), 224
Bartley (Ha), 348
Bartlow (C), 348
Basildon (Berks), 82
Bastwick (Nf), 82
Batcombe (So), 162
Batton (D), 162
Bayworth (Berks), 38
Belford (Nb), 236
Benham (Berks), 96
Bensington (O), xxi, 57, 196
Berrington (He), 84
Besford (Sa), 187
Beslow (Sa), 187
Bestnover (Sx), 48
Bestwall (Do), 48
Bibury (Gl), 38

Bisley (Gl), 97
Bladon (O), 11
Blawith Knott (La), 290
Bledington (Gl), 11
Blickling (Nf), 322
Bloxham (O), 98
Bloxholm (L), 98
Bloxwich (St), 98
Bloxworth (Do), 98
Blunt's Hall (Ess), 236
Boehill (D), 186
Bocking (Ess), 41
Bockleton (Sa), 41
Bonehill (St), 338
Bordesley (Wa), 365
Bowland Knotts (Y), 290
Boycott (Sa), 304
Boyland (Nf), 304
Boyton (W), 304
Boyton End (Sf), 304
Bozen Green (Herts), 365
Bradway (Db), 191
Breedon (Lei), 101
Brickworth (W), 190
Brighthampton (O), 190
Brightlingsea (Ess), 190
Brighton (Sx), 190
Broadway (Herts, So), 191
Brockhampton (Do, Gl, Ha, He, O), 33
Brookhampton (Sa, Wa), 33
Buckfast (D), 141
Bucklebury (Berks), 2
Burtle (So), 348

Cakeham al. Cackham (Sx), 236
Callingwood (St), 218
Cannings (W), 257
Cark (La), 38
Catshill (Sr), 339
Cavick (Nf), 236
Charingworth (Gl), 51
Chevington (Sr), 219
Chieveley (Berks), xxi, 219
Childerley (C), 50
Childwick (Herts), 50

Chirbury (Sa), 109
Chivenore (D), 219
Christon (So), 107
Churchdown (Gl), 109
Churchfield (Nth), 107, 109
Church Hill (So), 107
Churchill (D, O, So), 108
Cleeve, Bishop's (Gl), 314
Cloutsham Ball (So), 237
Clowes (K), 39
Cobham (K), 363
Cobley (Ha), 363
Codford (W), 117
Codnor (Db), 117
Coleshill (Wa), 10
Comberworth (L), 193
Cookbury (D), 312
Cookley (Sf), 312
Cooksland (St), 312
Cookworthy (D), 312
Cooling (K), 258
Copford (Ess), 308
Copley (So), 308
Copson (K), 308
Coreley (Sa), 54
Cornwood (D), 54
Coulston (W), 231
Cowdray (Sx), 73
Cowesfield (W), 231
Crapnell Fm (So), 106, 120
Creech (Do), 109
Creechbarrow Hill (So), 108
Creech St Michael (So), 107
Crichel (Do), 107
Crookham (Berks), 316
Crook Hill (Db), 108
Croom (Y), 316
Cropredy (O), 120
Croughton (Ch), 316
Crowhurst (Sx), 316
Crownest (Y), 91
Croydon (Sr), 316
Cruchfield (Berks), 109
Culham (O), 258
Cumberwood (Gl), 193
Cutcombe (So), 241
Cutslow (O), 241
Cutt Mill (O), 92
Cuxham (O), 312
Cuxton (K), 312

Dalch, R. (D), 47
Darmsden (Sf), 195
Dawlish (D), 47
Dinnington (Nb), 163

Dinton (W), 163
Dorchester (Do), 99
Dormers Well (Mx), 195
Dowlish (So), 47
Drakelow (Db), 258
Drockbridge (Ha), 170
Droxford (Ha), 222
Dulcote (So), 107

Ealing Bridge (Ess), 125
Earnley (Sx), 30
Earnshill (So), 30
East Wells (So), 48
Ebberston (Y), 184
Ebrington (Gl), 184
Eckington (Db, Sx), 195
Edington (Berks), 92
Edmondthorpe (Lei), 116
Edwinstowe (Nt), 222
Etchden (K), 90
Exton (Ha), 16, 116

Farwood (D), 276
Faulkland (So), 267
Fingay Hill (Y), 166
Fledborough (Nt), xxi, 126
Folkestone (K), 267
Fordon (Y), 276
Fore Wood (Sx), 276
Forty Fm (Mx), 203
Forty Hall (Mx), 202
Forwood (Wa), 276
Frankaborough (D), 347
Frankhill (D), 347
Frankton (Wa), 347
Frankton, English (Sa), 347
Freeford (St), 249
Fring (Nf), 249
Fullwich (Ch), 286
Furtho (Nth), 203, 276

Ganfield Hundred (Berks), 341
Gannah (He), 341
Gannow (La), 341
Garliford (D), 211
Gauze Brook (W), 198
Gilcote (So), 125
Gilmorton (Lei), 125
Glaisdale (Y), 34
Glazebrook (La), 34
Glazenwood (Ess), 34
Glendon (Nth), 43
Glenfield (Lei), 43
Greet, R. (Nt), 232
Grim's Dyke (W), 127

Guilden Morden (C), 125
Guilden Sutton (Ch), 125
Guiltcross Hundred (Nf), 125

Halam (Nt), 296
Hampton Lucy (Wa), 303
Harborough (Wa), 292
Harford (D), 134
Harpenden (Herts), 75
Harpford (D), 75
Harpley (Nf), 75
Harpsfield (Herts), 75
Harpsford (Sr), 75
Harpswell (L), 75
Harptree (So), 75
Hartlington (Y), 243
Haselor (Wa), 106
Haselour (St), 106
Hawkridge (Berks, K, Sx), 26
Hazelbury (W), 294
Henbury (Gl), 321
Hett (Du), 76
Hidcote (Gl), 348
Himley (St), 135
Holyoakes (Lei), 364
Honeychild (K), 12
Honeywell (D), 12
Honington (Wa), 297
Huddersfield (Y), xxiii
Hunningham (Wa), 297
Hurcott (So), 251
Hurdcote (W), 251
Hurdcott (W), 251

Immingham (L), 283
Intwood (Nt), 324
Iping (Sx), 319
Ipplepen (D), 319

Keckwick (Ch), 147
Kempston (Nf), 144
Kesgrave (Sf), 147
Keynor (Sx), 156
Keynsham (So), 222
Kidlington (O), 247
Kigbeare (D), 236
Kilmiston (Ha), 102
Kineton (Wa), 330
Kington (He), 330
Kinnerley (Sa), 228
Kinnersley (He), 228
Kinton (Sa), 330
Kinvaston (St), 238

Landmoth (Y), 166

Lapley (St), 298
Lapworth (Wa), 161, 298
Lawell Ho (D), 355
Lench (La), 65
Leystone (Herts), 31
Limber (L), 215
Linacre (K, La), 112
Lindridge (K, Lei), 57
Luckington (So, W), 28
Lynhurst (K), 343
Lypiatt (Gl), 244

Mamhead (D), 60
Mam Tor (Db), 60
Mardleybury (Herts), 62
Marlingford (Nf), 62
Marnham (Nt), 315
Martley (Sf), 62
Matson (Gl), 210
Mattersey (Nt), 210
Meanwood (Y), 59
Meering (Nt), 241
Menutton (Sa), 49
Merrington, Kirk (Du), 242
Methersham (Sx), 210
Minton (Sa), 49
Mitton (La, Wa), 102
Mondaytown (Sa), 49
Moreton Pinkney (Nth), 125
Mouldsworth (Ch), 112
Myndtown (Sa), 49
Mythe, The (Gl), 55
Myton (Y), 102
Mytton (Sa), 102

Nackington (K), 178
Naithwood (D), 48
Nanhurst (Sr), 186
Nateley (Ha), 189
Neen Savage (Sa), 14
Neen Sollars (Sa), 14
Nettlebed (O), 214
Nobold (Sa), 329
Notgrove (Gl), 189

Orleton (He), 67
Orwell, R. (Sf), 9
Otherton (St), 118

Packington (Ess), 100
Pardshaw (Cu), 113
Parret, R. (So), 13
Patching (Sx), 100, 133
Pendle (La), 68
Pennicott (D), 334

Pettridge (K), 221
Pibworth (Berks), xxii
Pickering (Y), xxii, 226
Piddle, R. (Do), 14
Pinbury (Gl), xxii, 223
Pinden (K), 334
Pinley (Wa), 223
Plealey (Sa), 158
Podmore (St), 264
Ponsworthy (D), 244
Portfield (O), 114
Portpool Lane (Mx), 291
Potheridge (D), 117
Potterspury (Nth), 202
Poughill (D), 224
Poynings (Sx), 244
Prickshaw (La), 64
Prixford (D), 64
Pucklechurch (Gl), 252
Pudmore Pond (Sr), 65
Purfleet (Ess), 291

Quinton (Gl), 42

Rabley (Herts), 254
Reddish (La), 365
Ribden (St), 254
Rishangles (Sf), 345
Robley (Ha), 254
Rock (Sx), 70
Rockmoor Pond (Ha), 169
Rowberry (He), 357
Rushock (He), 255
Ruswarpe (Y), 307

St Chloe (Gl), 37
Salford (O), 7
Sandling (K), 207
Sannacott (D), 238
Sarsden (O), 109
Seavington (So), 35
Sevenhampton (Gl, W), 35
Shareshill (St), 343
Shelley (Ess, Sf, Sx), 349
Sheraton (Du), 343
Sherford (So), 32
Sherholt (St), 212
Shitterton (Do), 32
Shrewton (W), 331
Shutterton (D), 32
Siddington (Ch, Gl), 61
Smite (Wa), 140
Smite, R. (Lei, Nt), 140
Snettisham (Nf), 166
Snodland (K), 230

Snodshill (W), 230
Snowdenham (Sr), 230
Spilsbury (O), 61
Stalybridge (Ch), 232
Stapenhill (St), 100
Staple (K, So, W), 226
Staveley (Db, La), 232
Stirton (Y), 357
Streetly (St), 357
Strensall (Y), 89
Stringston (So), xx, 229
Sturton (L, Nb, Nt, Y), 357
Swineshead Hundred (Gl), 162

Tarrant Hinton (Do), 107
Tettenhall (St), 168
Threapwood (Ch), 219
Threepwood (Nb), 219
Throcking (Herts), 52
Throckley (Nb), 52
Thurrock (Ess), 170
Tibberton (Gl), 170
Ticknall (Db), 41
Tisbury (W), 234
Toppesfield (Ess), 272
Toppinghoe (Ess), 272
Topsham (D), 272
Touchen End (Berks), 272
Tredington (Gl), 172
Trench Fm (Sa), 143
Trenthide (Do), 87
Trill Fm (Do), 16
Trimstone (D), 252
Trotsworth (Sr), 176
Trotterscliffe (K), 176
Trumpington (C), 252
Twembrook (Ch), 238
Twyning (Gl), 238
Tyberton (He), 170

Uckfield (Sx), 160
Uckington (Sa), 160
Ugford (W), 160
Ullenhall (Wa), 267

Vasterne (W), 140

Waddicar (La), 221
Waddon (Sr), 165
Warwick (Wa), 246
Weathergrove (So), 336
Weedon (Nth), 350
Weighton, Market (Y), 289
Wereham (Nf), 20
Wetheringsett (Sf), 336

Wetmoor (St), 183
Whiston (La, Y), 115
Whiston (Nth), xv
Whitehall Fm (O), 183
Whitestone (D), 115
Whitestone Hundred (So), 115
Whitstone Hundred (Gl), 115
Wichnor (St), xv
Wickham, Childs (Gl), 273
Wildersmoor (La), 209
Wilderswood (La), 209
Willey (Sr), 350
Windhill (Y), 27
Winford (So), 200
Winford Eagle (Do), 200
Winfrith Newburgh (Do), 16, 200
Witchley Green (R), xv

Witton (Ch), 289
Wollaston (Nth), 196
Woodhill (W), 221
Woollaston (St), 196
Woolstone (Gl), 52
Wrabness (Ess), 254
Wroughton (W), 75
Wyche, The (He), 8
Wyegate (Gl), 62
Wyre, R. (La), 20

Yagden's Lane (Sa), 26
Yagland (D), 26
Yardley (Ess, So, Y), 232
Yazor (He), 26
Yeading (Mx), 50